THE PHILIPPINES: CURRENT ISSUES AND HISTORICAL BACKGROUND

THE PHILIPPINES: CURRENT ISSUES AND HISTORICAL BACKGROUND

HARRY S. CALIT (EDITOR)

Nova Science Publishers, Inc.
New York

Senior Editors: Susan Boriotti and Donna Dennis
Coordinating Editor: Tatiana Shohov
Office Manager: Annette Hellinger
Graphics: Wanda Serrano
Editorial Production: Matthew Kozlowski and Maya Columbus
Circulation: Ave Maria Gonzalez, Raymond Davis and Vladimir Klestov
Communications and Acquisitions: Serge P. Shohov
Marketing: Cathy DeGregory

Library of Congress Cataloging-in-Publication Data
Available upon Request

ISBN 1-59033-576-7

Copyright © 2003 by Nova Science Publishers, Inc.
400 Oser Ave, Suite 1600
Hauppauge, New York 11788-3619
Tele. 631-231-7269   Fax 631-231-8175
e-mail: Novascience@earthlink.net
Web Site: http://www.novapublishers.com

Printed in the United States of America

CONTENTS

PREFACE

The Philippines, reported home of several terrorist groups and the site of innumerable bombings in recent years, presents a rather bright contrast to other countries in Asia.

Philippines, Republic of the (in Filipino, *Republikang Pilipinas*), republic in the western Pacific Ocean, comprising the Philippine Islands and forming part of the Malay Archipelago, an island grouping that extends southward to include Indonesia and Malaysia. The Philippines includes more than 7,100 islands, but most of the land area is shared among the 11 largest islands.

The majority of Philippine people are of Malay stock, descendants of Indonesians and Malays who migrated to the islands long before the Christian era. The most significant ethnic minority group is the Chinese, who have played an important role in commerce since the ninth century, when they first came to the islands to trade. As a result of intermarriage, many Filipinos have some Chinese and Spanish ancestry. Americans and Spaniards constitute the next largest alien minorities in the country.

About 90% of the people are Christian; most were converted and westernized to varying degrees during nearly 400 years of Spanish and American rule. The major non-Hispanicized groups are the Muslim population, concentrated in the Sulu Archipelago and in central and western Mindanao, and the mountain groups of northern Luzon. Small forest tribes live in the more remote areas of Mindanao.

About 87 native languages and dialects are spoken, all belonging to the Malay-Polynesian linguistic family. About 40 percent of the population lives in poverty while a wealthy minority holds most political power.

PART 1: CURRENT ISSUES

ABU SAYYAF: TARGET OF PHILIPPINE-U.S. ANTI–TERRORISM COOPERATION

Larry Niksch

THE PHILIPPINE RESPONSE TO SEPTEMBER 11

President Gloria Macapagal-Arroyo voiced strong support for the United States in the aftermath of the September 11, 2001 terrorist attack. The Philippines, she said, is prepared to "go every step of the way" with the United States. President Arroyo allowed U.S. military forces to use Filipino ports and airfields to support military operations in Afghanistan. She cited morality and Philippine national interests as reasons for her pro-U.S. stand. She defined the national interest as linking a struggle against international terrorism with the struggle against terrorism within the Philippines.[1]

Philippine terrorism has been multifaceted for at least three decades and has been carried out by different groups with different agendas. A significant communist insurgency, the New Peoples Army (NPA) in the 1970s and 1980s engaged in bombings, assassinations, and kidnappings. The communists today still have an estimated armed strength of over 10,000; and President Bush designated the NPA as a terrorist group in December 2001. Criminal syndicates have practiced widespread kidnappings for ransom. The target of President Arroyo's policy, however, is Muslim insurgency and terrorism.

This chapter provides an overview and policy analysis of the Abu Sayyaf terrorist group in the Philippines and the recently announced Philippine-U.S. program of against it. It examines the origins and operations of Abu Sayyaf, the efforts of the Philippine government and military to eliminate it, and the implications of a greater U.S. military role in attempts to suppress it.

---

[1] Landler, Mrk. Philippines Offers U.S. Its Troops and Bases. *New York Times*, October 2, 2002. P.5.

HISTORIC MUSLIM INSURGENCY

Located on the big southern island of Mindanao and the Sulu island chain southwest of Mindanao, Filipino Muslims, called since the time of Spanish rule, revolted against Spanish colonizers of the Philippines from the 17th century on, the American rulers of the early 20th century, and Philippine governments since independence in 1946. From 1899 to 1914, the U.S. military conducted a number of campaigns to suppress Muslim insurgents in the southern Philippines-campaigns, which were controversial because of heavy civilian casualties. Muslim grievances after 1946 focused on the growing settlement of Catholic Filipinos on Mindanao, which reduced the geographical area of a Muslim majority (there are about 7 million Filipino Muslims). Muslims revolted in the 1970s under a Moro National Liberation Front (MNLF), which demanded an independent Muslim state. An estimated 120,000 people were killed in the 1970s in heavy fighting between the MNLF and the Philippine armed forces (AFP).[2]

Since the late 1970s, there have been two trends in the Muslim problem. The first has been negotiations between the Philippine government and the MNLF. As a result, the MNLF abandoned its goal of an independent Muslim state. An agreement was reached in 1996 that created an autonomous Muslim region. This apparent positive trend was countered by the fragmentation of the Muslim movement. A segment of the MNLF broke away in 1978 and formed the Moro Islamic Liberation Front (MILF). The MILF demanded independence for Muslim populated regions and proclaimed that a Muslim state would be based on "Koranic principles." The MILF gained strength into the 1990s. By 1995-96, U.S. estimates placed armed MILF strength at 35,000-45,000 in seven provinces on Mindanao. The MILF had large base camps and functional governmental operations. Its operations included attacks on the AFP and planting bombs in Mindanao cities. A Bangsamoro Peoples Consultative Assembly of approximately 200,000 people was held in 1996 in MILF-held territory and called for an independent Muslim state.[3]

Stepped-up MILF military operations in 1998-99 prompted Philippine President Joseph Estrada to order an all-out military offensive against MILF base camps. The AFP captured the MILF's main base on Mindanao and damaged the MILF militarily. In 2001, Philippine government-MILF negotiations resulted in a tentative cease-fire. This success was offset, however, by the break between the government and MNLF leader, Nur Misuari. When the Philippine government opposed his re-election as governor of the Muslim autonomous region, MNLF forces attacked the AFP and took civilian hostages on Jolo Island in the Sulu chain and in the city of Zamboanga in west Mindanao. Nur Misuari fled to Malaysia where he was arrested by Malaysian authorities.

---

[2] Sales, Peter M. War in Mindanaao. *Asia-Pacific Defence Reporter*, October-November 2000, p.8,10.
[3] Tiglao, Rigoberto. Hidden Strength; Cresent Moon Rising. *Far Eastern Economic Review*, February 23, 1995. P. 22-28. Tiglao, Rigoberto. Moro Reprise. *Far Eastern Economic Review*, December 26, 1996-January 2, 1997. P. 22.

ABU SAYYAF: ORIGINS, STRENGTH, AND OPERATIONS

Abubakar Janjalani, the son of a fisherman on Basilan Island, formed Abu Sayyaf in 1990. Janjalani had become connected with a Muslim fundamentalist movement, Al Islamic Tabligh, in the 1980s. That organization received financial support from Saudi Arabia and Pakistan, including funds to send young Muslim men to schools in the Middle East. Janjalani studied in Saudi Arabia and Libya and became radicalized. When he returned to Basilan, he recruited two groups into Abu Sayyaf (meaning "sword bearer" in Arabic): dissidents from the MNLF and Filipinos who had fought with the Afghan mujaheddin rebels against the Soviet Union.[4]

Over the next five years, Abu Sayyaf staged ambushes, bombings, kidnappings, and executions, mainly against Filipino Christians on Basilan and the west coast of Mindanao. Its strength grew only slowly to an estimated 600 by 1995.[5] Abu Sayyaf operations declined for four years after 1995, partly as a result of the 1996 settlement between the Philippine government and the MNLF. In 1998, AFP troops killed Abubakar Janjalani. His brother, Khadaffy, and Ghalib Andang took command. Then in April 2000, Abu Sayyaf began kidnapping operations further a field geographically and aimed at foreigners, with a principle aim of extracting ransom payments. Abu Sayyaf forces commanded by Andang, aboard fast speedboats, attacked a tourist resort in the Malaysian state of Sabah and kidnapped 21 foreigners, including Malaysians, Frenchmen, Germans, Finns, and South Africans. In July 2000, Abu Sayyaf seized three French journalists. It released the hostages later in the year after it received ransom payments, including money reportedly from European governments funneled through the Libyan government. Estimates of the amount of this ransom range from $10 to $25 million.[6]

According to Philippine government officials, Abu Sayyaf used the 2000 ransom to recruit new members, raising its strength to an estimated 1,000 or more, and acquire new equipment, including communications equipment and more fast speedboats. Abu Sayyaf used speedboats again on May 27, 2000, in venturing 300 miles across the Sulu Sea to attack a tourist resort on Palawan, the Philippines' large, western-most island. Khadaffy Janjalani commanded the operation. Abu Sayyaf kidnapped 20 people, including three Americans. It took them to Basilan. Abu Sayyaf announced in June 2001 that it had beheaded one of the Americans, Guillermo Sobero, of Corono, California. As of January 2002, Abu Sayyaf holds Martin and Gracia Burnham, Christian missionaries of Wichita, Kansas, and Deborah Yap, a Filipino nurse. Most of the other abductees from Palawan were freed after more ransom was paid, reportedly as much as $1 million per person. Throughout 2000 and 2001, Abu Sayyaf kidnapped numerous Filipinos on Basilan and Mindanao, releasing some after ransom

---

[4] In Mindanao, the Islamic Fundamentalist Movement Appears to be Spearheaded by the Tabligh and Abu Sayyaf. *Philippine Daily Inquirer*, July 29, 1994. P. 1.

[5] Richburg, Keith. Spoilers of the Peace. *Washington Post*, May 25, 1995. P. A33.

[6] Fisk, Robert. The Double-Edged Sword of Gaddafi's Links with the Philippines. *London Independent* (internet version), August 22, 2000. Tan, Abby. Kidnappings a Blow to Philippine Image. *Christian Science Monitor*, June 6, 2001. P. 7.

payments and executing others. Ex-hostages claim Abu Sayyaf is demanding $2 million for the Burnhams.[7]

CONNECTIONS TO AL QAEDA AND OTHER FOREIGN LINKS

The *Wall Street Journal* of December 3, 2001, quoted Admiral Denis Blair, Commander-in-Chief of the U.S. Pacific Command, that "we're seeing increasing evidence that there are potential current links" between Abu Sayyaf and Osama bin Laden's Al Qaeda terrorist organization. Blair gave no details. There have been varying accounts regarding Abu Sayyaf's relationship with Al Qaeda. It is accepted that Abu Sayyaf received funding and support from Al Qaeda in the early 1990s. Money came from Mohammed Jamal Khalifa, a Saudi and brother-in-law of bin Laden, who operated a number of Islamic charities in the southern Philippines. Ramzi Yoesef, an Al Qaeda operative, came to the Philippines in 1994. He and other Al Qaeda operatives reportedly trained Abu Sayyaf fighters.[8] Yoesef established an Al Qaeda cell in Manila. Yoesuf used the cell to plan an assassination of Pope John Paul II, the planting of bombs aboard 12 U.S. airliners flying trans-Pacific routes, and the crashing of an airplane into the Central Intelligence Agency's headquarters in Langley, Virginia. Filipino police uncovered the cell in 1995 and provided information on the plot to the CIA and FBI. Yoesef later was arrested in Pakistan and extradited to the United States for trial over his complicity in the 1993 bombing of the World Trade Center.[9]

There is less information regarding Abu Sayyaf's recent relationship with Al Qaeda. Filipino officials close to President Arroyo have contended that the relationship declined after 1995 when the Ramzi Yoesuf plot was uncovered and Khalifa left the Philippines. Civilian officials assert that there is no hard evidence of current ties. They cite the decline in foreign financial support as a key reason for Abu Sayyaf's expanded kidnappings for ransom. In contrast, Filipino military officials claim that active links exist. A secret AFP intelligence report of early 2000 reportedly asserted that Abu Sayyaf received training, arms, and other support from Al Qaeda and other Middle East terrorist groups.[10] AFP officers subsequently reported that "foreign Muslims" were training Abu Sayyaf on Mindanao to conduct urban terrorism and that Osama bin Laden had ordered stepped-up aid to Abu Sayyaf, including possibly $3 million in 2000.[11] In July 2001, Philippine Senator Rudolfo Biazon, chairman of the Senate committee on national security and defense and a former highly decorated Marine

---

[7] Romero, Paolo. Abus Attempting a Robin Hood. *Philippine Star* (internet version), July 27, 2001. What Ransom? *Philippine Daily Inquirer* (internet version), June 18, 2001. Quezon City GMA 7 television broadcast, December 7, 2001.

[8] Police Hunt for Sudanese Terrorist in Mindanao. *Manila Chronicle*, December 15, 1995. P.3. Pomonti, Jean-Claude. Al Qaeda's Invisible Presence in Southeast Asia. *Le Monde*, November 4-5, 2001, P. 12.

[9] For a detailed account of the Ramzi Yousef bomb plot, see: Brzezinski, Matthew. Bust and Boom. *Washington Post Magazine*, December 31, 2001. P. 15-17, 27-28.

[10] Chandrasekaran, Rajiv. Terrorism War's New Front. *Washinton Post*, December 22, 2001. P. A1. Kurlantzick, Joshua. Muslim Separatists in Global Network of Terrorist Groups. *Washinton Times*, May 2, 2000. P. A13.

[11] Arquiza, Ray. Interpol Alerts RP on Bin Laden's Men. *Philippine Star* (internet version), July 10, 2001. Gomez, Jim. Philippine Rebels, bin Laden Linked. Agence France Presse report, June 20, 2000.

General, cited reports from United Nations sources that at least 50 Abu Sayyaf members were being trained in Afghanistan.[12]

Abu Sayyaf's other foreign links are with individuals and possibly groups in Malaysia and with Libya. A prominent Malaysian, Sairan Karno, helped to negotiate the release of the hostages in 2000. Libya's leader, Moammar Gadafi, was the key intermediary in hostage negotiations in 2000 and 2001 involving Abu Sayyaf and other Filipino Muslim groups. Libya was a conduit for ransoms paid to Abu Sayyaf by European governments and other parties. Libya has been accused of aiding the MILF, and it was involved in Philippine-MILF negotiations in 2001 for a truce. Libya also funds Muslim schools, mosques, and other facilities in the southern Philippines. It offered money for "livelihood projects" in its role in the 2000 hostage negotiations. Like the prior charities of Mohammed Khalifa, this raises the possibility that Libyan money gets channeled to Abu Sayyaf. Libya officially has condemned Abu Sayyaf kidnappings.[13]

LINKS TO THE MILF AND MNLF

Leaders of the MILF and MNLF have denied any supportive links with Abu Sayyaf. They have criticized Abu Sayyaf's terrorist attacks against civilians. The MILF rejected the Afghan Taliban's call for a jihad against the United States and condemned the September 11 attack.[14] There have been reports of links between the MILF and Al Qaeda. The latest was an allegation reportedly by Singapore officials that an MILF trainer and bomb specialist assisted the group of 13 Al Qaeda-linked terrorists arrested in Singapore in January 2002.[15] The claims that links exist and that elements of the MILF and MNLF give active aid to Abu Sayyaf.[16] There clearly is contact between Abu Sayyaf and units of the two larger organizations in the Sulu islands, Basilan, and western Mindanao, where all three groups operate. The MNLF's attack on AFP units on Jolo Island in November 2001 demonstrated the proximity of MNLF and Abu Sayyaf units. A number of MILF units operate on Basilan. Some Abu Sayyaf members were formerly with the MNLF. Several thousand MNLF members kept their weapons despite the 1996 agreement and operate as independent commands. Factions with the MILF and MNLF are hard-line advocates of Muslim independence and reject autonomy proposals; they undoubtedly would be inclined to cooperate with Abu Sayyaf under certain circumstances.[17] Moreover, the tenuous relations

---

[12] Nocum, Armand N. Talibans Training 50 Abu Members, says Biazon. *Philippine Daily Inquirer* (internet version), July 6, 2001.

[13] Mydans, Seth. Libyan Aid Helps to Free Hostage Held in Philippines. *New York Times*, October 21, 2001. P. A9. Sheehan, Deidre. Buying Trouble. *Far Eastern Economic Review*, September 7, 2000. P. 29.

[14] Mendez, Christina. MILF Rejects 'Holy War' vs. US. *Philippine Star* (internet version), September 17, 2001.

[15] Mydans, Seth. Suspects in Singapore Are Linked to Al Qaeda and Plans for Anti-U.S. Attacks. *New York Times*, January 12, 2002. P. A8. Marinay, Manny B. Philippine Military Bares MILF's Foreign Sources of Funds. *Manila Times (internet version), March 27, 2002.*

[16] Alipala, Inot. MILF, MNLF Aiding Abu, Military Charges. *Philippine Daily Inquirer* (internet version), July 5, 2001.

[17] Sheehan, Deidre. Swords into Ploughshares. *Far Eastern Economic Review*, September 20, 2001. P. 30-32. Lerner, Marc. Philippines Guerrilla Group has bin Laden Links. *Washington Times*, September 24, 2001. P. A13.

between the Philippine government and the MILF and MNLF raise the strong possibility of shifting linkages among the three Muslim groups.

PHILIPPINE GOVERNMENT AND AFP POLICIES AND OPERATIONS

The basic Philippine government policy since August 2000 has been constant military pressure on Abu Sayyaf In September 2000, President Estrada ordered the AFP to commit over 1,500 troops into Jolo to conduct operations against Abu Sayyaf units that had taken the foreign hostages in Malaysia. President Arroyo ordered the AFP into Basilan after the hostage-taking on Palawan. As many as 4,500 troops were deployed to Basilan in 2001. AFP operations apparently have reduced Abu Sayyaf strength from the level of over 1000 in early 2000. The AFP estimated in December 2001 that Abu Sayyaf strength on Basilan was below 100 and was about 500 on Jolo.

AFP operations have been limited by several factors. One is the mountainous, jungle terrain of the two islands pockmarked by underground caves. A second is the support civilians on Jolo and Basilan reportedly give Abu Sayyaf, although recent surveys of Muslims on Basilan suggested that many are disillusioned by Abu Sayyaf's violence. A third is the limited military equipment of the AFP, including an absence of night vision and other surveillance equipment and shortages of helicopters, mortars, naval patrol craft, surveillance aircraft, and even basic necessities like military boots. A fourth limitation appears to be the unevenness in the quality of the AFP. The attrition of Abu Sayyaf strength appears to reflect AFP successes, but there also have been failed operations. The most controversial was the failed encirclement of the Abu Sayyaf holding the Burnhams and Filipino hostages in a church in the town of Lamitan in June 2001. Several AFP units pulled out of their positions without explanation, allowing the Abu Sayyaf unit to break out of the encirclement. A Catholic priest and other witnesses charged that Abu Sayyaf had bribed AFP commanders to pull units from their positions, and Filipino Catholic bishops have called for an inquiry. A Philippine Senate Committee is investigating the Lamitan incident.[18]

A fifth limitation is the hostage situation itself. In 2000, European governments reportedly pressured the Philippine government to refrain from "excessive" military operations while Abu Sayyaf held the European hostages.[19] There are no reports of similar U.S. pressure regarding the Burnhams. Nevertheless, Arroyo Administration officials and AFP commanders say they are restrained from air bombing and using artillery and mortars out of concern over the safety of the hostages. A sixth limitation is the AFP deployment of most of its forces in the southern Philippines in the broader areas of Mindanao dominated by the MILF and MNLF. Only a small percentage of Filipino troops are committed against Abu Sayyaf. A final constraint is the danger of AFP operations producing a large numbers of civilian casualties or displaced civilians. The Estrada Administration came under criticism in 2000 over reports that the AFP offensive on Jolo caused civilian casualties and displacement among the island's more than 200,000 residents.

---

[18] Chandrasekaran, Rajiv. Rebels' Escape Draws Scrutiny. *Washington Post*, September 1, 2001, p. A 18.
[19] Sheehan, Buying Trouble, p. 529. See also Kyodo News Service (Tokyo) report, July 13, 2000; and the Agence France Presse report, July 12, 2000.

The Philippine government has opposed payment of ransom for hostages. The reality is that the government has allowed the payment of ransom from members of hostages' families and from European governments through Libya in 2000. Although the U.S. Government opposes the payment of ransom for hostages, Filipino officials asserted that unidentified parties are trying to negotiate a ransom deal for the Burnhams.[20]

The Arroyo Administration also is negotiating with Indonesia and Malaysia to form a mechanism for trilateral cooperation against terrorist groups. It appears to have some success in securing Malaysia's cooperation. Malaysia has increased its naval patrols in the Sulu Sea, and it arrested Nur Misuari after he fled to Malaysia in November 2001.

THE IMPLICATIONS OF U.S. INVOLVEMENT

Beginning in October 2001, the United States sent groups of military observers to Mindanao to assess AFP operations against Abu Sayyaf, render advice, and examine AFP equipment needs. President Bush extended $93 million in military aid to the Philippines when President Arroyo visited Washington in 2001, and he offered a direct U.S. military role in combating Abu Sayyaf. President Arroyo insisted that the U.S. military role should be advisory and that the AFP would retain full operational responsibility. By late December 2001, the AFP on Mindanao began to receive quantities of U.S. military equipment. Moreover, AFP commanders expressed frustration over the failure to rescue the hostages and suggested that they would support President Arroyo if she sought a more direct U.S. military role.[21] It was announced in January 2002 that the United States would deploy 650 troops to Mindanao and Basilan within a month. Support/maintenance personnel would number 500. Special Forces numbering 150 would perform training and advisory functions; and some of these would accompany AFP units on Basilan. U.S. military personnel would not conduct independent operations, but they would be armed and authorized to defend themselves. Such a role on Basilan would likely place U.S. Special Forces in direct combat situations in AFP-Abu Sayyaf encounters.

This enlarged U.S. military role has several implications. Successful military operations against Abu Sayyaf would extend U.S. successes beyond Afghanistan and reinforce the Bush Administration's message to governments everywhere that the United States is determined to fight terrorism on many fronts. The Philippine government's example could influence other governments to cooperate with the United States. Success against Abu Sayyaf would further revive the Philippine-U.S. security alliance, a goal of U.S. policy since the signing in 1998 of a Philippine-U.S. Visiting Forces Agreement. It undoubtedly will produce greater Philippine-U.S. cooperation against any future attempts by Al Qaeda to plant cells in Manila or elsewhere in the Philippines.

Other implications, however, are complex and contain uncertain outcomes. One is the likely heightened danger to American citizens and businesses in the Philippines, who could be targeted by Abu Sayyaf or Al Qaeda, or even by the communist NPA. Another is the issue of

---

[20] Echeminada, Roel and Romero, Paolo. The Military to Unmask Group Negotiating Abu Ransom. *Philippine Star* (internet version), December 21, 2001.

[21] More US 'Advisors' to Help Fight Sayyaf. *Manila Times*, January 4, 2002. P. 1. Ng-Gadil, Mirasol. AFP Admitted that Operation Against Abu Sayyuf Bandits is Difficult. *Manila Kabayan* (internet version), December 30, 2001.

military objectives, which Pentagon officials have not defined if the primary U.S. objective is the rescue of the hostages, the U.S. military likely would limit its role to precise operations targeting the Abu Sayyaf group on Basilan holding the hostages. Restraints on the use of bombing and artillery would have to continue. Training and advice probably would focus on a rescue operation on the ground and on prior surveillance and intelligence operations. However, if an objective of equal priority were to destroy Abu Sayyaf, U.S. military activities would be broader in scope and would have to be carried out on Jolo and areas of western Mindanao and include maritime surveillance and possibly maritime patrols.

Another implication relates to confining the mission to Abu Sayyaf, The Bush Administration reportedly wants to avoid military involvement with the MILF.[22] If the tenuous Philippine government truces with the MILF and MNLF should collapse, the AFP undoubtedly would use recently supplied U.S. military equipment against these groups. The Philippine government might want U.S. training and advice for AFP units committed against the MILF and/or MNLF. U.S. military personnel with the AFP could become involved in clashes with MILF or MNLF units in areas where these groups are in proximity with Abu Sayyaf. AFP operations against Abu Sayyaf, which used aerial bombing or artillery, could link the United States with potentially heavy civilian casualties. Finally, if reports of MRX-Al Qaeda links are validated, a strong case would emerge in U.S. policy deliberations to target the MILF as well as Abu Sayyaf In short, an enlarged U.S. role against Abu Sayyaf contains a high level risk of wider U.S. military involvement affecting large elements of the Muslim population of Mindanao. The risk was highlighted by threats in late January 2002 from MNLF elements loyal to Nur Misuari to attack American targets in Philippine cities, including Manila.

The enlarged U.S. military role also carries the risk of political backlashes. Muslims in neighboring Indonesia and Malaysia might react against the United States, especially if the U.S. military role expands beyond missions against Abu Sayyaf and if it becomes prolonged. Influential Filipino "nationalist" and leftist groups all ready are criticizing the U.S. military role, even though polls indicate overwhelming Filipino public support for it and the influential Catholic Bishops Conference endorsed it. Critics charge that the United States is plotting to restore a permanent U.S. military presence in the Philippines. They were influential in the Philippine government's decision in 1991 to order the United States to withdraw from the large U.S. military bases in the Philippines. The critics also are reviving accounts of the controversial American military campaigns of 1899-1914.

The U.S. military role also has implications for a U.S. political role on Mindanao. The Bush Administration will face sentiment and pressure to influence the political, social, and economic issues underlying Filipino Muslim discontent: the scope and extent of autonomy of the Muslim populated region; the role of Islam in education; and economic development issues. The likely U.S. involvement in these issues was evidenced by President Bush's promise to President Arroyo in November 2001 of $55 million in development aid for Mindanao.

---

[22] Landler, Mark. The Temperature's a Lot Warmer but the Mission's the Same: Hunting Down Terrorists. *New York Times*, November 4, 2001. P. B4.

Chapter 2

PHILIPPINE-U.S. SECURITY RELATIONS

Larry Niksch

Until 1992, the Philippines and the United States had an intimate security relationship based on a 1947 military bases agreement and a 1952 Mutual Defense Treaty. In the treaty, each party promises to "act to meet the common danger" of an armed attack on the other party "in accordance with its constitutional process." The treaty specifies that an armed attack includes "an armed attack on the metropolitan territory of either of the parties, or on the island territories under its jurisdiction in the Pacific, or on its armed forces, public vessels or aircraft in the Pacific."

The security relationship was frayed in 1991 when the Philippine Senate voted to reject ratification of a new U.S.-Philippines agreement to extend U.S. rights to military bases beyond 1992, the expiration date of the 1947 agreement. As a result, the United States withdrew from its bases by December 1992, including its huge naval base at Subic Bay. The security relationship was damaged further by cuts in U.S. military assistance to the Philippines and by a Philippine Supreme Court ruling in December 1996 that executive orders by President Fidel Ramos to continue provisions of the U.S.-Philippine Status of Forces Agreement (which also expired in 1992) were unconstitutional. The ruling ended the legal status of U.S. military personnel in the Philippines, and the Clinton Administration and the Pentagon responded by ending U.S.-Philippine joint military exercises and barring U.S. military personnel from entering the Philippines.

VISITING FORCES AGREEMENT AND NEW MILITARY SUPPORT PROGRAM

U.S. and Philippine responses to the Supreme Court ruling constituted the first step toward restoring a functioning security relationship. They negotiated a Visiting Forces Agreement (VFA), signed on February 10, 1998. The VFA restored a legal status for U.S. military personnel in the Philippines, including the nature of criminal jurisdiction over American military personnel accused of committing crime - a sensitive issue in negotiating the VFA. The Philippine Senate ratified it on May 27, 1999, by a vote of 18 to 5. The first joint military exercise on Philippine soil was held in January 2000.

A second step came in an agreement to begin a U.S. military support program for the Philippines. Secretary of Defense William Cohen and Philippine Secretary of Defense Orlando Mercado announced on October 3, 2000, "an exchange of defense experts to facilitate, coordinate and assist in meeting the equipment requirements of the AFP" (Armed Forces of the Philippines). This "defense assessment team" is to clarify the equipment needs of the AFP and to "set forth priorities" for an American assistance program.[1] It is scheduled to submit initial findings in October 2000.

ISSUES IN A RENEWED SECURITY RELATIONSHIP

The Philippine-U.S. agreements are within the context of at least three related security issues that will require Manila and Washington to make policy decisions in the course of implementing the VFA and the plan for U.S. military support.

The Form and Scope of Any New U.S. Military Support Program

The Philippines' main motive for seeking U.S. aid was its confrontation with China in the disputed South China Sea. In 1995, China, which claims the entire South China Sea basin, occupied Mischief Reef in the Philippine-claimed area of the Spratly Islands. Since then, the Philippine navy has confronted the Chinese when it appeared that China was seeking to expand its positions in the disputed area. Incidents have occurred in which the Philippine navy has fired warning shots and has rammed Chinese vessels. The Philippine government thus has sought U.S. assistance to strengthen AFP naval and air capabilities in the South China Sea.

The Philippines, however, has competing defense priorities related to the escalation of hostilities with Muslim insurgents in the southern Philippines in 2000. The insurgents seek independence for the Muslim regions of the Philippines. The heavy fighting on Mindanao against the Moro Islamic Liberation Front and the kidnaping of foreigners by Abu Sayyaf, a smaller Muslim group, appears to have shifted Philippine government priorities away from the South China Sea. By spring 2000, the AFP had deployed over 110,000 troops against the Muslims, 60 percent of total AFP strength.[2]

These defense priorities contrast with the weaknesses of the AFP and the lack of progress of the Philippine government in implementing a 15 year military modernization program, which it announced in 1995. The Philippine Air Force's combat assets consist of ten F-5 fighters over 30 years old. Naval vessels date back to World War II except for three gunboats purchased from Hong Kong in 1997. Logistics capabilities to service equipment is viewed by experts as deficient. The modernization program, estimated to cost $8.2 billion, stalled after 1997 when President Estrada imposed budget austerity measures, including constraints on

---

[1] Text of Joint Press Conference of Secretary of Defense Cohen and Secretary of National Defense Mercado, October 3, 2000.
[2] GMA Television (Manila) report, May 31, 2000.

defense spending. In 1999, the Philippines spent 52 billion pesos ($1.27 billion) on defense, 8.8 percent of total expenditures.[3]

The nature of Philippine defense needs and the uncertainty over the Philippine government's commitment to strengthening the AFP appear to create two apparent options in fashioning a U.S. military aid program. One is a program to create a specific naval and air force structure that would give the AFP the capability to carry out defined military missions in the South China Sea. Senator Rodolfo Biazon, Chairman of the Philippine Congress' Committee on National Defense and Security and a respected former Marine General, has recommended this kind of program.[4] Such a program would be analogous, in a smaller scale, to the U.S.-Japan defense program of the 1980s under which Japan undertook specific anti-Soviet naval and air missions in a geographically defined region in the Northwest Pacific and developed a force structure featuring agreed-upon types of weapons and equipment. Military missions likely would include intelligence gathering and surveillance; moving troops (Philippine Marines) to occupy islands and atolls; mounting a credible show of force at a particular time and place if it appeared that the Chinese were about to occupy another position; and successfully engaging the Chinese navy and air force if China resorted to military force.

Several types of U.S. weapons would be important in building up AFP capabilities to perform such missions: surveillance, strike, and transport aircraft; fast attack patrol naval craft; frigates armed with surface to surface and surface to air missiles; amphibious landing craft; and long range troop carrying helicopters. Such a force would not necessarily have to be large, given the limited number of islands and atolls in dispute and limits on China's ability to deploy military forces hundreds of miles from the Chinese mainland. Nevertheless, it would have to be well armed, well trained, with an effective logistics component. Because of the AFP's deficiencies in all these areas, the United States undoubtedly would have to assist in training for operations and logistics.

The second apparent option is a broader program aimed at a general improvement in all services of the AFP. Such a program would give more emphasis to supplying the Philippine army, the largest of the AFP's services. The program would be orientated more towards the war with Muslim insurgents. U.S. priorities to assist the Philippine army no doubt would include transportation aircraft, troop carrying helicopters, naval supply vessels, armored personnel carriers, infantry weapons, ammunition, and medical equipment. According to informed sources, the AFP is pressing the United States to provide such support. Secretary of Defense William Cohen stated on his trip to the Philippines in September 2000 that the United States could assist the AFP to develop counter-terrorism units.[5]

Unlike option one, the program would not seek to create a new, distinct force structure with the exception of counter-terrorism units. Decisions would be more on an on-going basis depending on the nature of the fighting on Mindanao and the needs of the Philippine army. This program, too, would appear to require a direct role for U.S. military personnel in training

---

[3] The Philippines. Foreign Military Markets: Asia, Australia, and Pacific Rim, April 2000. Simon, Sheldon. Asian Armed Forces: Internal Tasks and Capabilities. Seattle, The National Bureau of Asian Research, 2000. P. 20-22.

[4] Manila Urged to Use US Aid Against PRC, Not Insurgents. Philippine Star (internet version), March 14, 2000.

[5] News Briefing by Secretary of Defense William Cohen, September 14, 2000.

and logistics. Knowledgeable U.S. sources emphasized the need of this kind of U.S. role in developing an AFP capability to service and maintain equipment.

The effectiveness of any U.S. military support program will depend on the commitment of the Philippine government and the AFP to support it. According to U.S. officials, the Philippines would have to buy U.S. military equipment either on a commercial basis or on a credit basis through the U.S. foreign military sales program. This would entail a major financial expenditure for the Philippines. Other experts assert that the Philippines could take much greater advantage of the U.S. Excess Defense Articles program and acquire U.S. weaponry, including fighter aircraft and patrol boats and frigates, at no cost or at a depreciated price.[6] Regardless of the form of acquisition, sizeable Philippine government funds also would be required for training, logistics and maintenance of acquired weaponry, infrastructure, and possibly new military bases. The AFP would need to commit high level, competent officers to administer the program. Philippine priorities and ideas concerning the type of program would be important to dispel perceptions within Filipino political elites that the program was U.S.-imposed. Philippine congressional support for the program would be essential.

The U.S. Defense Commitment

The renewal of the security relationship has raised anew questions concerning the U.S. defense commitment to the Philippines and the U.S. military role in the Philippines. There has been much discussion over whether the 1952 Mutual Defense Treaty (MDT) covers the positions in the South China Sea in dispute between the Philippines and China (Spratly Islands and Scarborough Shoal). Successive U.S. administrations have stated that Article IV of the MDT, calling for responses to an armed attack on either of the signatories, does not cover the Spratly Islands;[7] but U.S. statements are more vague regarding Scarborough Shoal. U.S. officials, however, have stated that the United States opposes any country taking unilateral actions to assert territorial claims and that the United States would consult with the Philippines "on what action to take" if Philippines military forces in the Spratlys were attacked.[8] Article III of the MDT provides for consultations if either signatory is threatened by armed attack. Philippine government statements have indicated an acceptance of the U.S. position but also that the Philippines might invoke the MDT in case of a Chinese attack in the South China Sea in order to activate Article III regarding consultations.[9]

Statements regarding the defense commitment and U.S. military activities in or near the South China Sea also appear aimed at deterring Chinese aggressiveness. The first U.S.-

---

[6] U.S. Congressional Research Service. Excess Defense Articles: Grants and Sales to Allies and Friendly Countries. By Richard F. Grimmett. CRS Report RS20428. January 10,2000. P. 4-5. Statistics since 1995 show that the Philippines is not among the numerous countries that have made significant acquisitions of U.S. weaponry under the Excess Defense Articles program.

[7] Pablo, Carlito. Cohen Says US Defending RP Not Automatic. *Philippine Daily Inquirer,* August 4,1998. P. 1.

[8] Ibid. Joint Press Conference of Secretary of Defense Cohen and Secretary of National Defense Mercado, October 3,1999.

[9] Atienza, Deride. U.S. Defense of Philippines Could Apply to Spratlys. Kyodo News Agency (Japan) report, June 4, 1999. Estrada: U.S. Defense Pact Does Not Cover Spratlys. *Philippine Daily Inquirer* (internet version), February 14, 1999.

Philippine military exercise after Philippine ratification of the VFA took place on Palawan, a main Philippine island near the disputed area in the Spratlys. Admiral Joseph Prueher, Commander of U.S. Pacific Forces, stated in February 1999 that the U.S. navy would make "a little bigger show of our presence there [South China Sea] than we have in the past."[10] At that time, U.S. military intelligence officials began to disclose publicly details of Chinese military activities in the South China Sea and provided this information to the Philippine government.[11] The Palawan exercise and these other U.S. activities have drawn Chinese attention. Chinese officials criticized the Palawan exercise, and they have warned Southeast Asian countries against strengthening military cooperation with the United States.[12]

The MDT does not cover insurrection within the Philippines. However, longstanding U.S. policy supports the territorial integrity of the Philippines, and past U.S. military aid has been used against Filipino communist and Muslim insurgents. Current U.S. policy opposes worldwide Islamic terrorist groups; Philippine military intelligence claims that such groups are supporting the MILF and Abu Sayuyuf. A more direct U.S. role in the southern Philippines thus appears possible even if the intention is to avoid it. A U.S. military support program that assists the AFP in the South would heighten the danger of Muslim terrorist attacks against American targets in the Philippines, pointed up in August 2000 by the kidnaping of an American by Abu Sayyuf. Attacks against Americans, in turn, could.raise debate and issues in Washington regarding a more direct U.S. military involvement.

U.S. Diplomacy

A renewed security relationship also raises the policy issue of the role of U.S. diplomacy in the South China Sea dispute. The Clinton Administration did not give the South China Sea a priority in U.S. diplomacy until 1999. The Administration stressed only the right of free navigation. It did not raise this issue extensively in the U.S. bilateral dialogue with China. Moreover, it did not get involved in the negotiations since 1995 over concluding a code of conduct for the contesting countries in the South China Sea. Those negotiations, within the Association of Southeast Asian Nations (ASEAN) and between ASEAN and China, have focused on the types and scope of aggressive behavior that a code of conduct would prohibit. The Philippines has pressed its ASEAN partners since 1998 to draft a code of conduct that would prohibit any claimant from seizing additional islands and atolls.

At the meeting of the ASEAN Regional Forum (ARF) in July 1999, U.S. Secretary of State Madeleine Albright did not endorse a code of conduct (in contrast to the Australian Foreign Minister, who argued for one), but she did warn that "we cannot simply sit on the sidelines and watch" if a cycle were "to emerge in which each incident leads to another with potentially greater risks and graver consequences."[13]

---

[10] Halloran, Richard. Reading Beijing. *Far Eastern Economic Review,* February 25,1999. P. 28.
[11] Gertz, Bill. China Makes Upgrades to Island Base. *Washington Times,* February 11, 1999. P. Al. Manila Reports on More PRC Military Buildup in Spratlys. *Philippine Star* (internet version), April 16, 1999.
[12] Khumrungroj, Sa Nguan. PRC Official Warns ASEAN Against Boosting US Military Ties. *The Nation* (Bangkok, internet version), March 15,2000.
[13] Kyodo News Agency report, July 26, 1999. Pathan, Don. US Urges ARF to Ease Military Tension in South China Sea. *The Nation,* July 27, 1999. P. 1.

Diplomacy over a code of conduct faces two challenges. One is whether the ten members of ASEAN can present a unified proposal as tough as proposed by the Philippines. The second is whether China would accept such a code of conduct that specifically prohibited seizures of islands and atolls. It is argued among U.S. experts on Southeast Asia that a more assertive U.S. diplomacy would bolster ASEAN in its dealings with China. The Philippines favors a more assertive U.S. diplomacy. Other experts believe that ASEAN is too fragmented to be effective, and they warn against the United States making the South China Sea a contentious issue in U.S.-China relations.[14]

A failure of the code of conduct initiative could have serious implications for U.S.-Philippine security relations. In 1999, Malaysia, another claimant and ASEAN member, occupied two islands in the Spratlys. This intensified debate within the Philippine government over whether the AFP should occupy key positions in the Philippine-claimed area in the Spratlys. The Philippine Defense Ministry has proposed such action; but the Foreign Ministry opposes it, arguing that diplomacy should be given a further opportunity.[15] A collapse of the code of conduct initiative could tilt the debate in favor of the Defense Ministry. A move by the AFP to occupy positions in the Spratlys would create new issues and decisions for the United States in terms of the degree of U.S. security support for Manila. A collapse of the code of conduct initiative also could produce a chain reaction in which all the claimants moved to occupy islands and atolls. Either a singular Philippine reaction or a chain reaction could escalate the danger of military clashes in the South China Sea.

---

[14] McDevitt, Michael. China and the South China Sea: A Conference Summary Report. *PacNet.*, April 16, 1999.

[15] Espina, Rene. Foreign Policy Reviewed. *Manila Bulletin* (internet version), June 27, 1999. Tiglao, Rigoberto. Seaside Boom. *Far Eastern Economic Review,* July 8, 1999. P. 14.

Chapter 3

RELIGIOUS FREEDOM IN THE PHILIPPINES

Edward P. Lipton

The Constitution provides for freedom of religion, and the Government generally respects this right in practice, although there were a few exceptions. There was no change in the status of respect for religious freedom during the period covered by this report. Adherents of all faiths are free to exercise their religious beliefs in all parts of the country without government interference or restriction; however, socioeconomic disparity between the Christian majority and the Muslim minority has contributed to persistent conflict in certain provinces.

The principal remaining armed insurgent Muslim group continued to seek greater autonomy or an independent Islamic state. Peace talks between the Government and this group stalled during June 2000 as violent clashes claimed many lives on both sides. Negotiations began again after Gloria Macapagal-Arroyo became President in January 2001. In June 2001, the Government reached agreement with this group to implement a cease-fire agreement, cooperate in efforts to resettle displaced persons, and undertake development projects in areas of conflict. Militant Muslim splinter groups have engaged in terrorism. Moderate Muslim leaders strongly criticized these tactics. There is some ethnic and cultural discrimination against Muslims by Christians. This has led some Muslims to seek successfully a degree of political autonomy for Muslims in the southwestern part of the country. The U.S. Embassy discusses religious freedom issues with the Government in the context of its overall dialog and policy of promoting human rights.

SECTION I. RELIGIOUS DEMOGRAPHY

The Philippines has a land area of approximately 118,000 square miles, and its population is approximately 76.4 million. Over 85 percent of citizens of this former Spanish colony claim membership in the Roman Catholic Church, according to the most recent official census data on religious preference (1990). Other Christian denominations together comprise approximately 8.7 percent of the population. Followers of the Islamic faith totaled 4.6 percent and Buddhists 0.1 percent. Indigenous and other religious traditions accounted for

1.2 percent of those surveyed. Atheists and persons who did not designate a religious preference accounted for 0.3 percent of the population.

Some academic experts question the accuracy of the statistical sampling in the 1990 census. Some Muslim scholars argue that census takers seriously undercounted the number of Muslims because of security concerns in western Mindanao, where Muslims still are a majority, that often prevented them from conducting accurate counts outside urban areas. Current estimates place the number of Muslims at least 5 million, or approximately 7 percent of the population. Muslims reside principally in Mindanao and nearby islands and are the largest single minority religious group in the country. There is no available data on ''nominal'' members of religious organizations. Estimates of nominal members of the largest group, Roman Catholics, range from 60 to 65 percent of the total population. These estimates are based on regular church attendance. El Shaddai, a lay charismatic movement affiliated with the Roman Catholic Church, has grown rapidly in the last decade; it claims approximately 5 million active members within the country and an additional 300,000 members in other countries.

Most Muslims belong to the Sunni branch of Islam. There is a small number of Shi'a believers in the provinces of Lanao del Sur and Zamboanga del Sur. Approximately 19 percent of the population of Mindanao is Muslim, according to the 1990 census. Members of the Muslim minority are concentrated in five provinces of western Mindanao: Maguindanao; Lanao del Sur; Basilan; Sulu; and Tawi-Tawi. There also are significant Muslim communities in nearby Mindanao provinces, including Zamboanga del Sur, Zamboanga del Norte, Sultan Kudarat, Lanao del Norte, and North Cotabato. There are sizable Muslim neighborhoods in metropolitan Manila on Luzon, and in Palawan. Among Protestant and other Christian groups, there are numerous denominations, including Seventh Day-Adventists, United Church of Christ, United Methodist, Assemblies of God, and Philippine (Southern) Baptist denominations. In addition there are two churches established by Filipino religious leaders, the Independent Church of the Philippines or Aglipayan and the Iglesia ni Cristo (Church of Christ). A majority of the country's nearly 12 million indigenous people reportedly are Christians. However, observers note that many indigenous groups mix elements of their native religions with Christian beliefs and practices. Christian missionaries work in most parts of western Mindanao, often within Muslim communities.

SECTION II. STATUS OF RELIGIOUS FREEDOM

Legal/Policy Framework

The Constitution provides for freedom of religion, and the Government generally respects this right in practice, although there were a few exceptions. Although Christianity, particularly Roman Catholicism, is the dominant religion, there is no state religion. The Government generally does not restrict adherents of other religions from practicing their faith. Organized religions must register with the Securities and Exchange Commission as nonstock, nonprofit organizations and with the Bureau of Internal Revenue to establish their tax-exempt status. There were no reports of discrimination in the registration system during the period covered by this report. The Government provides no direct subsidies to institutions for religious purposes, including aid to the extensive school systems maintained by religious orders and church groups. The Office of Muslim affairs, funded through the Office of the President, generally limits its activities to fostering Islamic religious practices, although it also has the authority to coordinate projects for economic growth in predominantly Muslim areas. The office's Philippine Pilgrimage Authority helps coordinate the travel of religious pilgrimage groups to Mecca, in Saudi Arabia, by providing bus service to and from airports, hotel reservations, and guides. The Presidential Assistant for Muslim Affairs helps coordinate relations with countries that have large Islamic populations that have contributed to Mindanao's economic development and to the peace process with insurgent groups.

The four-province Autonomous Region in Muslim Mindanao (ARMM) was established in 1990 to respond to the demand of Muslims for local autonomy in areas where they are a majority or a substantial minority. The provinces comprising the ARMM are: Maguindanao; Lanao del Sur; Sulu; and Tawi-Tawi. In 1996 the Government signed a peace agreement with the Islamic Moro National Liberation Front (MNLF), concluding an often violent struggle that had lasted more than 20 years. A plebiscite on autonomy for an expanded autonomous region, promised in the 1996 peace agreement, again was postponed during the period covered by this report. The Government is working with the MNLF's leaders on a variety of development programs to reintegrate former MNLF fighters into the market economy through jobs and business opportunities. In addition the integration of ex- MNLF fighters into the armed forces and police has eased suspicion between Christians and Muslims.

Peace negotiations between the Government and the Moro Islamic Liberation Front (MILF), the chief remaining armed Muslim separatist group, stalled during June 2000. During the second half of 2000, government forces completed the military offensives begun during the first half of the year, overrunning most MILF strongholds. Negotiations began again after Gloria Macapagal-Arroyo became President in January 2001. In June 2001, the Government reached agreement with the MILF to implement a cease-fire agreement, cooperate in efforts to resettle displaced persons, and undertake development projects in areas of conflict.

In June 2000, following persistent reports that troops operating against Muslim separatists in Mindanao had desecrated mosques, the Secretary of National Defense ordered the AFP to refrain from such action. The Department of National Defense issued code-of-conduct instructions that included provisions that military offensives could not be begun during Muslim prayer hours "unless absolutely required." The Code of Muslim Personal Laws, enacted in 1977, recognizes the Shari'a (Islamic law) civil law system as part of national law; however, it applies only to Muslims, and applies regardless of their place of residence in the country. As part of their strategy for a moral and religious revival in western Mindanao, some Muslim religious leaders (ulamas) argue that the Government should allow Islamic courts to extend their jurisdiction to criminal law cases, a step beyond the many civil law cases that they already can settle as part of the judicial system in western Mindanao. Some ulamas also support the MILF's goal of forming an autonomous region governed in accordance with Islamic law.

Based on a traditional policy of promoting moral education, local public schools make available to church groups the opportunity to teach moral values during school hours. Attendance is not mandatory, and various churches rotate in sharing classroom space. In many parts of Mindanao, Muslim students routinely attend Catholic schools from elementary to university level. These students are not required to undertake Catholic religious instruction.

Restrictions on Religious Freedom

Muslims, who are concentrated in the most impoverished parts of western Mindanao, complained that the Government has not made sufficient effort toward economic development in those areas. Some Muslim religious leaders asserted that Muslims suffer from economic discrimination, which is reflected in the Government's failure to provide money to stimulate southwestern Mindanao's sluggish economic development. Leaders in both Christian and Muslim communities contend that economic disparities and ethnic tensions, more than religious differences, are at the root of the modern separatist movement that emerged in the early 1970's. Intermittent government efforts to integrate Muslims into political and economic society have achieved only limited success to date. Many Muslims claim that they continue to be underrepresented in senior civilian and military positions, and have cited the lack of proportional Muslim representation in the national government institutions.

At the end of the period covered by this report, there was one Muslim cabinet secretary and two Muslim senior presidential advisors, but no Muslim senators or Supreme Court justices. There are 7 Muslims in the 206-member House of Representatives. In July 2000, many Muslims complained of the Government's disrespect for Muslim religious practices when then-President Estrada celebrated an Armed Forces of the Philippines (AFP) military victory by holding a pork and beer feast at the former headquarters of the separatist MILF.

The Government placed responsibility on the MILF for mass killings on July 16, 2000 in Bumbaran, Lanao del Sur Province, but after subsequent investigation, the Commission on Human Rights stated that the perpetrators could have been non- MILF separatists posing as MILF members, or may have been renegade former members of the MNLF. MILF soldiers reportedly had forced approximately 33 civilians, all Christians, into a Muslim prayer house in the early morning. After a nearby battle during the day between the MILF and government forces, armed persons fired on the civilians in custody, killing 21 persons and injuring 9 others. The profit-oriented terrorist Abu Sayyaf Group (ASG) claims to seek the immediate establishment of an independent Islamic state in the southwestern part of the country. In fact, however, the ASG is a loose collection of criminal-terrorist gangs, and its religious affiliation is rejected by mainstream Muslim leaders. All ASG kidnap victims taken during 2000 except one had been released by mid-April 2001, but in late May the ASG kidnapped another 20 hostages, including several foreign nationals. More hostages were taken in June 2001, and several were beheaded by their captors. Most of those hostages remained in captivity at mid-year. Although many Muslims believe that discrimination against them is rooted in their religious culture, most do not favor the establishment of a separate state, and the overwhelming majority reject terrorism as a means of achieving a satisfactory level of autonomy. Mainstream Muslim leaders, both domestic and foreign, have strongly criticized the actions of the ASG and its renegade offshoots as ''un-Islamic.''

Forced Religious Conversions

There were no reports of forced religious conversion, including of minor U.S. citizens who had been abducted or illegally removed from the United States, or of the Government's refusal to allow such citizens to be returned to the United States.

SECTION III. SOCIETAL ATTITUDES

Religious affiliation is customarily a function of a person's family, ethnic group, or tribal membership. Historically, Muslims have been alienated socially from the dominant Christian majority, and there is some ethnic and cultural discrimination against Muslims. Christian and Muslim communities live in close proximity throughout central and western Mindanao and, in many areas, their relationship is harmonious. However, efforts by the dominant Christian population to resettle in traditionally Muslim areas, particularly over the past 60 years, have brought resentment from some Muslim residents. Muslims view Christian proselytizing as an extension of an historical effort by the Christian majority to deprive them of their homeland and cultural identity as well as their religion. Christian missionaries work in most parts of western Mindanao, often within Muslim communities.

On August 27, 2000, unidentified persons attacked a vehicle and killed 12 passengers, all Muslims, in Carmen, North Cotabato. The Government blamed the MILF, but the provincial governor stated that those responsible may have been civilians seeking revenge on Muslims. The national culture, with its emphasis on familial, tribal, and regional loyalties, creates informal barriers whereby access to jobs or resources is provided first to those of one's own family or group. Some employers have a biased expectation that Muslims have a lower educational level. Predominantly Muslim provinces in Mindanao continue to lag behind the rest of the island of Mindanao in almost all aspects of socioeconomic development.

Religious dialog and cooperation among the country's various religious communities generally are amicable. Many religious leaders are involved in ecumenical activities and also in interdenominational efforts to alleviate poverty. The Interfaith Group, which is registered as a non-governmental organization, includes Roman Catholic, Islamic, and Protestant church representatives who have joined together in an effort to support the Mindanao peace process through work with communities of former combatants. Besides social and economic support, the Interfaith Group seeks to encourage Mindanao communities to instill their faiths in their children. Amicable ties among religious groups are reflected in many nonofficial organizations. The leadership of human rights groups, trade union confederations, and industry associations represent many religious persuasions.

The Bishops-Ulamas Conference, which meets monthly to deepen mutual doctrinal understanding between Roman Catholic and Muslim leaders in Mindanao, helps further the Mindanao peace process. The co-chairs of the conference are the Archbishop of Davao, Ferdinand Capalla, and the president of the Ulama Association, Majid Mutilan, the outgoing governor of Lanao del Sur province. The conference seeks to foster exchanges at the local level between parish priests and local Islamic teachers. Paralleling the dialog fostered by religious leaders, the Silsila Foundation in Zamboanga City hosts a regional exchange among Muslim and Christian academics and local leaders meant to reduce bias and promote cooperation. The Government's National Ecumenical Commission (NEC) fosters interfaith dialog among the major religious groups—the Roman Catholic Church, Islam, Iglesia ni Cristo, the Philippine Independent Church (Aglipayan), and Protestant denominations. The Protestant churches are represented in the NEC by the National Council of Churches of the Philippines and the Council of Evangelical Churches of the Philippines. Members of the NEC met periodically with the President to discuss social and political questions.

PART 2: HISTORICAL BACKGROUND

Chapter 4

PHILIPPINES: FACTS AT A GLANCE

Ronald E. Dolan

Formal Name: Republic of the Philippines
Short Form: Philippines
Term for Citizens: Filipinos
Capital: Manila
Date of Independence: Attained full independence from United States July 4, 1946.

GEOGRAPHY

Location and Size: Archipelago off coast of Southeast Asia, total 300,000 square kilometers, land area 298,170 square kilometers.

Topography: Archipelago of 7,100 islands: Luzon, Mindanao, Palawan, and numerous smaller islands, all prone to earthquakes. Largely mountainous terrain, creating narrow coastal plains and interior valleys and plains. Major plains include those of Central Luzon, northeastern Cagayan Valley, and Agusan Basin in far south. Numerous dormant and active volcanos, notably Mount Pinatubo in Central Luzon. Highest point Mount Apo (2,954 meters).

Climate: Tropical marine; northeast monsoon (December to February), southwest monsoon (May to October). Mean annual sea-level temperatures rarely fall below 27° C. Frequent typhoons.

SOCIETY

Population: 66,117,284 in July 1990; average population density 220 persons per square kilometer; annual growth rate 2.5 percent; birth rate 29 per 1,000 (in 1991); death rate 7 per 1,000 (in 1991).

Ethnic Groups: 91.5 percent Christian Malay, almost 5 percent Muslim Malay, close to 1 percent Chinese, and 3 percent other, mainly upland tribal groups.

Language: Pilipino (based on Tagalog) and English (official languages). Eleven languages and eighty-seven dialects indigenous to archipelago.

Religion: In 1989 approximately 82 percent Roman Catholic, approximately 9 percent associated with Iglesia ni Kristo and various Protestant denominations, 5 percent Muslim, remainder Buddhist, Daoist (or Taoist), or other religions.

Education: In 1989 six years of compulsory, free elementary education provided to approximately 15 million students, more than 96 percent of age-group. Approximately 290,000 teachers in 34,000 elementary schools. Beginning at age 13, approximately 4 million students, more than 55 percent of age-group, enrolled in 5,500 secondary schools with approximately 80,000 teachers; 1.6 million enrolled in 1,675 institutions of higher education with 56,380 instructors. Supervised by Department of Education, Culture, and Sports. Literacy rate nearly 90 percent in 1990.

Health: In 1990 life expectancy 69 years for women, 63 years for men; infant mortality rate in 1989 was 51.6 deaths per 1,000 births. Main health hazards: pulmonary, cardiovascular, and gastrointestinal disorders. Health care system in 1989 adequate in urban areas, minimal in rural areas; 33,000 health professionals, including 9,500 physicians, and 1,700 hospitals with 85,000 beds concentrated in urban areas.

ECONOMY

Salient Features: Economy struggling under heavy foreign debt. Approximately 50 percent of population below poverty line; unemployment 10.3 percent in mid-1991, underemployment estimated at nearly twice that rate. Large overseas work force. Rapid economic growth of 1970s slowed considerably in 1980s. Prospects for 1990s uncertain.

Gross National Product (GNP): US$41.5 billion (1990); per capita GNP US$668 (1990).

Gross Domestic Product (GDP): Approximately US$43 billion (1990).

Resources: Ample manganese, nickel, cobalt, copper, gold, silver, and low-grade iron ores and coal. In late 1980s, petroleum and natural gas production provided less than half of energy needs. Excellent potential for hydroelectric and geothermal energy.

Industry: 33 percent of GNP and approximately 15 percent of work force in 1990. Major industries: textiles, food processing, chemicals, pharmaceuticals, wood products, and electronics equipment assembly.

Services: 44 percent of GNP and approximately 40 percent of work force in 1990.

Agriculture, Forestry, and Fishing: 23 percent of GNP and slightly more than 45 percent of work force in 1990. Intense cultivation of diminishing arable land, already in short supply. Major crops: rice, corn, coconuts, sugarcane, pineapples, and bananas. Rapidly declining timber resources. In 1990, 2 million ton fish catch provided more than half of domestic protein consumption.

Foreign Trade: Heavy importation of capital goods and high petroleum prices along with weak export growth resulted in large trade deficit increase.

Exports: Approximately US$8.1 billion in 1989. Major products: clothing, electronic components, nickel, coconut products, sugar, pineapples, bananas. Major partners: United States, European Community, Japan.

Imports: Approximately US$12.1 billion in 1989. Major products: fuels, lubricants, motor vehicles, consumer goods. Major partners: United States, Japan, Economic and Social Commission for Asia and the Pacific, European Community.

Balance of Payments: Current account deficit US$1.4 billion in 1989.

Exchange Rate: P24.96=US$1 (January 1992).

Fiscal Year: Calendar year.

TRANSPORTATION AND COMMUNICATIONS

Maritime: Extensive interisland transportation; 314 private and 622 public seaports, including major ports at Manila, Cebu, Iloilo, Cagayan de Oro, Zamboanga, and Davao.

Railroads: In 1990 one main line from Manila 266 kilometers north to San Fernando and La Union, 474 kilometers south to Legaspi City; 15 kilometers of Light Rail Transit system in Metro Manila.

Roads: In 1988 some 157,000 kilometers of various type roads; 26,000 kilometers designated national (arterial) roads. Somewhat less than 50 percent of national roads all-weather surfaces.

Airports: Total of 301 airports, 237 usable; international facilities at Manila (Ninoy Aquino) and near Cebu City (Mactan). Philippine Airlines serves domestic and international routes.

Telecommunications: In 1989, 380 radio stations and 42 television stations. In 1990, 872,900 telephones, mainly concentrated in Metro Manila; 4 million radio receivers, 6 million television receivers.

GOVERNMENT AND POLITICS

Government: Presidential form of government based on 1987 constitution with president and vice president elected separately by popular vote. Bicameral legislature (Congress: Senate--upper house; House of Representatives--lower house). President limited to one six-year term. Senators elected nationwide and limited to two consecutive six-year terms, representatives elected from 200 districts and limited to three consecutive three-year terms.

Politics: Numerous political parties. In 1992 main parties included PDP-LABAN, Lakas-NUCD, Nacionalista Party, and Liberal Party.

Administrative Divisions: 73 provinces and 61 chartered cities.

Judiciary: Civil law system heavily influenced by Spanish and Anglo-American law. Independent judiciary headed by Supreme Court, with anticorruption Sandiganbayan, Court of Tax Appeals, Intermediate Appellate Court, regional trial courts, and metropolitan and municipal courts.

Media: Freedom of expression constitutional right; about thirty daily newspapers in 1991.

Foreign Affairs: Diplomatic relations with virtually all countries of world. Member of international organizations, including Association of Southeast Asian Nations (ASEAN), Asian Development Bank, and United Nations and its affiliated agencies.

NATIONAL SECURITY

Armed Forces: Armed Forces of Philippines (AFP), with total active duty strength of 106,500 in late 1991: army 68,000, navy 23,000 (including 8,500 marines and 2,000 coast guard), and air force 15,500. Reserves totaled 128,000: army 100,000, navy 12,000, and air force 16,000.

Military Units: Six area unified commands, six naval districts, and thirteen air force squadrons.

Equipment: Army: light tanks, armored infantry fighting vehicles, armored personnel carriers, towed howitzers, mortars, and recoilless rifles. Navy: frigates, patrol and coastal combatants, amphibious ships and craft, auxiliaries, and rotary and fixed-wing aircraft. Air Force: fighters, reconnaissance aircraft, transport aircraft, helicopters, and training aircraft.

Military Budget: Approximately US$968.4 million in FY 1991.

Foreign Military Treaties: Mutual Defense Treaty Between the Republic of the Philippines and the United States of America (1951).

Insurgency: In 1992 New People's Army (NPA), military arm of Communist Party of the Philippines-Marxist Leninist a formidable threat, especially in Luzon; Moro National Liberation Front (MNLF) potential threat in the south.

Police: Philippine Constabulary combined with Integrated National Police on January 1, 1991, to form Philippine National Police under newly created Department of Interior and Local Government.

Chapter 5

PHILIPPINES: A COUNTRY STUDY

Ronald E. Dolan

INTRODUCTION

In early spring 1992, as President Corazon C. Aquino approached the end of her term, there was no doubt that her administration had restored a functioning democratic system to the Philippines. Aquino herself had decided not to seek another term as president even though the one-term presidency limitation imposed by the constitution did not apply to her. There was, however, no dearth of aspirants for the position. Eight candidates, including former First Lady Imelda Marcos, who had returned to the Philippines in the fall of 1991 to face embezzlement charges, were considered serious contenders.

In 1992, although its citizens had many reasons to hope for a brighter future, the Philippines was a nation beset with numerous economic and political problems. These problems has been compounded by a series of natural disasters: in the wake of a massive earthquake in northern Luzon in July 1990 and a devastating typhoon in the central Visyas in November 1990, the Mount Pinatubo volcano in Central Luzon erupted for the first time in 600 years in early June 1991. The eruption covered the surrounding countryside with molten ash and caused serious damage to the infrastructure of the region, including United States military facilities at Clark Air Base and Subic Bay Naval Base. The economy, which had slowed to a 3-percent gross national product (GNP--see Glossary) growth in 1990, fell by 0.6 percent in the first six months of 1991 and by slightly more than that in the third quarter. Inflation peaked at 19.3 percent in August 1991, declined to 15.8 percent by November, but remained far above the 9.5-percent International Monetary Fund (IMF--see Glossary) target for the year. Investment, up 19.7 percent from January to September 1991, was nearly offset by the inflation rate, resulting in only a marginal increase. Unemployment was 10.3 percent in July 1991, nearly two percentage points higher than the previous year, and most economists estimated underemployment to be at least twice that rate.

In the early 1990s, the Philippines was rather densely populated (220 persons per square kilometer), and the annual population growth rate was 2.5 percent. Approximately 57 percent of the population was under twenty years of age. Education was very highly regarded, as it had been throughout most of the twentieth century. The literacy rate of the total population approached 90 percent, and compulsory, free education reached nearly all elementary school-age children, even in the remotest areas. Health care was adequate in urban areas, less so in the countryside.

Corazon Aquino had been swept into the presidency by the February 1986 "People's Power" uprising amid high expectations that she would be able to right all of the wrongs in the Philippine body politic. It soon became evident, however, that her goals were essentially limited to restoring democratic institutions. She renounced the dictatorial powers that she had inherited from President Ferdinand E. Marcos and returned the Philippines to the rule of law, replacing the Marcos constitution with a democratic, progressive document that won overwhelming popular approval in a nationwide plebiscite, and scheduling national legislative and local elections. The new constitution, ratified in 1987, gives the Philippines a presidential system of government similar to that of the United States. The constitution provides the checks and balances of a three-branch government. It provides for the presidency; a two-house Congress, the Senate and the House of Representatives; and an independent judiciary capped by the Supreme Court. The constitution also provides for regular elections and contains a bill of rights guaranteeing the same political freedoms found in the United States Constitution. Fueled by a constitutionally guaranteed free and open press, the freewheeling political life that had existed before the martial law period (1972-81) soon resumed. But most of the political problems, including widespread corruption, human rights abuses, and inequitable distribution of wealth and power, remained.

Many of the most intractable problems in the Philippines can be traced to the country's colonial past. One major source of tension and instability stems from the great disparity in wealth and power between the affluent upper social stratum and the mass of low-income, often impoverished, Filipinos. In 1988 the wealthiest 10 percent of the population received nearly 36 percent of the income, whereas the poorest 30 percent of the population received less than 15 percent of the income.

The roots of the disparity between the affluent and the impoverished lie in the structure established under Spanish rule, lasting from the first settlement under Miguel López de Legazpi in 1565 to the beginning of United States rule in 1898. Friars of various Roman Catholic orders, acting as surrogates of the Spanish government, had integrated the scattered peoples of the *barangays* (see Glossary) into administrative entities and firmly implanted Roman Catholicism among them as the dominant faith--except in the southern Muslim-dominated portion of the archipelago. Over the centuries, these orders acquired huge landed estates and became wealthy, sometimes corrupt, and very powerful. Eventually, their estates were acquired by *principales* (literally, principal ones; a term for the indigenous local elite) and Chinese mestizos (see Glossary) eager to take advantage of expanding opportunities in agriculture and commerce. The children of these new entrepreneurs and landlords were provided education opportunities not available to the general populace and formed the nucleus of an emerging, largely provincially based, sociocultural elite--the *ilustrados* (see Glossary)-- who dominated almost all aspects of national life in later generations.

The peasants revolted from time to time against their growing impoverishment on the landed estates. They were aided by some reform-minded *ilustrados*, who made persistent demands for better treatment of the colony and its eventual assimilation with Spain. In the late nineteenth century, inflamed by various developments, including the martyrdom of three Filipino priests, a number of young *ilustrados* took up the nationalist banner in their writings, published chiefly in Europe. During the struggle for independence against Spain (1896-98), *ilustrados* and peasants made common cause against the colonial power, but not before a period of *ilustrado* vacillation, reflective of doubts about the outcome of a confrontation that had begun as a mass movement among workers and peasants around Manila. Once committed to the struggle, however, the ilustrados took over, becoming the articulators and leaders of the fight for independence--first against Spain, then against the United States.

Philippine peasant guerrilla forces contributed to the defeat of the Spanish. When the Filipinos were denied independence by the United States, they focused their revolutionary activity on United States forces, holding out in the hills for several years. The *ilustrado* leadership chose to accommodate to the seemingly futile situation. Once again, *ilustrados* found themselves in an intermediary position as arbiters between the colonial power and the rest of the population. *Ilustrados* responded eagerly to United States tutelage in democratic values and process in preparation for eventual Philippine self-rule, and, in return for their allegiance, United States authorities began to yield control to the *ilustrados*. Although a massive United States-sponsored popular education program exposed millions of Filipinos to the basic workings of democratic government, political leadership at the regional and national levels became almost entirely the province of families of the sociocultural elite. Even into the 1990s, most Philippine political leaders belonged to this group.

Members of the peasantry, for their part, continued to stage periodic uprisings in protest against their difficult situation. As the twentieth century progressed, their standard of living worsened as a result of population growth, usury, the spread of absentee landlordism, and the weakening of the traditional patron-client bonds of reciprocal obligation.

Whereas the economic legacy of colonialism, including the relative impoverishment of a very large segment of the population, left seeds of dissension in its wake, not all of the enduring features of colonial rule were destabilizing forces. Improvements in education and health had done much to enhance the quality of life. More important in the context of stabilizing influences was the profound impact of Roman Catholicism. The great majority of the Filipino people became Catholic, and the prelates of the church profoundly influenced the society.

Beginning with independence in 1946, the church was a source of stability to the infant nation. Throughout the period of constitutional government up to the declaration of martial law in 1972, however, the church remained outside of politics; its largely conservative clergy was occupied almost exclusively with religious matters.

Democracy functioned fairly well in the Philippines until 1972. National elections were held regularly under the framework of the 1935 constitution, which established checks and balances among the principal branches of government. Elections provided freewheeling, sometimes violent, exchanges between two loosely structured political parties, with one succeeding the other at the apex of power in a remarkably consistent cycle of alternation. Ferdinand Marcos, first elected to the presidency in 1965, was reelected by a large margin in 1969, the first president since independence to be elected to a second term.

Discontent rooted in economic disparity and religious differences grew in the late 1960s. The New People's Army (NPA), a guerrilla force formed in 1968 in Tarlac Province, north of Manila, by the newly established Communist Party of the Philippines-Marxist Leninist, soon spread to other parts of Luzon and throughout the archipelago. In the south, demands for Muslim autonomy and violence, often between indigenous Muslims and government-sponsored Christian immigrants who had begun to move down from the north, were on the rise. In 1969 the Moro National Liberation Front (MNLF) was organized as a guerrilla force for the Muslim cause. The volatile political situation came to a head when grenade explosions in the Plaza Miranda in Manila during an opposition Liberal Party rally on August 21, 1971, killed 9 people and wounded 100. Marcos blamed the leftists and suspended habeas corpus. Thirteen months later, on September 21, 1972, Marcos used a provision of the 1935 constitution to declare martial law after an attempt was reportedly made to assassinate Minister of National Defense Juan Ponce Enrile. In 1986, after Marcos's downfall, Enrile admitted that his unoccupied car had been riddled by machine-gun bullets fired by his own people.

Under the provisions of martial law, Marcos shut down Congress and most newspapers, jailed his major political opponents, assumed dictatorial powers, and ruled by presidential decree. During the early years of martial law, the economy improved, benefiting from increased business confidence and Marcos's appointment of talented technocrats to economic planning posts. But over the next few years, major segments of the economy gradually were brought under the control of the Marcos crony (see Glossary) group. Monopolies controlled by Marcos cronies were subsidized heavily, seriously depleting the national treasury. The previously apolitical, professional armed forces were used by Marcos to enforce martial law and ensure his political survival. Even after Marcos rescinded martial law in January 1981, he continued to rule with virtual dictatorial powers. Thus, it came as no surprise that Marcos won an overwhelming victory in the June 1981 presidential election, an election that was boycotted by most opposition forces.

In the late 1970s and early 1980s, as the economic and political situation deteriorated, opposition to the Marcos government grew. The Catholic Church, the country's strongest and most independent non-governmental institution, became increasingly critical of the government. Priests, nuns, and the church hierarchy, motivated by their commitment to human rights and social justice, became involved in redressing the sufferings of the common people through the political process. The business community became increasingly apprehensive during this period, as inflation and unemployment soared and the GNP stagnated and declined. Young military officers, desirous of a return to pre- martial law professionalism, allied with Minister of National Defense Enrile to oppose close Marcos associates in the military.

One of Marcos's first acts under martial law was to jail Senator Benigno "Ninoy" Aquino, his main opponent and most likely successor. But even in his imprisonment, Aquino maintained a large following, and when he was allowed to go to the United States for medical treatment in 1980, he became a more formidable leader of the opposition in exile. By 1983 the deteriorating economic and political situation and Marcos's worsening health convinced Aquino that in order to prevent civil war he must return to the Philippines to build a responsible united opposition and persuade Marcos to relinquish power.

Despite the obvious danger to his personal safety, Aquino returned. He was shot in the head and killed on August 21, 1983, as he was escorted off an airplane at Manila International Airport by soldiers of the Aviation Security Command. As a martyr, Aquino became the focus of popular indignation against the corrupt Marcos regime, a more formidable opponent in death than in life. The opposition, initially consisted primarily of the Catholic hierarchy, the business elite, and a faction of the armed forces. It grew into the People's Power movement with millions of rural, working class, middle class, and professional supporters, when Aquino's widow, Corazon "Cory" Aquino, returned to the Philippines to take over, first symbolically and then substantively, as leader of the opposition.

In November 1985, Marcos, still convinced that he had control of the political situation, announced a presidential election for February 7, 1986, one year before the expiration of his presidential term. Cardinal Jaime Sin, the archbishop of Manila, arranged a political alliance of convenience that ran the immensely popular Cory Aquino as candidate for president and politically astute Salvador "Doy" Laurel as vice president. The Aquino-Laurel ticket gained the support of the Catholic Church and a substantial part of the electorate and, despite widespread fraud by Marcos supporters, garnered a majority of votes in the election. Nevertheless, the Marcos-dominated National Assembly declared Marcos the winner on February 15.

Opposition at home and abroad was immediate and vociferous. On February 22, Minister of National Defense Juan Ponce Enrile and the commander of the Philippine Constabulary, Fidel V. Ramos, issued a joint statement demanding Marcos's resignation and set up a rebel headquarters inside Camp Aguinaldo and the adjoining Camp Crame in Metro Manila (see Glossary). When Marcos called out troops loyal to him to put down the rebellion, Cardinal Sin broadcast an appeal over the church-run Radio Veritas calling on the people to render nonviolent support to the rebels. Hundreds of thousands of unamed priests, nuns, and ordinary citizens faced down the tanks and machine guns of the government troops. Violent confrontation was prevented and many government troops turned back or defected. By the evening of February 25, Marcos and his family were enroute to exile in Hawaii, and Corazon Aquino had assumed power.

The Aquino government had been in office only five months when it was challenged by the first of six coup attempts led by dissatisfied armed forces factions. The first attempt, a relatively minor affair, was quickly put down, but later attempts in August 1987 and December 1989, led by the same reformist officers that had helped bring Aquino to power, came very close to toppling her government. In the 1989 attempt, elite rebel units seized a major air base in Cebu, held parts of army and air force headquarters and the international airport, and were preparing to move on armed forces headquarters in Camp Aguinaldo when they were turned back. The threat of another coup attempt hung over the capital in 1990, but as Aquino's term drew to a close in 1991 and 1992, the threat had considerably diminished. Most disaffected military officers seemed content to seek change through the political process, and many officers involved in earlier coup attempts had been persuaded to give themselves up, confident of lenient treatment.

In 1992 the threat from domestic insurgents was somewhat reduced. Although the MNLF and other Moro insurgent groups were a major threat in the southern Philippines in the early 1970s, since that time, internal divisions, reduced external support, pressure by the armed forces, and government accommodations-- including the creation of an Autonomous Region in Muslim Mindanao in 1990--had greatly reduced that threat. The communist NPA peaked in 1987, when there were 26,000 guerrillas active in the field. In 1992, with approximately 20,000 full-time guerrilla troops, the NPA remained a formidable threat to the government. Arrest of a number of top insurgent cadres and major internal purges, however, had greatly reduced its power.

Despite Filipinos' serious concern for maintaining national identity and avoiding any appearance of foreign subjugation, in 1992 congruent interests and a long history of friendly relations made it seem likely that the United States would remain the Philippines' closest ally—even after the long, difficult, and ultimately unsuccessful negotiations to extend the Military Bases Agreement. The original Military Bases Agreement of 1947, amended in 1959 and again in 1979, was scheduled to expire in 1991 unless an extension was negotiated. Negotiations for continued United States use of the two major bases in the Philippines--Clark Air Base in Pampanga Province and Subic Bay Naval Base in Zambales Province--had begun in 1990. The tenor of the negotiations changed significantly, however, in 1991, when the end of the Cold War made the bases less important and the eruption of the Mount Pinatubo volcano rendered Clark Air Base unusable. By the end of August 1991, United States and Philippine negotiators had agreed to extend the United States lease of Subic Bay Naval Base for another ten years in return for US$360 million in direct compensation for the first year and US$203 million for the remaining nine years of the lease. But in September 1991, the Philippine Senate rejected the agreement. As a result, the United States was expected to vacate Subic Bay Naval Base, its only remaining base in the Philippines, by the end of 1992.

In early spring 1992, everyone's attention was turned to the upcoming national elections. Who would be the first president elected since the restoration of democracy? What would be the composition of the new Congress? Would the new president and the new Congress strike out in bold new directions or would it be more business as usual? The future of the Philippines depended on the answers to these questions.

* * *

Fidel Ramos succeeded Corazon Aquino as president of the Philippines on June 30, 1992, after winning a 23.6 percent plurality in the May 11, 1992, general election. Ramos, secretary of national defense in the Aquino administration and handpicked by Aquino to succeed her, narrowly defeated Secretary of Agrarian Reform Miriam Defensor Santiago, who received 19.8 percent of the vote, and former Marcos crony Eduardo Cojuangco, who received 18.1 percent.

The election proved that Corazon Aquino had succeeded in the primary goal of her presidency, restoring democracy to the Philippines. Nearly 85 percent of eligible voters turned out to elect 17,205 officials, including the president, the vice president, 24 members of the Senate, 200 members of the House of Representatives, 73 governors, and 1,602 mayors. The election was relatively peaceful; there was no threat of a military coup before, during, or after the election and only 52 election-related deaths were reported, compared to 150 in the 1986 presidential election. Despite claims of election fraud from losing candidates, the Commission on Elections apparently exercised effective control and relatively few voting irregularities were substantiated. Ramos won the election on his appeal for stability and a continuation of Aquino policies, and Santiago received strong support for her anticorruption candidacy. Cojuangco's substantial support, however, suggested that a large share of the electorate favored a return to the economic policies and the traditional patronage system of the Marcos era.

Shortly after his inauguration, Ramos sought a reconciliation with his former rivals from the presidential election, Imelda Marcos and Eduardo Cojuangco. In the House of Representatives, Ramos gained the position of speaker of the House for Jose de Venecia, his close political ally and secretary of the Lakas ng Edsa-National Union of Christian Democrats (Lakas-NUCD). Ramos received support from the fifty-one members of the House elected under the banner of the Lakas-NUCD alliance, which he had formed when he failed to get the nomination of the Laban Demokratikong Pilipino (LDP) party. In part because of his conciliatory approach, Ramos was also able to marshal support from a substantial share of LDP members, from members of Eduardo Cojuangco's Nationalist People's Party, and from members of the Liberal Party. He was less successful in the Senate, where LDP chairman Neptali Gonzales was elected president. Ramos seemed likely to face a major challenge getting his program to stimulate economic growth and restore order to the Philippines through a divided and potentially hostile Congress.

The Philippine economy showed some improvement in early 1992, spurred by increases in agricultural production and in consumer and government spending. Budget deficits were well within IMF guidelines--P3.2 billion in the first two months. At the end of April, the treasury posted a P5.5 billion surplus as a result of higher than programmed revenue receipts, mainly from the sale of Philippine Airlines. The increased revenue permitted the early repeal of the 5 percent import surcharge, stimulating both import spending and export growth. The money supply grew more rapidly than desired, but was kept under control. Treasury bill rates fell to 17.3 percent in March 1992 from 23 percent in November 1991, and inflation was down to 9.4 percent for the first quarter of 1992, from 18.7 percent in 1991.

One of the greatest threats to the Philippine economy in 1992 was the power shortage. The fall in the water level in Lake Lanao caused a 50 percent reduction in the power supply to Mindanao in December 1991, and the resumption of full power was not expected until almost the end of 1992. The power shortage in Luzon continued to be chronic. Power cuts of four to five hours per day have been common; in May they reached six hours on some days in Manila, the country's industrial hub. To help to meet this chronic shortage, the government reactivated the contract with Westinghouse Corporation to restart construction on a 620 megawatt nuclear power plant on the Bataan Peninsula that had been abandoned in 1986. This plant, however, will not be on line until 1995.

The conversion to civilian use of the military bases vacated by the United States poses another major economic challenge. The United States forces departed from the huge Subic Bay Naval Base on September 30, 1992, and the United States was expected to leave Cubi Point Naval Air Station, its last base in the Philippines, in November 1992. The Philippine Congress ratified a base conversion bill in February 1992 that created five special economic zones at the vacated United States bases under the Base Conversion Development Authority. The authority, which will exist for five years, will sell the land connected with the bases within six months and use half the proceeds to convert the bases to civilian use. One plan envisions converting the former Subic Bay Naval Base into a tourist center, industrial zone, container port, and commercial shipyard. But this plan will be hampered by the United States removal of major equipment, including three dry docks, from the base.

In late 1992, a new Philippine president and a new Congress, the first elected under the 1987 constitution, faced major economic and political challenges. An anxious Philippine citizenry waited to see how well its leader and elected representatives would cooperate in an attempt to meet these challenges.

HISTORICAL SETTING

On August 21, 1983, Benigno Aquino, leader of the Philippines democratic opposition, was assassinated as he left the airplane that had brought him back home after three years' exile in the United States. The explanation of the killing by the government of President Ferdinand E. Marcos, placing responsibility on a lone communist gunman, who himself was shot by government troops, aroused skepticism and was even rejected by a government appointed commission. It was evident to a majority of Filipinos that Aquino had been killed by the armed forces and that ultimate responsibility lay, if not with Ferdinand Marcos, with his powerful wife Imelda Romualdez Marcos and her close ally, General Fabian Ver. The killing exposed the Marcoses to massive popular indignation, even more than the communist and Muslim insurgencies in the countryside, economic distress, corruption of political institutions, and the incompetence and brutality of the military. Aquino's widow, Corazon Cojuangco Aquino, became a powerful symbol of democratic resurgence. Following a February 7, 1986, presidential election hopelessly compromised by regimeperpetuated abuses, she was brought to power by a popular movement that encompassed practically every major social group. Her struggle against Marcos was more than a political campaign and assumed the proportions of a moral crusade, backed by the Roman Catholic Church.

Ferdinand Marcos had been elected president in 1965 and won a second term in 1969. But, largely in order to perpetuate his regime, he felt constrained to impose martial law in September 1972. Long-established democratic institutions were shut down or coopted by the Marcos dictatorship. While the economies of neighboring states, such as Malaysia, Thailand, and Indonesia, flourished, or at least adequately weathered uncertainties during the late 1970s and early 1980s, the Philippine economy stagnated. The Aquino assassination caused any remaining confidence in business to evaporate. For ordinary Filipinos, this situation meant high inflation, unemployment, and declines in already low living standards.

The Marcos era from 1965 to 1986 and the ensuing democratic resurgence under Corazon Aquino revealed both the strengths and weaknesses of the nation's democratic institutions. A Spanish colony since the sixteenth century, the Philippines became a United States possession after the 1898 Spanish-American War, although local patriots wanted to establish an independent republic and fought a bitter guerrilla war against the new colonizers. Representative institutions were established in the first decade of United States rule in order to prepare the people for eventual independence. Particularly when compared with other Western colonies in Asia, progress in this direction was rapid. On November 15, 1935, the self-governing Commonwealth of the Philippines was established. Despite a harsh Japanese occupation during World War II, which inflicted tremendous suffering on the population, independence was achieved, on schedule, on July 4, 1946.

The independent Philippines had firmly established democratic institutions: a two-party system, an independent judiciary, a free press, and regularly scheduled national and local elections. Although there were electoral abuses, the candidates and the citizenry abided by the results. But social values emphasized the importance of personal relations over the rule of law, and the political system and economy since early American colonial days had been dominated by a small landholding elite that opposed meaningful social change, including land reform. The rural and urban poor lacked political power. Many joined communist insurgencies. By the early 1980s, a nation rich in natural resources had extreme poverty in some regions, such as the sugar growing island of Negros, and gaps between rich and poor were wider than in most of the other developing countries of Southeast Asia and East Asia (see fig. 1).

When Marcos declared martial law in September 1972, he promised to eliminate poverty and injustice and create a "New Society." Instead, he destroyed democratic institutions that would have acted as a brake on abuses of power by him, his wife, and their close associates. Corazon Aquino assumed power on February 25, 1986, amidst an atmosphere of hope and enthusiasm. But the obstacles she faced--communist insurgency, years of economic mismanagement, and an indigenous ethic that persistently emphasized group loyalties and patron-client relationships over the national welfare--were formidable.

Early History

Negrito, proto-Malay, and Malay peoples were the principal peoples of the Philippine archipelago. The Negritos are believed to have migrated by land bridges some 30,000 years ago, during the last glacial period. Later migrations were by water and took place over several thousand years in repeated movements before and after the start of the Christian era.

The social and political organization of the population in the widely scattered islands evolved into a generally common pattern. Only the permanent-field rice farmers of northern Luzon had any concept of territoriality. The basic unit of settlement was the *barangay* (see Glossary), originally a kinship group headed by a *datu* (chief). Within the *barangay*, the broad social divisions consisted of nobles, including the *datu*; freemen; and a group described before the Spanish period as dependents. Dependents included several categories with differing status: landless agricultural workers; those who had lost freeman status because of indebtedness or punishment for crime; and slaves, most of whom appear to have been war captives.

Islam was brought to the Philippines by traders and proselytizers from the Indonesian islands. By 1500 Islam was established in the Sulu Archipelago and spread from there to Mindanao; it had reached the Manila area by 1565. Muslim immigrants introduced a political concept of territorial states ruled by rajas or sultans who exercised suzerainty over the *datu*. Neither the political state concept of the Muslim rulers nor the limited territorial concept of the sedentary rice farmers of Luzon, however, spread beyond the areas where they originated. When the Spanish arrived in the sixteenth century, the majority of the estimated 500,000 people in the islands still lived in *barangay* settlements.

The Early Spanish Period, 1521-1762

The first recorded sighting of the Philippines by Europeans was on March 16, 1521, during Ferdinand Magellan's circumnavigation of the globe. Magellan landed on Cebu, claimed the land for Charles I of Spain, and was killed one month later by a local chief. The Spanish crown sent several expeditions to the archipelago during the next decades. Permanent Spanish settlement was finally established in 1565 when Miguel López de Legazpi, the first royal governor, arrived in Cebu from New Spain (Mexico). Six years later, after defeating a local Muslim ruler, he established his capital at Manila, a location that offered the excellent harbor of Manila Bay, a large population, and proximity to the ample food supplies of the central Luzon rice lands. Manila remained the center of Spanish civil, military, religious, and commercial activity in the islands. The islands were given their present name in honor of Philip II of Spain, who reigned from 1556 to 1598.

Spain had three objectives in its policy toward the Philippines, its only colony in Asia: to acquire a share in the spice trade, to develop contacts with China and Japan in order to further Christian missionary efforts there, and to convert the Filipinos to Christianity. Only the third objective was eventually realized, and this not completely because of the active resistance of both the Muslims in the south and the Igorot, the upland tribal peoples in the north. Philip II explicitly ordered that pacification of the Philippines be bloodless, to avoid a repetition of Spain's sanguinary conquests in the Americas. Occupation of the islands was accomplished with relatively little bloodshed, partly because most of the population (except the Muslims) offered little armed resistance initially.

Church and state were inseparably linked in carrying out Spanish policy. The state assumed administrative responsibility--funding expenditures and selecting personnel--for the new ecclesiastical establishments. Responsibility for conversion of the indigenous population to Christianity was assigned to several religious orders: the Dominicans, Franciscans, and Augustinians, known collectively as the friars--and to the Jesuits. At the lower levels of colonial administration, the Spanish built on traditional village organization by co-opting the traditional local leaders, thereby ruling indirectly.

This system of indirect rule helped create in rural areas a Filipino upper class, referred to as the *principalía* or the *principales* (principal ones). This group had local wealth; high status and prestige; and certain privileges, such as exemption from taxes, lesser roles in the parish church, and appointment to local offices. The *principalía* was larger and more influential than the preconquest nobility, and it created and perpetuated an oligarchic system of local control. Among the most significant and enduring changes that occurred under Spanish rule was that the Filipino idea of communal use and ownership of land was replaced with the concept of private, individual ownership and the conferring of titles on members of the *principalía*.

Religion played a significant role in Spain's relations with and attitudes toward the indigenous population. The Spaniards considered conversion through baptism to be a symbol of allegiance to their authority. Although they were interested in gaining a profit from the colony, the Spanish also recognized a responsibility to protect the property and personal rights of these new Christians.

The church's work of converting Filipinos was facilitated by the absence of other organized religions, except for Islam, which predominated in the south. The missionaries had their greatest success among women and children, although the pageantry of the church had a wide appeal, reinforced by the incorporation of Filipino social customs into religious observances, for example, in the fiestas celebrating the patron saint of a local community (see Religious Life). The eventual outcome was a new cultural community of the main Malay lowland population, from which the Muslims (known by the Spanish as Moros, or Moors) and the upland tribal peoples of Luzon remained detached and alienated.

The Spanish found neither spices nor exploitable precious metals in the Philippines. The ecology of the islands was little changed by Spanish importations and technical innovations, with the exception of corn cultivation and some extension of irrigation in order to increase rice supplies for the growing urban population. The colony was not profitable, and a long war with the Dutch in the seventeenth century and intermittent conflict with the Moros nearly bankrupted the colonial treasury. Annual deficits were made up by a subsidy from Mexico.

Colonial income derived mainly from entrepôt trade: The "Manila galleons" sailing from Acapulco on the west coast of Mexico brought shipments of silver bullion and minted coin that were exchanged for return cargoes of Chinese goods, mainly silk textiles. There was no direct trade with Spain. Failure to exploit indigenous natural resources and investment of virtually all official, private, and church capital in the galleon trade were mutually reinforcing tendencies. Loss or capture of the galleons or Chinese junks en route to Manila represented a financial disaster for the colony.

The thriving entrepôt trade quickly attracted growing numbers of Chinese to Manila. The Chinese, in addition to managing trade transactions, were the source of some necessary provisions and services for the capital. The Spanish regarded them with mixed distrust and acknowledgment of their indispensable role. During the first decades of Spanish rule, the Chinese in Manila became more numerous than the Spanish, who tried to control them with residence restrictions, periodic deportations, and actual or threatened violence that sometimes degenerated into riots and massacres of Chinese during the period between 1603 and 1762.

The Decline of Spanish Rule, 1762-1898

In 1762 Spain became involved in the Seven Years' War (1756-63) on the side of France against Britain; in October 1762, forces of the British East India Company captured Manila after fierce fighting. Spanish resistance continued under Lieutenant Governor Simón de Anda, based at Bacolor in Pampanga Province, and Manila was returned to the Spanish in May 1764 in conformity with the Treaty of Paris, which formally ended the war. The British occupation nonetheless marked, in a very significant sense, the beginning of the end of the old order.

Spanish prestige suffered irreparable damage because of the defeat at British hands. A number of rebellions broke out, of which the most notable was that of Diego Silang in the Ilocos area of northern Luzon. In December 1762, Silang expelled the Spanish from the coastal city of Vigan and set up an independent government. He established friendly relations with the British and was able to repulse Spanish attacks on Vigan, but he was assassinated in May 1763. The Spanish, tied down by fighting with the British and the rebels, were unable to control the raids of the Moros of the south on the Christian communities of the Visayan Islands and Luzon. Thousands of Christian Filipinos were captured as slaves, and Moro raids continued to be a serious problem through the remainder of the century. The Chinese community, resentful of Spanish discrimination, for the most part enthusiastically supported the British, providing them with laborers and armed men who fought de Anda in Pampanga.

After Spanish rule was restored, José Basco y Vargas one of the ablest of Spanish administrators, was the governor from 1778 to 1787, and he implemented a series of reforms designed to promote the economic development of the islands and make them independent of the subsidy from New Spain. In 1781 he established the Economic Society of Friends of the Country, which, throughout its checkered history extending over the next century, encouraged the growth of new crops for export--such as indigo, tea, silk, opium poppies, and abaca (hemp)--and the development of local industry. A government tobacco monopoly was established in 1782. The monopoly brought in large profits for the government and made the Philippines a leader in world tobacco production.

The venerable galleon trade between the Philippines and Mexico continued as a government monopoly until 1815, when the last official galleon from Acapulco docked at Manila. The Royal Company of the Philippines, chartered by the Spanish king in 1785, promoted direct trade from that year on between the islands and Spain. All Philippine goods were given tariff-free status, and the company, together with Basco's Economic Society, encouraged the growth of a cash-crop economy by investing a portion of its early profits in the cultivation of sugar, indigo, peppers, and mulberry trees for silk, as well as in textile factories.

Trade with Europe and America

As long as the Spanish empire on the eastern rim of the Pacific remained intact and the galleons sailed to and from Acapulco, there was little incentive on the part of colonial authorities to promote the development of the Philippines, despite the initiatives of José Basco y Vargas during his career as governor in Manila. After his departure, the Economic Society was allowed to fall on hard times, and the Royal Company showed decreasing profits. The independence of Spain's Latin American colonies, particularly Mexico in 1821, forced a fundamental reorientation of policy. Cut off from the Mexican subsidies and protected Latin American markets, the islands had to pay for themselves. As a result, in the late eighteenth century commercial isolation became less feasible.

Growing numbers of foreign merchants in Manila spurred the integration of the Philippines into an international commercial system linking industrialized Europe and North America with sources of raw materials and markets in the Americas and Asia. In principle, non-Spanish Europeans were not allowed to reside in Manila or elsewhere in the islands, but in fact British, American, French, and other foreign merchants circumvented this prohibition by flying the flags of Asian states or conniving with local officials. In 1834 the crown abolished the Royal Company of the Philippines and formally recognized free trade, opening the port of Manila to unrestricted foreign commerce.

By 1856 there were thirteen foreign trading firms in Manila, of which seven were British and two American; between 1855 and 1873 the Spanish opened new ports to foreign trade, including Iloilo on Panay, Zamboanga in the western portion of Mindanao, Cebu on Cebu, and Legaspi in the Bicol area of southern Luzon. The growing prominence of steam over sail navigation and the opening of the Suez Canal in 1869 contributed to spectacular increases in the volume of trade. In 1851 exports and imports totaled some US$8.2 million; ten years later, they had risen to US$18.9 million and by 1870 were US$53.3 million. Exports alone grew by US$20 million between 1861 and 1870. British and United States merchants dominated Philippine commerce, the former in an especially favored position because of their bases in Singapore, Hong Kong, and the island of Borneo.

By the late nineteenth century, three crops--tobacco, abaca, and sugar--dominated Philippine exports. The government monopoly on tobacco had been abolished in 1880, but Philippine cigars maintained their high reputation, popular throughout Victorian parlors in Britain, the European continent, and North America. Because of the growth of worldwide shipping, Philippine abaca, which was considered the best material for ropes and cordage, grew in importance and after 1850 alternated with sugar as the islands' most important export. Americans dominated the abaca trade; raw material was made into rope, first at plants in New England and then in the Philippines. Principal regions for the growing of abaca were the Bicol areas of southeastern Luzon and the eastern portions of the Visayan Islands.

Sugarcane had been produced and refined using crude methods at least as early as the beginning of the eighteenth century. The opening of the port of Iloilo on Panay in 1855 and the encouragement of the British vice consul in that town, Nicholas Loney (described by a modern writer as "a one-man whirlwind of entrepreneurial and technical innovation"), led to the development of the previously unsettled island of Negros as the center of the Philippine sugar industry, exporting its product to Britain and Australia. Loney arranged liberal credit terms for local landlords to invest in the new crop, encouraged the migration of labor from the neighboring and overpopulated island of Panay, and introduced stream-driven sugar refineries that replaced the traditional method of producing low-grade sugar in loaves. The population of Negros tripled. Local "sugar barons"--- the owners of the sugar plantations--became a potent political and economic force by the end of the nineteenth century.

Chinese and Chinese Mestizos

In the late eighteenth and early nineteenth centuries, deep-seated Spanish suspicion of the Chinese gave way to recognition of their potentially constructive role in economic development. Chinese expulsion orders issued in 1755 and 1766 were repealed in 1788. Nevertheless, the Chinese remained concentrated in towns around Manila, particularly Binondo and Santa Cruz. In 1839 the government issued a decree granting them freedom of occupation and residence.

In the latter half of the nineteenth century, immigration into the archipelago, largely from the maritime province of Fujian on the southeastern coast of China, increased, and a growing proportion of Chinese settled in outlying areas. In 1849 more than 90 percent of the approximately 6,000 Chinese lived in or around Manila, whereas in 1886 this proportion decreased to 77 percent of the 66,000 Chinese in the Philippines at that time, declining still further in the 1890s. The Chinese presence in the hinterland went hand in hand with the transformation of the insular economy. Spanish policy encouraged immigrants to become agricultural laborers. Some became gardeners, supplying vegetables to the towns, but most shunned the fields and set themselves up as small retailers and moneylenders. The Chinese soon gained a central position in the cash-crop economy on the provincial and local levels.

Of equal, if not greater, significance for subsequent political, cultural, and economic developments were the Chinese mestizos (see Glossary). At the beginning of the nineteenth century, they composed about 5 percent of the total population of around 2.5 million and were concentrated in the most developed provinces of Central Luzon and in Manila and its environs. A much smaller number lived in the more important towns of the Visayan Islands, such as Cebu and Iloilo, and on Mindanao. Converts to Catholicism and speakers of Filipino languages or Spanish rather than Chinese dialects, the mestizos enjoyed a legal status as subjects of Spain that was denied the Chinese. In the words of historian Edgar Vickberg, they were considered, unlike the mixed-Chinese of other Southeast Asian countries, not "a special kind of local Chinese" but "a special kind of Filipino."

The eighteenth-century expulsion edicts had given the Chinese mestizos the opportunity to enter retailing and the skilled craft occupations formerly dominated by the Chinese. The removal of legal restrictions on Chinese economic activity and the competition of new Chinese immigrants, however, drove a large number of mestizos out of the commercial sector in mid-nineteenth century. As a result, many Chinese mestizos invested in land, particularly in Central Luzon. The estates of the religious orders were concentrated in this region, and mestizos became *inquilinos* (lessees) of these lands, subletting them to cultivators; a portion of the rent was given by the *inquilino* to the friary estate. Like the Chinese, the mestizos were moneylenders and acquired land when debtors defaulted.

By the late nineteenth century, prominent mestizo families, despite the inroads of the Chinese, were noted for their wealth and formed the major component of a Filipino elite. As the export economy grew and foreign contact increased, the mestizos and other members of this Filipino elite, known collectively as *ilustrados* (see Glossary), obtained higher education (in some cases abroad), entered professions such as law or medicine, and were particularly receptive to the liberal and democratic ideas that were beginning to reach the Philippines despite the efforts of the generally reactionary--and friar-dominated--Spanish establishment.

The Friarocracy

The power of religious orders remained one of the great constants, over the centuries, of Spanish colonial rule. Even in the late nineteenth century, the friars of the Augustinian, Dominican, and Franciscan orders conducted many of the executive and control functions of government on the local level. They were responsible for education and health measures, kept the census and tax records, reported on the character and behavior of individual villagers, supervised the selection of local police and town officers, and were responsible for maintaining public morals and reporting incidences of sedition to the authorities. Contrary to the principles of the church, they allegedly used information gained in confession to pinpoint troublemakers. Given the minuscule number of Spanish living outside the capital even in the nineteenth century, the friars were regarded as indispensable instruments of Spanish rule that contemporary critics labeled a "friarocracy" (frialocracia).

Controversies over visitation and secularization were persistent themes in Philippine church history. Visitation involved the authority of the bishops of the church hierarchy to inspect and discipline the religious orders, a principle laid down in church law and practiced in most of the Catholic world. The friars were successful in resisting the efforts of the archbishop of Manila to impose visitation; consequently, they operated without formal supervision except that of their own provincials or regional superiors. Secularization meant the replacement of the friars, who came exclusively from Spain, with Filipino priests ordained by the local bishop. This movement, again, was successfully resisted, as friars through the centuries kept up the argument, often couched in crude racial terms, that Filipino priests were too poorly qualified to take on parish duties. Although church policy dictated that parishes of countries converted to Christianity be relinquished by the religious orders to indigenous diocesan priests, in 1870 only 181 out of 792 parishes in the islands had Filipino priests. The national and racial dimensions of secularization meant that the issue became linked with broader demands for political reform.

The economic position of the orders was secured by their extensive landholdings, which generally had been donated to them for the support of their churches, schools, and other establishments. Given the general lack of interest on the part of Spanish colonials--clustered in Manila and dependent on the galleon trade--in developing agriculture, the religious orders had become by the eighteenth century the largest landholders in the islands, with their estates concentrated in the Central Luzon region. Land rents--paid often by Chinese mestizo inquilinos, who planted cash crops for export--provided them with the sort of income that enabled many friars to live like princes in palatial establishments.

Central to the friars' dominant position was their monopoly of education at all levels and thus their control over cultural and intellectual life. In 1863 the Spanish government decreed that a system of free public primary education be established in the islands, which could have been interpreted as a threat to this monopoly. By 1867 there were 593 primary schools enrolling 138,990 students; by 1877 the numbers had grown to 1,608 schools and 177,113 students; and in 1898 there were 2,150 schools and over 200,000 students out of a total population of approximately 6 million. The friars, however, were given the responsibility of supervising the system both on the local and the national levels. The Jesuits were given control of the teacher-training colleges. Except for the Jesuits, the religious orders were strongly opposed to the teaching of modern foreign languages, including Spanish, and scientific and technical subjects to the indios (literally, Indians; the Spanish term for Filipinos). In 1898 the University of Santo Tomás taught essentially the same courses that it did in 1611, when it was founded by the Dominicans, twenty-one years before Galileo was brought before the Inquisition for publishing the idea that the earth revolved around the sun.

The friarocracy seems to have had more than its share of personal irregularities, and the priestly vow of chastity often was honored in the breach. In the eyes of educated Filipino priests and laymen, however, most inexcusable was the friars' open attitude of contempt toward the people. By the late nineteenth century, their attitude was one of blatant racism. In the words of one friar, responding to the challenge of the ilustrados, "the only liberty the Indians want is the liberty of savages. Leave them to their cock-fighting and their indolence, and they will thank you more than if you load them down with old and new rights."

Apolinario de la Cruz, a Tagalog (see Glossary) who led the 1839-41 Cofradía de San José revolt, embodied the religious aspirations and disappointments of the Filipinos. A pious individual who sought to enter a religious order, he made repeated applications that were turned down by the racially conscious friars, and he was left with no alternative but to become a humble lay brother performing menial tasks at a charitable institution in Manila. While serving in that capacity, he started the cofradía (confraternity or brotherhood), a society to promote Roman Catholic devotion among Filipinos. From 1839 to 1840, Brother Apolinario sent representatives to his native Tayabas, south of Laguna de Bay, to recruit members, and the movement rapidly spread as cells were established throughout the southern Tagalog area. Originally, it was apparently neither anti-Spanish nor nativist in religious orientation, although native elements were prevalent among its provincial followers. Yet its emphasis on secrecy, the strong bond of loyalty its members felt for Brother Apolinario, and, above all, the fact that it barred Spanish and mestizos from membership aroused the suspicions of the authorities. The cofradía was banned by the authorities in 1840.

In the autumn of 1841 Brother Apolinario left Manila and gathered his followers, then numbering several thousands armed with rifles and bolos (heavy, single-bladed knives), at bases in the villages around the town of Tayabas; as a spiritual leader, he preached that God would deliver the Tagalog people from slavery. Although the rebel force, aided by Negrito hill tribesmen, was able to defeat a detachment led by the provincial governor in late October, a much larger Spanish force composed of soldiers from Pampanga Province--the elite of the Philippine military establishment and traditional enemies of the Tagalogs--took the cofradía camp at Alitao after a great slaughter on November 1, 1841.

The insurrection effectively ended with the betrayal and capture of Brother Apolinario. He was executed on November 5, 1841. Survivors of the movement became remontados (those who go back into the mountains), leaving their villages to live on the slopes of the volcanic Mount San Cristobal and Mount Banahao, within sight of Alitao. These mountains, where no friar ventured, became folk religious centers, places of pilgrimage for lowland peasants, and the birthplace of religious communities known as colorums (see Glossary).

The Development of a National Consciousness
Religious movements such as the cofradía and colorums expressed an inchoate desire of their members to be rid of the Spanish and discover a promised land that would reflect

memories of a world that existed before the coming of the colonists. Nationalism in the modern sense developed in an urban context, in Manila and the major towns and, perhaps more significantly, in Spain and other parts of Europe where Filipino students and exiles were exposed to modern intellectual currents. Folk religion, for all its power, did not form the basis of the national ideology. Yet the millenarian tradition of rural revolt would merge with the Europeanized nationalism of the ilustrados to spur a truly national resistance, first against Spain in 1896 and then against the Americans in 1899.

Following the Spanish revolution of September 1868, in which the unpopular Queen Isabella II was deposed, the new government appointed General Carlos María de la Torre governor of the Philippines. An outspoken liberal, de la Torre extended to Filipinos the promise of reform. In a break with established practice, he fraternized with Filipinos, invited them to the governor's palace, and rode with them in official processions. Filipinos in turn welcomed de la Torre warmly, held a "liberty parade" to celebrate the adoption of the liberal 1869 Spanish constitution, and established a reform committee to lay the foundations of a new order. Prominent among de la Torre's supporters in Manila were professional and business leaders of the ilustrado community and, perhaps more significantly, Filipino secular priests. These included the learned Father José Burgos, a Spanish mestizo, who had published a pamphlet, Manifesto to the Noble Spanish Nation, criticizing those racially prejudiced Spanish who barred Filipinos from the priesthood and government service. For a brief time, the tide seemed to be turning against the friars. In December 1870, the archbishop of Manila, Gregorio Melitón Martínez, wrote to the Spanish regent advocating secularization and warning that discrimination against Filipino priests would encourage anti-Spanish sentiments.

According to historian Austin Coates, "1869 and 1870 stand distinct and apart from the whole of the rest of the period as a time when for a brief moment a real breath of the nineteenth century penetrated the Islands, which till then had been living largely in the seventeenth century." De la Torre abolished censorship of newspapers and legalized the holding of public demonstrations, free speech, and assembly--rights guaranteed in the 1869 Spanish constitution. Students at the University of Santo Tomás formed an association, the Liberal Young Students (Juventud Escolar Liberal), and in October 1869 held demonstrations protesting the abuses of the university's Dominican friar administrators and teachers.

The liberal period came to an abrupt end in 1871. Friars and other conservative Spaniards in Manila managed to engineer the replacement of de la Torre by a more conservative figure, Rafael de Izquierdo, who, following his installation as governor in April 1871, reimposed the severities of the old regime. He is alleged to have boasted that he came to the islands "with a crucifix in one hand and a sword in the other." Liberal laws were rescinded, and the enthusiastic Filipino supporters of de la Torre came under political suspicion.

The heaviest blow came after a mutiny on January 20, 1872, when about 200 Filipino dock workers and soldiers in Cavite Province revolted and killed their Spanish officers, apparently in the mistaken belief that a general uprising was in progress among Filipino regiments in Manila. Grievances connected with the government's revocation of old privileges--particularly exemption from tribute service--inspired the revolt, which was put down by January 22. The authorities, however, began weaving a tale of conspiracy between the mutineers and prominent members of the Filipino community, particularly diocesan priests. The governor asserted that a secret junta, with connections to liberal parties in Spain, existed in Manila and was ready to overthrow Spanish rule.

A military court sentenced to death the three Filipino priests most closely associated with liberal reformism--José Burgos, Mariano Gomez, and Jacinto Zamora--and exiled a number of prominent ilustrados to Guam and the Marianas (then Spanish possessions), from which they escaped to carry on the struggle from Hong Kong, Singapore, and Europe. Archbishop Martínez requested that the governor commute the priests' death sentences and refused the governor's order that they be defrocked. Martínez's efforts were in vain, however, and on February 17, 1872, they were publicly executed with the brutal garrote on the Luneta (the broad park facing Manila Bay). The archbishop ordered that Manila church bells toll a requiem for the victims, a requiem that turned out to be for Spanish rule in the islands as well. Although a policy of accommodation would have won the loyalty of peasant and ilustrado alike, intransigence--particularly on the question of the secularization of the clergy--led increasing numbers of Filipinos to question the need for a continuing association with Spain.

José Rizal and the Propaganda Movement

Between 1872 and 1892, a national consciousness was growing among the Filipino émigrés who had settled in Europe. In the freer atmosphere of Europe, these émigrés--liberals exiled in 1872 and students attending European universities--formed the Propaganda Movement. Organized for literary and cultural purposes more than for political ends, the Propagandists, who included upper-class Filipinos from all the lowland Christian areas, strove to "awaken the sleeping intellect of the Spaniard to the needs of our country" and to create a closer, more equal association of the islands and the motherland. Among their specific goals were representation of the Philippines in the Cortes, or Spanish parliament; secularization of the clergy; legalization of Spanish and Filipino equality; creation of a public school system independent of the friars; abolition of the polo (labor service) and vandala (forced sale of local products to the government); guarantee of basic freedoms of speech and association; and equal opportunity for Filipinos and Spanish to enter government service.

The most outstanding Propagandist was José Rizal, a physician, scholar, scientist, and writer. Born in 1861 into a prosperous Chinese mestizo family in Laguna Province, he displayed great intelligence at an early age. After several years of medical study at the University of Santo Tomás, he went to Spain in 1882 to finish his studies at the University of Madrid. During the decade that followed, Rizal's career spanned two worlds: Among small communities of Filipino students in Madrid and other European cities, he became a leader and eloquent spokesman, and in the wider world of European science and scholarship--particularly in Germany--he formed close relationships with prominent natural and social scientists. The new discipline of anthropology was of special interest to him; he was committed to refuting the friars' stereotypes of Filipino racial inferiority with scientific arguments. His greatest impact on the development of a Filipino national consciousness, however, was his publication of two novels--Noli Me Tangere (Touch me not) in 1886 and El Filibusterismo (The reign of greed) in 1891. Rizal drew on his personal experiences and depicted the conditions of Spanish rule in the islands, particularly the abuses of the friars. Although the friars had Rizal's books banned, they were smuggled into the Philippines and rapidly gained a wide readership.

Other important Propagandists included Graciano Lopez Jaena, a noted orator and pamphleteer who had left the islands for Spain in 1880 after the publication of his satirical short novel, Fray Botod (Brother Fatso), an unflattering portrait of a provincial friar. In 1889 he established a biweekly newspaper in Barcelona, La Solidaridad (Solidarity), which became the principal organ of the Propaganda Movement, having audiences both in Spain and in the islands. Its contributors included Rizal; Dr. Ferdinand Blumentritt, an Austrian geographer and ethnologist whom Rizal had met in Germany; and Marcelo del Pilar, a reformminded lawyer. Del Pilar was active in the anti-friar movement in the islands until obliged to flee to Spain in 1888, where he became editor of La Solidaridad and assumed leadership of the Filipino community in Spain.

In 1887 Rizal returned briefly to the islands, but because of the furor surrounding the appearance of Noli Me Tangere the previous year, he was advised by the governor to leave. He returned to Europe by way of Japan and North America to complete his second novel and an edition of Antonio de Morga's seventeenth-century work, Sucesos de las Islas Filipinas (History of the Philippine Islands). The latter project stemmed from an ethnological interest in the cultural connections between the peoples of the pre-Spanish Philippines and those of the larger Malay region (including modern Malaysia and Indonesia) and the closely related political objective of encouraging national pride. De Morga provided positive information about the islands' early inhabitants, and reliable accounts of pre-Christian religion and social customs.

After a stay in Europe and Hong Kong, Rizal returned to the Philippines in June 1892, partly because the Dominicans had evicted his father and sisters from the land they leased from the friars' estate at Calamba, in Laguna Province. He also was convinced that the struggle for reform could no longer be conducted effectively from overseas. In July he established the Liga Filipina (Philippine League), designed to be a truly national, nonviolent organization. It was dissolved, however, following his arrest and exile to the remote town of Dapitan in northwestern Mindanao.

The Propaganda Movement languished after Rizal's arrest and the collapse of the Liga Filipina. La Solidaridad went out of business in November 1895, and in 1896 both del Pilar and Lopez Jaena died in Barcelona, worn down by poverty and disappointment. An attempt was made to reestablish the Liga Filipina, but the national movement had become split between ilustrado advocates of reform and peaceful evolution (the compromisarios, or compromisers) and a plebeian constituency that wanted revolution and national independence. Because the Spanish refused to allow genuine reform, the initiative quickly passed from the former group to the latter.

The Katipunan

After Rizal's arrest and exile, Andres Bonifacio, a self-educated man of humble origins, founded a secret society, the Katipunan, in Manila. This organization, modeled in part on Masonic lodges, was committed to winning independence from Spain. Rizal, Lopez Jaena, del Pilar, and other leaders of the Propaganda Movement had been Masons, and Masonry was regarded by the Catholic Church as heretical. The Katipunan, like the Masonic lodges, had secret passwords and ceremonies, and its members were organized into ranks or degrees, each having different colored hoods, special passwords, and secret formulas. New members went through a rigorous initiation, which concluded with the pacto de sangre, or blood compact.

The Katipunan spread gradually from the Tondo district of Manila, where Bonifacio had founded it, to the provinces, and by August 1896--on the eve of the revolt against Spain--it had some 30,000 members, both men and women. Most of them were members of the lower- and lower-middle-income strata, including peasants. The nationalist movement had effectively moved from the closed circle of prosperous *ilustrados* to a truly popular base of support.

The 1896 Uprising and Rizal's Execution

During the early years of the Katipunan, Rizal remained in exile at Dapitan. He had promised the Spanish governor that he would not attempt an escape, which, in that remote part of the country, would have been relatively easy. Such a course of action, however, would have both compromised the moderate reform policy that he still advocated and confirmed the suspicions of the reactionary Spanish. Whether he came to support Philippine independence during his period of exile is difficult to determine.

He retained, to the very end, a faith in the decency of Spanish "men of honor," which made it difficult for him to accept the revolutionary course of the Katipunan. Revolution had broken out in Cuba in February 1895, and Rizal applied to the governor to be sent to that yellow fever-infested island as an army doctor, believing that it was the only way he could keep his word to the governor and yet get out of his exile. His request was granted, and he was preparing to leave for Cuba when the Katipunan revolt broke out in August 1896. An informer had tipped off a Spanish friar about the society's existence, and Bonifacio, his hand forced, proclaimed the revolution, attacking Spanish military installations on August 29, 1896. Rizal was allowed to leave Manila on a Spanish steamship. The governor, however, apparently forced by reactionary elements, ordered Rizal's arrest en route, and he was sent back to Manila to be tried by a military court as an accomplice of the insurrection.

The rebels were poorly led and had few successes against colonial troops. Only in Cavite Province did they make any headway. Commanded by Emilio Aguinaldo, the twenty-seven-year-old mayor of the town of Cavite who had been a member of the Katipunan since 1895, the rebels defeated Civil Guard and regular colonial troops between August and November 1896 and made the province the center of the revolution.

Under a new governor, who apparently had been sponsored as a hard-line candidate by the religious orders, Rizal was brought before a military court on fabricated charges of involvement with the Katipunan. The events of 1872 repeated themselves. A brief trial was held on December 26 and--with little chance to defend himself--Rizal was found guilty and sentenced to death. On December 30, 1896, he was brought out to the Luneta and executed by a firing squad.

Rizal's death filled the rebels with new determination, but the Katipunan was becoming divided between supporters of Bonifacio, who revealed himself to be an increasingly ineffective leader, and its rising star, Aguinaldo. At a convention held at Tejeros, the Katipunan's headquarters in March 1897, delegates elected Aguinaldo president and demoted Bonifacio to the post of director of the interior. Bonifacio withdrew with his supporters and formed his own government. After fighting broke out between Bonifacio's and Aguinaldo's troops, Bonifacio was arrested, tried, and on May 10, 1897, executed by order of Aguinaldo.

As 1897 wore on, Aguinaldo himself suffered reverses at the hands of Spanish troops, being forced from Cavite in June and retreating to Biak-na-Bato in Bulacan Province. The futility of the struggle was becoming apparent, however, on both sides. Although Spanish troops were able to defeat insurgents on the battlefield, they could not suppress guerrilla activity. In August armistice negotiations were opened between Aguinaldo and a new Spanish governor. By mid-December, an agreement was reached in which the governor would pay Aguinaldo the equivalent of US$800,000, and the rebel leader and his government would go into exile. Aguinaldo established himself in Hong Kong, and the Spanish bought themselves time. Within the year, however, their more than three centuries of rule in the islands would come to an abrupt and unexpected end.

Spanish-American War and Philippine Resistance

Outbreak of War, 1898

Spain's rule in the Philippines came to an end as a result of United States involvement with Spain's other major colony, Cuba. American business interests were anxious for a resolution--with or without Spain--of the insurrection that had broken out in Cuba in February 1895. Moreover, public opinion in the United States had been aroused by newspaper accounts of the brutalities of Spanish rule. When the United States declared war on Spain on April 25, 1898, acting Secretary of the Navy Theodore Roosevelt ordered Commodore George Dewey, commander of the Asiatic Squadron, to sail to the Philippines and destroy the Spanish fleet anchored in Manila Bay. The Spanish navy, which had seen its apogee in the support of a global empire in the sixteenth century, suffered an inglorious defeat on May 1, 1898, as Spain's antiquated fleet, including ships with wooden hulls, was sunk by the guns of Dewey's flagship, the *Olympia*, and other United States warships. More than 380 Spanish sailors died, but there was only one American fatality.

As Spain and the United States had moved toward war over Cuba in the last months of 1897, negotiations of a highly tentative nature began between United States officials and Aguinaldo in both Hong Kong and Singapore. When war was declared, Aguinaldo, a partner, if not an ally, of the United States, was urged by Dewey to return to the islands as quickly as possible. Arriving in Manila on May 19, Aguinaldo reassumed command of rebel forces. Insurrectionists overwhelmed demoralized Spanish garrisons around the capital, and links were established with other movements throughout the islands.

In the eyes of the Filipinos, their relationship with the United States was that of two nations joined in a common struggle against Spain. As allies, the Filipinos provided American forces with valuable intelligence (e.g., that the Spanish had no mines or torpedoes with which to sink warships entering Manila Bay), and Aguinaldo's 12,000 troops kept a slightly larger Spanish force bottled up inside Manila until American troop reinforcements could arrive from San Francisco in late June. Aguinaldo was unhappy, however, that the United States would not commit to paper a statement of support for Philippine independence.

By late May, the United States Department of the Navy had ordered Dewey, newly promoted to Admiral, to distance himself from Aguinaldo lest he make untoward commitments to the Philippine forces. The war with Spain still was going on, and the future of the Philippines remained uncertain. The immediate objective was to capture Manila, and it was thought best to do that without the assistance of the insurgents. By late July, there were some 12,000 United States troops in the area, and relations between them and rebel forces deteriorated rapidly.

By the summer of 1898, Manila had become the focus not only of the Spanish-American conflict and the growing suspicions between the Americans and Filipino rebels but also of a rivalry that encompassed the European powers. Following Dewey's victory, Manila Bay was filled with the warships of Britain, Germany, France, and Japan. The German fleet of eight ships, ostensibly in Philippine waters to protect German interests (a single import firm), acted provocatively--cutting in front of United States ships, refusing to salute the United States flag (according to naval courtesy), taking soundings of the harbor, and landing supplies for the besieged Spanish. Germany, hungry for the ultimate status symbol, a colonial empire, was eager to take advantage of whatever opportunities the conflict in the islands might afford. Dewey called the bluff of the German admiral, threatening a fight if his aggressive activities continued, and the Germans backed down.

The Spanish cause was doomed, but Fermín Jaudenes, Spain's last governor in the islands, had to devise a way to salvage the honor of his country. Negotiations were carried out through British and Belgian diplomatic intermediaries. A secret agreement was made between the governor and United States military commanders in early August 1898 concerning the capture of Manila. In their assault, American forces would neither bombard the city nor allow the insurgents to take part (the Spanish feared that the Filipinos were plotting to massacre them all). The Spanish, in turn, would put up only a show of resistance and, on a prearranged signal, would surrender. In this way, the governor would be spared the ignominy of giving up without a fight, and both sides would be spared casualties. The mock battle was staged on August 13. The attackers rushed in, and by afternoon the United States flag was flying over Intramuros, the ancient walled city that had been the seat of Spanish power for over 300 years.

The agreement between Jaudenes and Dewey marked a curious reversal of roles. At the beginning of the war, Americans and Filipinos had been allies against Spain in all but name; now Spanish and Americans were in a partnership that excluded the insurgents. Fighting between American and Filipino troops almost broke out as the former moved in to dislodge the latter from strategic positions around Manila on the eve of the attack. Aguinaldo was told bluntly by the Americans that his army could not participate and would be fired upon if it crossed into the city. The insurgents were infuriated at being denied triumphant entry into their own capital, but Aguinaldo bided his time. Relations continued to deteriorate, however, as it became clear to Filipinos that the Americans were in the islands to stay.

The Malolos Constitution and the Treaty of Paris

After returning to the islands, Aguinaldo wasted little time in setting up an independent government. On June 12, 1898, a declaration of independence, modeled on the American one, was proclaimed at his headquarters in Cavite. It was at this time that Apolinario Mabini, a lawyer and political thinker, came to prominence as Aguinaldo's principal adviser. Born into a poor *indio* family but educated at the University of Santo Tomás, he advocated "simultaneous external and internal revolution," a philosophy that unsettled the more conservative landowners and *ilustrados* who initially supported Aguinaldo. For Mabini, true independence for the Philippines would mean not simply liberation from Spain (or from any other colonial power) but also educating the people for self-government and abandoning the paternalistic, colonial mentality that the Spanish had cultivated over the centuries. Mabini's *The True Decalogue*, published in July 1898 in the form of ten commandments, used this medium, somewhat paradoxically, to promote critical thinking and a reform of customs and attitudes. His *Constitutional Program for the Philippine Republic*, published at the same time, elaborated his ideas on political institutions.

On September 15, 1898, a revolutionary congress was convened at Malolos, a market town located thirty-two kilometers north of Manila, for the purpose of drawing up a constitution for the new republic. A document was approved by the congress on November

29, 1898. Modeled on the constitutions of France, Belgium, and Latin American countries, it was promulgated at Malolos on January 21, 1899, and two days later Aguinaldo was inaugurated as president.

American observers traveling in Luzon commented that the areas controlled by the republic seemed peaceful and well governed. The Malolos congress had set up schools, a military academy, and the Literary University of the Philippines. Government finances were organized, and new currency was issued. The army and navy were established on a regular basis, having regional commands. The accomplishments of the Filipino government, however, counted for little in the eyes of the great powers as the transfer of the islands from Spanish to United States rule was arranged in the closing months of 1898.

In late September, treaty negotiations were initiated between Spanish and American representatives in Paris. The Treaty of Paris was signed on December 10, 1898. Among its conditions was the cession of the Philippines, Guam, and Puerto Rico to the United States (Cuba was granted its independence); in return, the United States would pay Spain the sum of US$20 million. The nature of this payment is rather difficult to define; it was paid neither to purchase Spanish territories nor as a war indemnity. In the words of historian Leon Wolff, "it was . . . a gift. Spain accepted it. Quite irrelevantly she handed us the Philippines. No question of honor or conquest was involved. The Filipino people had nothing to say about it, although their rebellion was thrown in (so to speak) free of charge."

The Treaty of Paris aroused anger among Filipinos. Reacting to the US$20 million sum paid to Spain, *La Independencia* (Independence), a newspaper published in Manila by a revolutionary, General Antonio Luna, stated that "people are not to be bought and sold like horses and houses. If the aim has been to abolish the traffic in Negroes because it meant the sale of persons, why is there still maintained the sale of countries with inhabitants?" Tension and ill feelings were growing between the American troops in Manila and the insurgents surrounding the capital. In addition to Manila, Iloilo, the main port on the island of Panay, also was a pressure point. The Revolutionary Government of the Visayas was proclaimed there on November 17, 1898, and an American force stood poised to capture the city. Upon the announcement of the treaty, the radicals, Mabini and Luna, prepared for war, and provisional articles were added to the constitution giving President Aguinaldo dictatorial powers in times of emergency. President William McKinley issued a proclamation on December 21, 1898, declaring United States policy to be one of "benevolent assimilation" in which "the mild sway of justice and right" would be substituted for "arbitrary rule." When this was published in the islands on January 4, 1899, references to "American sovereignty" having been prudently deleted, Aguinaldo issued his own proclamation that condemned "violent and aggressive seizure" by the United States and threatened war.

War of Resistance

Hostilities broke out on the night of February 4, 1899, after two American privates on patrol killed three Filipino soldiers in a suburb of Manila. Thus began a war that would last for more than two years. Some 126,000 American soldiers would be committed to the conflict; 4,234 American and 16,000 Filipino soldiers, part of a nationwide guerrilla movement of indeterminate numbers, died.

The Filipino troops, armed with old rifles and bolos and carrying *anting-anting* (magical charms), were no match for American troops in open combat, but they were formidable opponents in guerrilla warfare. For General Ewell S. Otis, commander of the United States forces, who had been appointed military governor of the Philippines, the conflict began auspiciously with the expulsion of the rebels from Manila and its suburbs by late February and the capture of Malolos, the revolutionary capital, on March 31, 1899. Aguinaldo and his government escaped, however, establishing a new capital at San Isidro in Nueva Ecija Province. The Filipino cause suffered a number of reverses. The attempts of Mabini and his successor as president of Aguinaldo's cabinet, Pedro Paterno, to negotiate an armistice in May 1899 ended in failure because Otis insisted on unconditional surrender.

Still more serious was the murder of Luna, Aguinaldo's most capable military commander, in June. Hot-tempered and cruel, Luna collected a large number of enemies among his associates, and, according to rumor, his death was ordered by Aguinaldo. With his best commander dead and his troops suffering continued defeats as American forces pushed into northern Luzon, Aguinaldo dissolved the regular army in November 1899 and ordered the establishment of decentralized guerrilla commands in each of several military zones. More than ever, American soldiers knew the miseries of fighting an enemy that was able to move at will within the civilian population in the villages. The general population, caught between Americans and rebels, suffered horribly.

According to historian Gregorio Zaide, as many as 200,000 civilians died, largely because of famine and disease, by the end of the war. Atrocities were committed on both sides. Although Aguinaldo's government did not have effective authority over the whole archipelago and resistance was strongest and best organized in the Tagalog area of Central Luzon, the notion entertained by many Americans that independence was supported only by the "Tagalog tribe" was refuted by the fact that there was sustained fighting in the Visayan Islands and in Mindanao. Although the ports of Iloilo on Panay and Cebu on Cebu were captured in February 1899, and Tagbilaran, capital of Bohol, in March, guerrilla resistance continued in the mountainous interiors of these islands. Only on the sugar-growing island of Negros did the local authorities peacefully accept United States rule. On Mindanao the United States Army faced the determined opposition of Christian Filipinos loyal to the republic.

Aguinaldo was captured at Palanan on March 23, 1901, by a force of Philippine Scouts loyal to the United States and was brought back to Manila. Convinced of the futility of further resistance, he swore allegiance to the United States and issued a proclamation calling on his compatriots to lay down their arms. Yet insurgent resistance continued in various parts of the Philippines until 1903.

The Moros on Mindanao and on the Sulu Archipelago, suspicious of both Christian Filipino insurrectionists and Americans, remained for the most part neutral. In August 1899, an agreement had been signed between General John C. Bates, representing the United States government, and the sultan of Sulu, Jamal-ul Kiram II, pledging a policy of noninterference on the part of the United States. In 1903, however, a Moro province was established by the American authorities, and a more forward policy was implemented: slavery was outlawed, schools that taught a non-Muslim curriculum were established, and local governments that challenged the authority of traditional community leaders were organized. A new legal system replaced the sharia, or Islamic law. United States rule, even more than that of the Spanish, was seen as a challenge to Islam. Armed resistance grew, and the Moro province remained under United States military rule until 1914, by which time the major Muslim groups had been subjugated (see Islam).

The First Phase of United States Rule, 1898-1935

On January 20, 1899, President McKinley appointed the First Philippine Commission (the Schurman Commission), a five-person group headed by Dr. Jacob Schurman, president of Cornell University, and including Admiral Dewey and General Otis, to investigate conditions in the islands and make recommendations. In the report that they issued to the president the following year, the commissioners acknowledged Filipino aspirations for independence; they declared, however, that the Philippines was not ready for it. Specific recommendations included the establishment of civilian government as rapidly as possible (the American chief executive in the islands at that time was the military governor), including establishment of a bicameral legislature, autonomous governments on the provincial and municipal levels, and a system of free public elementary schools.

The Second Philippine Commission (the Taft Commission), appointed by McKinley on March 16, 1900, and headed by William Howard Taft, was granted legislative as well as limited executive powers. Between September 1900 and August 1902, it issued 499 laws. A judicial system was established, including a Supreme Court, and a legal code was drawn up to replace antiquated Spanish ordinances. A civil service was organized. The 1901 municipal code provided for popularly elected presidents, vice presidents, and councilors to serve on municipal boards. The municipal board members were responsible for collecting taxes, maintaining municipal properties, and undertaking necessary construction projects; they also elected provincial governors. In July 1901 the Philippine Constabulary was organized as an archipelago-wide police force to control brigandage and deal with the remnants of the insurgent movement. After military rule was terminated on July 4, 1901, the Philippine Constabulary gradually took over from United States army units the responsibility for suppressing guerrilla and bandit activities.

From the very beginning, United States presidents and their representatives in the islands defined their colonial mission as tutelage: preparing the Philippines for eventual independence. Except for a small group of "retentionists," the issue was not whether the Philippines would be granted self-rule, but when and under what conditions. Thus political development in the islands was rapid and particularly impressive in light of the complete lack of representative institutions under the Spanish. The Philippine Organic Act of July 1902 stipulated that, with the achievement of peace, a legislature would be established composed of a lower house, the Philippine Assembly, which would be popularly elected, and an upper house consisting of the Philippine Commission, which was to be appointed by the president of the United States. The two houses would share legislative powers, although the upper house alone would pass laws relating to the Moros and other non-Christian peoples. The act also provided for extending the United States Bill of Rights to Filipinos and sending two Filipino resident commissioners to Washington to attend sessions of the United States Congress. In July 1907, the first elections for the assembly were held, and it opened its first session on October 16, 1907. Political parties were organized, and, although open advocacy of independence had been banned during the insurgency years, criticism of government policies in the local newspapers was tolerated.

Taft, the Philippines' first civilian governor, outlined a comprehensive development plan that he described as "the Philippines for the Filipinos . . . that every measure, whether in the form of a law or an executive order, before its adoption, should be weighed in the light of this question: Does it make for the welfare of the Filipino people, or does it not?" Its main features included not only broadening representative institutions but also expanding a system of free public elementary education and designing economic policies to promote the islands' development. Filipinos widely interpreted Taft's pronouncements as a promise of independence.

The 1902 Philippine Organic Act disestablished the Catholic Church as the state religion. The United States government, in an effort to resolve the status of the friars, negotiated with the Vatican. The church agreed to sell the friars' estates and promised gradual substitution of Filipino and other non-Spanish priests for the friars. It refused, however, to withdraw the religious orders from the islands immediately, partly to avoid offending Spain. In 1904 the administration bought for US$7.2 million the major part of the friars' holdings, amounting to some 166,000 hectares, of which one-half was in the vicinity of Manila. The land was eventually resold to Filipinos, some of them tenants but the majority of them estate owners.

A Collaborative Philippine Leadership

The most important step in establishing a new political system was the successful coaptation of the Filipino elite--called the "policy of attraction." Wealthy and conservative ilustrados, the self-described "oligarchy of intelligence," had been from the outset reluctant revolutionaries, suspicious of the Katipunan and willing to negotiate with either Spain or the United States. Trinidad H. Pardo de Tavera, a descendant of Spanish nobility, and Benito Legarda, a rich landowner and capitalist, had quit Aguinaldo's government in 1898 as a result of disagreements with Mabini. Subsequently, they worked closely with the Schurman and Taft commissions, advocating acceptance of United States rule.

In December 1900, de Tavera and Legarda established the Federalista Party, advocating statehood for the islands. In the following year they were appointed the first Filipino members of the Philippine Commission of the legislature. In such an advantageous position, they were able to bring influence to bear to achieve the appointment of Federalistas to provincial governorships, the Supreme Court, and top positions in the civil service. Although the party boasted a membership of 200,000 by May 1901, its proposal to make the islands a state of the United States had limited appeal, both in the islands and in the United States, and the party was widely regarded as being opportunistic. In 1905 the party revised its program over the objections of its leaders, calling for "ultimate independence" and changing its name to the National Progressive Party (Partido Nacional Progresista).

The Nacionalista Party, established in 1907, dominated the Philippine political process until after World War II. It was led by a new generation of politicians, although they were not ilustrados and were by no means radical. One of the leaders, Manuel Quezon, came from a family of moderate wealth. An officer in Aguinaldo's army, he studied law, passed his bar examination in 1903, and entered provincial politics, becoming governor of Tayabas in 1906 before being elected to the Philippine Assembly the following year. His success at an early age was attributable to consummate political skills and the support of influential Americans. His Nacionalista Party associate and sometime rival was Sergio Osmeña, the college-educated son of a shopkeeper, who had worked as a journalist. The former journalist's thoroughness and command of detail made him a perfect complement to Quezon. Like Quezon, Osmeña had served as a provincial governor (in his home province of Cebu) before being elected in 1907 to the assembly and, at age twenty-nine, selected as its first speaker.

Although the Nacionalista Party's platform at its founding called for "immediate independence," American observers believed that Osmeña and Quezon used this appeal only to get votes. In fact, their policy toward the Americans was highly accommodating. In 1907 an understanding was reached with an American official that the two leaders would block any attempt by the Philippine Assembly to demand independence. Osmeña and Quezon, who were the dominant political figures in the islands up to World War II, were genuinely committed to independence. The failure of Aguinaldo's revolutionary movement, however, had taught them the pragmatism of adopting a conciliatory policy.

The appearance of the Nacionalista Party in 1907 marked the emergence of the party system, although the party was without an effective rival from 1916 for most of the period until the emergence of the Liberal Party in 1946. Much of the system's success (or, rather, the success of the Nacionalistas) depended on the linkage of modern political institutions with traditional social structures and practices. Most significantly, it involved the integration of local-level elite groups into the new political system. Philippine parties have been described by political scientist Carl Landé as organized "upward" rather than "downward." That is, national followings were put together by party leaders who worked in conjunction with local elite groups--in many cases the descendants of the principalía of Spanish times--who controlled constituencies tied to them in patron-client relationships. The issue of independence, and the conditions and timing under which it would be granted, generated considerable passion in the national political arena. According to Landé, however, the decisive factors in terms of popular support were more often local and particularistic issues rather than national or ideological concerns. Filipino political associations depended on intricate networks of personal ties, directed upward to Manila and the national legislature.

The linchpins of the system created under United States tutelage were the village- and province-level notables--often labeled bosses or caciques by colonial administrators--who garnered support by exchanging specific favors for votes. Reciprocal relations between inferior and superior (most often tenants or sharecroppers with large landholders) usually involved the concept of utang na loob (repayment of debts) or kinship ties, and they formed the basis of support for village-level factions led by the notables (see The Social Values and Organization). These factions decided political party allegiance. The extension of voting rights to all literate males in 1916, the growth of literacy, and the granting of women's suffrage in 1938 increased the electorate considerably. The elite, however, was largely successful in monopolizing the support of the newly enfranchised, and a genuinely populist alternative to the status quo was never really established.

The policy of attraction ensured the success of what colonial administrators called the political education of the Filipinos. It was, however, also the cause of its greatest failure. Osmeña and Quezon, as the acknowledged representatives, were not genuinely interested in social reform, and serious problems involving land ownership, tenancy, and the highly unequal distribution of wealth were largely ignored. The growing power of the Nacionalista Party, particularly in the period after 1916 when it gained almost complete control of a bicameral Filipino legislature, barred the effective inclusion of non-elite interests in the political system. Not only revolution but also moderate reform of the social and economic systems were precluded. Discussions of policy alternatives became less salient to the political process than the dynamics of personalism and the ethic of give and take.

The Jones Act
The term of Governor General Francis Burton Harrison (1913-21) was one of particularly harmonious collaboration between Americans and Filipinos. Harrison's attitudes (he is

described as having regarded himself as a "constitutional monarch" presiding over a "government of Filipinos") reflected the relatively liberal stance of Woodrow Wilson's Democratic Party administration. In 1913 Wilson had appointed five Filipinos to the Philippine Commission of the legislature, giving it a Filipino majority for the first time. Harrison undertook rapid "Filipinization" of the civil service, much to the anger and distress of Americans in the islands, including superannuated officials. In 1913 there had been 2,623 American and 6,363 Filipino officials; in 1921 there were 13,240 Filipino and 614 American administrators. Critics accused Harrison of transforming a "colonial government of Americans aided by Filipinos" into a "government of Filipinos aided by Americans" and of being the "plaything and catspaw of the leaders of the Nacionalista Party."

A major step was taken in the direction of independence in 1916, when the United States Congress passed a second organic law, commonly referred to as the Jones Act, which replaced the 1902 law. Its preamble stated the intent to grant Philippine independence as soon as a stable government was established. The Philippine Senate replaced the Philippine Commission as the upper house of the legislature. Unlike the commission, all but two of the Senate's twenty-four members (and all but nine of the ninety representatives in the lower house, now renamed the House of Representatives) were popularly elected. The two senators and nine representatives were appointed by the governor general to represent the non-Christian peoples. The legislature's actions were subject to the veto of the governor general, and it could not pass laws affecting the rights of United States citizens. The Jones Act brought the legislative branch under Filipino control. The executive still was firmly under the control of an appointed governor general, and most Supreme Court justices, who were appointed by the United States president, still were Americans in 1916.

Elections were held for the two houses in 1916, and the Nacionalista Party made an almost clean sweep. All but one elected seat in the Senate and eighty-three out of ninety elected seats in the House were won by their candidates, leaving the National Progressive Party (the former Federalista Party) a powerless opposition. Quezon was chosen president of the Senate, and Osmeña continued as speaker of the House.

The Jones Act remained the basic legislation for the administration of the Philippines until the United States Congress passed new legislation in 1934 which became effective in 1935, establishing the Commonwealth of the Philippines. Provisions of the Jones Act were differently interpreted, however, by the governors general. Harrison rarely challenged the legislature by his use of the veto power. His successor, General Leonard Wood (1921-27), was convinced that United States withdrawal from the islands would be as disastrous for the Filipinos as it would be for the interests of the United States in the western Pacific. He aroused the intense opposition of the Nacionalistas by his use of the veto power 126 times in his six years in office. The Nacionalista Party created a political deadlock when ranking Filipino officials resigned in 1923 leaving their positions vacant until Wood's term ended with his death in 1927. His successors, however, reversed Wood's policies and reestablished effective working relations with Filipino politicians.

Although the Jones Act did not transfer responsibility for the Moro regions (reorganized in 1914 under the Department of Mindanao and Sulu) from the American governor to the Filipino controlled legislature, Muslims perceived the rapid Filipinization of the civil service and United States commitment to eventual independence as serious threats. In the view of the Moros, an independent Philippines would be dominated by Christians, their traditional enemies. United States policy from 1903 had been to break down the historical autonomy of the Muslim territories. Immigration of Christian settlers from Luzon and the Visayan Islands to the relatively unsettled regions of Mindanao was encouraged, and the new arrivals began supplanting the Moros in their own homeland. Large areas of the island were opened to economic exploitation. There was no legal recognition of Muslim customs and institutions. In March 1935, Muslim datu petitioned United States president Franklin D. Roosevelt, asking that "the American people should not release us until we are educated and become powerful because we are like a calf who, once abandoned by its mother, would be devoured by a merciless lion." Any suggestion of special status for or continued United States rule over the Moro regions, however, was vehemently opposed by Christian Filipino leaders who, when the Commonwealth of the Philippines was established, gained virtually complete control over government institutions.

Economic and Social Developments
The Taft Commission, appointed in 1900, viewed economic development, along with education and the establishment of representative institutions, as one of the three pillars of the United States program of tutelage. Its members had ambitious plans to build railroads and highways, improve harbor facilities, open greater markets for Philippine goods through the lowering or elimination of tariffs, and stimulate foreign investment in mining, forestry, and cash-crop cultivation. In 1901 some 93 percent of the islands' total land area was public land, and it was hoped that a portion of this area could be sold to American investors. Those plans were frustrated, however, by powerful agricultural interests in the United States Congress who feared competition from Philippine sugar, coconut oil, tobacco, and other exports. Although Taft argued for more liberal terms, the United States Congress, in the 1902 Land Act, set a limit of 16 hectares of Philippine public land to be sold or leased to American individuals and 1,024 hectares to American corporations. This act and tight financial markets in the United States discouraged the development of large-scale, foreign-owned plantations such as were being established in British Malaya, the Dutch East Indies, and French Indochina.

The Taft Commission argued that tariff relief was essential if the islands were to be developed. In August 1909, Congress passed the Payne Aldrich Tariff Act, which provided for free entry to the United States of all Philippine products except rice, sugar, and tobacco. Rice imports were subjected to regular tariffs, and quotas were established for sugar and tobacco. In 1913 the Underwood Tariff Act removed all restrictions. The principal result of these acts was to make the islands increasingly dependent on American markets; between 1914 and 1920, the portion of Philippine exports going to the United States rose from 50 to 70 percent. By 1939 it had reached 85 percent, and 65 percent of imports came from the United States.

In 1931 there were between 80,000 and 100,000 Chinese in the islands active in the local economy; many of them had arrived after United States rule had been established. Some 16,000 Japanese were concentrated largely in the Mindanao province of Davao (the incorporated city of Davao was labeled by local boosters the "Little Tokyo of the South") and were predominant in the abaca industry. Yet the immigration of foreign laborers never reached a volume sufficient to threaten indigenous control of the economy or the traditional social structure as it did in British Malaya and Burma.

The Tenancy Problem

The limited nature of United States intervention in the economy and the Nacionalista Party's elite dominance of the Philippine political system ensured that the status quo in landlord and tenant relationships would be maintained, even if certain of its traditional aspects changed. A government attempt to establish homesteads modeled on those of the American West in 1903 did little to alter landholding arrangements. Although different regions of the archipelago had their own specific arrangements and different proportions of tenants and small proprietors, the kasama (sharecropper) system, was the most prevalent, particularly in the rice-growing areas of Central Luzon and the Visayan Islands.

Under this arrangement, the landowners supplied the seed and cash necessary to tide cultivators over during the planting season, whereas the cultivators provided tools and work animals and were responsible for one-half the expense of crop production. Usually, owner and sharecropper each took one-half of the harvest, although only after the former deducted a portion for expenses. Terms might be more liberal in frontier areas where owners needed to attract cultivators to clear the land. Sometimes land tenancy arrangements were three tiered. An original owner would lease land to an inquilino, who would then sublet it to kasamas. In the words of historian David R. Sturtevant: "Thrice removed from their proprietario, affected taos [peasants] received ever-diminishing shares from the picked-over remains of harvests."

Cultivators customarily were deep in debt, for they were dependent on advances made by the landowner or inquilino and had to pay steep interest rates. Principal and interest accumulated rapidly, becoming an impossible burden. It was estimated in 1924 that the average tenant family would have to labor uninterruptedly for 163 years to pay off debts and acquire title to the land they worked. The kasama system created a class of peons or serfs; children inherited the debts of their fathers, and over the generations families were tied in bondage to their estates. Contracts usually were unwritten, and landowners could change conditions to their own advantage.

Two factors led to a worsening of the cultivators' position. One was the rapid increase in the national population (from 7.6 million in 1905 to 16 million in 1939) brought about through improvements in public health, which put added pressure on the land, lowered the standard of living, and created a labor surplus. Closely tied to the population increase was the erosion of traditional patron-client ties. The landlord-tenant relationship was becoming more impersonal. The landlord's interest in the tenants' welfare was waning. Landlords ceased providing important services and used profits from the sale of cash crops to support their urban life-styles or to invest in other kinds of enterprises. Cultivators accused landowners of being shameless and forgetting the principle of utang na loob, demanding services from tenants without pay and giving nothing in return.

As the area under cultivation increased from 1.3 million hectares in 1903 to 4 million hectares in 1935--stimulated by United States demand for cash crops and by the growing population--tenancy also increased. In 1918 there were roughly 2 million farms, of which 1.5 million were operated by their owners; by 1939 these figures had declined to 1.6 million and 800,000, respectively, as individual proprietors became tenants or migrant laborers. Disparities in the distribution of wealth grew. By 1939 the wealthiest 10 percent of the population received 40 percent of the islands' income. The elite and the cultivators were separated culturally and geographically, as well as economically; as new urban centers rose, often with an Americanized culture, the elite left the countryside to become absentee landlords, leaving estate management in the hands of frequently abusive overseers. The Philippine Constabulary played a central role in suppressing anti-landlord resistance.

Resistance Movements

The tradition of rural revolt, often with messianic overtones, continued under United States rule. *Colorum* sects, derived from the old Cofradía de San José, had spread throughout the Christian regions of the archipelago and by the early 1920s competed with the Roman Catholic establishment and the missionaries of Gregorio Aglipay's Independent Philippine Church (Iglesia Filipina Independiente). A *colorum*-led revolt broke out in northeastern Mindanao early in 1924, sparked by a sect leader's predictions of an imminent judgment day. In 1925 Florencio Entrencherado, a shopkeeper on the island of Panay, proclaimed himself Florencio I, Emperor of the Philippines, somewhat paradoxically running for the office of provincial governor of Iloilo that same year on a platform of tax reduction, measures against Chinese and Japanese merchants, and immediate independence. Although he lost the election, the campaign made him a prominent figure in the western Visayan Islands and won him the sympathies of the poor living in the sugar provinces of Panay and Negros. Claiming semi-divine attributes (that he could control the elements and that his charisma had been granted him by the Holy Spirit and the spirits of Father Burgos and Rizal), Florencio had a following of some 10,000 peasants on Negros and Panay by late 1926. In May 1927, his supporters, heeding his call that "the hour will come when the poor will be ordered to kill all the rich," launched an abortive insurrection.

Tensions were highest in Central Luzon, where tenancy was most widespread and population pressures were the greatest. The 1931 Tayug insurrection north of Manila was connected with a *colorum* sect and had religious overtones, but traditionally messianic movements gradually gave way to secular, and at times revolutionary, ones. One of the first of these movements was the Association of the Worthy Kabola (Kapisanan Makabola Makasinag), a secret society that by 1925 had some 12,000 followers, largely in Nueva Ecija Province. Its leader, Pedro Kabola, called for liberation of the Philippines and promised the aid of the Japanese. The Tangulang (Kapatiran Tangulang Malayang Mamamayang--Association for an Offensive for Our Future Freedom) movement founded in 1931 was both urban and rural based and had as many as 40,000 followers.

The most important movement, however, was that of the Sakdalistas. Founded in 1933 by Benigno Ramos, a former Nacionalista Party member and associate of Quezon who broke with him over the issue of collaboration, the Sakdal Party (*sakdal* means to accuse) ran candidates in the 1934 election on a platform of complete independence by the end of 1935, redistribution of land, and an end to caciquism. Sakdalistas were elected to a number of seats in the legislature and to provincial posts, and by early 1935 the party may have had as many as 200,000 members. Because of poor harvests and frustrations with the government's lack of response to peasant demands, Sakdalistas took up arms and seized government buildings in a number of locations on May 2-3, 1935. The insurrection, suppressed by the Philippine Constabulary, resulted in approximately 100 dead and Benigno Ramos fled into exile to Japan.

Through the 1930s, tenant movements in Central Luzon became more active, articulate, and better organized. In 1938 the Socialist Party joined in a united front with the Communist Party of the Philippines (Partido Komunista ng Pilipinas--PKP), which was prominent in supporting the demands of tenants for better contracts and working conditions. As the depression wore on and prices for cash crops collapsed, tenant strikes and violent confrontations with landlords, their overseers, and the Philippine Constabulary escalated.

In response to deteriorating conditions, commonwealth president Quezon launched the "Social Justice" program, which included regulation of rents but achieved only meager results. There were insufficient funds to carry out the program, and implementation was sabotaged on the local level by landlords and municipal officials. In 1939 and 1940, thousands of cultivators were evicted by landlords because they insisted on enforcement of the 1933 Rice Share Tenancy Act, which guaranteed larger shares for tenants.

The Commonwealth and the Japanese Occupation

Commonwealth Politics, 1935-41
The constellation of political forces in the United States that assisted in the resolution of the independence question formed an odd community of interests with the Filipino nationalists. Principal among these were the agricultural interests. American sugar beet, tobacco, and dairy farmers feared the competition of low-tariff insular products, and the hardships suffered in a deepening depression in the early 1930s led them to seek protection through a severance of the colonial relationship. In this they had the support of Cuban sugar interests, who feared the loss of markets to Philippine sugarcane. United States labor unions, particularly on the West Coast, wanted to exclude Filipino labor. A number of American observers saw the Philippines as a potential flash point with an expansive Japan and argued for a withdrawal across the Pacific to Hawaii.

In the climate generated by these considerations, Osmeña and Manuel Roxas, a rising star in the Nacionalista Party and Osmeña's successor as speaker of the House, successfully campaigned for passage of the Hare-Hawes-Cutting Independence Bill, which Congress approved over President Herbert Hoover's veto in January 1933. Quezon opposed the legislation, however, on the grounds that clauses relating to trade and excluding Filipino immigrants were too stringent and that the guarantees of United States bases on Philippine soil and powers granted a United States high commissioner compromised independence. After the bill was defeated in the Philippine legislature, Quezon himself went to Washington and negotiated the passage of a revised independence act, the Tydings-McDuffie Act, in March 1934.

The Tydings-McDuffie Act provided for a ten-year transition period to independence, during which the Commonwealth of the Philippines would be established. The commonwealth would have its own constitution and would be self-governing, although foreign policy would be the responsibility of the United States. Laws passed by the legislature affecting immigration, foreign trade, and the currency system had to be approved by the United States president.

If the Tydings-McDuffie Act marked a new stage in Filipino-American partnership, it remained a highly unequal one. Although only fifty Filipino immigrants were allowed into the United States annually under the arrangement, American entry and residence in the islands were unrestricted. Trade provisions of the act allowed for five years' free entry of Philippine goods during the transition period and five years of gradually steepening tariff duties thereafter, reaching 100 percent in 1946, whereas United States goods could enter the islands unrestricted and duty free during the full ten years. Quezon had managed to obtain more favorable terms on bases; the United States would retain only a naval reservation and fueling stations. The United States would, moreover, negotiate with foreign governments for the neutralization of the islands.

The country's first constitution was framed by a constitutional convention that assembled in July 1934. Overwhelmingly approved by plebiscite in May 1935, this document established the political institutions for the intended ten-year commonwealth period that began that year and after July 1946 became the constitution of the independent Republic of the Philippines. The first commonwealth election to the new Congress was held in September 1935. Quezon and Osmeña, reconciled after their disagreements over the independence act, ran on a Coalition Party ticket and were elected president and vice president, respectively.

World War II, 1941-45

Japan launched a surprise attack on the Philippines on December 8, 1941, just ten hours after the attack on Pearl Harbor. Initial aerial bombardment was followed by landings of ground troops both north and south of Manila. The defending Philippine and United States troops were under the command of General Douglas MacArthur, who had been recalled to active duty in the United States Army earlier in the year and was designated commander of the United States Armed Forces in the Asia-Pacific region. The aircraft of his command were destroyed; the naval forces were ordered to leave; and because of the circumstances in the Pacific region, reinforcement and resupply of his ground forces were impossible. Under the pressure of superior numbers, the defending forces withdrew to the Bataan Peninsula and to the island of Corregidor at the entrance to Manila Bay. Manila, declared an open city to prevent its destruction, was occupied by the Japanese on January 2, 1942.

The Philippine defense continued until the final surrender of United States-Philippine forces on the Bataan Peninsula in April 1942 and on Corregidor in May. Most of the 80,000 prisoners of war captured by the Japanese at Bataan were forced to undertake the infamous "Death March" to a prison camp 105 kilometers to the north. It is estimated that as many as 10,000 men, weakened by disease and malnutrition and treated harshly by their captors, died before reaching their destination. Quezon and Osmeña had accompanied the troops to Corregidor and later left for the United States, where they set up a government in exile. MacArthur was ordered to Australia, where he started to plan for a return to the Philippines.

The Japanese military authorities immediately began organizing a new government structure in the Philippines. Although the Japanese had promised independence for the islands after occupation, they initially organized a Council of State through which they directed civil affairs until October 1943, when they declared the Philippines an independent republic. Most of the Philippine elite, with a few notable exceptions, served under the Japanese. Philippine collaboration in Japanese-sponsored political institutions--which later became a major domestic political issue--was motivated by several considerations. Among them was the effort to protect the people from the harshness of Japanese rule (an effort that Quezon himself had advocated), protection of family and personal interests, and a belief that Philippine nationalism would be advanced by solidarity with fellow Asians. Many collaborated to pass information to the Allies. The Japanese-sponsored republic headed by President José P. Laurel proved to be unpopular.

Japanese occupation of the Philippines was opposed by increasingly effective underground and guerrilla activity that ultimately reached large-scale proportions. Postwar investigations showed that about 260,000 people were in guerrilla organizations and that members of the anti-Japanese underground were even more numerous. Their effectiveness was such that by the end of the war, Japan controlled only twelve of the forty-eight provinces. The major element of resistance in the Central Luzon area was furnished by the Huks (see Glossary), Hukbalahap, or the People's Anti-Japanese Army organized in early 1942 under the leadership of Luis Taruc, a communist party member since 1939. The Huks armed some 30,000 people and extended their control over much of Luzon. Other guerrilla units were attached to the United States Armed Forces Far East.

MacArthur's Allied forces landed on the island of Leyte on October 20, 1944, accompanied by Osmeña, who had succeeded to the commonwealth presidency upon the death of Quezon on August 1, 1944. Landings then followed on the island of Mindoro and around the Lingayen Gulf on the west side of Luzon, and the push toward Manila was initiated. Fighting was fierce, particularly in the mountains of northern Luzon, where Japanese troops had retreated, and in Manila, where they put up a last-ditch resistance. Guerrilla forces rose up everywhere for the final offensive. Fighting continued until Japan's formal surrender on September 2, 1945. The Philippines had suffered great loss of life and tremendous physical destruction by the time the war was over (see The Armed Forces in National Life). An estimated 1 million Filipinos had been killed, a large proportion during the final months of the war, and Manila was extensively damaged.

Independence and Constitutional Government, 1945-72

Demoralized by the war and suffering rampant inflation and shortages of food and other goods, the Philippine people prepared for the transition to independence, which was scheduled for July 4, 1946. A number of issues remained unresolved, principally those concerned with trade and security arrangements between the islands and the United States. Yet in the months following Japan's surrender, collaboration became a virulent issue that split the country and poisoned political life. Most of the commonwealth legislature and leaders, such as Laurel, Claro Recto, and Roxas, had served in the Japanese-sponsored government. While the war was still going on, Allied leaders had stated that such "quislings" and their counterparts on the provincial and local levels would be severely punished. Harold Ickes, who as United States secretary of the interior had civil authority over the islands, suggested that all officials above the rank of schoolteacher who had cooperated with the Japanese be purged and denied the right to vote in the first postwar elections. Osmeña countered that each case should be tried on its own merits.

Resolution of the problem posed serious moral questions that struck at the heart of the political system. Collaborators argued that they had gone along with the occupiers in order to shield the people from the harshest aspects of Japanese rule. Before leaving Corregidor in March 1942, Quezon had told Laurel and José Vargas, mayor of Manila, that they should stay behind to deal with the Japanese but refuse to take an oath of allegiance. Although president of a "puppet" republic, Laurel had faced down the Japanese several times and made it clear that his loyalty was first to the Philippines and second to the Japanese-sponsored Greater East Asia Coprosperity Sphere.

Critics accused the collaborators of opportunism and of enriching themselves while the people starved. Anti-collaborationist feeling, moreover, was fueled by the people's resentment of the elite. On both the local and the national levels, it had been primarily the landlords, important officials, and the political establishment that had supported the Japanese, largely because the latter, with their own troops and those of a reestablished Philippine Constabulary, preserved their property and forcibly maintained the rural status quo. Tenants felt the harshest aspects of Japanese rule. Guerrillas, particularly those associated with the Husk, came from the ranks of the cultivators, who organized to defend themselves against Philippine Constabulary and Japanese depredations.

The issue of collaboration centered on Rosa, prewar Nacionalista speaker of the House of Representatives, who had served as minister without portfolio and was responsible for rice procurement and economic policy in the wartime Laurel government. A close prewar associate of MacArthur, he maintained contact with Allied intelligence during the war and in 1944 had unsuccessfully attempted to escape to Allied territory, which exonerated him in the general's eyes. MacArthur supported Roxas in his ambitions for the presidency when he announced himself as a candidate of the newly formed Liberal Party (the liberal wing of the Nacionalista Party) in January 1946. MacArthur's favoritism aroused much criticism, particularly because other collaborationist leaders were held in jail, awaiting trial. A presidential campaign of great vindictiveness ensued, in which Roxas's wartime role was a central issue. Roxas outspent and outspoke his Nacionalista opponent, the aging and ailing Osmeña. In the April 23, 1946, election, Roxas won 54 percent of the vote, and the Liberal Party won a majority in the legislature.

On July 4, 1946, Roxas became the first president of the independent Republic of the Philippines. In 1948 he declared an amnesty for arrested collaborators--only one of whom had been indicted--except for those who had committed violent crimes. The resiliency of the prewar elite, although remarkable, nevertheless had left a bitter residue in the minds of the people. In the first years of the republic, the issue of collaboration became closely entwined with old agrarian grievances and produced violent results.

Economic Relations with the United States after Independence

If the inauguration of the Commonwealth of the Philippines in November 1935 marked the high point of Philippine-United States relations, the actual achievement of independence was in many ways a disillusioning anticlimax. Economic relations remained the most salient issue. The Philippine economy remained highly dependent on United States markets--more dependent, according to United States high commissioner Paul McNutt, than any single state was dependent on the rest of the country. Thus a severance of special relations at independence was unthinkable, and large landowners, particularly those with hectarage in sugar, campaigned for an extension to free trade. The Philippine Trade Act, passed by the United States Congress in 1946 and commonly known as the Bell Act, stipulated that free trade be continued until 1954; thereafter, tariffs would be increased 5 percent annually until full amounts were reached in 1974. Quotas were established for Philippine products both for free trade and tariff periods. At the same time, there would be no restrictions on the entry of United States products to the Philippines, nor would there be Philippine import duties. The Philippine peso (for value of the peso--see Glossary) was tied at a fixed rate to the United States dollar.

The most controversial provision of the Bell Act was the "parity" clause that granted United States citizens equal economic rights with Filipinos, for example, in the exploitation of natural resources. If parity privileges of individuals or corporations were infringed upon, the president of the United States had the authority to revoke any aspect of the trade agreement. Payment of war damages amounting to US$620 million, as stipulated in the Philippine Rehabilitation Act of 1946, was made contingent on Philippine acceptance of the parity clause.

The Bell Act was approved by the Philippine legislature on July 2, two days before independence. The parity clause, however, required an amendment relating to the 1935 constitution's thirteenth article, which reserved the exploitation of natural resources for Filipinos. This amendment could be obtained only with the approval of three-quarters of the members of the House and Senate and a plebiscite. The denial of seats in the House to six members of the leftist Democratic Alliance and three Nacionalistas on grounds of fraud and violent campaign tactics during the April 1946 election enabled Roxas to gain legislative approval on September 18. The definition of three-quarters became an issue because three-quarters of the sitting members, not the full House and Senate, had approved the amendment, but the Supreme Court ruled in favor of the administration's interpretation.

In March 1947, a plebiscite on the amendment was held; only 40 percent of the electorate participated, but the majority of those approved the amendment. The Bell Act, particularly the parity clause, was seen by critics as an inexcusable surrender of national sovereignty. The pressure of the sugar barons, particularly those of Roxas's home region of the western Visayan Islands, and other landowner interests, however, was irresistible. In 1955 a revised United States-Philippine Trade Agreement (the Laurel-Langley Agreement) was negotiated. This treaty abolished the United States authority to control the exchange rate of the peso, made parity privileges reciprocal, extended the sugar quota, and extended the time period for the reduction of other quotas and for the progressive application of tariffs on Philippine goods exported to the United States.

Security Agreements

The Philippines became an integral part of emerging United States security arrangements in the western Pacific upon approval of the Military Bases Agreement in March 1947. The United States retained control of twenty-three military installations, including Clark Air Base and the extensive naval facilities at Subic Bay, for a lease period of ninety-nine years. United States rather than Philippine authorities retained full jurisdiction over the territories covered by the military installations, including over collecting taxes and trying offenders, including Filipinos, in cases involving United States service personnel. Base rights remained a controversial issue in relations between the two countries into the 1990s (see Foreign Affairs).

The Military Assistance Agreement also was signed in March 1947. This treaty established a Joint United States Military Advisory Group to advise and train the Philippine armed forces and authorized the transfer of aid and matériel--worth some US$169 million by 1957. Between 1950 and the early 1980s, the United States funded the military education of nearly 17,000 Filipino military personnel, mostly at military schools and training facilities in the United States. Much United States aid was used to support and reorganize the Philippine Constabulary in late 1947 in the face of growing internal unrest. A contingent of Philippine troops was sent to Korea in 1950. In August 1951 the two nations signed the Mutual Defense Treaty Between the Republic of the Philippines and the United States of America.

The Huk Rebellion

At the end of World War II, most rural areas, particularly in Central Luzon, were tinderboxes on the point of incineration. The Japanese occupation had only postponed the farmers' push for better conditions. Tensions grew as landlords who had fled to urban areas during the fighting returned to the villages in late 1945, demanded back rent, and employed military police and their own armed contingents to enforce these demands. Food and other goods were in short supply. The war had sharpened animosities between the elite, who in large numbers had supported the Japanese, and those tenants who had been part of the guerrilla resistance. Having had weapons and combat experience and having lost friends and relatives to the Japanese and the wartime Philippine Constabulary, guerrilla veterans and those close to them were not as willing to be intimidated by landlords as they had been before 1942.

MacArthur had jailed Taruc and Casto Alejandrino, both Huk leaders, in 1945 and ordered United States forces to disarm and disband Huk guerrillas. Many guerrillas, however, concealed their weapons or fled into the mountains. The Huks were closely identified with the emerging Pambansang Kaisahan ng mga Magbubukid (PKM--National Peasant Union), which was strongest in the provinces of Pampanga, Bulacan, Nueva Ecija, and Tarlac and had as many as 500,000 members. As part of the left-wing Democratic Alliance, which also included urban left-wing groups and labor unions, the PKM supported Osmeña and the Nacionalistas against Roxas in the 1946 election campaign. They did so not only because Roxas had been a collaborator but also because Osmeña had promised a new law giving tenants 60 percent of the harvest, rather than the 50 percent or less that had been customary.

Six Democratic Alliance candidates won congressional seats, including Taruc, who had been released from jail along with other leaders, but their exclusion from the legislature on charges of using terrorist methods during the campaign provoked great unrest in the districts that had elected them. Continued landlord- and police-instigated violence against peasant activities, including the murder of PKM leader Juan Feleo in August 1946, provoked the Huk veterans to dig up their weapons and incite a rebellion in the Central Luzon provinces. The name of the HUK movement was changed from the People's Anti-Japanese Army to the People's Liberation Army (Hukbong Mapagpalaya ng Bayan).

Roxas's policy toward the Huks alternated between gestures of negotiation and harsh suppression. His administration established an Agrarian Commission and passed a law giving tenants 70 percent of the harvest, although this was extremely difficult to enforce in the countryside. The Huks in turn demanded reinstatement of the Democratic Alliance members of Congress; disbandment of the military police, which in the 1945-48 period had been the equivalent of the old Philippine Constabulary; and a general amnesty. They also refused to give up their arms. In March 1948, Roxas declared the Huks an illegal and subversive organization and stepped up counterinsurgency activities.

Following Roxas's death from a heart attack in April 1948, his successor, Elpidio Quirino, opened negotiations with Huk leader Taruc, but nothing was accomplished. That same year the communist PKP decided to support the rebellion, overcoming its reluctance to rely on peasant movements. Although it lacked a peasant following, the PKP declared that it would lead the Huks on all levels and in 1950 described them as the "military arm" of the revolutionary movement to overthrow the government. From its inception, the government considered the Huk movement to have been communist instigated, an extension onto the Luzon Plain of the international revolutionary strategy of the Cominform (see Glossary) in Moscow. Yet the rebellion's main impetus was peasant grievances, not Leninist designs. The principal factors were continuous tenant-landlord conflicts, in which the government actively took the part of the latter, dislocations caused by the war, and perhaps an insurrectionist tradition going back several centuries. According to historian Benedict Kerkvliet, "the PKP did not inspire or control the peasant movement . . . . What appears closer to the truth is that the PKP, as an organization, moved back and forth between alliance and non-alliance with the peasant movement in Central Luzon." Most farmers had little interest in or knowledge of socialism. Most wanted better conditions not redistribution of land or collectivization. The landlord-tenant relationship itself was not challenged, just its more exploitive and impersonal character in the contemporary period.

Huk fortunes reached their peak between 1949 and 1951. Violence associated with the November 1949 presidential election, in which Quirino was reelected on the Liberal Party ticket, led many farmers to support the Huks, and after that date there were between 11,000 and 15,000 armed Huks. Although the core of the rebellion remained in Central Luzon, Huk regional committees also were established in the provinces of Southern Tagalog, in northern Luzon, in the Visayan Islands, and in Mindanao. Antigovernment activities spread to areas outside the movement's heartland.

Beginning in 1951, however, the momentum began to slow. This was in part the result of poor training and the atrocities perpetrated by individual Huks. Their mistreatment of Negrito peoples made it almost impossible for them to use the mountain areas where these tribespeople lived, and the assassination of Aurora Quezon, President Quezon's widow, and of her family by Huks outraged the nation. Many Huks degenerated into murderers and bank robbers. Moreover, in the words of one guerrilla veteran, the movement was suffering from "battle fatigue." Lacking a hinterland, such as that which the Democratic Republic of Vietnam (North Vietnam) provided for Viet Cong guerrillas or the liberated areas established by the Chinese Communists before 1949, the Huks were constantly on the run. Also the Huks were mainly active in Central Luzon, which permitted the government to concentrate its forces. Other decisive factors were the better quality of United States-trained Philippine armed forces and the more conciliatory policy adopted by the Quirino government toward the peasants.

The Magsaysay, Garcia, and Macapagal Administrations, 1953- 65

Ramon Magsaysay, a member of Congress from Zambales Province and veteran of a non-Huk guerrilla unit during the war, became secretary of defense in 1950. He initiated a campaign to defeat the insurgents militarily and at the same time win popular support for the government. With United States aid and advisers he was able to improve the quality of the armed forces, whose campaign against the Huks had been largely ineffective and heavy-handed. In 1950 the constabulary was made part of the armed forces (it had previously been under the secretary of the interior) with its own separate command. All armed forces units were placed under strict discipline, and their behavior in the villages was visibly more restrained. Peasants felt grateful to Magsaysay for ending the forced evacuations and harsh pacification tactics that some claimed had been worse than those of the Japanese occupation.

Nominated as Nacionalista Party presidential candidate in April 1953, Magsaysay won almost two-thirds of the vote over his opponent, Quirino, in November. Often compared to United States president Andrew Jackson, Magsaysay styled himself as a man of the people. He invited thousands of peasants and laborers to tour the Malacañang Palace--the presidential residence in Manila--and encouraged farmers to send him telegrams, free of charge, with their complaints. In the countryside a number of small-scale but highly visible projects had been started, including the building of bridges, roads, irrigation canals, and artesian "liberty wells";

the establishment of special courts for landlord-tenant disputes; agricultural extension services; and credit for farmers. The Economic Development Corps project settled some 950 families on land that the government had purchased on Mindanao. In the ensuing years, this program, in various forms, promoted the settlement of poor people from the Christian north in traditionally Muslim areas. Although it relieved population pressures in the north, it also exacerbated centuries-old Muslim Christian hostilities. The capture and killing of Huk leaders, the dissolution of Huk regional committees, and finally the surrender of Taruc in May 1954 marked the waning of the Huk threat.

Magsaysay's vice president, Carlos P. Garcia, succeeded to the presidency after Magsaysay's death in an airplane crash in March 1957 and was shortly thereafter elected to the office. Garcia emphasized the nationalist themes of "Filipino First" and attainment of "respectable independence." Further discussions with the United States on the question of the military bases took place in 1959. Early agreement was reached on United States relinquishment of large land areas initially reserved for bases but no longer required for their operation. As a result, the United States turned over to Philippine administration the town of Olongapo on Subic Bay, north of Manila, which previously had been under the jurisdiction of the United States Navy.

The 1957 election had resulted, for the first time, in a vice president of a party different from that of the president. The new vice president, Diosdado Macapagal, ran as the candidate of the Liberal Party, which followers of Magsaysay had joined after unsuccessful efforts to form an effective third party. By the time of the 1961 presidential election, the revived Liberal Party had built enough of a following to win the presidency for Macapagal. In this election, the returns from each polling place were reported by observers (who had been placed there by newspapers) as soon as the votes were counted. This system, known as Operation Quick Count, was designed to prevent fraud.

The issue of jurisdiction over United States service personnel in the Philippines, which had not been fully settled after the 1959 discussions, continued to be a problem in relations between the two countries. A series of incidents in the 1960-65 period, chiefly associated with Clark Air Base, aroused considerable anti-American feelings and demonstrations. Negotiations took place and resulted in an August 1965 agreement to adopt provisions similar to the status of forces agreement of the North Atlantic Treaty Organization regarding criminal jurisdiction. In the next four years, agreements were reached on several other matters relating to the bases, including a 1966 amendment to the 1947 agreement, which moved the expiration date of the fixed term for United States use of the military facilities up to 1991.

Philippine foreign policy under Macapagal sought closer relations with neighboring Asian peoples. In July 1963, he convened a summit meeting in Manila consisting of the Philippines, Indonesia, and Malaysia. An organization called MAPHILINDO was proposed; much heralded in the local press as a realization of Rizal's dream of bringing together the Malay peoples, MAPHILINDO was described as a regional association that would approach issues of common concern in the spirit of consensus. MAPHILINDO was quickly shelved, however, in the face of the continuing confrontation between Indonesia and newly established Malaysia and the Philippines' own claim to Sabah, the territory in northeastern Borneo that had become a Malaysian state in 1963.

Marcos and the Road to Martial Law, 1965-72

In the presidential election of 1965, the Nacionalista candidate, Ferdinand E. Marcos (1917-90), triumphed over Macapagal. Marcos dominated the political scene for the next two decades, first as an elected president in 1965 and 1969, and then as a virtual dictator after his 1972 proclamation of martial law. He was born in Ilocos Norte Province at the northwestern tip of Luzon, a traditionally poor and clannish region. He was a brilliant law student, who successfully argued before the Philippine Supreme Court in the late 1930s for a reversal of a murder conviction against him (he had been convicted of shooting a political rival of his father). During World War II, Marcos served in the Battle of Bataan and then claimed to have led a guerrilla unit, the Maharlikas. Like many other aspects of his life, Marcos's war record, and the large number of United States and Philippine military medals that he claimed (at one time including the Congressional Medal of Honor), came under embarrassing scrutiny during the last years of his presidency. His stories of wartime gallantry, which were inflated by the media into a personality cult during his years in power, enthralled not only Filipino voters but also American presidents and members of Congress.

In 1949 Marcos gained a seat in the Philippine House of Representatives; he became a senator in 1959. His 1954 marriage to former beauty queen Imelda Romualdez provided him with a photogenic partner and skilled campaigner. She also had family connections with the powerful Romualdez political dynasty of Leyte in the Visayas.

During his first term as president, Marcos initiated ambitious public works projects-- roads, bridges, schools, health centers, irrigation facilities, and urban beautification projects-- that improved the quality of life and also provided generous pork barrel benefits for his friends. Massive spending on public works was, politically, a cost-free policy not only because the pork barrel won him loyal allies but also because both local elites and ordinary people viewed a new civic center or bridge as a benefit. By contrast, a land reform program-- part of Marcos's platform as it had been that of Macapagal and his predecessors--would alienate the politically all-powerful landowner elite and thus was never forcefully implemented.

Marcos lobbied rigorously for economic and military aid from the United States but resisted pressure from President Lyndon Johnson to become significantly involved in the Second Indochina War. Marcos's contribution to the war was limited to a 2,000- member Philippine Civic Action Group sent to the Republic of Vietnam (South Vietnam) between 1966 and 1969. The Philippines became one of the founding members of the Association of Southeast Asian Nations (ASEAN), established in 1967. Disputes with fellow ASEAN member Malaysia over Sabah in northeast Borneo, however, continued, and it was discovered, after an army mutiny and murder of Muslim troops in 1968 (the "Corregidor Incident"), that the Philippine army was training a special unit to infiltrate Sabah (see Relations with Asian Neighbors).

Although Marcos was elected to a second term as president in 1969--the first president of the independent Philippines to gain a second term--the atmosphere of optimism that characterized his first years in power was largely dissipated. Economic growth slowed. Ordinary Filipinos, especially in urban areas, noted a deteriorating quality of life reflected in spiraling crime rates and random violence. Communist insurgency, particularly the activity of the Huks--had degenerated into gangsterism during the late 1950s, but the Communist Party of the Philippines-Marxist Leninist, usually referred to as the CPP, was "reestablished" in 1968 along Maoist lines in Tarlac Province north of Manila, leaving only a small remnant of the original PKP. The CPP's military arm, the New People's Army (NPA), soon spread from Tarlac to other parts of the archipelago. On Mindanao and in the Sulu Archipelago, violence between Muslims and Christians, the latter often recent government-sponsored immigrants from the north, was on the rise. In 1969 the Moro National Liberation Front (MNLF) was organized on Malaysian soil. The MNLF conducted an insurrection supported by Malaysia and certain Islamic states in the Middle East, including Libya.

The carefully crafted "Camelot" atmosphere of Marcos's first inauguration, in which he cast himself in the role of John F. Kennedy with Imelda as his Jackie, gave way in 1970 to general dissatisfaction with what had been one of the most dishonest elections in Philippine history and fears that Marcos might engineer change in the 1935 constitution to maintain himself in power. On January 30, 1970, the "Battle of Mendiola," named after a street in front of the Malacañang Palace, the presidential mansion, pitted student demonstrators, who tried to storm the palace, against riot police and resulted in many injuries.

Random bombings, officially attributed to communists but probably set by government agents provocateurs, occurred in Manila and other large cities. Most of these only destroyed property, but grenade explosions in the Plaza Miranda in Manila during an opposition Liberal Party rally on August 21, 1971, killed 9 people and wounded 100 (8 of the wounded were Liberal Party candidates for the Senate). Although it has never been conclusively shown who was responsible for the bombing, Marcos blamed leftists and suspended habeas corpus--a prelude to martial law. But evidence subsequently pointed, again, to government involvement.

Government and opposition political leaders agreed that the country's constitution, American-authored during the colonial period, should be replaced by a new document to serve as the basis for thorough-going reform of the political system. In 1967 a bill was passed providing for a constitutional convention, and three years later, delegates to the convention were elected. It first met in June 1971.

The 1935 constitution limited the president to two terms. Opposition delegates, fearing that a proposed parliamentary system would allow Marcos to maintain himself in power indefinitely, prevailed on the convention to adopt a provision in September 1971 banning Marcos and members of his family from holding the position of head of state or government under whatever arrangement was finally established. But Marcos succeeded, through the use of bribes and intimidation, in having the ban nullified the following summer. Even if Marcos had been able to contest a third presidential term in 1973, however, both the 1971 mid-term elections and subsequent public opinion polls indicated that he or a designated successor-- Minister of National Defense Juan Ponce Enrile or the increasingly ambitious Imelda Marcos- -would likely be defeated by his arch-rival, Senator Benigno "Ninoy" Aquino.

Proclamation 1081 and Martial Law

On September 21, 1972, Marcos issued Proclamation 1081, declaring martial law over the entire country. Under the president's command, the military arrested opposition figures, including Benigno Aquino, journalists, student and labor activists, and criminal elements. A total of about 30,000 detainees were kept at military compounds run by the army and the Philippine Constabulary. Weapons were confiscated, and "private armies" connected with prominent politicians and other figures were broken up. Newspapers were shut down, and the mass media were brought under tight control. With the stroke of a pen, Marcos closed the Philippine Congress and assumed its legislative responsibilities. During the 1972-81 martial law period, Marcos, invested with dictatorial powers, issued hundreds of presidential decrees, many of which were never published.

Like much else connected with Marcos, the declaration of martial law had a theatrical, smoke-and-mirrors quality. The incident that precipitated Proclamation 1081 was an attempt, allegedly by communists, to assassinate Minister of National Defense Enrile. As Enrile himself admitted after Marcos's downfall in 1986, his unoccupied car had been riddled by machinegun bullets fired by his own men on the night that Proclamation 1081 was signed.

Most Filipinos--or at least those well positioned within the economic and social elites-- initially supported the imposition of martial law. The rising tide of violence and lawlessness was apparent to everyone. Although still modest in comparison with the Huk insurgency of the early 1950s, the New People's Army was expanding, and the Muslim secessionist movement continued in the south with foreign support. Well-worn themes of communist conspiracy--Marcos claimed that a network of "front organizations" was operating "among our peasants, laborers, professionals, intellectuals, students, and mass media personnel"-- found a ready audience in the United States, which did not protest the demise of Philippine democracy.

The New Society

Marcos claimed that martial law was the prelude to creating a "New Society" based on new social and political values. He argued that certain aspects of personal behavior, attributed to a colonial mentality, were obstacles to effective modernization. These included the primacy of personal connections, as reflected in the ethic of *utang na loob*, and the importance of maintaining in-group harmony and coherence, even at the cost to the national community. A new spirit of self-sacrifice for the national welfare was necessary if the country were to equal the accomplishments of its Asian neighbors, such as Taiwan and the Republic of Korea (South Korea). Despite Marcos's often perceptive criticisms of the old society, Marcos, his wife, and a small circle of close associates, the crony (see Glossary) group, now felt free to practice corruption on an awe-inspiring scale.

Political, economic, and social policies were designed to neutralize Marcos's rivals within the elite. The old political system, with its parties, rough-and-tumble election campaigns, and a press so uninhibited in its vituperative and libelous nature that it was called "the freest in the world," had been boss-ridden and dominated by the elite since early American colonial days, if not before. The elite, however, composed of local political dynasties, had never been a homogeneous group. Its feuds and tensions, fueled as often by assaults on *amor proprio* (self-esteem) as by disagreement on ideology or issues, made for a pluralistic system.

Marcos's self-proclaimed "revolution from the top" deprived significant portions of the old elite of power and patronage. For example, the powerful Lopez family, who had fallen out of Marcos's favor (Fernando Lopez had served as Marcos's first vice president), was stripped of most of its political and economic assets. Although always influential, during the martial law years, Imelda Marcos built her own power base, with her husband's support. Concurrently the governor of Metro Manila (see Glossary) and minister of human settlements (a post created for her), she exercised significant powers.

Crony Capitalism

During the first years of martial law, the economy benefited from increased stability, and business confidence was bolstered by Marcos's appointment of talented technocrats to economic planning posts. Despite the 1973 oil price rise shock, the growth of the gross national product (GNP--see Glossary) was respectable, and the oil-pushed inflation rate, reaching 40 percent in 1974, was trimmed back to 10 percent the following year. Between 1973 and the early 1980s, dependence on imported oil was reduced by domestic finds and successful energy substitution measures, including one of the world's most ambitious geothermal energy programs. Claiming that "if land reform fails, there is no New Society," Marcos launched highly publicized new initiatives that resulted in the formal transfer of land to some 184,000 farming families by late 1975. The law was filled with loopholes, however, and had little impact on local landowning elites or landless peasants, who remained desperately poor.

The largest, most productive, and technically most advanced manufacturing enterprises were gradually brought under the control of Marcos's cronies. For example, the huge business conglomerate owned by the Lopez family, which included major newspapers, a broadcast network, and the country's largest electric power company, was broken up and distributed to Marcos loyalists including Imelda Marcos's brother, Benjamin "Kokoy" Romualdez, and another loyal crony, Roberto Benedicto. Huge monopolies and semi-monopolies were established in manufacturing, construction, and financial services. When these giants proved unprofitable, the government subsidized them with allocations amounting to hundreds of millions of pesos. Philippine Airlines, the nation's international and domestic air carrier, was nationalized and turned into what one author has called a "virtual private commuter line" for Imelda Marcos and her friends on shopping excursions to New York and Europe (see Transportation).

Probably the most negative impact of crony capitalism, however, was felt in the traditional cash-crop sector, which employed millions of ordinary Filipinos in the rural areas. (The coconut industry alone brought income to an estimated 15 million to 18 million people.) Under Benedicto and Eduardo Cojuangco, distribution and marketing monopolies for sugar and coconuts were established. Farmers on the local level were obliged to sell only to the monopolies and received less than world prices for their crops; they also were the first to suffer when world commodity prices dropped. Millions of dollars in profits from these monopolies were diverted overseas into Swiss bank accounts, real estate deals, and purchases of art, jewelry, and antiques. On the island of Negros in the Visayas, the region developed by Nicholas Loney for the sugar industry in the nineteenth century, sugar barons continued to live lives of luxury, but the farming community suffered from degrees of malnutrition rare in other parts of Southeast Asia.

Ferdinand Marcos was responsible for making the previously nonpolitical, professional Armed Forces of the Philippines, which since American colonial times had been modeled on the United States military, a major actor in the political process. This subversion occurred done in two ways. First, Marcos appointed officers from the Ilocos region, his home province, to its highest ranks. Regional background and loyalty to Marcos rather than talent or a distinguished service record were the major factors in promotion. Fabian Ver, for example, had been a childhood friend of Marcos and later his chauffeur, rose to become chief of staff of the armed forces and head of the internal security network. Secondly, both officers and the rank and file became beneficiaries of generous budget allocations. Officers and enlisted personnel received generous salary increases. Armed forces personnel increased from about 58,000 in 1971 to 142,000 in 1983. Top-ranking military officers, including Ver, played an important policy-making role. On the local level, commanders had opportunities to exploit the economy and establish personal patronage networks, as Marcos and the military establishment evolved a symbiotic relationship under martial law.

A military whose commanders, with some exceptions, were rewarded for loyalty rather than competence proved both brutal and ineffective in dealing with the rapidly growing communist insurgency and Muslim separatist movement. Treatment of civilians in rural areas was often harsh, causing rural people, as a measure of self-protection rather than ideological commitment, to cooperate with the insurgents. The communist insurgency, after some reverses in the 1970s, grew quickly in the early 1980s, particularly in some of the poorest regions of the country. The Muslim separatist movement reached a violent peak in the mid-1970s and then declined greatly, because of divisions in the leadership of the movement and reduced external support brought about by the diplomatic activity of the Marcos government.

Relations with the United States remained most important for the Philippines in the 1970s, although the special relationship between the former and its ex-colony was greatly modified as trade, investment, and defense ties were redefined (see Relations with the United States). The Laurel-Langley Agreement defining preferential United States tariffs for Philippine exports and parity privileges for United States investors expired on July 4, 1974, and trade relations were governed thereafter by the international General Agreement on Tariffs and Trade (GATT). During the martial law period, foreign investment terms were substantially liberalized, despite official rhetoric about foreign "exploitation" of the economy. A policy promoting "nontraditional" exports such as textiles, footwear, electronic components, and fresh and processed foods was initiated with some success. Japan increasingly challenged the United States as a major foreign participant in the Philippine economy.

The status of United States military bases was redefined when a major amendment to the Military Bases Agreement of 1947 was signed on January 6, 1979, reaffirming Philippine sovereignty over the bases and reducing their total area. At the same time, the United States administration promised to make its "best effort" to obtain congressional appropriations for military and economic aid amounting to US$400 million between 1979 to 1983. The amendment called for future reviews of the bases agreement every fifth year. Although the administration of President Jimmy Carter emphasized promoting human rights worldwide, only limited pressure was exerted on Marcos to improve the behavior of the military in rural areas and to end the death-squad murder of opponents. (Pressure from the United States, however, did play a role in gaining the release of Benigno Aquino in May 1980, and he was allowed to go to the United States for medical treatment after spending almost eight years in prison, including long stretches of time in solitary confinement.)

On January 17, 1981, Marcos issued Proclamation 2045, formally ending martial law. Some controls were loosened, but the ensuing New Republic proved to be a superficially liberalized version of the crony-dominated New Society. Predictably, Marcos won an overwhelming victory in the June 1981 presidential election, boycotted by the main opposition groups, in which his opponents were nonentities.

From Aquino's Assassination to People's Power

Benigno "Ninoy" Aquino was, like his life-long rival Ferdinand Marcos, a consummate politician, Philippine-style. Born in 1932, he interrupted his college studies to pursue a journalistic career, first in wartime Korea and then in Vietnam, Malaya, and other parts of Southeast Asia. Like Marcos, a skilled manager of his own public image, he bolstered his popularity by claiming credit for negotiating the May 1954 surrender of Huk leader Luis Taruc. The Aquino family was to Tarlac Province in Central Luzon what the Marcos family was to Ilocos Norte and the Romualdez family was to Leyte: a political dynasty. Aquino became the governor of Tarlac Province in 1963, and a member of the Senate in 1967. His marriage to Corazon Cojuangco, a member of one of the country's richest and most prominent Chinese mestizo families, was, like Marcos's marriage to Imelda Romualdez, a great help to his political career. If martial law had not been declared in September 1972, Aquino would probably have defeated Marcos or a hand-picked successor in the upcoming presidential election. Instead, he was one of the first to be jailed when martial law was imposed.

Aquino's years in jail--physical hardship, the fear of imminent death at the hands of his jailers, and the opportunity to read and meditate--seemed to have transformed the fast-talking political operator into a deeper and more committed leader of the democratic opposition. Although he was found guilty of subversion and sentenced to death by a military court in November 1977, Aquino, still in prison, led the LABAN (Lakas Ng Bayan--Strength of the Nation) party in its campaign to win seats in the 1978 legislative election and even debated Marcos's associate, Enrile, on television. The vote was for seats in the legislature called the National Assembly, initiated in 1978, which was, particularly in its first three years essentially a rubber-stamp body designed to pass Marcos's policies into law with the appearance of correct legal form. (The LABAN was unsuccessful, but it gained 40 percent of the vote in Metro Manila.)

Allowed to go to the United States for medical treatment in 1980, Benigno Aquino, accompanied by his wife, became a major leader of the opposition in exile. In 1983 Aquino was fully aware of the dangers of returning to the Philippines. Imelda Marcos had pointedly advised him that his return would be risky, claiming that communists or even some of Marcos's allies would try to kill him. The deterioration of the economic and political situation and Marcos's own worsening health, however, persuaded Aquino that the only way his country could be spared civil war was either by persuading the president to relinquish power voluntarily or by building a responsible, united opposition. In his view, the worst possible outcome was a post-Marcos regime led by Imelda and backed by the military under Ver.

Aquino was shot in the head and killed as he was escorted off an airplane at Manila International Airport by soldiers of the Aviation Security Command on August 21, 1983. The government's claim that he was the victim of a lone communist gunman, Rolando Galman (who was conveniently killed by Aviation Security Command troops after the alleged act), was unconvincing. A commission appointed by Marcos and headed by jurist Corazon Agrava concluded in their findings announced in late October 1984, that the assassination was the result of a military conspiracy. Marcos's credibility, both domestically and overseas, was mortally wounded when the Sandiganbayan, a high court charged with prosecuting government officials for crimes, ignored the Agrava findings, upheld the government's story, and acquitted Ver and twenty-four other military officers and one civilian in December 1985.

Although ultimate responsibility for the act still had not been clearly determined in the early 1990s, on September 28, 1990, a special court convicted General Luther Custodio and fifteen other officers and enlisted members of the Aviation Security Command of murdering Aquino and Galman. Most observers believed, however, that Imelda Marcos and Fabian Ver wanted Aquino assassinated. Imelda's remarks, both before and after the assassination, and the fact that Ver had become her close confidant, cast suspicion on them.

For the Marcoses, Aquino became a more formidable opponent dead than alive. His funeral drew millions of mourners in the largest demonstration in Philippine history. Aquino became a martyr who focused popular indignation against a corrupt regime. The inevitable outcome--Marcos's overthrow--could be delayed but not prevented.

The People's Power (see Glossary) movement, which bore fruit in the ouster of Marcos on February 25, 1986, was broad-based but primarily, although not exclusively, urban-based, indeed the movement was commonly known in Manila as the EDSA Revolution (see Glossary). People's Power encompassed members of the Roman Catholic hierarchy, the business elite, and a faction of the armed forces. Its millions of rural, working-class, middle-class, and professional supporters were united not by ideology or class interests, but by their esteem for Aquino's widow, Corazon, and their disgust with the Marcos regime. After her husband's assassination, Corazon Aquino assumed first a symbolic and then a substantive role as leader of the opposition. A devout Catholic and a shy and self-styled "simple housewife," Mrs. Aquino inspired trust and devotion. Some, including top American policy makers, regarded her as inexperienced and naive. Yet in the events leading up to Marcos's ouster she displayed unexpected shrewdness and determination.

The Old Political Opposition

Martial law had emasculated and marginalized the opposition, led by a number of traditional politicians who attempted, with limited success, to promote a credible, noncommunist alternative to Marcos. The most important of these was Salvador H. "Doy" Laurel. Laurel organized a coalition of ten political groups, the United Nationalist Democratic Organization (UNIDO), to contest the 1982 National Assembly elections. Although he included Benigno Aquino as one of UNIDO's twenty "vice presidents," Laurel and Aquino were bitter rivals.

The Catholic Church

During the martial law and post-martial law periods, the Catholic Church was the country's strongest and most independent non-governmental institution. It traditionally had been conservative and aligned with the elites. Parish priests and nuns, however, witnessed the sufferings of the common people and often became involved in political, and even communist, activities. One of the best-known politicized clergy was Father Conrado Balweg, who led a New People's Army guerrilla unit in the tribal minority regions of northern Luzon. Although Pope John Paul II had admonished the clergy worldwide not to engage in active political struggle, the pope's commitment to human rights and social justice encouraged the Philippine hierarchy to criticize the Marcos regime's abuses in the late 1970s and early 1980s. Church-state relations deteriorated as the state controlled media accused the church of being infiltrated by communists. Following Aquino's assassination, Cardinal Jaime Sin, archbishop of Manila and a leader of the Catholic Bishops Conference of the Philippines, gradually shifted the hierarchy's stance from one of "critical collaboration" to one of open opposition.

A prominent Catholic layman, José Concepcion, played a major role in reviving the National Movement for Free Elections (NAMFREL) with church support in 1983 in order to monitor the 1984 National Assembly elections. Both in the 1984 balloting and the February 7, 1986, presidential election, NAMFREL played a major role in preventing, or at least reporting, regime-- instigated irregularities. The backbone of its organization was formed by parish priests and nuns in virtually every part of the country.

The Business Elite

The Aquino assassination shattered business confidence at a time when the economy was suffering from years of mismanagement under the cronies and unfavorable international conditions. Business leaders, especially those excluded from regime-nurtured monopolies, feared that a continuation of the status quo would cause a collapse of the economy. Their apprehensions were shared by foreign creditors and international agencies such as the International Monetary Fund (IMF--see Glossary). Inflation and unemployment were soaring. The country's GNP became stagnant by 1983, and then it contracted--by -6.8 percent in 1984, and -3.8 percent in 1985, according to the IMF. There was a steep decline both in domestic and foreign investment. Outward capital flows reached as high as US$2 million a day in the panic that followed Aquino's death. The Makati area of Manila, with its banks, brokerage houses, luxury hotels, and upper-class homes, became a center of vocal resistance to the Marcos regime.

The Left

Left-wing groups, affiliated directly or indirectly with the Communist Party of the Philippines, played a prominent role in anti-regime demonstrations after August 1983. While the New People's Army was spreading in rural areas, the communists, through the National Democratic Front, gained influence, if not control, over some labor unions, student groups, and other urban based organizations. Leftists demanding radical political change established the New Nationalist Alliance (Bagging Alyansang Makabayan--BAYAN), in the early 1980s, but their political influence suffered considerably from their decision to boycott the presidential election of February 1986.

The Armed Forces

Corruption and demoralization of the armed forces led to the emergence, in the early 1980s, of a faction of young officers, mostly graduates of the elite Philippine Military Academy, known as the Reform the Armed Forces Movement (RAM--see Political Role). RAM supported a restoration of pre-martial law "professionalism" and was closely allied with Minister of National Defense Enrile, long a Marcos loyalist yet increasingly unhappy with Ver's ascendancy over the armed forces.

United States Reactions

Given its past colonial association and continued security and economic interests in the Philippines, the United States never was a disinterested party in Philippine politics. On June 1, 1983, the United States and the Philippines signed a five-year memorandum of agreement on United States bases, which committed the United States administration to make "best efforts" to secure US$900 million in economic and military aid for the Philippines between 1984 and 1988. The agreement reflected both United States security concerns at a time of increased Soviet-Western tension in the Pacific and its continued faith in the Marcos regime.

The assassination of Aquino shocked United States diplomats in Manila, but conservative policy makers in the administration of President Ronald Reagan remained, until almost the very end, supportive of the Marcoses, because no viable alternative seemed available. In hindsight, United States support for the moderate People's Power movement under Corazon Aquino, backed by church and business groups, would seem to be self-evident common sense. Yet in the tense days and weeks leading up to Marcos's ouster, many policy makers feared that she was not tough or canny enough to survive a military coup d'état or a communist takeover.

The Snap Election and Marcos's Ouster

Indicative of the importance of United States support for his regime, Marcos announced his decision to hold a "snap" presidential election on an American television talk show, "This Week with David Brinkley," in November 1985. He promised skeptical Americans access for observer teams, setting February 7, 1986, a year before his six-year presidential term ran out, as the date for the election. He believed his early reelection would solidify United States support, silence his critics in the Philippines and the United States, and perhaps banish the ghost of Benigno Aquino. Marcos's smoothly running, well-financed political machine and the divided nature of the opposition promised success, but his decision proved to be a monumental blunder.

Cardinal Sin, an astute negotiator described by one diplomat as "one of the best politicians in the Philippines," arranged a political alliance of convenience between Corazon Aquino and Salvador Laurel, who had announced his own candidacy but agreed to run as Aquino's vice-presidential candidate. Aquino had immense popular support and Laurel brought his superior organizational skills to the campaign. Their agreement to run together was arranged just in time for the deadline for submission of candidacies in early December. The church hierarchy gave its moral support to the opposition ticket. Cardinal Sin, realizing that poor people would not refuse money offered for votes and that the ethic of utang na loob would oblige them to vote for the briber, admonished the voters that an immoral contract was not binding and that they should vote according to their consciences.

On the day of the election, NAMFREL guarded ballot boxes and tried to get a rapid tally of the results in order to prevent irregularities. A team of United States observers, which included a joint congressional delegation, issued a mild criticism of electoral abuses, but individual members expressed shock and indignation: Senator Richard Lugar claimed that between 10 and 40 percent of the voters had been disenfranchised by the removal of their names from registration rolls. The results tabulated by the government's Commission on Elections (COMELEC) showed Marcos leading, whereas NAMFREL figures showed a majority for the Aquino-Laurel ticket. On February 9, computer operators at COMELEC observed discrepancies between their figures and those officially announced and walked out in protest, at some risk to their lives. The church condemned the election as fraudulent, but on February 15, the Marcos-dominated National Assembly proclaimed him the official winner. Despite the election fraud, the Reagan administration's support for Marcos remained strong, as did its uncertainty concerning Corazon Aquino. Yet a consensus of policy makers in the White House, Department of State, Pentagon, and Congress was emerging and advised the withdrawal of support from Marcos.

On February 22, Enrile and General Fidel Ramos, commander of the Philippine Constabulary, issued a joint statement demanding Marcos's resignation. They established their rebel headquarters inside Camp Aguinaldo and the adjoining Camp Crame in Metro Manila, which was guarded by several hundred troops. Marcos ordered loyal units to suppress the uprising, but Cardinal Sin, broadcasting over the Catholic-run Radio Veritas (which became the voice of the revolution), appealed to the people to bring food and supplies for the rebels and to use nonviolence to block pro-Marcos troop movements.

Hundreds of thousands responded. In the tense days that followed, priests, nuns, ordinary citizens, and children linked arms with the rebels and faced down, without violence, the tanks and machine guns of government troops. Many of the government troops defected, including the crews of seven helicopter gunships, which seemed poised to attack the massive crowd on February 24 but landed in Camp Crame to announce their support for People's Power. Violent confrontations were prevented. The Philippine troops did not want to wage war on their own people.

Although Marcos held an inauguration ceremony at Malacañang Palace on February 25, it was boycotted by foreign ambassadors (with the exception, in an apparently unwitting gaffe, of a new Soviet ambassador). It was, for the Marcoses, the last, pathetic hurrah. Advised by a United States senator, Paul Laxalt, who had close ties to Reagan, to "cut and cut cleanly," Marcos realized that he had lost United States support for any kind of arrangement that could keep him in power. By that evening, the Marcoses had quit the palace that had been their residence for two decades and were on their way to exile in the United States. Manila's population surged into Malacañang to view the evidence of the Marcos's extravagant life-style (including Imelda's much publicized hundreds of pairs of expensive, unworn shoes). An almost bloodless revolution brought Corazon Aquino into office as the seventh president of the Republic of the Philippines (see The Rise of Corazon Aquino).

* * *

David Joel Steinberg's The Philippines provides a good general introduction to the country and pays considerable attention to historical background. For good discussions of the Spanish period, see John L. Phelan's The Hispanicization of the Philippines and Robert Reed's Colonial Manila. Austin Coate's Rizal provides a well-written account of one of the most extraordinary lives of modern times. On the American annexation of the islands, Stuart C. Miller's Benevolent Assimilation is a valuable work. Peter W. Stanley's Reappraising an Empire is a good study of the American colonial period, and Theodore Friend's The Blue Eyed Enemy discusses the Japanese occupation in comparison with neighboring Indonesia. One of the best accounts of the insurgency is Benedict J. Kerkvliet's The Huk Rebellion.

Crisis in the Philippines, a collection of essays edited by John Bresnan, provides an excellent academic discussion of the Marcos years and the events that brought Corazon Aquino to the presidency. Waltzing with a Dictator, by Raymond Bonner, discusses Marcos's relations with the United States, martial law, and the collapse of the Marcos regime. People Power, edited by Monina Allarey Mercado, describes the tense and exuberant atmosphere surrounding the mass movement that toppled Marcos. (For additional information and complete citations, see Bibliography.)

THE SOCIETY AND ITS ENVIRONMENT

The Philippines continued to be primarily a rural society in 1990, despite increasing signs of urbanization. The family remained the prime unit of social awareness, and ritual kin relations and associations of a patron-client nature still were the basis for social groupings beyond the nuclear family, rather than horizontal ties forged among members of economically based social classes. Because of a common religious tradition and the spread of Pilipino as a widely used, if not thoroughly accepted, national language, Filipinos were a relatively homogeneous population, with the important exceptions of the Muslim minority on Mindanao and in Sulu and southern Palawan provinces, and the upland tribal minorities sprinkled throughout the islands. Filipinos shared a common set of values emphasizing social acceptance as a primary virtue and a common world view in which education served as the principal avenue for upward social mobility. Cleavages in the society were based primarily on religious (in the case of Muslims versus Christians), sociocultural (in the case of upland tribes versus lowland coastal Filipinos), and urban-rural differences, rather than ethnic or racial considerations.

Improvements in the national transportation system and in mass communications in most parts of the archipelago in the 1970s and 1980s tended to reduce ethnolinguistic and regional divisions among lowland Filipinos, who made up more than 90 percent of the population. Some resistance to this cultural homogeneity remained, however, and continued regional identification was manifested in loyalty to regional languages and in opposition to the imposition of a national language based largely on Tagalog, the language of the Manila area.

Large numbers of rural migrants continued to flow into the huge metropolitan areas, especially Metro Manila (see Glossary). Filipinos also migrated in substantial numbers to the United States and other countries. Many of these migrants, especially those to the Middle East, migrated only to find temporary employment and retained their Philippine domiciles.

There has been a significant shift in the composition of the elite as a result of political and economic policies following the end of the administration of President Ferdinand E. Marcos in 1986. Some of the elite families displaced by the Marcos regime regained wealth and influence, and many of the families enjoying power, privilege, and prestige in the early 1990s were not the same as those enjoying similar status a decade earlier. The abolition of monopolistic marketing boards, along with some progress in privatization, has eliminated the economic base of some of Marcos's powerful associates.

As a result of economic policies that permitted fruit and logging companies to expand their landholdings, previously formed by tribal people, and to push farther and farther into the mountains to exploit timber resources, upland tribal people have been threatened and dislocated, and the country's rich rain forests have suffered. Despite government efforts to instill respect for cultural diversity, it remained to be seen whether minorities and the ecosystem they shared would survive the onslaught of powerful economic forces that include the migration of thousands of lowland Filipinos to the frontier areas on Mindanao, as well as the intrusion of corporate extractive industries. Even if these influences were held in check, the attraction of lowland society might wean the tribal people from their customary way of life.

Although it would seem that the continued high rate of population growth aggravated the state of the Philippine economy and health care, population growth did not seem to be a major concern of the government. Roman Catholic clergy withdrew cooperation from the Population Control Commission (Popcom) and sought its elimination. The commission was retained, and government efforts to reduce population growth continued but hardly on a scale likely to produce major results.

Physical Setting

The Philippine archipelago lies in Southeast Asia in a position that has led to its becoming a cultural crossroads, a place where Malays, Chinese, Spaniards, Americans, and others have interacted to forge that unique cultural and racial blend known to the world as Filipino. The archipelago numbers some 7,100 islands and the nation claims an exclusive economic zone (EEZ--see Glossary) of 200 nautical miles from its shores. The Philippines occupies an area that stretches for 1,850 kilometers from about the fifth to the twentieth parallels north latitude. The total land area is almost 300,000 square kilometers. Only approximately 1,000 of its islands are populated, and fewer than one-half of these are larger than 2.5 square kilometers. Eleven islands make up 94 percent of the Philippine landmass, and two of these--Luzon and Mindanao--measure 105,000 and 95,000 square kilometers, respectively. They, together with the cluster of the Visayan Islands that separate them, represent the three principal regions of the archipelago that are identified by the three stars on the Philippine flag. Topographically, the Philippines is broken up by the sea, which gives it one of the longest coastlines of any nation in the world (see fig. 2). Most Filipinos live on or near the coast, where they can easily supplement their diet from approximately 2,000 species of fish.

Off the coast of eastern Mindanao is the Philippine Trough, which descends to a depth of 10,430 meters. The Philippines is part of a western Pacific arc system that is characterized by active volcanoes. Among the most notable peaks are Mount Mayon near Legaspi, Taal Volcano south of Manila, and Mount Apo on Mindanao. All of the Philippines islands are prone to earthquakes. The northern Luzon highlands, or Cordillera Central, rise to between 2,500 and 2,750 meters, and, together with the Sierra Madre in the northeastern portion of Luzon and the mountains of Mindanao, boast rain forests that provide refuge for numerous upland tribal groups. The rain forests also offer prime habitat for more than 500 species of birds, including the Philippine eagle (or monkey-eating eagle), some 800 species of orchids, and some 8,500 species of flowering plants.

The country's most extensive river systems are the Pulangi (Rio Grande), which flows into the Mindanao River; the Agusan, in Mindanao which flows north into the Mindanao Sea; the Cagayan in northern Luzon; and the Pampanga, which flows south from east Central Luzon into Manila Bay. Laguna de Bay, southeast of Manila Bay, is the largest freshwater lake in the Philippines. Several rivers have been harnessed for hydroelectric power.

The Climate

The Philippines has a tropical marine climate dominated by a rainy season and a dry season. The summer monsoon brings heavy rains to most of the archipelago from May to October, whereas the winter monsoon brings cooler and drier air from December to February. Manila and most of the lowland areas are hot and dusty from March to May. Even at this time, however, temperatures rarely rise above 37° C. Mean annual sea-level temperatures rarely fall below 27° C. Annual rainfall measures as much as 5,000 millimeters in the mountainous east coast section of the country, but less than 1,000 millimeters in some of the sheltered valleys.

Monsoon rains, although hard and drenching, are not normally associated with high winds and waves. But the Philippines does sit astride the typhoon belt, and it suffers an annual onslaught of dangerous storms from July through October. These are especially hazardous for northern and eastern Luzon and the Bicol and Eastern Visayas regions, but Manila gets devastated periodically as well.

In the last decade, the Philippines has suffered severely from natural disasters. In 1990 alone, Central Luzon was hit by both a drought, which sharply curtailed hydroelectric power, and by a typhoon that flooded practically all of Manila's streets. Still more damaging was an earthquake that devastated a wide area in Luzon, including Baguio and other northern areas. The city of Cebu and nearby areas were struck by a typhoon that killed more than a hundred people, sank vessels, destroyed part of the sugar crop, and cut off water and electricity for several days.

Building construction is undertaken with natural disasters in mind. Most rural housing has consisted of nipa huts that are easily damaged but are inexpensive and easy to replace. Most urban buildings are steel and concrete structures designed (not always successfully) to resist both typhoons and earthquakes. Damage is still significant, however, and many people are displaced each year by typhoons, earthquakes, and other natural disasters. In 1987 alone the Department of Social Welfare and Development helped 2.4 million victims of natural disasters.

Population

Population Growth

The Philippine population in the early 1990s continued to grow at a rapid, although somewhat reduced rate from that which had prevailed in the preceding decades. In 1990 the Philippine population was more than 66 million, up from 48 million in 1980. This figure represents an annual growth rate of 2.5 percent, down from 2.6 percent in 1980 and from more than 3 percent in the 1960s. Even at the lower growth rate, the Philippine population will increase to an estimated 77 million by the year 2000 and will double every twenty-nine years into the next century. Moreover, in 1990 the population was still a youthful one, with 57 percent under the age of twenty. The birth rate in early 1991 was 29 per 1,000, and the death rate was 7 per 1,000. The infant mortality rate was 48 deaths per 1,000 live births. Population density increased from 160 per square kilometer in 1980 to 220 in 1990. The rapid population growth and the size of the younger population has required the Philippines to double the amount of housing, schools, and health facilities every twenty-nine years just to maintain a constant level.

Migration

There were two significant migration trends that affected population figures in the 1970s and the 1980s. First was a trend of migration from village to city, which put extra stress on urban areas. As of the early 1980s, thirty cities had 100,000 or more residents, up from twenty-one in 1970. Metro Manila's population was 5,924,563, up from 4,970,006 in 1975, marking an annual growth rate of 3.6 percent. This figure was far above the national average of 2.5 percent. Within Metro Manila, the city of Manila itself was growing more slowly, at a rate of only 1.9 percent per annum, but two other cities within this complex, Quezon City and Caloocan, were booming at rates of 4 percent and 3.5 percent, respectively.

A National Housing Authority report revealed that, in the early 1980s, one out of four Metro Manila residents was a squatter. This figure represented a 150 percent increase in a decade in the number of people living in shantytown communities, evidence of continuing, virtually uncontrolled, rural-urban migration. The city of Manila had more than 500,000 inhabitants and Quezon City had 371,000 inhabitants in such neighborhoods. Moreover, rural-urban migrants, responding to better employment opportunities in peripheral metropolitan cities such as Navotas, had boosted the percentage of squatters in that city's total population.

A second major migration pattern consisted of resettlement from the more densely to the less densely populated regions. As a result of a population-land ratio that declined from about one cultivated hectare per agricultural worker in the 1950s to about 0.5 hectare by the early 1980s, thousands of Filipinos had migrated to the agricultural frontier on Mindanao. According to the 1980 census, six of the twelve fastest growing provinces were in the western, northern, or southern Mindanao regions, and a seventh was the frontier province of Palawan. Sulu, South Cotabato, Misamis Oriental, Surigao del Norte, Agusan del Norte, and Agusan del Sur provinces all had annual population growth rates of 4 percent or more, a remarkable statistic given the uncertain law-and-order situation on Mindanao. Among the fastest growing cities in the late 1970s were General Santos (10 percent annual growth rate), Iligan (6.9), Cagayan de Oro (6.7), Cotabato (5.7), Zamboanga (5.4), Butuan (5.4), and Dipolog (5.1)--all on Mindanao.

By the early 1980s, the Mindanao frontier had ceased to offer a safety valve for land-hungry settlers. Hitherto peaceful provinces had become dangerous tinderboxes in which mounting numbers of Philippine army troops and New People's Army insurgents carried on a sporadic shooting war with each other and with bandits, "lost commands," millenarian religious groups, upland tribes, loggers, and Muslims (see The Counterinsurgency Campaign). Population pressures also created an added obstacle to land reform. For years, there had been demands to restructure land tenure so that landlords with large holdings could be eliminated and peasants could become farm owners. In the past, land reform had been opposed by landlords. In the 1990s there simply was not enough land to enable a majority of the rural inhabitants to become landowners. International migration has offered better economic opportunities to a number of Filipinos without, however, reaching the point where it would relieve population pressure. Since the liberalization of United States immigration laws in 1965, the number of people in the United States having Filipino ancestry had grown substantially to 1,406,770 according to the 1990 United States census. In the fiscal year ending September 30, 1990, the United States Embassy in Manila issued 45,189 immigrant and 85,128 temporary visas, the largest number up to that time.

In addition to permanent residents, in the late 1980s and early 1990s, more than half a million temporary migrants went abroad to work but maintained a Philippine residence. This number included contract workers in the Middle East and domestic servants in Hong Kong and Singapore, as well as nurses and physicians who went to the United States for training and work experience, a fair proportion of whom managed to become permanent residents. The remittances sent back to the Philippines by migrants have been a substantial source of foreign exchange.

Population Control

Popcom was the government agency with primary responsibility for controlling population growth. In 1985 Popcom set a target for reducing the growth rate to 1 percent by 2000. To reach that goal in the 1990s, Popcom recommended that families have a maximum of two children, that they space the birth of children at three-year intervals, and that women delay marriage to age twenty-three and men to age twenty-five.

During the Marcos regime (1965-86), there was a rather uneasy accommodation between the Catholic hierarchy and the government population control program. Bishops served on Popcom, and the rhythm method was included by clinics as a birth-control method about which they could give information. A few Catholic priests, notably Frank Lynch, even called for energetic support of population limitation.

The fall of Marcos coincided with a general rise of skepticism about the relation between population growth and economic development. It became common to state that exploitation, rather than population pressure, was the cause of poverty. The bishops withdrew from the Popcom board, opposed an effort to reduce the number of children counted as dependents for tax purposes, secured the removal of the population-planning clause from the draft of the Constitution, and attempted to end government population programs. Attacks on the government population program were defeated, and efforts to popularize family planning, along with the provision of contraceptive materials, continued. In the early 1990s, however, the program generally lacked the firm government support needed to make it effective.

Ethnicity, Regionalism, and Language

Historical Development of Ethnic Identities

Philippine society was relatively homogeneous in 1990, especially considering its distribution over some 1,000 inhabited islands. Muslims and upland tribal peoples were obvious exceptions, but approximately 90 percent of the society remained united by a common cultural and religious background. Among the lowland Christian Filipinos, language was the main point of internal differentiation, but the majority interacted and intermarried regularly across linguistic lines. Because of political centralization, urbanization, and extensive internal migration, linguistic barriers were eroding, and government emphasis on Pilipino and English (at the expense of local dialects) also reduced these divisions. Nevertheless, national integration remained incomplete.

Through centuries of intermarriage, Filipinos had become a unique blend of Malay, Chinese, Spanish, Negrito, and American. Among the earliest inhabitants were Negritos, followed by Malays, who deserve most of the credit for developing lowland Philippine agricultural life as it is known in the modern period (see Early History). As the Malays spread throughout the archipelago, two things happened. First, they absorbed, through intermarriage, most of the Negrito population, although a minority of Negritos remained distinct by retreating to the mountains. Second, they dispersed into separate groups, some of which became relatively isolated in pockets on Mindanao, northern Luzon, and some of the other large islands. Comparative linguistic analysis suggests that most groups may once have spoken a form of "proto-Manobo," but that each group developed a distinct vernacular that can be traced to its contact over the centuries with certain groups and its isolation from others.

With the advent of Islam in the southern Philippines during the fifteenth century, separate sultanates developed on Mindanao and in the Sulu Archipelago. By the middle of the sixteenth century, Islamic influence had spread as far north as Manila Bay.

Spain colonized the Philippines in the sixteenth century and succeeded in providing the necessary environment for the development of a Philippine national identity; however, Spain never completely vitiated Muslim autonomy on Mindanao and in the Sulu Archipelago, where the separate Muslim sultanates of Sulu, Maguindanao, and Maranao remained impervious to Christian conversion. Likewise, the Spanish never succeeded in converting upland tribal groups, particularly on Luzon and Mindanao. The Spanish influence was strongest among lowland groups and emanated from Manila. Even among these lowland peoples, however, linguistic differences continued to outweigh unifying factors until a nationalist movement emerged to question Spanish rule in the nineteenth century.

Philippine national identity emerged as a blend of diverse ethnic and linguistic groups, when lowland Christians, called *indios* by the Spaniards, began referring to themselves as "Filipinos," excluding Muslims, upland tribal groups, and ethnic Chinese who had not been assimilated by intermarriage and did not fit the category. In the very process of defining a national identity, the majority was also drawing attention to a basic societal cleavage among the groups (see The Development of a National Consciousness). In revolting against Spanish rule and, later, fighting United States troops, the indigenous people became increasingly conscious of a national unity transcending local and regional identities. A public school system that brought at least elementary-level education to all but the most remote barrios and *sitios* (small clusters of homes) during the early twentieth century also served to dilute religious, ethnic, and linguistic or regional differences, as did improvements in transportation and communication systems and the spread of English as a lingua franca (see The First Phase of United States Rule, 1898-1935).

Language Diversity and Uniformity

Some eleven languages and eighty-seven dialects were spoken in the Philippines in the late 1980s. Eight of these--Tagalog, Cebuano, Ilocano, Hiligaynon, Bicolano, Waray-Waray, Pampangan, and Pangasinan--were native tongues for about 90 percent of the population. All eight belong to the Malay-Polynesian language family and are related to Indonesian and Malay, but no two are mutually comprehensible. Each has a number of dialects and all have impressive literary traditions, especially Tagalog, Cebuano, and Ilocano. Some of the languages have closer affinity than others. It is easier for Ilocanos and Pangasinans to learn each other's language than to learn any of the other six. Likewise, speakers of major Visayan Island languages--Cebuano, Ilongo, and Waray-Waray--find it easier to communicate with each other than with Tagalogs, Ilocanos, or others.

Language divisions were nowhere more apparent than in the continuing public debate over national language. The government in 1974 initiated a policy of gradually phasing out English in schools, business, and government, and replacing it with Pilipino, based on the Tagalog language of central and southern Luzon. Pilipino had spread throughout the nation, the mass media, and the school system. In 1990 President Corazon Aquino ordered that all government offices use Pilipino as a medium of communication, and 200 college executives asked that Pilipino be the main medium of college instruction rather than English. Government and educational leaders hoped that Pilipino would be in general use throughout the archipelago by the end of the century. By that time, it might have enough grass-roots support in non-Tagalog-speaking regions to become a national language. In the early 1990s, however, Filipinos had not accepted a national language at the expense of their regional languages. Nor was there complete agreement that regional languages should be subordinated to a national language based on Tagalog.

The role of English was also debated. Some argued that English was essential to economic progress because it opened the Philippines to communication with the rest of the world, facilitated foreign commerce, and made Filipinos desirable employees for international firms both in the Philippines and abroad. Despite census reports that nearly 65 percent of the populace claimed some understanding of English, as of the early 1990s competence in English appeared to have deteriorated. Groups also debated whether "Filipinization" and the resulting shifting of the language toward "Taglish" (a mixture of Tagalog and English) had made the language less useful as a medium of international communication. Major newspapers in the early 1990s, however, were in English, English language movies were popular, and English was often used in advertisements.

Successful Filipinos were likely to continue to be competent in Pilipino and English. Speakers of another regional language would most likely continue to use that language at home, Pilipino in ordinary conversation in the cities, and English for commerce, government, and international relations. Both Pilipino, gaining use in the media, and English continued in the 1990s to be the languages of education.

The Lowland Christian Population

Although lowland Christians maintained stylistic differences in dress until the twentieth century and had always taken pride in their unique culinary specialties, they continued to be a remarkably homogeneous core population of the Philippines. In 1990 lowland Christians, also known as Christian Malays, made up 91.5 percent of the population and were divided into several regional groups. Because of their regional base in Metro Manila and adjacent provinces to the north, east, and south, Tagalogs tended to be more visible than other groups. Cebuanos, whose language was the principal one in the Visayan Island area, inhabited Cebu, Bohol, Siquijor, Negros Oriental, Leyte, and Southern Leyte provinces, and parts of Mindanao. Ilocanos had a reputation for being ready migrants, leaving their rocky northern Luzon homeland not just for more fertile parts of the archipelago but for the United States as well. The home region of the Ilongos (speakers of Hiligaynon) included most of Panay, Negros Occidental Province, and the southern end of Mindoro. Their migration in large numbers to the Cotabato and Lanao areas of Mindanao led to intense friction between them and the local Muslim inhabitants and the outbreak of fighting between the two groups in the 1970s. The homeland of the Bicolanos, or "Bicolandia" was the southeastern portion of Luzon together with the islands of Catanduanes, Burias, and Ticao, and adjacent parts of Masbate. The Waray-Warays lived mostly in eastern Leyte and Samar in the Eastern Visayas. The Pampangan homeland was the Central Luzon Plain and especially Pampanga Province. Speakers of Pangasinan were especially numerous in the Lingayen Gulf region of Luzon, but they also had spread to the Central Luzon Plain where they were interspersed with Tagalogs, Ilocanos, and Pampangans.

As migrants to the city, these lowland Christians clustered together in neighborhoods made up primarily of people from their own regions. Multi-lingualism generally characterized these neighborhoods; the language of the local area was used, as a rule, for communicating with those native to the area, and English or Pilipino was used as a supplement. Migrants to cities and to agricultural frontiers were remarkably ready and willing to learn the language of their new location while retaining use of their mother tongue within the home.

Muslim Filipinos

Muslims, about 5 percent of the total population, were the most significant minority in the Philippines. Although undifferentiated racially from other Filipinos, in the 1990s they remained outside the mainstream of national life, set apart by their religion and way of life. In the 1970s, in reaction to consolidation of central government power under martial law, which began in 1972, the Muslim Filipino, or Moro (see Glossary) population increasingly identified with the worldwide Islamic community, particularly in Malaysia, Indonesia, Libya, and Middle Eastern countries. Longstanding economic grievances stemming from years of governmental neglect and from resentment of popular prejudice against them contributed to the roots of Muslim insurgency (see The Moros).

Moros were confined almost entirely to the southern part of the country--southern and western Mindanao, southern Palawan, and the Sulu Archipelago. Ten subgroups could be identified on the basis of language. Three of these groups made up the great majority of Moros. They were the Maguindanaos of North Cotabato, Sultan Kudarat, and Maguindanao provinces; the Maranaos of the two Lanao provinces; and the Tausugs, principally from Jolo Island. Smaller groups were the Samals and Bajaus, principally of the Sulu Archipelago; the Yakans of Zamboanga del Sur Province; the Ilanons and Sangirs of Southern Mindanao Region; the Melabugnans of southern Palawan; and the Jama Mapuns of the tiny Cagayan Islands.

Muslim Filipinos traditionally have not been a closely knit or even allied group. They were fiercely proud of their separate identities, and conflict between them was endemic for centuries. In addition to being divided by different languages and political structures, the separate groups also differed in their degree of Islamic orthodoxy. For example, the Tausugs, the first group to adopt Islam, criticized the more recently Islamicized Yakan and Bajau peoples for being less zealous in observing Islamic tenets and practices. Internal differences among Moros in the 1980s, however, were outweighed by commonalities of historical experience vis-à-vis non-Muslims and by shared cultural, social, and legal traditions.

The traditional structure of Moro society focused on a sultan who was both a secular and a religious leader and whose authority was sanctioned by the Quran. The *datu* were communal leaders who measured power not by their holdings in landed wealth but by the numbers of their followers. In return for tribute and labor, the *datu* provided aid in emergencies and advocacy in disputes with followers of another chief. Thus, through his *agama* (court--actually an informal dispute-settling session), a *datu* became basic to the smooth function of Moro society. He was a powerful authority figure who might have as many as four wives and who might enslave other Muslims in raids on their villages or in debt bondage. He might also demand revenge (*maratabat*) for the death of a follower or upon injury to his pride or honor.

The *datu* continued to play a central role in Moro society in the 1980s. In many parts of Muslim Mindanao, they still administered the sharia (sacred Islamic law) through the *agama*. They could no longer expand their circle of followers by raiding other villages, but they achieved the same end by accumulating wealth and then using it to provide aid, employment, and protection for less fortunate neighbors. *Datu* support was essential for government programs in a Muslim *barangay* (see Glossary). Although a *datu* in modern times rarely had more than one wife, polygamy was permitted so long as his wealth was sufficient to provide for more than one. Moro society was still basically hierarchical and familial, at least in rural areas.

The national government policies instituted immediately after independence in 1946 abolished the Bureau for Non-Christian Tribes used by the United States to deal with minorities and encouraged migration of Filipinos from densely settled areas such as Central Luzon to the "open" frontier of Mindanao. By the 1950s, hundreds of thousands of Ilongos, Ilocanos, Tagalogs, and others were settling in North Cotabato and South Cotabato and Lanao del Norte and Lanao del Sur provinces, where their influx inflamed Moro hostility. The crux of the problem lay in land disputes. Christian migrants to the Cotabatos, for example, complained that they bought land from one Muslim only to have his relatives refuse to recognize the sale and demand more money. Muslims claimed that Christians would title land through government agencies unknown to Muslim residents, for whom land titling was a new institution. Distrust and resentment spread to the public school system, regarded by most Muslims as an agency for the propagation of Christian teachings. By 1970, a terrorist organization of Christians called the Ilagas (Rats) began operating in the Cotabatos, and Muslim armed bands, called Blackshirts, appeared in response. The same thing happened in the Lanaos, where the Muslim Barracudas began fighting the Ilagas. Philippine army troops sent in to restore peace and order were accused by Muslims of siding with the Christians. When martial law was declared in 1972, Muslim Mindanao was in turmoil (see Marcos and the Road to Martial Law, 1965-72).

The Philippine government discovered shortly after independence that there was a need for some kind of specialized agency to deal with the Muslim minority and so set up the Commission for National Integration in 1957, which was later replaced by the Office of Muslim Affairs and Cultural Communities. Filipino nationalists envisioned a united country in which Christians and Muslims would be offered economic advantages and the Muslims would be assimilated into the dominant culture. They would simply be Filipinos who had their own mode of worship and who refused to eat pork. This vision, less than ideal to many Christians, was generally rejected by Muslims who feared that it was a euphemistic equivalent of assimilation. Concessions were made to Muslim religion and customs. Muslims were exempted from Philippine laws prohibiting polygamy and divorce, and in 1977 the government attempted to codify Muslim law on personal relationships and to harmonize Muslim customary law with Philippine law. A significant break from past practice was the 1990 establishment of the Autonomous Region in Muslim Mindanao, which gave Muslims in the region control over some aspects of government, but not over national security and foreign affairs (see Local Government).

There were social factors in the early 1990s that militated against the cultural autonomy sought by Muslim leaders. Industrial development and increased migration outside the region brought new educational demands and new roles for women. These changes in turn led to greater assimilation and, in some cases, even intermarriage. Nevertheless, Muslims and Christians generally remained distinct societies often at odds with one another.

Upland Tribal Groups
Another minority, the more than 100 upland tribal groups, in 1990 constituted approximately 3 percent of the population. As lowland Filipinos, both Muslim and Christian, grew in numbers and expanded into the interiors of Luzon, Mindoro, Mindanao, and other

islands, they isolated upland tribal communities in pockets. Over the centuries, these isolated tribes developed their own special identities. The folk art of these groups was, in a sense, the last remnant of an indigenous tradition that flourished everywhere before Islamic and Spanish contact.

Technically, the upland tribal groups were a blend in ethnic origin like other Filipinos, although they did not, as a rule, have as much contact with the outside world. They displayed great variety in social organization, cultural expression, and artistic skills that showed a high degree of creativity, usually employed to embellish utilitarian objects, such as bowls, baskets, clothing, weapons, and even spoons. Technologically, these groups ranged from the highly sophisticated Bontocs and Ifugaos, who engineered the extraordinary rice terraces, to more primitive groups. They also covered a wide spectrum in terms of their integration and acculturation with lowland Christian Filipinos. Some, like the Bukidnons of Mindanao, had intermarried with lowlanders for almost a century, whereas others, like the Kalingas on Luzon, remained more isolated from lowland influences.

There were ten principal cultural groups living in the Cordillera Central of Luzon in 1990. The name Igorot, the Tagalog word for mountaineer, was often used with reference to all groups. At one time it was employed by lowland Filipinos in a pejorative sense, but in recent years it came to be used with pride by youths in the mountains as a positive expression of their separate ethnic identity vis-à-vis lowlanders. Of the ten groups, the Ifugaos of Ifugao Province, the Bontocs of Mountain and Kalinga-Apayao provinces, and the Kankanays and Ibalois of Benguet Province were all wet-rice farmers who worked the elaborate rice terraces they had constructed over the centuries. The Kankanays and Ibalois were the most influenced by Spanish and American colonialism and lowland Filipino culture because of the extensive gold mines in Benguet, the proximity of Baguio, good roads and schools, and a consumer industry in search of folk art. Other mountain peoples of Luzon were the Kalingas of Kalinga-Apayao Province and the Tinguians of Abra Province, who employed both wet-rice and dry-rice growing techniques. The Isnegs of northern Kalinga-Apayao Province, the Gaddangs of the border between Kalinga-Apayao and Isabela provinces, and the Ilongots of Nueva Vizcaya Province all practiced shifting cultivation. Negritos completed the picture for Luzon. Although Negritos formerly dominated the highlands, by the early 1980s they were reduced to small groups living in widely scattered locations, primarily along the eastern ranges of the mountains.

South of Luzon, upland tribal groups were concentrated on Mindanao, although there was an important population of mountain peoples with the generic name Mangyan living on Mindoro. Among the most important groups on Mindanao were the Manobos (a general name for many tribal groups in southern Bukidnon and Agusan del Sur provinces); the Bukidnons of Bukidnon Province; the Bagobos, Mandayas, Atas, and Mansakas, who inhabited mountains bordering the Davao Gulf; the Subanuns of upland areas in the Zamboanga provinces; the Mamanuas of the Agusan-Surigao border region; and the Bila-ans, Tirurays, and T-Bolis of the area of the Cotabato provinces. Tribal groups on Luzon were widely known for their carved wooden figures, baskets, and weaving; Mindanao tribes were renowned for their elaborate embroidery, appliqué, and bead work.

The Office of Muslim Affairs and Cultural Communities succeeded in establishing a number of protected reservations for tribal groups. Residents were expected to speak their tribal language, dress in their traditional tribal clothing, live in houses constructed of natural materials using traditional architectural designs, and celebrate their traditional ceremonies of propitiation of spirits believed to be inhabiting their environment. They also were encouraged to reestablish their traditional authority structure in which, as in Moro society, tribal datu were the key figures. These men, chosen on the basis of their bravery and their ability to settle disputes, were usually, but not always, the sons of former datu. Often they were also the ones who remembered the ancient oral epics of their people. The datu sang these epics to reawaken in tribal youth an appreciation for the unique and semi-sacred history of the tribal group.

Contact between primitive and modern groups usually resulted in weakening or destroying tribal culture without assimilating the tribal groups into modern society. It seemed doubtful that the shift of government policy from assimilation to cultural pluralism could reverse the process. James Eder, an anthropologist who has studied several Filipino tribes, maintains that even the protection of tribal land rights tends to lead to the abandonment of traditional culture because land security makes it easier for tribal members to adopt the economic practices of the larger society and facilitates marriage with outsiders. Government bureaus could not preserve tribes as social museum exhibits, but with the aid of various private organizations, they hoped to be able to help the tribes adapt to modern society without completely losing their ethnic identity.

The Chinese

In 1990 the approximately 600,000 ethnic Chinese made up less than 1 percent of the population. Because Manila is close to Taiwan and the mainland of China, the Philippines has for centuries attracted both Chinese traders and semi-permanent residents. The Chinese have been viewed as a source of cheap labor and of capital and business enterprise. Government policy toward the Chinese has been inconsistent. Spanish, American, and Filipino regimes alternately welcomed and restricted the entry and activities of the Chinese (see Chinese and Chinese Mestizos). Most early Chinese migrants were male, resulting in a sex ratio, at one time, as high as 113 to 1, although in the 1990s it was more nearly equal, reflecting a population based more on natural increase than on immigration.

There has been a good deal of intermarriage between the Chinese and lowland Christians, although the exact amount is impossible to determine. Although many prominent Filipinos, including José Rizal, President Corazon Aquino, and Cardinal Jaime Sin have mixed Chinese ancestry, intermarriage has not necessarily led to ethnic understanding. Mestizos (see Glossary), over a period of years, tended to deprecate their Chinese ancestry and to identify as Filipino. The Chinese tended to regard their culture as superior and sought to maintain it by establishing a separate school system in which about half the curriculum consisted of Chinese literature, history, and language.

Intermarriage and changing governmental policies made it difficult to define who was Chinese. The popular usage of "Chinese" included Chinese aliens, both legal and illegal, as well as those of Chinese ancestry who had become citizens. "Ethnic Chinese" was another term often used but hard to define. Mestizos could be considered either Chinese or Filipino, depending on the group with which they associated to the greatest extent.

Research indicates that Chinese were one of the least accepted ethnic groups. The common Filipino perception of the Chinese was of rich businessmen backed by Chinese cartels who stamped out competition from other groups. There was, however, a sizable Chinese working class in the Philippines, and there was a sharp gap between rich and poor Chinese.

Social Values and Organization

The great majority of the Philippine population is bound together by common values and a common religion. Philippine society is characterized by many positive traits. Among these are strong religious faith, respect for authority, and high regard for *amor proprio* (self-esteem) and smooth interpersonal relationships. Philippine respect for authority is based on the special honor paid to elder members of the family and, by extension, to anyone in a position of power. This characteristic is generally conducive to the smooth running of society, although, when taken to extreme, it can develop into an authoritarianism that discourages independent judgment and individual responsibility and initiative. Filipinos are sensitive to attacks on their own self-esteem and cultivate a sensitivity to the self-esteem of others as well. Anything that might hurt another's self-esteem is to be avoided or else one risks terminating the relationship. One who is insensitive to others is said to lack a sense of shame and embarrassment, the principal sanction against improper behavior. This great concern for self-esteem helps to maintain harmony in society and within one's particular circle, but it also can give rise to clannishness and a willingness to sacrifice personal integrity to remain in the good graces of the group. Strong personal faith enables Filipinos to face great difficulties and unpredictable risks in the assurance that "God will take care of things." But, if allowed to deteriorate into fatalism, even this admirable characteristic can hinder initiative and stand in the way of progress.

Social organization generally follows a single pattern, although variations do occur, reflecting the influence of local traditions. Among lowland Christian Filipinos, social organization continues to be marked primarily by personal alliance systems, that is, groupings composed of kin (real and ritual), grantors and recipients of favors, friends, and partners in commercial exchanges.

Philippine personal alliance systems are anchored by kinship, beginning with the nuclear family. A Filipino's loyalty goes first to the immediate family; identity is deeply embedded in the web of kinship. It is normative that one owes support, loyalty, and trust to one's close kin and, because kinship is structured bilaterally with affinal as well as consanguineal relatives, one's kin can include quite a large number of people. Still, beyond the nuclear family, Filipinos do not assume the same degree of support, loyalty, and trust that they assume for immediate family members for whom loyalty is nothing less than a social imperative. With respect to kin beyond this nuclear family, closeness in relationship depends very much on physical proximity.

Bonds of ritual kinship, sealed on any of three ceremonial occasions--baptism, confirmation, and marriage--intensify and extend personal alliances. This mutual kinship system, known as *compadrazgo*, meaning godparenthood or sponsorship, dates back at least to the introduction of Christianity and perhaps earlier. It is a primary method of extending the group from which one can expect help in the way of favors, such as jobs, loans, or just simple gifts on special occasions. But in asking a friend to become godparent to a child, a Filipino is also asking that person to become a closer friend. Thus it is common to ask acquaintances who are of higher economic or social status than oneself to be sponsors. Such ritual kinship cannot be depended on in moments of crisis to the same extent as real kinship, but it still functions for small and regular acts of support such as gift giving.

A dyadic bond--between two individuals--may be formed based on the concept of *utang na loob*. Although it is expected that the debtor will attempt repayment, it is widely recognized that the debt (as in one's obligation to a parent) can never be fully repaid and the obligation can last for generations. Saving another's life, providing employment, or making it possible for another to become educated are "gifts" that incur *utang na loob*. Moreover, such gifts initiate a long-term reciprocal interdependency in which the grantor of the favor can expect help from the debtor whenever the need arises and the debtor can, in turn, ask other favors. Such reciprocal personal alliances have had obvious implications for the society in general and the political system in particular. In 1990 educated Filipinos were less likely to feel obligated to extend help (thereby not initiating an *utang na loob* relationship) than were rural dwellers among whom traditional values remained strong. Some observers believed that as Philippine society became more modernized and urban in orientation, *utang na loob* would become less important in the political and social systems.

In the commercial context, *suki* relationships (market-exchange partnerships) may develop between two people who agree to become regular customer and supplier. In the marketplace, Filipinos will regularly buy from certain specific suppliers who will give them, in return, reduced prices, good quality, and, often, credit. *Suki* relationships often apply in other contexts as well. For example, regular patrons of restaurants and small neighborhood retail shops and tailoring shops often receive special treatment in return for their patronage. *Suki* does more than help develop economic exchange relationships. Because trust is such a vital aspect, it creates a platform for personal relationships that can blossom into genuine friendship between individuals.

Patron-client bonds also are very much a part of prescribed patterns of appropriate behavior. These may be formed between tenant farmers and their landlords or between any patron who provides resources and influence in return for the client's personal services and general support. The reciprocal arrangement typically involves the patron giving a means of earning a living or of help, protection, and influence and the client giving labor and personal favors, ranging from household tasks to political support. These relationships often evolve into ritual kinship ties, as the tenant or worker may ask the landlord to be a child's godparent. Similarly, when favors are extended, they tend to bind patron and client together in a network of mutual obligation or a long-term interdependency.

Filipinos also extend the circle of social alliances with friendship. Friendship often is placed on a par with kinship as the most central of Filipino relationships. Certainly ties among those within one's group of friends are an important factor in the development of personal alliance systems. Here, as in other categories, a willingness to help one another provides the prime rationale for the relationship.

These categories--real kinship, ritual kinship, *utang na loob* relationships, *suki* relationships, patron-client bonds, and friendship--are not exclusive. They are interrelated components of the Filipino's personal alliance system. Thus two individuals may be cousins, become friends, and then cement their friendship through godparenthood. Each of their social networks will typically include kin (near and far, affinal and consanguineal), ritual kin, one or two patron-client relationships, one or more other close friends (and a larger number of social friends), and a dozen or more market-exchange partners. *Utang na loob* may infuse any or all of these relationships. One's network of social allies may include some eighty or more people, integrated and interwoven into a personal alliance system.

In 1990 personal alliance systems extended far beyond the local arena, becoming pyramidal structures going all the way to Manila, where members of the national political elite represented the tops of numerous personal alliance pyramids. The Philippine elite was composed of weathly landlords, financiers, businesspeople, high military officers, and national political figures. Made up of a few families often descended from the *ilustrados* (see Glossary), or enlightened ones, of the Spanish colonial period, the elite controlled a high percentage of the nations's wealth. The lavish life-styles of this group usually included owning at least two homes (one in Manila and one in the province where the family originated), patronizing expensive shops and restaurants, belonging to exclusive clubs, and having a retinue of servants. Many counted among their social acquaintances a number of rich and influential foreigners, especially Americans, Spaniards, and other Europeans. Their children attended exclusive private schools in Manila and were often sent abroad, usually to the United States, for higher education. In addition, by 1990 a new elite of businesspeople, many from Hong Kong and Taiwan, had developed.

In the cities, there existed a considerable middle-class group consisting of small entrepreneurs, civil servants, teachers, merchants, small property owners, and clerks whose employment was relatively secure. In many middle-class families, both spouses worked. They tended to place great value on higher education, and most had a college degree. They also shared a sense of common identity derived from similar educational experiences, facility in using English, common participation in service clubs such as the Rotary, and similar economic standing.

Different income groups lived in different neighborhoods in the cities and lacked the personal contact essential to the patron-client relationship. Probably the major social division was between those who had a regular source of income and those who made up the informal sector of the economy. The latter subsisted by salvaging material from garbage dumps, begging, occasional paid labor, and peddling. Although their income was sometimes as high as those in regular jobs, they lacked the protection of labor legislation and had no claim to any type of social insurance (see Employment and Labor Relations; Economic Welfare).

Urban Social Patterns

The Philippines, like most other Southeast Asian nations, has one dominant city that is in a category all by itself as a "primate city." In the mid-1980s, Metro Manila produced roughly half of the gross national product (GNP--see Glossary) of the Philippines and contained two-thirds of the nation's vehicles. Its plethora of wholesale and retail business establishments, insurance companies, advertising companies, and banks of every description made the region the unchallenged hub of business and finance.

Because of its fine colleges and universities, including the University of the Philippines, Ateneo de Manila University, and De La Salle University, some of the best in Southeast Asia, the Manila area was a magnet for the best minds of the nation. In addition to being the political and judicial capital, Manila was the entertainment and arts capital, with all the glamour of first-class international hotels and restaurants. Because Manila dominated the communications and media industry, Filipinos everywhere were constantly made aware of economic, cultural, and political events in Manila. Large numbers of rural Filipinos moved to Manila in search of economic and other opportunities. More than one-half of the residents of Metro Manila were born elsewhere.

In the early 1990s, Manila, especially the Makati section, had a modern superstructure of hotels and banks, supermarkets, malls, art galleries, and museums. Beneath this structure, however, was a substructure of traditional small neighborhoods and a wide spectrum of life-styles ranging from traditional to modern, from those of the inordinately wealthy to those of the abjectly poor. Metro Manila offered greater economic extremes than other urban areas: poverty was visible in thousands of squatters' flimsy shacks and wealth was evident in the elegant, guarded suburbs with expensive homes and private clubs. But in Manila, unlike urban centers in other countries, these economic divisions were not paralleled by racial or linguistic residential patterns. Manila and other Philippine cities were truly melting pots, in which wealth was the only determinant for residence.

Whether in poor squatter and slum communities or in middleclass sections of cities, values associated primarily with rural *barangays* continued to be important in determining expectations, if not always actions. Even when it was clearly impossible to create a warm and personal community in a city neighborhood, Filipinos nevertheless felt that traditional patterns of behavior conducive to such a community should be followed. Hospitality, interdependence, patron-client bonds, and real kinship all continued to be of importance for urban Filipinos.

Still another indication that traditional Philippine values remained functional for city dwellers was that average household size in the 1980s was greater in urban than in rural areas. Observers speculated that, as Filipinos moved to the city, they had fewer children but more extended family members and non-relatives in their households. This situation might have been caused by factors such as the availability of more work opportunities in the city, the tendency of urban Filipinos to marry later so that there were more singles, the housing industry's inability to keep pace with urbanization, and the high urban unemployment rates that caused families to supplement their incomes by taking in boarders. Whatever the reason, it seemed clear that kinship and possibly other personal alliance system ties were no weaker for most urban Filipinos than for their rural kin.

Urban squatters have been a perennial problem or, perhaps, a sign of a problem. Large numbers of people living in makeshift housing, often without water or sewage, indicated that cities had grown in population faster than in the facilities required. In fact, the growth in population even exceeded the demand for labor so that many squatters found their living by salvaging material from garbage dumps, peddling, and performing irregular day work.

Most squatters were long-time residents, who found in the absence of rent a way of coping with economic problems. The efforts of the government in the late 1980s to beautify and modernize the Manila area led inevitably to conflict with the squatters who had settled most of the land that might be utilized in such projects. The forced eviction of squatters and the destruction of their shacks were frequent occurrences.

Two types of organizations have intervened in support of squatters: non-governmental organizations (NGOs) and syndicates. The NGOs had a variety of programs, each one representing only a small minority of the actual squatters, but they sustained pressure on the government and demanded land titles and an end to forced evictions as well as help in housing construction. The syndicates were extra-legal entities that provided an informal type of government in the late 1980s, levying fees of as much as 3 billion pesos (for value of peso--see Glossary) a year, or about US$120 million. The syndicates allocated land for lots, built roads and sidewalks of sorts, maintained order, and occasionally even provided water and light. In other words, they acted like private developers, although their only claim to the land was forcible seizure. Both the authoritarian Marcos government and the democratic Aquino government found it hard to handle the squatter problem. All proposed solutions contained difficulties, and probably only a major economic recovery in both rural and urban areas would provide a setting in which a degree of success would be possible.

The growth of other urban centers in the late 1980s and early 1990s, could signal a slowdown in the expansion of Metro Manila. This situation has been caused, at least in part, by the policies of both the Marcos and the Aquino administrations. The Marcos administration encouraged industrial decentralization and prohibited the erection of new factories within fifty kilometers of Manila. In an effort to relieve unemployment, the Aquino administration spent billions of pesos on rural infrastructure, which helped to expand business in the nearby cities. Cities such as Iligan, Cagayan de Oro, and General Santos on Mindanao, and especially Cebu on Cebu Island experienced economic growth in the 1980s far exceeding that of Manila.

The Role and Status of the Filipina

Women have always enjoyed greater equality in Philippine society than was common in other parts of Southeast Asia. Since pre-Spanish times, Filipinos have traced kinship bilaterally. A woman's rights to legal equality and to inherit family property have not been questioned. Education and literacy levels in 1990 were higher for women than for men. President Aquino often is given as an example of what women can accomplish in Philippine society. The appearance of women in important positions, however, is not new or even unusual in the Philippines. Filipino women, usually called Filipinas, have been senators, cabinet officers, Supreme Court justices, administrators, and heads of major business enterprises. Furthermore, in the early 1990s women were found in more than a proportionate share of many professions although they predominated in domestic service (91 percent), professional and technical positions (59.4 percent), and sales (57.9 percent). Women also were often preferred in assembly-type factory work. The availability of the types of employment in which women predominated probably explains why about two-thirds of the rural to urban migrants were female. Although domestic service is a low-prestige occupation, the other types of employment compare favorably with opportunities open to the average man.

This favorable occupational distribution does not mean that women were without economic problems. Although women were eligible for high positions, these were more often obtained by men. In 1990 women represented 64 percent of graduate students but held only 159 of 982 career top executive positions in the civil service. In the private sector, only about 15 percent of top-level positions were held by women.

According to many observers, because men relegated household tasks to women, employed women carried a double burden. This burden was moderated somewhat by the availability of relatives and servants who functioned as helpers and child caretakers, but the use of servants and relatives has sometimes been denounced as the equivalent of exploiting some women to free others.

Since the Spanish colonial period, the woman has been the family treasurer, which, at least to some degree, gave her the power of the purse. Nevertheless, the Spanish also established a tradition of subordinating women, which is manifested in women's generally submissive attitudes and in a double standard of sexual conduct. The woman's role as family treasurer, along with a woman's maintenance of a generally submissive demeanor, has changed little, but the double standard of sexual morality is being challenged. Male dominance also has been challenged, to some extent, in the 1987 constitution. The constitution contains an equal rights clause--although it lacks specific provisions that might make that clause effective.

As of the early 1990s, divorce was prohibited in the Philippines. Under some circumstances, legal separation was permitted, but no legal remarriage was possible. The family code of 1988 was somewhat more liberal. Reflective of Roman Catholic Church law, the code allowed annulment for psychological incapacity to be a marital partner, as well as for repeated physical violence against a mate or pressure to change religious or political affiliation. Divorce obtained abroad by an alien mate was recognized. Although the restrictive divorce laws might be viewed as an infringement on women's liberty to get out of a bad marriage, indications were that many Filipinas viewed them as a protection against abandonment and loss of support by wayward husbands.

Religious Life

Religion holds a central place in the life of most Filipinos, including Catholics, Muslims, Buddhists, Protestants, and animists. It is central not as an abstract belief system, but rather as a host of experiences, rituals, ceremonies, and adjurations that provide continuity in life, cohesion in the community, and moral purpose for existence. Religious associations are part of the system of kinship ties, patron client bonds, and other linkages outside the nuclear family.

Christianity and Islam have been superimposed on ancient traditions and acculturated. The unique religious blends that have resulted, when combined with the strong personal faith of Filipinos, have given rise to numerous and diverse revivalist movements. Generally characterized by millenarian goals, anti-modern bias, supernaturalism, and authoritarianism in the person of a charismatic messiah figure, these movements have attracted thousands of Filipinos, especially in areas like Mindanao, which have been subjected to extreme pressure of change over a short period of time. Many have been swept up in these movements, out of a renewed sense of fraternity and community. Like the highly visible examples of flagellation and reenacted crucifixion in the Philippines, these movements may seem to have little in common with organized Christianity or Islam. But in the intensely personalistic Philippine religious context, they have not been aberrations so much as extreme examples of how religion retains its central role in society.

The religious composition of the Philippines remained predominantly Catholic in the late 1980s. In 1989 approximately 82 percent of the population was Roman Catholic; Muslims accounted for only 5 percent. The remaining population was mostly affiliated with other Christian churches, although there were also a small number of Buddhists, Daoists (or Taoists), and tribal animists. Christians were to be found throughout the archipelago. Muslims remained largely in the south and were less integrated than other religious minorities into the mainstream of Philippine culture. Although most Chinese were members of Christian churches, a minority of Chinese worshipped in Daoist or in Buddhist temples, the most spectacular of which was an elaborate Daoist temple on the outskirts of Cebu.

Historical Background

Spanish colonialism had, from its formal inception in 1565 with the arrival of Miguel López de Legazpi, as its principal raison d'être the conversion of the inhabitants to Christianity. When Legazpi embarked on his conversion efforts, most Filipinos were still practicing a form of polytheism, although some as far north as Manila had converted to Islam. For the majority, religion still consisted of sacrifices and incantations to spirits believed to be inhabiting field and sky, home and garden, and other dwelling places both human and natural. Malevolent spirits could bring harm in the form of illness or accident, whereas benevolent spirits, such as those of one's ancestors, could bring prosperity in the form of good weather and bountiful crops. Shamans were called upon to communicate with these spirits on behalf of village and family, and propitiation ceremonies were a common part of village life and ritual. Such beliefs continued to influence the religious practices of many upland tribal groups in the modern period.

The religious system that conquistadors and priests imported in the sixteenth and seventeenth centuries was superimposed on this polytheistic base. Filipinos who converted to Catholicism did not shed their earlier beliefs but superimposed the new on the old. Saints took primacy over spirits, the Mass over propitiation ceremonies, and priests over shamans. This mixing of different religious beliefs and practices marked Philippine Catholicism from the start.

From its inception, Catholicism was deeply influenced by the prejudices, strategies, and policies of the Catholic religious orders. Known collectively as friars, the orders of the Augustinians, Dominicans, Franciscans, and others, and the Jesuits turned out to be just about the only Caucasians willing to dedicate their lives to converting and ministering to Spain's subject population in the Philippines. They divided the archipelago into distinct territories, learned the vernaculars appropriate to each region, and put down roots in the rural Philippines where they quickly became founts of wisdom for uneducated and unsophisticated local inhabitants (see The Friarocracy). Because most secular colonial officials had no intention of living so far from home any longer than it took to turn a handsome profit, friars took on the roles of the crown's representatives and interpreters of government policies in the countryside.

The close relationship between church and state proved to be a liability when the Philippines was swept by nationalistic revolt in the late nineteenth century and Filipino priests seized churches and proclaimed the Independent Philippine Church (Iglesia Filipina Independiente). After the American occupation, Protestant missionaries came and established churches and helped to spread American culture.

Roman Catholicism

The Catholic Church made a remarkable comeback in the Philippines in the twentieth century, primarily because the Vatican agreed to divest itself of massive church estates and to encourage Filipinos to join in the clergy. This resurgence was so successful that Protestant mission efforts, led by large numbers of American missionaries during the period of American colonial rule, made little headway. In the early 1990s, the clergy were predominantly Filipino, all of the diocesan hierarchy were Filipino, and the church was supported by an extensive network of parochial schools.

Catholicism, as practiced in the Philippines in the 1990s, blended official doctrine with folk observance. In an intensely personal way, God the Father was worshiped as a father figure and Jesus as the loving son who died for the sins of each individual, and the Virgin was venerated as a compassionate mother. In the words of scholar David J. Steinberg, "This framework established a cosmic *compadrazgo*, and an *utang na loob* to Christ, for his sacrifice transcended any possible repayment . . . . To the devout Filipino, Christ died to save him; there could be no limit to an individual's thanksgiving." As in other Catholic countries, Filipinos attended official church services (men usually not as regularly as women) such as Masses, novenas, baptisms, weddings, and funerals. They supplemented these official services with a number of folk-religious ceremonies basic to the community's social and religious calendar and involving just about everyone in the community.

Perhaps the single event most conducive to community solidarity each year is the fiesta. Celebrated on the special day of the patron saint of a town or *barangay*, the fiesta is a time for general feasting. Houses are opened to guests, and food is served in abundance. The fiesta always includes a Mass, but its purpose is unabashedly social. The biggest events include a parade, dance, basketball tournament, cockfights, and other contests, and perhaps a carnival, in addition to much visiting and feasting.

Christmas is celebrated in a manner that blends Catholic, Chinese, Philippine, and American customs. For nine days, people attend *misas de gallo* (early morning Christmas Mass). They hang elaborate lanterns (originally patterned after the Chinese lanterns) and other decorations in their homes and join with friends in caroling. On Christmas Eve, everyone attends midnight Mass, the climax of the *misas de gallo* and the year's high point of church attendance. After the service, it is traditional to return home for a grand family meal. The remaining days of the Christmas season are spent visiting kin, especially on New Year's Day and Epiphany, January 6. The Christmas season is a time of visiting and receiving guests. It is also a time for reunion with all types of kin--blood, affinal, and ceremonial. Children especially are urged to visit godparents.

During the Lenten season, most communities do a reading of the Passion narrative and a performance of a popular Passion play. The custom of reading or chanting of the Passion could be an adaptation of a pre-Spanish practice of chanting lengthy epics, but its continuing importance in Philippine life probably reflects the popular conception of personal indebtedness to Christ for His supreme sacrifice. At least one observer has suggested that Filipinos have, through the Passion, experienced a feeling of redemption that has been the basis for both millennial dreams and historical revolutionary movements for independence.

Indigenous Christian Churches

Iglesia Filipina Independiente

The Iglesia Filipina Independiente (Independent Philippine Church), founded by Gregorio Aglipay (1860-1940), received the support of revolutionary leader Emilio Aguinaldo during the revolt against Spain and subsequent conflicts with American forces. It rode the tide of anti-friar nationalism in absorbing Filipino Roman Catholic clergy and forcibly seizing church property at the beginning of the twentieth century. One out of every sixteen diocesan priests and one out of four Philippine Catholics followed Aglipay into the Iglesia Filipina Independiente in those years of violent national and religious catharsis. The Iglesia Filipina Independiente, formally organized in 1902, thus enjoyed approximately five years of rapid growth, before a temporary decline in Philippine nationalism sent its fortunes into precipitous decline.

Many followers returned to Catholicism, especially after Americans and then Filipinos replaced Spanish priests. Among those who remained in the new church, a crippling schism emerged over doctrinal interpretation, especially after 1919 when members were suddenly instructed to discard earlier church statements concerning the divinity of Christ. To some extent, the schism was caused by Aglipay himself, who shifted his theological views between 1902 and 1919. At first, he deemphasized doctrinal differences between his church and Roman Catholicism, and most of the independent church's priests followed Roman Catholic ritual-- saying Mass, hearing confession, and presiding over folk religious-Catholic ceremonies just as always. Later, Aglipay moved closer to Unitarianism.

In 1938 the church formally split. The faction opposing Aglipay later won a court decision giving it the right to both the name and property of the Iglesia Filipina Independiente. Followers of Aglipay, however, continued to argue that they represented true Aglipayanism. In the early 1990s, those Aglipayans who rejected the Unitarian stance and adhered to the concept of the Trinity were associated with the Protestant Episcopal church of the United States.

Iglesia ni Kristo

In the 1990s, all over Luzon, the Visayan Islands, and even northern Mindanao, unmistakable Iglesia ni Kristo (Church of Christ) places of worship, all similar in design and architecture, were being constructed for a rapidly growing membership. Founded by Felix Manalo Ysagun in 1914, the Iglesia ni Kristo did not attract much notice until after World War II, when its highly authoritarian organization and evangelical style began to fill a need for urban and rural families displaced by rapid changes in Philippine society. The church, led by clergy with little formal education, requires attendance at twice-weekly services conducted in local Philippine languages, where guards take attendance and forbid entrance to nonmembers. Membership dues, based on ability to pay, are mandatory. Members are expected to be "disciplined, clean, and God-fearing." Gamblers and drunks face the possibility of being expelled. The church forbids (on penalty of expulsion) marriage to someone of another faith and membership in a labor union. The Iglesia ni Kristo also tells its members how to vote and is even respected for its ability to get out the vote for candidates of its choice.

There are a number of reasons why so many Filipinos have joined such an authoritarian church, not the least of which is the institution's ability to stay the decline of traditional Philippine vertical patron-client relationships, especially in urban areas. The church also has been successful in attracting potential converts through its use of mass rallies similar to Protestant revival meetings. The message is always simple and straightforward--listeners are told that the Iglesia ni Kristo is the mystical body of Christ, outside of which there can be no salvation. Roman Catholicism and Protestant churches are denounced--only through membership in the Iglesia ni Kristo can there be hope for redemption.

Although the original appeal of the Iglesia ni Kristo was to members of the lower socioeconomic class, its puritanical precepts encouraged social mobility; and many of its members were climbing the economic ladder. Whether the church would be able to maintain its puritanical, authoritarian stance when more of its members reached middle-class status was difficult to predict. The church gave neither a count nor an estimate of its membership, but the rapid construction of elaborate buildings, including a campus for an Iglesia ni Kristo college adjacent to the University of the Philippines, would indicate that it was expanding.

Protestantism

From the start, Protestant churches in the Philippines were plagued by disunity and schisms. At one point after World War II, there were more than 200 denominations representing less than 3 percent of the populace. Successful mergers of some denominations into the United Church of Christ in the Philippines and the formation of the National Council of Churches in the Philippines (NCCP) brought a degree of order. In the 1990s, there remained a deep gulf and considerable antagonism, however, between middleclass -oriented NCCP churches and the scores of more evangelical denominations sprinkled throughout the islands.

Protestantism has always been associated with United States influence in the Philippines. All major denominations in the United States, and some minor ones, sent missions to the Philippines, where they found the most fertile ground for conversions among some of the upland tribes not yet reached by Catholic priests and among the urban middle class. Most American school teachers who pioneered in the new Philippine public school system also were Protestants, and they laid the groundwork for Protestant churches in many lowland barrios. Filipinos who converted to Protestantism often experienced significant upward social mobility in the American colonial period. Most were middle-level bureaucrats, servants, lawyers, or small entrepreneurs, and some became nationally prominent despite their minority religious adherence.

Protestant missionaries made major contributions in the fields of education and medicine. Throughout the islands, Protestant churches set up clinics and hospitals. They also constructed private schools, including such outstanding institutions of higher education as Central Philippine University, Silliman University, Philippine Christian College, and Dansalan Junior College in Marawi.

The denominations planted by the early missionaries numbered among their adherents about 2 percent of the population in the late 1980s. Their influence was supplemented, if not overshadowed, by a number of evangelical and charismatic churches and para-religious groups, such as New Tribes Mission, World Vision, and Campus Crusade for Christ, which became active after World War II. Increased activity by these religious groups did not mean that the country had ceased to be primarily Catholic or that the older Protestant churches had lost their influence. It did indicate that nominal Catholics might be less involved in parish activities than ever, that the older Protestant churches had new rivals, and that, in general, religious competition had increased.

An indication of this trend is seen in the change in the affiliation of missionaries coming to the Philippines. In 1986 there were 1,931 non-Roman Catholic missionaries, not counting those identified with the Church of Jesus Christ and Latter Day Saints. Of these, only sixty-three were from the denominations that sent missionaries in the early 1900s. The rest were from fundamentalist churches or para-church groups (the terms are not necessarily exclusive).

Islam

In the early 1990s, Filipino Muslims were firmly rooted in their Islamic faith. Every year many went on the hajj (pilgrimage) to the holy city of Mecca; on return men would be addressed by the honoritic "hajj" and women the honorific "hajji". In most Muslim communities, there was at least one mosque from which the muezzin called the faithful to prayer five times a day. Those who responded to the call to public prayer removed their shoes before entering the mosque, aligned themselves in straight rows before the minrab (niche), and offered prayers in the direction of Mecca. An imam, or prayer leader, led the recitation in Arabic verses from the Quran, following the practices of the Sunni (see Glossary) sect of Islam common to most of the Muslim world. It was sometimes said that the Moros often neglected to perform the ritual prayer and did not strictly abide by the fast (no food or drink in daylight hours) during Ramadan, the ninth month of the Muslim calendar, or perform the duty of almsgiving. They did, however, scrupulously observe other rituals and practices and celebrate great festivals of Islam such as the end of Ramadan; Muhammad's birthday; the night of his ascension to heaven; and the start of the Muslim New Year, the first day of the month of Muharram.

Islam in the Philippines has absorbed indigenous elements, much as has Catholicism. Moros thus make offerings to spirits (diwatas), malevolent or benign, believing that such spirits can and will have an effect on one's health, family, and crops. They also include pre-Islamic customs in ceremonies marking rites of passage--birth, marriage, and death. Moros share the essentials of Islam, but specific practices vary from one Moro group to another. Although Muslim Filipino women are required to stay at the back of the mosque for prayers (out of the sight of men), they are much freer in daily life than are women in many other Islamic societies.

Because of the world resurgence of Islam since World War II, Muslims in the Philippines have a stronger sense of their unity as a religious community than they had in the past. Since the early 1970s, more Muslim teachers have visited the nation and more Philippine Muslims have gone abroad--either on the hajj or on scholarships--to Islamic centers than ever before. They have returned revitalized in their faith and determined to strengthen the ties of their fellow Moros with the international Islamic community. As a result, Muslims have built many new mosques and religious schools, where students (male and female) learn the basic rituals and principles of Islam and learn to read the Quran in Arabic. A number of Muslim institutions of higher learning, such as the Jamiatul Philippine al-Islamia in Marawi, also offer advanced courses in Islamic studies.

Divisions along generational lines have emerged among Moros since the 1960s. Many young Muslims, dissatisfied with the old leaders, asserted that datu and sultans were unnecessary in modern Islamic society. Among themselves, these young reformers were divided between moderates, working within the system for their political goals, and militants, engaging in guerrilla-style warfare. To some degree, the government managed to isolate the militants, but Muslim reformers, whether moderates or militants, were united in their strong religious adherence. This bond was significant, because the Moros felt threatened by the continued expansion of Christians into southern Mindanao and by the prolonged presence of Philippine army troops in their homeland.

Ecumenical Developments

The coming of Protestant missionaries was not welcomed by Catholic clergy, and, for several years, representatives of Catholic and Protestant churches engaged in mutual recrimination. Catholics were warned against involvement in Protestant activities, even in groups like the Young Men's Christian Association and the Young Women's Christian Association. Since the 1970s, hostility between Catholics and many Protestant churches had lessened; churches emphasized the virtues rather than the alleged defects of other churches; and priests and pastors occasionally cooperated. Although the ecumenical emphasis did not eliminate competition and gained far more hold among older Protestant churches than among groups that had entered the Philippines more recently, the trend had significantly moderated religious tensions.

Some tentative efforts toward ecumenical understanding also were made in relations between Christians and Muslims, delineating common ground in the mutual acceptance of much of the Old Testament and New Testament of the Bible. Occasional conferences were held in an attempt to expand understanding. Their success by the early 1990s was limited but might indicate that, even in this tense area, improvement was possible.

Church and State

Church and state were officially separate in the 1990s, but religious instruction could, at the option of parents, be provided in public schools. The Catholic Church's influence on the government was quite evident in the lack of resources devoted to family planning and the prohibition of divorce.

The Catholic Church and, to a lesser extent, the Protestant churches engaged in a variety of community welfare efforts. These efforts went beyond giving relief and involved attempts to alter the economic position of the poor. Increasingly in the 1970s, these attempts led the armed forces of President Marcos to suspect that church agencies were aiding the communist guerrillas. In spite of reconciliation efforts, the estrangement between the churches and Marcos grew; it culminated in the call by Cardinal Jaime Sin for the people to go to the streets to block efforts of Marcos to remain in office after the questionable election of 1986 (see From Aquino's Assassination to People's Power; Political Role). The resulting nonviolent uprising was known variously as People's Power and as the EDSA Revolution (see Glossary).

The good feeling that initially existed between the church and the government of President Aquino lasted only a short time after her inauguration. Deep-seated divisions over the need for revolutionary changes again led to tension between the government and some elements in the churches.

Catholics fell into three general groups: conservatives who were suspicious of social action and held that Christian love could best be expressed through existing structures; moderates, probably the largest group, in favor of social action but inclined to cooperate with government programs; and progressives, who did not trust the government programs, were critical both of Philippine business and of American influence, and felt that drastic change was needed. Progressives were especially disturbed at atrocities accompanying the use of vigilantes. They denied that they were communists, but some of their leaders supported communist fronts, and a few priests actually joined armed guerrilla bands. There appeared to be more progressives among religious-order priests than among diocesan priests.

The major Protestant churches reflected the same three-way division as the Catholics. The majority of clergy and missionaries probably were moderates. A significant number, however, sided with the Catholic progressives in deploring the use of vigilante groups against the guerrillas, asking for drastic land reform, and opposing American retention of military bases. They tended to doubt that a rising economy would lessen social ills and often opposed the type of deflationary reform urged by the IMF (International Monetary Fund--see Glossary).

Education

In 1991 the education system was reaching a relatively large part of the population, at least at the elementary level. According to 1988 Philippine government figures, which count as literate everyone who has completed four years of elementary school, the overall literacy rate was 88 percent, up from 82.6 percent in 1970. Literacy rates were virtually the same for women and men. Elementary education was free and, in the 1987 academic year, was provided to some 15 million schoolchildren, 96.4 percent of the age-group. High school enrollment rates were approximately 56 percent nationwide but were somewhat lower on Mindanao and in Eastern Visayas region. Enrollment in institutions of higher learning exceeded 1.6 million.

Filipinos have a deep regard for education, which they view as a primary avenue for upward social and economic mobility. From the onset of United States colonial rule, with its heavy emphasis on mass public education, Filipinos internalized the American ideal of a democratic society in which individuals could get ahead through attainment of a good education. Middle-class parents make tremendous sacrifices in order to provide secondary and higher education for their children.

Philippine education institutions in the late 1980s varied in quality. Some universities were excellent, others were considered "diploma mills" with low standards. Public elementary schools often promoted students regardless of achievement, and students, especially those in poor rural areas, had relatively low test scores.

The proportion of the national government budget going to education has varied from a high of 31.53 percent in 1957 to a low of 7.61 percent in 1981. It stood at 15.5 percent in 1987. The peso amount, however, has steadily increased, and the lower percentage reflects the effect of a larger total government budget. Although some materials were still in short supply, by 1988 the school system was able to provide one textbook per subject per student. In 1991 the Philippine government and universities had numerous scholarship programs to provide students from low-income families with access to education. The University of the Philippines followed a "socialized tuition" plan whereby students from higher income families paid higher fees and students from the lowest income families were eligible for free tuition plus a living allowance.

Historical Background

Many of the Filipinos who led the revolution against Spain in the 1890s were *ilustrados*. *Ilustrados*, almost without exception, came from wealthy Filipino families that could afford to send them to the limited number of secondary schools (*colegios*) open to non-Spaniards. Some of them went on to the University of Santo Tomás in Manila or to Spain for higher education. Although these educational opportunities were not available to most Filipinos, the Spanish colonial government had initiated a system of free, compulsory primary education in 1863. By 1898 enrollment in schools at all levels exceeded 200,000 students.

Between 1901 and 1902, more than 1,000 American teachers, known as "Thomasites" for the S.S. *Thomas*, which transported the original groups to the Philippines, fanned out across the archipelago to open *barangay* schools. They taught in English and, although they did not completely succeed in Americanizing their wards, instilled in the Filipinos a deep faith in the general value of education. Almost immediately, enrollments began to mushroom from a total of only 150,000 in 1900-1901 to just under 1 million in elementary schools two decades later.

After independence in 1946, the government picked up this emphasis on education and opened schools in even the remotest areas of the archipelago during the 1950s and the 1960s.

Education in the Modern Period

The expansion in the availability of education was not always accompanied by qualitative improvements. Therefore, quality became a major concern in the 1970s and early 1980s. Data for the 1970s show significant differences in literacy for different regions of the country and between rural and urban areas. Western Mindanao Region, for example, had a literacy rate of 65 percent as compared with 90 percent for Central Luzon and 95 percent for Metro Manila. A survey of elementary-school graduates taken in the mid-1970s indicated that many of the respondents had failed to absorb much of the required course work and revealed major deficiencies in reading, mathematics, and language. Performance was poorest among respondents from Mindanao and only somewhat better for those from the Visayan Islands, whereas the best performance was in the Central Luzon and Southern Tagalog regions.

Other data revealed a direct relationship between literacy levels, educational attainment, and incidence of poverty. As a rule, families with incomes below the poverty line could not afford to educate their children beyond elementary school. Programs aimed at improving work productivity and family income could alleviate some of the problems in education, such as the high dropout rates that reflected, at least in part, family and work needs. Other problems, such as poor teacher performance, reflected overcrowded classrooms, lack of particular language skills, and low wages. These problems, in turn, resulted in poor student performance and high repeater rates and required direct action.

Vocational education in the late 1980s was receiving greater emphasis then in the past. Traditionally, Filipinos have tended to equate the attainment of education directly with escape from manual labor. Thus it has not been easy to win general popular support for vocational training.

Catholic and Protestant churches sponsored schools, and there were also proprietary (privately owned, nonsectarian) schools. Neither the proprietary nor the religious schools received state aid except for occasional subsidies for special programs. Only about 6 percent of elementary students were in private schools, but the proportion rose sharply to about 63 percent at the secondary level and approximately 85 percent at the tertiary level. About a third of the private school tertiary-level enrollment was in religiously affiliated schools.

In 1990 over 10,000 foreign students studied in the Philippines, mostly in the regular system, although there were three schools for international students--Brent in Baguio and Faith Academy and the International School in Manila. These schools had some Filipino students and faculty, but the majority of the students and faculty were foreign, mostly American. Faith Academy served primarily the children of missionaries, although others were admitted as space was available.

Chinese in the Philippines have established their own system of elementary and secondary schools. Classes in the morning covered the usual Filipino curriculum and were taught by Filipino teachers. In the afternoon, classes taught by Chinese teachers offered instruction in Chinese language and literature.

In 1990 the education system offered six years of elementary instruction followed by four years of high school. Children entered primary school at the age of seven. Instruction was bilingual in Pilipino and English, although it was often claimed that English was being slighted. Before independence in 1946, all instruction was in English; since then, the national language, Pilipino, has been increasingly emphasized. Until the compulsory study of Spanish was abolished in 1987, secondary and higher education students had to contend with three languages--Pillion, English, and Spanish.

In 1991 all education was governed by the Department of Education, Culture, and Sports, which had direct supervision over public schools and set mandatory policies for private schools as well. Bureaus of elementary, secondary, and higher education supervised functional and regional offices. District supervisors exercised direct administrative oversight of principals and teachers in their district. There was a separate office for non-formal education, which served students not working for a graduation certificate from a conventional school. Financing for public schools came from the national treasury, although localities could supplement national appropriations.

Education policies fluctuated constantly and were likely to be changed before teachers became accustomed to them. Areas of disagreement among Filipinos produced educational change as one faction or another gained control of a highly centralized public education administration. One example was the community school program that sought to involve schools in agricultural improvement. It was pushed vigorously in the 1950s, but little has been heard about it since. Another policy issue was the choice of a language of instruction. Until independence, English was, at least in theory, the language of instruction from first grade through college. The emphasis on English was followed by a shift toward local languages (of which there were eighty-seven), with simultaneous instruction in English and Pillion in later grades. Then, at least in official directives, in 1974 schools were told to drop the local language, and a bilingual--English and Pillion--program was adopted.

One of the most serious problems in the Philippines in the 1980s and early 1990s concerned the large number of students who completed college but then could not find a job commensurate with their educational skills. If properly utilized, these trained personnel could facilitate economic development, but when left idle or forced to take jobs beneath their qualifications, this group could be a major source of discontent.

Health and Living Standards

The struggle against disease has progressed considerably over the years. Health conditions in the Philippines in 1990 approximated to those in other Southeast Asian countries but lagged behind those in the West. Life expectancy, for instance, increased from 51.2 years in 1960 to 69 years for women and 63 years for men in 1990 (see fig. 4). Infant mortality was 101 per 1,000 in 1950 and had dropped to 51.6 per 1,000 in 1989. In 1923 approximately 76 percent of deaths were caused by communicable diseases. By 1980 deaths from communicable diseases had declined to about 26 percent.

In 1989 the ratio of physicians and hospitals to the total population was similar to that in a number of other Southeast Asian countries, but considerably below that in Europe and North America. Most health care personnel and facilities were concentrated in urban areas. There was substantial migration of physicians and nurses to the United States in the 1970s and 1980s, but there are no reliable figures to indicate what effect this had on the Philippines. Hospital equipment often did not function because there were insufficient technicians capable of maintaining it, but the 1990 report of the Department of Health said that centers for the repair and maintenance of hospital equipment expected to alleviate this problem.

In 1987 a little more than one-half of the infants and children received a complete series of immunization shots, a major step in preventive medicine, but obviously far short of a desirable goal. The problem was especially difficult in rural areas. The Department of Health had made efforts to provide every *baronage* with at least minimum health care, but doing so was both difficult and expensive, and the more remote areas inevitably received less attention.

Although very few Filipinos have been infected with acquired immune deficiency syndrome (AIDS), concern about the disease has caused authorities to give it considerable attention. By April 1979, only three people had died from AIDS, two of whom were overseas Filipinos visiting the homeland and one an American civilian who had contracted the disease outside the Philippines. In 1985 the Department of Health and the United States Naval Medical Research unit tested more than 17,000 people, including some 14,000 hospitality girls in Olangapo and a number of other Filipino cities. They identified twenty-one women as human immunodeficiency virus (HIV) carriers. The American sponsorship of the study was seized upon as argument for ending the Military Bases Agreement with the United States (see Foreign Military Relations). A June 1990 Philippine government study reported that at that time AIDS was growing at the rate of four cases a month and that twenty people had died from the disease. The study indicated that most AIDS cases in the Philippines were transmitted by heterosexual activity. An April 30, 1991, Department of Health report indicated that 240 Filipinos were infected with AIDS.

Like many other countries, the Philippines has a problem with illicit drugs. Official Philippine government statistics for 1989 indicate only 1,733 addicts, but the assumption was that the real number was from ten to a hundred times as great. The government has instituted both education and treatment programs, but it was uncertain how effective these programs would be. There also was a problem with inadequately tested legal drugs. In 1983, more than 265 pharmaceutical products were sold in the Philippines that were banned in many other countries. The Department of Health succeeded in eliminating 128 of them by 1988. Attempts to eliminate others have been blocked by the courts, which ruled that the department had acted without due process.

Malnutrition has been a perennial concern of the Philippine government and health care professionals. In 1987 the Department of Health reported that 2.8 percent of preschoolers were suffering from third-degree malnutrition and 17.6 percent from second-degree malnutrition. To alleviate this problem, the government targeted food assistance for nearly 500,000 preschoolers and lactating mothers.

Nutrition has shown some improvement. In 1955 government statistics estimated the daily per capita available food supply at only 80 percent of sufficiency. In 1986 it had improved to 101.8 percent. In the same period, the consumption of milk nearly tripled and the consumption of fats and oils more than doubled.

The Philippines has a dual health care system consisting of modern (Western) and traditional medicine. The modern system is based on the germ theory of disease and has scientifically trained practitioners. The traditional approach assumes that illness is caused by a breach of taboos set by supernatural forces. It is not unusual for an individual to alternate between the two forms of medicine. If the benefits of modern medicine are immediately obvious--eyeglasses, for instance--then there is little argument. If there is no immediate cure, the impulse to turn to the traditional healer is often strong.

One type of traditional healer that attracted the attention of foreigners as well as Filipinos was the so-called psychic surgeon, who professed to be able to operate without using a scalpel or drawing blood. Some practitioners attracted a considerable clientele and established lucrative practices. Travel agents in the United States credited these "surgeons" with generating travel to the Philippines.

Although medical treatment had improved and services had expanded, pervasive poverty and lack of access to family planning detracted from the general health of the Philippine people. In 1990 approximately 50 percent of the population was listed below the poverty line (down from 59 percent in 1985). A high rate of childbirth tended both to deplete family resources and to be injurious to the health of the mother. The main general health hazards were pulmonary, cardiovascular, and gastrointestinal disorders.

The Philippines had a social security system including medicare with wide coverage of the regularly employed urban workers. It offered a partial shield against disaster, but was limited both by the generally low level of incomes, which reduced benefits, and by the exclusion of most workers in agriculture. In April 1989, out of more than 22 million employed individuals, a little more than 10.5 million were covered by social security. In health care and social security, as with other services, the Philippines entered the 1990s as a modernizing society struggling with limited success against heavy odds to apply scarce financial resources to provide its people with a better life.

* * *

One of the best recent books synthesizing the social and geographic aspects of the Philippines is Jim Richardson's *The Philippines*. Robert Youngblood's *Marcos Against the Church* gives an excellent overview of contentious issues between church and government in the Marcos era and beyond. *Religion, Politics and Rationality in a Philippine Community*, by Raul Pertierra, is an insightful portrayal of socio-religious interaction on the *barangay* level. Kenneth Bauzon's *Liberalism and the Quest for Islamic Identity in the Philippines* clarifies the basic difference in political thinking between Muslim and Christian, and W.K. Che Man's *Muslim Separatism* is an excellent work on that subject.

Language Policy Formulation, Programming, Implementation, and Evaluation in Philippine Education (1565-1974), by Emma Bernabe, combines a historical approach to the language controversy with contemporary analysis and *The Role of English and Its Maintenance in the Philippines*, edited by Andrew B. Gonzales, provides a detailed report on that subject.

Philippine Society and the Individual: Selected Essays of Frank Lynch 1949-1976, edited by Aram A. Yengoyan and Perla Q. Makil, offers a careful treatment of Philippine values. James F. Eder's *On the Road to Extinction: Depopulation, Deculturation, and Adaptive Well-Being Among the Batak of the Philippines* is a provocative book on the upland tribes.

For information on the physical setting of the Philippines, the major work is still Frederick L. Wernstedt and J. E. Spencer's, *The Philippine Island World: A Physical, Cultural, and Regional Geography*.

The following periodicals also are excellent sources of information on contemporary Philippine society: *The Philippine Sociological Review, Solidarity, Philippine Quarterly of Culture and Society, Philippine Studies*, and *Pilipinas*. (For further references and complete citations, see Bibliography.)

THE ECONOMY

The Philippine economy experienced considerable difficulty in the 1980s. Real gross national product (GNP--see Glossary) grew at an annual average of only 1.8 percent, less than the 2.5 percent rate of population increase. The US$668 GNP per capita income in 1990 was below the 1978 level, and approximately 50 percent of the population lived below the poverty line. The 1988 unemployment rate of 8.3 percent (12.3 percent in urban areas) peaked at 11.4 percent in early 1989, and the underemployment rate, particularly acute for poor, less-educated, and elderly people, was approximately twice that of unemployment. In 1988, about 470,000 Filipinos left the country to work abroad in contract jobs or as merchant seamen.

The economy had grown at a relatively high average annual rate of 6.4 percent during the 1970s, financed in large part by foreign-currency borrowing. External indebtedness grew from $2.3 billion in 1970 to $24.4 billion in 1983, much of which was owed to transnational commercial banks.

In the early 1980s, the economy began to run into difficulty because of the declining world market for Philippine exports, trouble in borrowing on the international capital market, and a domestic financial scandal. The problem was compounded by the excesses of President Ferdinand E. Marcos's regime and the bailing out by government-owned financial institutions of firms owned by those close to the president that encountered financial difficulties. In 1983 the country descended into a political and economic crisis in the aftermath of the assassination of Marcos's chief rival, former Senator Benigno Aquino, and circumstances had not improved when Marcos fled the country in February 1986.

Economic growth revived in 1986 under the new president, Corazon C. Aquino, reaching 6.7 percent in 1988. But in 1988 the economy once again began to encounter difficulties. The trade deficit and the government budget deficit were of particular concern. In 1990 the economy continued to experience difficulties, a situation exacerbated by several natural disasters, and growth declined to 3 percent.

The structure of the economy evolved slowly over time. The agricultural sector in 1990 accounted for 23 percent of GNP and slightly more than 45 percent of the work force. About 33 percent of output came from industry, which employed about 15 percent of the work force. The manufacturing subsector had developed rapidly during the 1950s, but then it leveled off and did not increase its share of either output or employment. In 1990, 24 percent of GNP and 12 percent of employment were derived from manufacturing. The services sector, a residual employer, increased its share of the work force from about 25 percent in 1960 to 40 percent in 1990. In 1990 services accounted for 44 percent of GNP.

The Philippines is rich in natural resources. Land planted in rice and corn accounted for about 50 percent of the 4.5 million hectares of field crops in 1990. Another 25 percent of the cultivated area was taken up by coconuts, a major export crop. Sugarcane, pineapples, and Cavendish bananas also were important earners of foreign exchange. Forest reserves have been extensively exploited to the point of serious depletion. Archipelagic Philippines is surrounded by a vast aquatic resource base. In 1990 fish and other seafood from the surrounding seas provided more than half the protein consumed by the average Filipino household. The Philippines also had vast mineral deposits. In 1988 the country was the world's tenth largest producer of copper, the sixth largest producer of chromium, and the ninth largest producer of gold. The country's only nickel mining company was expected to resume operation in 1991 and again produce large quantities of that metal. Petroleum exploration continued but discoveries were minimal, and the country was required to import most of its oil.

Prior to 1970, Philippine exports consisted mainly of agricultural or mineral products in raw or minimally processed form. In the 1970s, the country began to export manufactured commodities, especially garments and electronic components, and the prices of some traditional exports declined. By 1988 nontraditional exports comprised 75 percent of the total value of goods shipped abroad.

Political Economy of Development

Economic Development Until 1970

In the mid-nineteenth century, a Filipino landowning elite developed on the basis of the export of abaca (Manila hemp), sugar, and other agricultural products. At the onset of the United States power in the Philippines in 1898-99, this planter group was cultivated as part of the United States military and political pacification program. The democratic process imposed on the Philippines during the American colonial period remained under the control of this elite. Access to political power required an economic basis, and in turn provided the means for enhancing economic power. The landowning class was able to use its privileged position directly to further its economic interests as well as to secure a flow of resources to garner political support and ensure its position as the political elite. Otherwise, the state played a minimal role in the economy, so that no powerful bureaucratic group arose that could pursue a development program independent of the wishes of the landowning class. This situation remained basically unchanged in the early 1990s.

At the time of independence in 1946, and in the aftermath of a destructive wartime occupation by Japan, Philippine reliance on the United States was even more apparent (see Economic Relations with the United States after Independence). To gain access to reconstruction assistance from the United States, the Philippines agreed to maintain its prewar exchange rate with the United States dollar and not to restrict imports from the United States. For a while the aid inflow from the United States offset the negative balance of trade, but by 1949, the economy had entered a crisis. The Philippine government responded by instituting import and foreign-exchange controls that lasted until the early 1960s.

Import restrictions stimulated the manufacturing sector. Manufacturing net domestic product (NDP--see Glossary) at first grew rapidly, averaging 12 percent growth per annum in real terms during the first half of the 1950s, contributing to an average 7.7 percent growth in the GNP, a higher rate than in any subsequent five-year period. The Philippines had entered an import-substitution stage of industrialization, largely as the unintended consequence of a policy response to balance-of-payments pressures. In the second half of the 1950s, the growth rate of manufacturing fell by about a third to an average of 7.7 percent, and real GNP growth was down to 4.9 percent. Import demand outpaced exports, and the allocation of foreign exchange was subject to corruption. Pressure mounted for a change of policy.

In 1962 the government devalued the peso (for value of the peso--see Glossary) and abolished import controls and exchange licensing. The peso fell by half to P3.90 to the dollar. Traditional exports of agricultural and mineral products increased; however, the growth rate of manufacturing declined even further. Substantial tariffs had been put in place in the late 1950s, but they apparently provided insufficient protection. Pressure from industrialists, combined with renewed balance of payments problems, resulted in the reimposition of exchange controls in 1968. Manufacturing recovered slightly, growing an average of 6.1 percent per year in the second half of the decade. However, the sector was no longer the engine of development that it had been in the early 1950s. Overall real GNP growth was mediocre, averaging somewhat under 5 percent in the second half of decade; growth of agriculture was more than a percentage point lower (see table 2). The limited impact of manufacturing also affected employment. The sector's share of the employed labor force, which had risen rapidly during the 1950s to over 12 percent, plateaued (see table 3). Import substitution had run its course.

Table 1. Metric Conversion Coefficients and Factors

When you kow	Multiply by	To find
Millimeters	0.04	inches
Centimeters	0.39	inches
Meters	3.3	feet
Kilometers	0.62	miles
Hectares	2.47	acres
Square kilometers	0.39	square miles
Cubic meters	35.3	cubic feet
Liters	0.26	gallons
Kilograms	2.2	pounds
Metric tons	0.98	long tons
1.1	short tons	
2,204	pounds	
Degrees Celsius (Centigrade)	1.8 and add 32	degrees Fahrenheit

Table 2. Rate of Growth of Gross National Product (GNP) by Sector, 1965-90*(in percentages)

Sector	1965-70	1970-75	1975-80	1980-85	1985-90	1989-90
Agriculture, forestry, and fishing	3.5	3.9	5.2	2.1	2.4	2.2
Industry	4.9	7.5	7.5	-2.8	4.5	1.9
Mining	15.3	5.2	8.4	-4.6	-2.0	2.5
Manufacturing	6.1	6.0	6.0	-1.5	4.8	1.4
Construction	3.1	14.8	12.5	-9.8	3.9	4.2
Services	4.8	4.8	5.8	-0.4	4.9	3.3
GNP	4.8	6.5	6.3	-1.0	4.6	3.1

*Sectoral products from 1965 to 1975 are net domestic product.
Source: Based on information from Philippines, National Economic and Development Authority, *1989 Philippine Statistical Yearbook,* Manila, 1989, Tables 3.9 and 3.10; Philippines, National Economic and Development Authority, *1981 Philippine Statistical Yearbook,* Manila, 1981, Tables 3.9 and 3.13; and Philippines, National Statistical Coordination Board, *The National Accounts of the Philippines: CY1988 to CY1990,* Manila, n.d., Tables 5-7.

Table 3. Distribution of Employment by Sector, Selected Years, 1956-88 (in percentages)

Sector	1956	1961	1968	1975	1980	1985	1988
Agriculture, forestry, and fishing	59.0	60.6	53.8	53.8	51.4	49.0	46.1
Industry							
Manufacturing	12.5	11.3	11.8	11.4	11.0	9.7	10.4
Other	3.3	3.1	4.0	3.8	4.5	4.6	5.2
Total industry	15.8	14.4	15.8	15.2	15.5	14.3	15.6
Services	24.5	24.6	30.0	31.0	33.0	36.8	38.2
TOTAL*	100.0	100.0	100.0	100.0	100.0	100.0	100.0

*Figures may not add to total because of rounding.
Sources: Based on information from Philippines, National Economic and Development Authority, *1989 Philippine Statistical Yearbook,* Manila, 1989, Tables 11.1 and 11.2; and Philippines, National Economic and Development Authority, *1981 Philippine Statistical Yearbook,* Manila, 1981, Table 11.8.

To stimulate industrialization, technocrats within the government worked to rationalize and improve incentive structures, to move the country away from import substitution, and to reduce tariffs. Movements to reduce tariffs, however, met stiff resistance from industrialists, and government efforts to liberalize the economy and emphasize export-led industrialization (see Glossary) were largely unsuccessful.

Martial Law and its Aftermath, (1972-86)

The Philippines found itself in an economic crisis in early 1970, in large part the consequence of the profligate spending of government funds by President Marcos in his reelection bid. The government, unable to meet payments on its US$2.3 billion international debt, worked out a US$27.5 million standby credit arrangement with the International Monetary Fund (IMF--see Glossary) that involved renegotiating the country's external debt and devaluing the Philippine currency to P6.40 to the United States dollar. The government, unwilling and unable to take the necessary steps to deal with economic difficulties on its own, submitted to the external dictates of the IMF. It was a pattern that would be repeated with increasing frequency in the next twenty years.

In September 1972, Marcos declared martial law, claiming that the country was faced with revolutions from both the left and the right (see Proclamation 1081 and Martial Law). He gathered around him a group of businessmen, used presidential decrees and letters of instruction to provide them with monopoly positions within the economy, and began channeling resources to himself and his associates, instituting what came to be called "crony capitalism." By the time Marcos fled the Philippines in February 1986, monopolization and corruption had severely crippled the economy.

In the beginning, this tendency was not so obvious. Marcos's efforts to create a "New Society" were supported widely by the business community, both Filipino and foreign, by Washington, and, *de facto,* by the multilateral institutions. Foreign investment was encouraged: an export-processing zone was opened; a range of additional investment incentives was created, and the Philippines projected itself onto the world economy as a country of low wages and industrial peace. The inflow of international capital increased dramatically.

A general rise in world raw material prices in the early 1970s helped boost the performance of the economy; real GNP grew at an average of almost 7 percent per year in the five years after the declaration of martial law, as compared with approximately 5 percent annually in the five preceding years. Agriculture performed better that it did in the 1960s. New rice technologies introduced in the late 1960s were widely adopted. Manufacturing was able to maintain the 6 percent growth rate it achieved in the late 1960s, a rate, however, that was below that of the economy as a whole. Manufactured exports, on the other hand, did quite well, growing at a rate twice that of the country's traditional agricultural exports. The public sector played a much larger role in the 1970s, with the extent of government expenditures in GNP rising by 40 percent in the decade after 1972. To finance the boom, the government extensively resorted to international debt, hence the characterization of the economy of the Marcos era as "debt driven."

In the latter half of the 1970s, heavy borrowing from transnational commercial banks, multilateral organizations, and the United States and other countries masked problems that had begun to appear on the economic horizon with the slowdown of the world economy. By 1976 the Philippines was among the top 100 recipients of loans from the World Bank and was considered a "country of concentration." Its balance of payments problem was solved and growth facilitated, at least temporarily, but at the cost of having to service an external debt that rose from US$2.3 billion in 1970 to more than US$17.2 billion in 1980.

There were internal problems as well, particularly in respect of the increasingly visible mismanagement of crony enterprises. A financial scandal in January 1981 in which a businessman fled the country with debts of an estimated P700 million required massive amounts of emergency loans from the Central Bank of the Philippines and other government-owned financial institutions to some eighty firms. The growth rate of GNP fell dramatically, and from then the economic ills of the Philippines proliferated. In 1980 there was an abrupt change in economic policy, related to the changing world economy and deteriorating internal conditions, with the Philippine government agreeing to reduce the average level and dispersion of tariff rates and to eliminate most quantitative restrictions on trade, in exchange for a US$200 million structural adjustment loan (see Glossary) from the World Bank (see Glossary). Whatever the merits of the policy shift, the timing was miserable. Exports did not increase substantially, while imports increased dramatically. The result was growing debt-service payments; emergency loans were forthcoming, but the hemorrhaging did not cease.

It was in this environment in August 1983 that President Marcos's foremost critic, former Senator Benigno Aquino, returned from exile and was assassinated. The country was thrown into an economic and political crisis that resulted eventually, in February 1986, in the ending of Marcos's twenty-one-year rule and his flight from the Philippines. In the meantime, debt repayment had ceased. Real GNP fell more than 11 percent before turning back up in 1986, and real GNP per capita fell 17 percent from its high point in 1981. In 1990 per capita real GNP was still 7 percent below the 1981 level.

The Aquino Government

In 1986 Corazon Aquino focused her presidential campaign on the misdeeds of Marcos and his cronies. The economic correctives that she proposed emphasized a central role for private enterprise and the moral imperative of reaching out to the poor and meeting their needs. Reducing unemployment, encouraging small-scale enterprise, and developing the neglected rural areas were the themes.

Aquino entered the presidency with a mandate to undertake a new direction in economic policy. Her initial cabinet contained individuals from across the political spectrum. Over time, however, the cabinet became increasingly homogeneous, particularly with respect to economic perspective, reflecting the strong influence of the powerful business community and international creditors. The businesspeople and technocrats who directed the Central Bank and headed the departments of finance and trade and industry became the decisive voices in economic decision making. Foreign policy also reflected this power relationship, focusing on attracting more foreign loans, aid, trade, investment, and tourists (see Foreign Affairs).

It soon became clear that the plight of the people had been subordinated largely to the requirements of private enterprise and the world economy. As the president noted in her state-of- the-nation address in June 1989, the poor had not benefited from the economic recovery that had taken place since 1986. The gap between the rich and poor had widened, and the proportion of malnourished preschool children had grown.

The most pressing problem in the Philippine international political economy at the time Aquino took office was the country's US$28 billion external debt. It was also one of the most vexatious issues in her administration. Economists within the economic planning agency, the National Economic and Development Authority (NEDA), argued that economic recovery would be difficult, if not impossible, to achieve in a relatively short period if the country did not reduce the size of the resource outflows associated with its external debt. Large debt-service payments and moderate growth (on the order of 6.5 percent per year) were thought to be incompatible. A two-year moratorium on debt servicing and selective repudiation of loans where fraud or corruption could be shown were recommended. Business-oriented groups and their representatives in the president's cabinet vehemently objected to taking unilateral action on the debt, arguing that it was essential that the Philippines not break with its major creditors in the international community. Ultimately, the president rejected repudiation; the Philippines would honor all its debts.

Domestically, land reform was a highly contentious issue, involving economics as well as equity. NEDA economists argued that broad-based spending increases were necessary to get the economy going again; more purchasing power had to be put in the hands of the masses. Achieving this objective required a redistribution of wealth downward, primarily through land reform. Given Aquino's campaign promises, there were high expectations that a meaningful program would be implemented. Prior to the opening session of the first Congress under the country's 1987 constitution, the president had the power and the opportunity to proclaim a substantive land reform program (see Constitutional Framework). Waiting until the last moment before making an announcement, she chose to provide only a broad framework. Specifics were left to the new Congress, which she knew was heavily represented by landowning interests. The result--a foregone conclusion--was the enactment of a weak, loophole-ridden piece of legislation (see Unsolved Political Problems).

The most immediate task for Aquino's economic advisers was to get the economy moving, and a turn around was achieved in 1986. Economic growth was low (1.9 percent), but it was positive. For the next two years, growth was more respectable--5.9 and 6.7 percent, respectively. In 1986 and 1987, consumption led the growth process, but then investment began to increase. In 1985 industrial capacity utilization had been as low as 40 percent, but by mid-1988 industries were working at near full capacity. Investment in durable goods grew almost 30 percent in both 1988 and 1989, reflecting the buoyant atmosphere. The international community was supportive. Like domestic investment, foreign investment did not respond immediately after Aquino took office, but in 1987 it began to pick up. The economy also was helped by foreign aid. The 1989 and 1991 meetings of the aid plan called the Multilateral Aid Initiative, also known as the Philippine Assistance Plan, a multinational initiative to provide assistance to the Philippines, pledged a total of US$6.7 billion.

Economic successes, however, generated their own problems. The trade deficit rose rapidly, as both consumers and investors attempted to regain what had been lost in the depressed atmosphere of the 1983-85 period. Although debt-service payments on external debt were declining as a proportion of the country's exports, they remained above 25 percent. And the government budget deficit ballooned, hitting 5.2 percent of GNP in 1990.

The 1988 GNP grew 6.7 percent, slightly more than the government plan target. Growth fell off to 5.7 percent in 1989, then plummeted in 1990 to just over 3 percent. Many factors contributed to the 1990 decline. The country was subjected to a prolonged drought, which resulted in the increased need to import rice. In July a major earthquake hit Northern Luzon, causing extensive destruction, and in November a typhoon did considerable damage in the Visayas. There were other, more human, troubles also. The country was attempting to regain a semblance of order in the aftermath of the December 1989 coup attempt. Brownouts became a daily occurrence, as the government struggled to overcome the deficient power-generating capacity in the Luzon grid, a deficiency that in the worst period was below peak demand by more than 300 megawatts and resulted in outages of four hours and more (see Energy). Residents of Manila suffered both from a lack of public transportation and clogged and overcrowded roadways; garbage removal was woefully inadequate; and, in general, the city's infrastructure was in decline. Industrial growth fell from 6.9 percent in 1989 to 1.9 percent in 1990; growth investment in 1990 in both fixed capital and durable equipment declined by half when compared with the previous year. Government construction, which grew at 10 percent in 1989, declined by 1 percent in 1990.

The Aquino administration appeared to be unable to work with the Congress to enact an economic package to overcome the country's economic difficulties. In July, as the government deficit soared Secretary of Finance Jesus Estanislao introduced a package of new tax measures. Then in October, stalemated with Congress, Aquino agreed to seek a reduction in the budget gap without new taxes. The agreement met with resistance from the Congress for being an onerous imposition on an economy in crisis, growth would be stifled and the poor would be impacted negatively. The willingness of the Congress to pass the tax package called for in the IMF agreement was in doubt. In 1990 Congress placed a 9 percent levy on all imports to provide revenues until an agreement could be reached with the administration on a tax package. In February 1991, however, it was learned that in its agreement with the IMF for new standby credits, the government had promised that it would indeed implement new taxes.

Accusations were widespread in Manila's press about the 1990-91 impasse. On the one hand, it was claimed that Aquino and her advisers had no economic plan; on the other hand, the Congress was said to be unwilling to work with the president. Traditional political patterns appeared to be reasserting themselves, and the technocrats had little ultimate influence. One study of the first Congress elected under the 1987 constitution showed that only 31 out of 200 members of the House of Representatives, were not previously elected officials or directly related to the leader of a traditional political clan. Business interests directly influenced the president to overrule already established policies, as in the 1990 program to simplify the tariff structure. Business and politics have always been deeply interwoven in the Philippines; crony capitalism was not a deviant model, but rather the logical extreme of a traditional pattern. As the Philippines entered the 1990s, the crucial question for the economy was whether the elite would limit its political activities to jockeying for economic advantage or would forge its economic and political interests in a fashion that would create a dynamic economy.

Economic Planning and Policy

The Philippines has traditionally had a private enterprise economy both in policy and in practice. The government intervened primarily through fiscal and monetary policy and in the exercise of its regulatory authority. Although expansion of public sector enterprises occurred during the Marcos presidency, direct state participation in economic activity has generally been limited. The Aquino government set a major policy initiative of consolidating and privatizing government-owned and government-controlled firms. Economic planning was limited largely to establishing targets for economic growth and other macroeconomic goals, engaging in project planning and implementation, and advising the government in the use of capital funds for development projects.

Development Planning

The responsibility for economic planning was vested in the National Economic and Development Authority. Created in January 1973, the authority assumed the mandate both for macroeconomic planning that had been undertaken by its predecessor organization, the National Economic Council, and project planning and implementation, previously undertaken by the Presidential Economic Staff. National Economic and Development Authority plans calling for the expansion of employment, maximization of growth, attainment of fiscal responsibility and monetary stability, provision of social services, and equitable distribution of income were produced by the Marcos administration for 1974-77, 1978-82, and 1983-88, and by the Aquino administration for 1987-92. Growth was encouraged largely through the provision of infrastructure and incentives for investment by private capital. Equity, a derivative goal, was to be achieved as the result of a dynamic economic expansion within an appropriate policy environment that emphasized labor-intensive production.

The National Economic and Development Authority Medium-Term Development Plan, 1987-92 reflected Aquino's campaign themes: elimination of structures of privilege and monopolization of the economy; decentralization of power and decision making; and reduction of unemployment and mass poverty, particularly in rural areas. The private sector was described as both the "initiator" and "prime mover" of the country's development; hence, the government was "to encourage and support private initiative," and state participation in the economy was to be minimized and decentralized. Goals included alleviation of poverty, generation of more productive employment, promotion of equity and social justice, and attainment of sustainable economic growth. Goals were to be achieved through agrarian reforms; strengthening the collective bargaining process; undertaking rural, labor-intensive infrastructure projects; providing social services; and expanding education and skill training. Nevertheless, as with previous plans, the goals and objectives were to be realized, trickle-down fashion, as the consequence of achieving a sustainable economic growth, albeit a growth more focused on the agricultural sector.

The plan also involved implementing more appropriate, market-oriented fiscal and monetary polices, achieving a more liberal trade policy based on comparative advantage, and improving the efficiency and effectiveness of the civil service, as well as better enforcement of government laws and regulations. Proper management of the country's external debt to allow an acceptable rate of growth and the establishment of a "pragmatic," development-oriented foreign policy were extremely important.

Economic performance fell far short of plan targets. For example, the real GNP growth rate from 1987 to 1990 averaged 25 percent less than the targeted rate, the growth rate of real exports was one-third less, and the growth rate of real imports was well over double. The targets, however, did provide a basis for discussion of consistency of official statements and whether the plan growth rates were compatible with the maintenance of external debt-repayment obligations. The plan also set priorities. Both Aquino's campaign pronouncements and the policies embodied in the planning document emphasized policies that would favorably affect the poor and the rural sector. But, because of dissension within the cabinet, conflicts with Congress, and presidential indecisiveness, policies such as land and tax reform either were not implemented or were implemented in an impaired fashion. In addition, the Philippines curtailed resources available for development projects and the provision of government services in order to maintain good relations with international creditors.

The Philippine government has undertaken to provide incentives to firms, both domestic and foreign, to invest in priority areas of the economy since the early 1950s. In 1967 an Investment Incentives Act, administered by a Board of Investments (BOI), was passed to encourage and direct investment more systematically. Three years later, an Export Incentives Act was passed, furthering the effort to move the economy beyond import substitution manufacturing. The incentive structure in the late 1960s and 1970s was criticized for favoring capital-intensive investment as against investments in agriculture and export industries, as well as not being sufficiently large. Export incentives were insufficient to overcome other biases against exports embodied in the structure of tariff protection and the overvaluation of the peso.

The investment incentive system was revised in 1983, and again in 1987, with the goal of rewarding performance, particularly exporting and labor-intensive production. As a results of objections made by the United States and other industrial nations to export-subsidy provisions contained in the 1983 Investment Code, much of the specific assistance to exporters was removed in the 1987 version. The 1987 Investment Code delegates considerable discretionary power over foreign investment to the government Board of Investments when foreign participation in an enterprise exceeds 40 percent. Legislation under consideration by the Philippine Congress in early 1991 would limit this authority. Under the new proposal, foreign participation exceeding 40 percent would be allowed in any area not covered by a specified "negative list."

Fiscal Policy

Historically, the government has taken a rather conservative stance on fiscal activities. Until the 1970s, national government expenditures and taxation generally were each less than 10 percent of GNP. (Total expenditures of provincial, city, and municipal governments were small, between 5 and 10 percent of national government expenditures in the 1980s.) Under the Marcos regime, national government activity increased to between 15 and 17 percent of GNP, largely because of increased capital expenditures and, later, growing debt-service payments. In 1987 and 1988, the ratio of government expenditure to GNP rose above 20 percent (see table 4). Tax revenue, however, remained relatively stable, seldom rising above 12 percent of GNP (see table 5). Chronic government budget deficits were covered by international borrowing during the Marcos era and mainly by domestic borrowing during the Aquino administration. Both approaches contributed to the vicious circle of deficits generating the need for borrowing, and the debt service on those loans creating greater deficits and the need to borrow even more. At 5.2 percent of GNP, the 1990 government deficit was a major consideration in the 1991 standby agreement between Manila and the IMF.

Table 4. Government Expenditures, 1980, 1985, and 1989 (in millions of pesos)

	1980	1985	1989
Economic services			
Agriculture, forestry, and fishing	2,475	4,606	16,217
Industry, trade, labor, and tourism	1,424	1,915	1,343
Utilities and infrastructure	11,822	13,378	22,309
Other	---	11,474	4,885
Total economic services	15,721	31,373	44,754
Social services			
Education	4,204	10,976	29,909
Health	1,333	3,220	7,353
Social security and welfare	442	1,875	3,720
Housing and community development	1,371	5,505	374
Other	267	183	2,632
Total social services	7,617	21,759	43,988
Defense	4,760	7,123	20,770
General public services	6,528	9,986	18,989
Debt-service fund	3,562	22,269	100,439
TOTAL	38,188	92,510	228,940

---means negligible.
*For value of the peso--see Glossary.
Source: Based on information from Philippines, National Economic and Development Authority, *1989 Philippine Statistical Yearbook,* Manila, 1989, Table 15.3.

Over time, the apportionment of government spending has changed considerably (see table 6). In 1989 the largest portion of the national government budget (43.9 percent) went for debt servicing. Most of the rest covered economic services and social services, including education. Only 9.1 percent of the budget was allocated for defense. The Philippines devoted a smaller proportion of GNP to defense than did any other country in Southeast Asia.

Table 5. Government Revenues, 1980, 1985, and 1988 (in millions of pesos)*

	1980	1985	1988
Tax revenue			
Taxes on income and profit	8,761	18,655	27,409
Taxes on property	196	173	384
Taxes on goods and services	9,332	22,677	33,207
Taxes on international trade and transactions	9,904	17,444	25,580
Other	640	1,304	3,772
Total tax revenue	28,833	60,253	90,352
Nontax revenue			
Nontax revenue proper	5,020	7,322	20,723
Capital revenue	2	3	11
Grants	222	380	1,775
Total nontax revenue	5,244	7,705	22,509
TOTAL	34,077	67,958	112,861

*For value of the peso--see Glossary.
Source: Based on information from Philippines, National Economic and Development Authority, *1989 Philippine Statistical Yearbook,* Manila, 1989, Table 15.2.

Table 6. Distribution of Government Expenditures, Selected Years, 1965-89 (in percentages)

	1965	1972	1980	1985	1989
Economic services	16.7	33.8	41.2	33.9	19.5
Social services					
Education	36.5	25.1	11.0	11.9	13.1
Other	7.7	6.5	8.9	11.6	6.1
Total social services	44.2	31.6	19.9	23.5	19.2
Defense	16.7	15.7	12.5	7.7	9.1
General public services	22.2	18.8	17.1	10.8	8.3
Debt-service fund	n.a.	n.a.	9.3	24.1	43.9
TOTAL*	100.0	100.0	100.0	100.0	100.0

n.a.--not applicable.
*Figures may not add to total because of rounding.
Source: Based on information from Philippines, National Economic and Development Authority, *1989 Philippine Statistical Yearbook,* Manila, 1989, Table 15.3; and Philippines, National Economic and Development Authority, *1981 Philippine Statistical Yearbook,* Manila, 1981, Table 16.5.

The Aquino government formulated a tax reform program in 1986 that contained some thirty new measures. Most export taxes were eliminated; income taxes were simplified and made more progressive; the investment incentives system was revised; luxury taxes were imposed; and, beginning in 1988, a variety of sales taxes were replaced by a 10 percent value-added tax--the central feature of the administration's tax reform effort. Some administrative improvements also were made. The changes, however, did not effect an appreciable rise in the tax revenue as a proportion of GNP.

Problems with the Philippine tax system appear to have more to do with collections than with the rates. Estimates of individual income tax compliance in the late 1980s ranged between 13 and 27 percent. Assessments of the magnitude of tax evasion by corporate income tax payers in 1984 and 1985 varied from as low as P1.7 billion to as high as P13 billion. The latter figure was based on the fact that only 38 percent of registered firms in the country actually filed a tax return in 1985. Although collections in 1989 were P10.1 billion, a 70 percent increase over 1988, they remained P1.4 billion below expectations. Tax evasion was compounded by mismanagement and corruption. A 1987 government study determined that 25 percent of the national budget was lost to graft and corruption.

Low collection rates also reinforced the regressive structure of the tax system. The World Bank calculated that effective tax rates (taxes paid as a proportion of income) of low-income families were about 50 percent greater than those of high-income families in the mid-1980s. Middle-income families paid the largest percentage. This situation was caused in part by the government's heavy reliance on indirect taxes. Individual income taxes accounted for only 8.9 percent of tax collections in 1989, and corporate income taxes were only 18.5 percent. Taxes on goods and services and duties on international transactions made up 70 percent of tax revenue in 1989, about the same as in 1960.

The consolidated public sector deficit--the combined deficit of national government, local government, and public-sector enterprise budgets--which had been greatly reduced in the first two years of the Aquino administration, rose to 5.2 of GNP by the end of 1990. In June 1990, the government proposed a comprehensive new tax reform package in an attempt to control the public sector deficit. About that time, the IMF, World Bank, and Japanese government froze loan disbursements because the Philippines was not complying with targets in the standby agreement with the IMF. As a result of the 1990-91 Persian Gulf crisis, petroleum prices increased and the Oil Price Stabilization Fund put an additional strain on the budget. The sudden cessation of dollar remittances from contract workers in Kuwait and Iraq and increased interest rates on domestic debt of the government also contributed to the deficit.

Negotiations between the Aquino administration and Congress on the administration's tax proposals fell through in October 1990, with the two sides agreeing to focus on improved tax collections, faster privatization of government-owned and government-controlled corporations, and the imposition of a temporary import levy. A new standby agreement between the government and the IMF in early 1991 committed the government to raise taxes and energy prices. Although the provisions of the agreement were necessary in order to secure fresh loans, the action increased the administration's already fractious relations with Congress.

Monetary Policy

The Central Bank of the Philippines was established in June 1948 and began operation the following January. It was charged with maintaining monetary stability; preserving the value and convertibility of the peso; and fostering monetary, credit, and exchange conditions conducive to the economic growth of the country. In 1991 the policy-making body of the Central Bank was the Monetary Board, composed of the governor of the Central Bank as chairman, the secretary of finance, the director general of the National Economic and Development Authority, the chairman of the Board of Investment, and three members from the private sector. In carrying out its functions, the Central Bank supervised the commercial banking system and managed the country's foreign currency system.

From 1975 to 1982, domestic saving (including capital consumption allowance) averaged 25 percent of GNP, about 5 percentage points less than annual gross domestic capital formation. This resource gap was filled with foreign capital. Between 1983 and 1989, domestic saving as a proportion of GNP declined on the average by a third, initially because of the impact of the economic crisis on personal savings and later more because of negative government saving. Investment also declined, so that for three of these years, domestic savings actually exceeded gross investment.

From the time it began operations until the early 1980s, the Central Bank intervened extensively in the country's financial life. It set interest rates on both bank deposits and loans, often at rates that were, when adjusted for inflation, negative. Central Bank credit was extended to commercial banks through an extensive system of rediscounting. In the 1970s, the banking system resorted, with the Central Bank's assistance, to foreign credit on terms that generally ignored foreign-exchange risk. The combination of these factors mitigated against the development of financial intermediation in the economy, particularly the growth of long-term saving. The dependence of the banking system on funds from the Central Bank at low interest rates, in conjunction with the discretionary authority of the bank, has been cited as a contributing factor to the financial chaos that occurred in the 1980s. For example, the proportion of Central Bank loans and advances to government-owned financial institutions increased from about 25 percent of the total in 1970 to 45 percent in 1981-82. Borrowings of the government-owned Development Bank of the Philippines from the Central Bank increased almost 100-fold during this period. Access to resources of this sort, in conjunction with subsidized interest rates, enabled Marcos cronies to obtain loans and the later bailouts that contributed to the financial chaos.

At the start of the 1980s, the government introduced a number of monetary measures built on 1972 reforms to enhance the banking industry's ability to provide adequate amounts of long-term finance. Efforts were made to broaden the capital base of banks through encouraging mergers and consolidations. A new class of banks, referred to as "expanded commercial banks" or "unibanks," was created to enhance competition and the efficiency of the banking industry and to increase the flow of long-term saving. Qualifying banks--those with a capital base in excess of P500 million--were allowed to expand their operations into a range of new activities, combining commercial banking with activities of investment houses. The functional division among other categories of banks was reduced, and that between rural banks and thrift banks eliminated.

Interest rates were deregulated during the same period, so that by January 1983 all interest rate ceilings had been abolished. Rediscounting privileges were reduced, and rediscount rates were set in relation to the cost of competing funds. Although the short-term response seemed favorable, there was little long-term change. The ratio of the country's money supply, broadly defined to include savings and time deposits, to GNP, around 0.2 in the 1970s, rose to 0.3 in 1983, but then fell again to just above 0.2 in the late 1980s. This ratio was among the lowest in Southeast Asia.

Monetary and fiscal policies that were set by the government in the early 1980s, contributed to large intermediation margins, the difference between lending and borrowing rates. In 1988, for example, loan rates averaged 16.8 percent, whereas rates on savings deposits were only slightly more than 4 percent. The Central Bank traditionally maintained relatively high reserve requirements (the proportion of deposits that must remain in reserve), in excess of 20 percent. In 1990 the reserve requirement was revised upward twice, going from 21 percent to 25 percent. In addition, the government levied both a 5 percent gross tax on bank receipts and a 20 percent tax on deposit earnings, and borrowed extensively to cover budget deficits and to absorb excess growth in the money supply.

In addition to large intermediation margins, Philippine banks offered significantly different rates for deposits of different amounts. For instance, in 1988 interest rates on six-month time deposits of large depositors averaged almost 13 percent, whereas small savers earned only 4 percent on their savings. Rates offered on six-month and twelve-month time deposits differed by only 1 percentage point, and the rate differential for foreign currency deposits of all available maturities was within a single percentage point range. Because savings deposits accounted for approximately 60 percent of total bank deposits and alternatives for small savers were few, the probability of interest rate discrimination by the commercial banking industry between small, less-informed depositors and more affluent savers, was quite high. Interest rates of time deposits also were bid up to reduce capital flight. This discrimination coupled with the large intermediation margins, gave rise to charges by Philippine economists and the World Bank that the Philippine commercial banking industry was highly oligopolistic.

Money supply growth has been highly variable, expanding during economic and political turmoil and then contracting when the Philippines tried to meet IMF requirements (see table 7). Before the 1969, 1984, and 1986 elections, the money supply grew rapidly. The flooding of the economy with money prior to the 1986 elections was one reason why the newly installed Aquino administration chose to scrap the existing standby arrangement with the IMF in early 1986 and negotiate a new agreement. The Central Bank released funds to stabilize the financial situation following a financial scandal in early 1981, after the onset of an economic crisis in late 1983, and after a coup attempt in 1989. The money was then repurchased by the Treasury and the Central Bank--the so-called Jobo bills, named after then Central Bank Governor Jose Fernandez--at high interest rates, rates that peaked in October 1984 at 43 percent and were approaching 35 percent in late 1990. The interest paid on this debt necessitated even greater borrowing. By contrast, in 1984 and 1985, in order to regain access to external capital, the growth rate of the money supply was very tight. IMF dictates were met, very high inflation abated, and the current account (see Glossary) was in surplus. Success, however, was obtained at the expense of a steep fall in output and high unemployment.

Privatization

When Aquino assumed the presidency in 1986, P31 billion, slightly more than 25 percent of the government's budget, was allocated to public sector enterprises--government-owned or government-controlled corporations--in the form of equity infusions, subsidies, and loans. Aquino also found it necessary to write off P130 billion in bad loans granted by the government's two major financial institutions, the Philippine National Bank and the Development Bank of the Philippines, "to those who held positions of power and conflicting interest under Marcos." The proliferation of inefficient and unprofitable public sector enterprises and bad loans held by the Philippine National Bank, the Development Bank of the Philippines, and other government entities, was a heavy legacy of the Marcos years.

**Table 7. Annual Rate of Growth of Money Supply and
Rate of Inflation, 1950-90 (in percentages)**

Year	Money Supply Growth Rate	Inflation Rate
1950-60	4.4	0.8
1960-70	9.9	5.4
1970-75	16.8	16.1
1975-80	17.0	11.7
1981	4.4	13.1
1982	-0.1	10.3
1983	38.3	10.0
1984	3.5	50.3
1985	6.5	23.1
1986	19.1	0.8
1987	22.1	3.8
1988	14.6	8.8
1989	31.5	10.6
1990	n.a.	12.7

n.a.--not available.
Source: Based on information from Philippines, National Economic and Development Authority, *1989 Philippine Statistical Yearbook,* Manila, 1989, Tables 2.11 and 16.1; "Central Bank Chief Outlines Goals for 1991," *Business World* [Manila], February 1, 1991, Foreign Broadcast Information Service, *Daily Report: East Asia,* February 8, 1991, 54; and Central Bank of the Philippines, *1989 Annual Report,* Manila, 1990, 34.

Burdened with 296 public sector enterprises, plus 399 other non-performing assets transferred to the government by the Philippine National Bank and the Development Bank of the Philippines, the Aquino administration established the Asset Privatization Trust in 1986 to dispose of government-owned and government-controlled properties. By early 1991, the Asset Privatization Trust had sold 230 assets with net proceeds of P14.3 billion. Another seventy-four public sector enterprises that were created with direct government investment were put up for sale; fifty-seven enterprises were sold wholly or in part for a total of about P6 billion. The government designated that about 30 percent of the original public sector enterprises be retained and expected to abolish another 20 percent. There was widespread controversy over the fairness of the divestment procedure and its potential to contribute to an even greater concentration of economic power in the hands of a few wealthy families.

Agriculture, Forestry, and Fishing

Agricultural Geography

In the late 1980s, nearly 8 million hectares--over 25 percent of total land--were under cultivation, 4.5 million hectares in field crops, and 3.2 million hectares in tree crops. Population growth reduced the amount of arable land per person employed in agriculture from about one hectare during the 1950s to around 0.5 hectare in the early 1980s. Growth in agricultural output had to come largely from multicropping and increasing yields. In 1988 double-cropping and intercropping resulted in 13.4 million hectares of harvested area, a total that was considerably greater than the area under cultivation. Palay (unhusked rice) and corn, the two cereals widely grown in the Philippines, accounted for about half of total crop area. Another 25 percent of the production area was taken up by coconuts, a major export earner. Sugarcane, pineapples, and Cavendish bananas (a dwarf variety) were also important earners of foreign exchange, although they accounted for a relatively small portion of cultivated area.

Climatic conditions are a major determinant of crop production patterns (see The Climate). For example, coconut trees need a constant supply of water and do not do well in areas with a prolonged dry season. Sugarcane, on the other hand, needs moderate rainfall spread out over a long growing period and a dry season for ripening and harvesting. Soil type, topography, government policy, and regional conflict between Christians and Muslims were also determinants in the patterns of agricultural activity.

Agricultural Production and Government Policy

The percentage of the population living in rural areas declined from 68 percent in 1970 to 57 percent in 1990, and the share of the labor force engaged in agriculture, forestry, and fishing also decreased to less than 50 percent by the late 1980s. Roughly two-thirds of agricultural households farmed their own land or were tenants; the others were landless agricultural workers. Some 75 percent of agricultural value added (see Glossary) came from crops and livestock. The remaining 25 percent came from forestry and fishing (see table 8). Value added in agricultural crops grew rapidly in the early 1970s, averaging growth rates of 7.7 percent (see table 9). In the 1980s, however, with the exception of corn, which was in growing demand as an animal feed, the growth rate of agricultural production declined and was sometimes negative for bananas and sugarcane. Low world prices combined with the high cost of inputs such as fertilizers were two of the most important reasons.

Table 8. Value Added in Agriculture, Forestry, and Fishing by Sector, Selected Years, 1970- 90 (in percentages)

Sector	1970	1975	1980	198 5	1988	1989	1990
Agricultural crops	55.1	62.5	58.8	60.8	56.2	57.3	56.2
Livestock							
Poultry	3.8	3.9	5.9	9.1	10.0	9.9	10.6
Other	11.3	8.2	6.2	6.2	7.3	7.7	8.4
Total livestock	15.1	12.1	12.1	15.3	17.3	17.6	19.0
Forestry	13.9	8.5	10.9	6.7	6.9	5.4	5.2
Fishing	15.8	16.8	18.1	17.2	19.6	19.6	19.5
TOTAL*	100.0	100.0	100.0	100.0	100.0	100.0	100.0

*Figures may not add to total because of rounding.
Source: Based on information from Philippines, National Economic and Development Authority, *1981 Philippine Statistical Yearbook* Manila, 1981, Table 3.16; Philippines, National Economic and Development Authority, *1989 Philippine Statistical Yearbook,* Manila, 1989, Table 3.13; and Philippines, National Statistical Coordination Board, *The National Accounts of the Philippines: CY1988 to CY1990,* Manila, n.d., Table 26.

Table 9. Rates of Growth of Value Added in Agriculture, Forestry, and Fishing by Sector, 1970- 90* (in percentages)

Sector	1970-75	1975-80	1980- 85	1985-90
Agricultural crops				
Palay (unhusked rice)	3.7	4.4	2.3	0.6
Corn	6.5	3.3	3.3	4.5
Coconut and copra	7.8	2.9	1.6	2.0
Sugarcane	6.6	- 0.5	-8.9	0.3
Bananas	11.1	15.6	2.4	- 2.7
All agricultural crops	7.7	5.7	1.9	0.5
Livestock	-0.7	1.6	2.8	8.5
Poultry	7.1	13.6	9.5	7.3
Forestry	-8.6	1.9	-12.6	- 3.4
Fishing	4.3	3.9	2.7	3.9
Agriculture, Forestry, and Fishing	4.5	5.2	2.1	2.4

*At 1972 prices.

Source: Based on information from Philippines, National Economic and Development Authority, *1981 Philippine Statistical Yearbook,* Manila, 1981, Table 3.16; Philippines, National Economic and Development Authority, *1989 Philippine Statistical Yearbook,* Manila, 1989, Table 3.13; and Philippines, National Statistical Coordination Board, *The National Accounts of the Philippines: CY1988 to CY1990,* Manila, n.d., Table 26.

The government pursued sometimes contradictory goals of maintaining cheap food and raw material prices, high farm income, food security, and stable prices, at times through direct intervention in agricultural markets. In 1981 the National Food Authority was created. It was empowered to regulate the marketing of all food and given monopoly privileges to import grains, soybeans, and other foodstuffs. The ability of the National Food Authority and its predecessor organizations to stabilize prices and keep them within the established price bands, at either the farm gate or the retail market, has been quite limited because of insufficient funds to affect the market, strict purchasing requirements, and corrupt practices among authority personnel. In 1985 the role of the National Food Authority was reduced, and price ceilings on rice were lifted. Beginning in the 1950s, government efforts to stimulate industrial development, such as tariffs on manufactured goods, overvaluation of the currency, export taxes on agricultural commodities, and price controls had a deleterious effect on the agricultural sector, making it relatively unprofitable. On the other hand, irrigation water was distributed at below-cost prices, and fertilizer manufacturing was subsidized.

Beginning in the latter half of the 1970s, the Marcos regime gave increased attention to agriculture and the rural sector in general, including agribusiness development. The Aquino government continued that emphasis, although its policy evolved from a commodity-specific orientation to a general, crop diversification approach that relied more on market signals to guide crop selection. The rice-price stabilization program remained in effect, and a program was implemented to increase small-farmer access to post-harvest facilities such as warehouses, rice mills, driers, and threshers.

Providing credit to the agricultural sector, particularly to small-sized and medium-sized farmers had been a government policy since the early 1950s, one that met with mixed success at best. By the early 1980s, there were approximately 900 privately owned, rural banks, which were the principal implementors of government-sponsored, supervised credit schemes. The Masagana 99 program was initiated in the early 1970s to encourage adoption of new, high-yielding rice varieties. No-collateral, low-interest loans were made available to small farmers, mainly by privately owned, rural banks, with the government guaranteeing 85 percent of any losses suffered by the banks. In general, however, regulated interest rates made rural banks unattractive to depositors.

In 1975 more than 500,000 farmers participated in the Masagana 99 program. By 1985, however, the program had expired because of high arrearage and the tight monetary policy instituted as part of an agreement with the IMF. The program was revived in the Aquino administration's Medium-Term Development Plan, 1987-92. According to a government report, however, as of 1988 the program had not yet reached most of the intended beneficiaries. Government efforts were also underway to rehabilitate rural banks, the majority of which had experienced severe difficulties during the economic crisis of the early 1980s and the subsequent monetary squeeze.

Rice and the Green Revolution
Rice is the most important food crop, a staple food in most of the country. It is produced extensively in Luzon, the Western Visayas, Southern Mindanao, and Central Mindanao (see fig. 5). In 1989 nearly 9.5 billion tons of palay were produced. In 1990 palay accounted for 27 percent of value added in agriculture and 3.5 percent of GNP. Per hectare yields have generally been low in comparison with other Asian countries. Since the mid-1960s, however, yields have increased substantially as a result of the cultivation of high-yielding varieties developed in the mid-1960s at the International Rice Research Institute located in the Philippines. The proportion of "miracle" rice in total output rose from zero in 1965-66 to 81 percent in 1981-82. Average productivity increased to 2.3 tons per hectare (2.8 tons on irrigated farms) by 1983. By the late 1970s, the country had changed from a net importer to a net exporter of rice, albeit on a small scale.

This "green revolution" was accompanied by an expanded use of chemical inputs. Total fertilizer consumption rose from 668 tons in 1976 to 1,222 tons in 1988, an increase of more than 80 percent. To stimulate productivity, the government also undertook a major expansion of the nation's irrigation system. The area under irrigation grew from under 500,000 hectares in the mid-1960s to 1.5 million hectares in 1988, almost half of the potentially irrigable land.

In the 1980s, however, rice production encountered problems. Average annual growth for 1980-85 declined to a mere 0.9 percent, as contrasted with 4.6 percent for the preceding fifteen years. Growth of value added in the rice industry also fell in the 1980s. Tropical storms and droughts, the general economic downturn of the 1980s, and the 1983-85 economic crisis all contributed to this decline. Crop loans dried up, prices of agricultural inputs increased, and palay prices declined. Fertilizer and plant nutrient consumption dropped 15 percent. Farmers were squeezed by rising debts and declining income. Hectarage devoted to rice production, level during the latter half of the 1970s, fell an average of 2.4 percent per annum during the first half of the 1980s, with the decline primarily in marginal, non-irrigated farms. As a result, in 1985, the last full year of the Marcos regime, the country imported 538,000 tons of rice. The situation improved somewhat in the late 1980s, and smaller amounts of rice were imported. However, in 1990 the country experienced a severe drought. Output fell by 1.5 percent, forcing the importation of an estimated 400,000 tons of rice.

Coconut Industry

The Philippines is the world's second largest producer of coconut products, after Indonesia. In 1989 it produced 11.8 million tons. In 1989, coconut products, coconut oil, copra (dried coconut), and desiccated coconut accounted for approximately 6.7 percent of Philippine exports. About 25 percent of cultivated land was planted in coconut trees, and it is estimated that between 25 percent and 33 percent of the population was at least partly dependent on coconuts for their livelihood. Historically, the Southern Tagalog and Bicol regions of Luzon and the Eastern Visayas were the centers of coconut production. In the 1980s, Western Mindanao and Southern Mindanao also became important coconut-growing regions.

In the early 1990s, the average coconut farm was a medium-sized unit of less than four hectares. Owners, often absentee, customarily employed local peasants to collect coconuts rather than engage in tenancy relationships. The villagers were paid on a piece-rate basis. Those employed in the coconut industry tended to be less educated and older than the average person in the rural labor force and earned lower-than-average incomes.

Land devoted to cultivation of coconuts increased by about 6 percent per year during the 1960s and 1970s, a response to devaluations of the peso in 1962 and 1970 and increasing world demand. Responding to the world market, the Philippine government encouraged processing of copra domestically and provided investment incentives to increase the construction of coconut oil mills. The number of mills rose from twenty-eight in 1968 to sixty-two in 1979, creating substantial excess capacity. The situation was aggravated by declining yields because of the aging of coconut trees in some regions.

In 1973 the martial law regime merged all coconut-related, government operations within a single agency, the Philippine Coconut Authority (PCA). The PCA was empowered to collect a levy of P0.55 per 100 kilograms on the sale of copra to be used to stabilize the domestic price of coconut-based consumer goods, particularly cooking oil. In 1974 the government created the Coconut Industry Development Fund (CIDF) to finance the development of a hybrid coconut tree. To finance the project, the levy was increased to P20.

Also in 1974, coconut planters, led by the Coconut Producers Federation (Cocofed), an organization of large planters, took control of the PCA governing board. In 1975 the PCA acquired a bank, renamed the United Coconut Planters Bank, to service the needs of coconut farmers, and the PCA director, Eduardo Cojuangco, a business associate of Marcos, became its president. Levies collected by the PCA were placed in the bank, initially interest-free. In 1978 the United Coconut Planters Bank was given legal authority to purchase coconut mills, ostensibly as a measure to cope with excess capacity in the industry. At the same time, mills not owned by coconut farmers--that is, Cocofed members or entities it controlled through the PCA--were denied subsidy payments to compensate for the price controls on coconut-based consumer products. By early 1980, it was reported in the Philippine press that the United Coconut Oil Mills, a PCA-owned firm, and its president, Cojuangco, controlled 80 percent of the Philippine oil-milling capacity. Minister of Defense Juan Ponce Enrile also exercised strong influence over the industry as chairman of both the United Coconut Planters Bank and United Coconut Oil Mills and honorary chairman of Cocofed. An industry composed of some 0.5 million farmers and 14,000 traders was, by the early 1980s, highly monopolized.

In principle, the coconut farmers were to be the beneficiaries of the levy, which between March 1977 and September 1981 stabilized at P76 per 100 kilograms. Contingent benefits included life insurance, educational scholarships, and a cooking oil subsidy, but few actually benefited. The aim of the replanting program, controlled by Cojuangco, was to replace aging coconut trees with a hybrid of a Malaysian dwarf and West African tall varieties. The new palms were to produce five times the weight per year of existing trees. The target of replanting 60,000 trees a year was not met. In 1983, 25 to 30 percent of coconut trees were estimated to be at least sixty years old; by 1988, the proportion had increased to between 35 and 40 percent.

When coconut prices began to fall in the early 1980s, pressure mounted to alter the structure of the industry. In 1985 the Philippine government agreed to dismantle the United Coconut Oil Mills as part of an agreement with the IMF to bail out the Philippine economy. Later a 1988 United States law requiring foods using tropical oils to be labeled indicating the saturated fat content had a negative impact on an already ailing industry and gave rise to protests from coconut growers that similar requirements were not levied on oils produced in temperate climates.

Sugar

From the mid-nineteenth century to the mid-1970s, sugar was the most important agricultural export of the Philippines, not only because of the foreign exchange earned, but also because sugar was the basis for the accumulation of wealth of a significant segment of the Filipino elite. The principal sugarcane-growing region is the Western Visayas, particularly the island of Negros. In 1980 the region accounted for half the area planted in cane and two-thirds of the production of sugar. Unlike the cultivation of rice, corn, and coconuts, sugarcane is typically grown on large farms or haciendas. In the mid-1980s, more than 60 percent of total production and about 80 percent of Negros's output came from farms twenty-five hectares or larger. Countrywide, tenancy arrangements existed for approximately half the sugarcane farms; however, they were generally the smaller ones, averaging 2.5 hectares in size and accounting for only slightly more than 20 percent of land planted in the crop. Elsewhere, laborers were employed, generally at very low wages. A survey undertaken in 1990 by the governor of Negros Occidental found that only one-third of the island's sugar planters were paying the then-mandated minimum wage of P72.50 per day. The contrast between the sumptuous lifestyles of Negros *hacenderos* and the poverty of their workers, particularly migrant laborers known as *sacadas*, epitomized the vast social and economic gulf separating the elite in the Philippines from the great mass of the population.

In the 1950s and 1960s, sugar accounted for more than 20 percent of Philippine exports. Its share declined somewhat in the 1970s and plummeted in the first half of the 1980s to around 7 percent. The sugar industry was in a crisis. Part of the problem was a depressed market for sugar. A dramatic increase in the world price of sugar had occurred in 1974, peaking at US$0.67 per pound in December of that year. The following two years, however, saw prices fall to less than US$0.10 a pound and remain there for a few years before moving upward again toward the end of the decade. Sugar prices fell again in the early 1980s, bottoming in May 1985 at less than US$0.03 per pound and averaging US$0.04 per pound for the year as a whole. In early 1990, prices had recovered to US$0.14 cents per pound then declined to approximately US$0.08 to US$0.09 per pound.

Historically, the Philippines was protected to a certain degree from vicissitudes of the world price of sugar by the country's access to a protected and subsidized United States market. In 1913 the United States Congress established free trade with its Philippine colony, providing Filipino sugar producers unlimited access to the American market. Later, in 1934, a quota system on sugar was enacted and remained in force until 1974. Although Philippine sugar exports to the United States were restricted during this period, the country continued to enjoy a relatively privileged position. Philippine quotas for the United States market in the early 1970s accounted for between 25 and 30 percent of the total, double that of other significant suppliers such as the Dominican Republic, Mexico, and Brazil. After the quota law expired in 1974, Philippine sugar was sold on the open market, generally to unrestricted destinations. As a consequence, shipments to the United States declined.

On May 5, 1982, the United States reestablished a quota system for the importation of sugar. Allocations were based on a country's share in sugar trade with the United States during the 1975-81 period, the period during which Philippine sugar exports to the United States had dwindled. The Philippine allotment was 13.5 percent. Efforts by the Philippine government to have it raised to 25 percent, the country's approximate share during the previous quota period, were unsuccessful. The loss of sales imposed by the reduced quota share was compounded by a dramatic 40 percent drop in total United States imports of sugar in the mid-1980s as compared with the early 1970s. Philippine sugar exports to the United States that had averaged just under 1.3 million tons per year in the 1968-71 period averaged only 284,000 tons from 1983 to 1988, falling to approximately 161,000 tons in 1988. In 1988 only 273 thousand hectares were planted in sugar, about half that of the early 1970s.

During the earlier quota period, Philippine producers enjoyed high profits, but operations were inefficient and lacking in mechanization. Sugar yields in the Philippines were among the lowest in the world. Increases in production occurred through expansion of land area devoted to sugarcane. With falling prices and the end of the United States quota, attempts to improve productivity through mechanization increased yields, but caused a dramatic fall in labor requirements, initially by 50 percent and, over a longer period, by an estimated 90 percent. In an island economy such as that of Negros, where sugar has accounted directly for 25 percent of employment, the consequent actual and potential lost livelihood was disastrous.

The decline of the sugar industry was complicated by the monopolization that took place during the martial law period, a process not dissimilar to what occurred in the coconut industry. In 1976, as a reaction to the precipitous decline in sugar prices, Marcos established the Philippine Sugar Commission (Philsucom), placing at the head his close associate Roberto Benedicto. Philsucom was given sole authority to buy and sell sugar, to set prices paid to planters and millers, and to purchase companies connected to the sugar industry. A bank was set up in 1978, and the construction of seven new sugar mills was authorized at a cost of US$40 million per mill.

By the 1980s, considerable resistance to Philsucom and its trading subsidiary, the National Sugar Trading Corporation (Nasutra) had been generated. As with the monopoly in the coconut industry, the government acquiesced in its 1985 agreement with the IMF to dismantle Nasutra. But the damage had been done. In a study undertaken by a group of University of the Philippines economists, losses to sugar producers between 1974 and 1983 were estimated to be between P11 billion and P14 billion. Aquino established the Sugar Regulatory Authority in 1986 to take over the institutions set up by Benedicto.

Land Tenancy and Land Reform

An important legacy of the Spanish colonial period was the high concentration of land ownership, and the consequent widespread poverty and agrarian unrest (see The Decline of Spanish Rule). United States administrators and several Philippine presidential administrations launched land reform programs to maintain social stability in the countryside. Lack of sustained political will, however, as well as landlord resistance, severely limited the impact of the various initiatives.

Farm size is a significant indicator of concentration of ownership. Although nationwide approximately 50 percent of farms in 1980 were less than two hectares, these small farms made up only 16 percent of total farm area. On the other hand, only about 3 percent of farms were over ten hectares, yet they covered approximately 25 percent of farm area. Farms also varied in size based on crops cultivated. Rice farms tended to be smaller; only 9 percent of rice land was on farms as large as ten hectares. Coconut farms tended to be somewhat larger; approximately 28 percent of the land planted in coconuts was on farms larger than ten hectares. Sugarcane, however, generally was planted on large farms. Nearly 80 percent of land planted in sugarcane was on farms larger than ten hectares. Pineapple plantations were a special case. Because the two largest producers were subsidiaries of transnational firms--Del Monte and Castle and Cooke--they were not permitted to directly own land. The transnationals circumvented this restriction, however, by leasing land. In 1987 subsidiaries of these two companies leased 21,400 hectares, 40 percent of the total hectarage devoted to pineapple production.

In September 1972, the second presidential decree that Marcos issued under martial law declared the entire Philippines a land reform area. A month later, he issued Presidential Decree No. 27, which contained the specifics of his land reform program. On paper, the program was the most comprehensive ever attempted in the Philippines, notwithstanding the fact that only rice and corn land were included. Holdings of more than seven hectares were to be purchased and parceled out to individual tenants (up to three hectares of irrigated, or five hectares of unirrigated, land), who would then pay off the value of the land over a fifteen-year period. Sharecroppers on holdings of less than seven hectares were to be converted to leaseholders, paying fixed rents.

The Marcos land reform program succeeded in breaking down many of the large haciendas in Central Luzon, a traditional center of agrarian unrest where landed elite and Marcos allies were not as numerous as in other parts of the country. In the country as a whole, however, the program was generally considered a failure. Only 20 percent of rice and corn land, or 10 percent of total farm land, was covered by the program, and in 1985, thirteen years after Marcos's proclamation, 75 percent of the expected beneficiaries had not become owner-cultivators. By 1988 less than 6 percent of all agricultural households had received a certificate of land transfer, indicating that the land they were cultivating had been registered as a land transfer holding. About half of this group, 2.4 percent, had received titles, referred to as emancipation patents. Political commitment on the part of the government waned rather quickly, after Marcos succeeded in undermining the strength of land elites who had opposed him. Even where efforts were made, implementation was selective, mismanaged, and subject to considerable graft and corruption.

The failure of the Marcos land reform program was a major theme in Aquino's 1986 presidential campaign, and she gave land reform first priority: "Land-to-the-tiller must become a reality, instead of an empty slogan." The issue was of some significance inasmuch as one of the largest landholdings in the country was her family's 15,000-hectare Hacienda Luisita. But the candidate was quite clear; the land reform would apply to Hacienda Luisita as well as to any other landholding. She did not actually begin to address the land reform question, however, until the issue was brought to a head in January 1987, when the military attacked a group of peasants marching to Malacañang, the presidential residence, to demand action on the promised land reform killing 18 and wounding more than 100 of them. The event galvanized the government into action: a land reform commission was formed, and in July 1987, one week before the new Congress convened and her decree-making powers would be curtailed, Aquino proclaimed the Comprehensive Agrarian Reform Program. More than 80 percent of cultivated land and almost 65 percent of agricultural households were to be included in a phased process that would consider the type of land and size of holding. In conformity with the country's new Constitution, provisions for "voluntary land sharing" and just compensation were included. The important details of timing, priorities, and minimum legal holdings, however, were left to be determined by the new Congress, the majority of whose members were connected to landed interests.

Criticism of Aquino's plan came from both sides. Landowners thought that it went too far, and peasant organizations complained that the program did not go far enough and that by leaving the details to a landlord-dominated Congress, the program was doomed to failure. A World Bank mission was quite critical of a draft of the land reform program. In its report, the mission suggested that in order to limit efforts to subvert the process, the Comprehensive Agrarian Reform Program needed to be carried out swiftly rather than in stages, and land prices should be determined using a mechanical formula rather than subjective valuation. The World Bank mission also was critical of a provision allowing incorporated farm entities to distribute stock to tenants and workers rather than the land itself. The scheme would be attractive, the mission argued, "to those landowners who believed that they would not have to live up to the agreement to transfer the land to the beneficiaries." The mission's recommendations were largely ignored in the final version of the government's program.

On June 10, 1988, a year after the proclamation, Congress passed the Comprehensive Agrarian Reform Law. Landowners were allowed to retain up to five hectares plus three hectares for each heir at least fifteen years of age. The program was to be implemented in phases. The amount of land that could be retained was to be gradually decreased, and a non-land-transfer, profit-sharing program could be used as an alternative to actual land transfer.

Especially controversial was the provision that allowed large landowners to transfer a portion of the respective corporation's total assets equivalent in value to that of its land assets, in lieu of the land being subdivided and distributed to tenants and farm laborers. In May 1989, the 7,000 tenants of the Aquino family estate, Hacienda Luisita, agreed to take a 33 percent share of the hacienda's corporate stock rather than a portion of the land itself. Because the remaining two-thirds of the stock (the value of non-land corporate assets) remained with Aquino's family, effective control of the land did not pass to the tillers. Proponents of land reform considered the stock-ownership provision a loophole in the law, and one that many large landowners would probably use. Following the example of the Hacienda Luisita, thirty-four agrocorporations had requested approval for a stock transfer as of mid-1990. Although legal, the action of the president's family raised questions as to the president's commitment to land reform.

It is difficult to estimate the cost allowing for inflation of the Comprehensive Agrarian Reform Program. Early on, in 1988 estimates ranged between P170 billion and P220 billion; the following year they were as high as P332 billion, of which P83 billion was for land acquisition and P248 billion for support services and infrastructure. The lowest mentioned figure averages to P17 billion a year, 2.1 percent of 1988 GNP in the Philippines and 8.9 percent of government expenditure that year. The sum was well beyond the capacity of the country, unless tax revenues were increased substantially and expenditure priorities reordered. To circumvent this difficulty, the Aquino government planned to obtain 50 to 60 percent of the funding requirements from foreign aid. As of 1990, however, success had been minimal.

Government claims that in the first three years of implementation the Comprehensive Agrarian Reform Program met with considerable success were open to question. Between July 1987 and March 1990, 430,730 hectares were distributed. About 80 percent of this, however, was from the continuation of the Marcos land reform program. Distribution of privately owned lands other than land growing rice and corn, 3,470 hectares, was insignificant not only in absolute terms, but it was also only 2 percent of what had been targeted. The inability of the Department of Agrarian Reform to spend its budget also indicated implementation difficulties. As of June 1990, the department had utilized only 44 percent of the P14.2 billion allocated to it for the period January 1988-June 1990. In part because of Supreme Court rulings, the Department of Agrarian Reform cut its land acquisition target in late 1990 by almost half from 400,000 hectares to 250,000 hectares.

Livestock

In 1990 the livestock industry, consisting primarily of cattle, carabao (water buffalo), hogs, and chickens, accounted for almost 20 percent of value added in the agricultural sector, up from 12 percent in 1980. Much of the growth came from the rapid expansion of poultry raising, which had begun to develop as a commercial industry in the 1960s. Chicken raising accounted for half of livestock value added in 1990 as compared with a quarter in 1970. Beginning in the late 1980s, commercial hog raisers also attempted to enter the international market by exporting live hogs to Hong Kong. Although carabao production increased as a result of an intensified livestock dispersal program run by the government, the carabao and cattle industries remained primarily backyard ventures.

In the late 1980s, hogs provided 60 percent of total domestic meat production; chickens provided 15 percent; and cattle and carabao, about 20 percent. The country was relatively self-sufficient in hog and chicken production but imported approximately 4,500 tons of beef annually. The economic difficulties of the 1980s made the lower-priced chicken and carabao attractive substitutes for higher-priced pork and beef, but carabao raising remained oriented primarily toward providing work animals. The dairy industry in the Philippines also was quite small. Liquid milk generally was not available in the market, and virtually all canned and dry milk was imported.

Forestry

Logging was a profitable business at the end of the 1980s. Actual forested land was estimated to be about 6.5 million hectares--more than 21.5 percent of Philippine territory--and much of that was in higher elevations and on steep slopes. The government facilitated the exploitation of the country's forest resources for the first three decades after independence by allocating the bulk of unclassified land as public forest land eligible to be licensed for logging, and by implementing policies of low forest charges and export taxes. Logs were a major foreign-exchange earner. By 1977, 8.3 million hectares of forest area were licensed for logging. In the late 1970s, the government became aware of the dangers of deforestation and began to impose restrictions. The amount of forested land and the volume of forest exports declined. By 1988, 120 licensed loggers, operating on a total area of 4.74 million hectares, cut an estimated 4.2 millon cubic meters of logs and exported 644 million board feet. The contribution of logs and lumber to total Philippine exports declined from 25 percent in 1969 to 2 percent in 1988.

In addition to the officially sanctioned logging industry, there has been considerable illegal logging. The full extent of this activity was difficult to determine, but the discrepancy between Philippine and Japanese statistics on log exports from the Philippines to Japan provided one source of information. From 1955 through 1986, log imports from the Philippines, according to Japanese statistics, averaged about 50 percent more than log exports to Japan according to Philippines statistics. In 1987 and 1988, the discrepancy was considerably reduced, perhaps an indication of the Aquino government's stricter enforcement policy.

Another cause of deforestation was swidden agriculture, called *kaingin* in the Philippines. The method involves burning a portion of forest area to produce a fertilizing effect, planting a series of crops for two or three years, and then, after the soil has become depleted of nutrients, moving on to another location to allow the burned out area to rejuvenate. Often referred to as slash-and-burn agriculture, swidden as practiced by upland Filipino groups was ecologically sound as long as land was relatively plentiful. But since the 1960s, increased use of land for logging and migration of landless peasants from lowland areas has caused a scarcity of land. Burned-over areas were not allowed to lay fallow for a sufficient period, and the new migrants often had no knowledge of sound swidden practice. As a result, new growth was not allowed to mature before being burned over again; extensive erosion occurred, and once-forested areas were transformed into grasslands.

The widespread deforestation caused massive ecological destruction. Beginning in the early 1980s, the government instituted reforestation programs to stem the destruction. In 1981 Marcos made the granting of timber concessions conditional on the concessionaire's reforesting. After his ouster, however, the new secretary of the Department of Environment and Natural Resources reported that 90 percent of the 170 logging companies with concessions had failed to implement reforestation activities. The Aquino administration also launched a reforestation program to replant 100,000 hectares per year, but it too met with limited success. In 1988, two years into the program, the government reforested 32,000 hectares and awarded reforestation contracts for another 4,500 hectares. Other initiatives included a program to employ upland dwellers in reforestation, limiting the extent of timber concessions, and controlling exports of forest products. Non-government, environmental organizations also became involved in forest preservation efforts. One official noted that with more than 5 million hectares of forests already denuded, and with a deforestation rate of 119,000 hectares per year, the country would be facing a timber famine within a decade. Second-growth forests were too young to cut, so timber requirements for the near term would have to be met from the remaining old-forest stands, leaving inadequate reserves for the medium term.

Fishing

The Philippines is surrounded by a vast aquatic resource base (see Physical Setting). In 1976 the government adopted a 200-nautical-mile exclusive economic zone covering some 2.2 million square kilometers. However, the country's traditional fishing grounds constituted a relatively small 126,500-squarekilometer area. Fish and other seafood provided more than half the protein consumed by the average Filipino household. Total fish production in 1989 was 2.3 million tons. Of this, 46 percent was caught by some 574,000 municipal and subsistence fishermen, who operated small boats in shallow water, customarily no more than three kilometers offshore. These fishermen were among the poorest of the poor, with incomes averaging only 25 percent of the national average. Another 27 percent of the catch came from the approximately 45,000 commercial fishermen. An equal proportion of the total catch was provided by the fast-growing aquaculture industry. Prawn production, mostly aquaculture, developed rapidly in the 1980s, averaging 31,000 tons during the 1984-87 period. In 1988 exports of fishery products amounted to US$407 million, approximately 6 percent of total exports.

During much of the 1980s, the livelihood of small municipal and subsistence fishermen was undermined by low production, stagnating at approximately 1 million tons per year. A number of factors contributed to the low production: encroachment of commercial fishermen into shallow waters, destruction of the marine environment, over-fishing, and an increasing number of fish ponds. A large proportion of the mangrove forests was cleared to construct fishponds, seriously damaging the coastal ecological system. Coral reefs sustained serious damage from illegal fishing with dynamite and cyanide, and from the muro-ami fishing technique by which young swimmers pound the coral with rocks attached to ropes to drive the fish into nets. Coral also was damaged by silting from erosion caused by deforestation, and inland freshwater lakes were polluted from industrial and agricultural wastes.

Industry

Manufacturing

Immediately after independence, the government concentrated its efforts on reconstructing and rehabilitating the war-damaged economy. In 1949 import and foreign exchange controls were imposed to alleviate a balance of payments problem. Imports fell dramatically, providing a stimulus for the development of light industry oriented toward the domestic market. Manufacturing growth was rapid, averaging 9.9 percent per year during the 1950s. Initially, textiles, food manufactures, tobacco, plastics, and light fabrication of metals dominated. There also was some assembly of automobiles and trucks and construction of truck and bus bodies. By the early 1960s, however, manufacturing growth declined to slightly less than the growth of GNP. The share of the labor force in manufacturing in 1988 was 10.4 percent, less than it was in 1956, although the share had grown to 12 percent in 1990.

By the late 1980s, and in part the consequence of local content laws that were intended to enhance linkage among various manufacturing industries and increase self-sufficiency, the industrial structure had become more complex, with intermediate and capital goods industries relatively large for a country at the Philippines' stage of development (see table 10). By the mid-1980s, an ambitious US$6 billion industrial development program originally undertaken by the Marcos regime in 1979 had resulted in operational copper smelter-refinery, cocochemical manufacturing, and phosphatic fertilizer projects. A cement-industry rehabilitation and expansion program and an integrated iron and steel mill project were still underway. A petrochemical complex appeared about to be undertaken in 1990, but was bogged down in a dispute over location and financing.

Table 10. Structure of Manufacturing Sector, 1970, 1980, and 1987 (in percentages)

Major Group	1970	1980	1987
Food products	24.4	22.3	23.6
Beverages	5.3	2.7	6.7
Tobacco	5.6	3.2	5.3
Textiles	7.0	7.2	5.2
Footwear and wearing apparel	1.8	2.9	3.3
Wood and cork	4.2	4.0	2.6
Furniture and fixtures	0.4	1.0	0.7
Paper	3.2	2.9	2.5
Printing	1.9	1.5	1.2
Leather	0.2	0.2	0.1
Rubber	2.5	1.6	1.5
Chemicals	13.7	11.5	11.0
Petroleum	8.7	15.9	15.1
Nonmetallic minerals	2.9	1.0	2.7
Basic metals	5.7	3.9	7.7
Metal products	3.2	2.5	1.5
Machinery (except electrical)	0.7	1.3	0.8
Electrical machinery	3.3	4.0	6.4
Transport equipment	4.0	4.6	1.5
Other	1.6	0.8	0.5
TOTAL	100.0[1]	100.0[2]	100.0[1]

[1] Figures may not add to total because of rounding.
[2] Sum of entries in source is 95 percent.
Source: Based on information from Philippines, National Economic and Development Authority, *1989 Philippine Statistical Yearbook,* Manila, 1989, Table 6.4.

Manufacturing output fell in the political and economic crisis of 1983, and industry in 1985 was working at as low as 40 percent of capacity. By the middle of 1988, after economic pump priming by the Aquino regime, industries were again working at full capacity. In 1990 the Board of Investments approved investment projects valued at US$3.75 billion, including US$1.48 billion targeted to the manufacturing sector.

Manufacturing production is geographically concentrated. In 1990, 50 percent of industrial output came from Metro Manila (see Glossary) and another 20 percent from the adjoining regions of Southern Tagalog and Central Luzon (see fig. 6). Prior to 1986, government efforts to distribute industry more evenly were largely ineffective. In the post-Marcos economic recovery, however, investment grew in small and medium-sized firms producing handicrafts, furniture, electronics, garments, footwear, and canned goods in areas outside of Metro Manila, particularly in Cebu City and Davao City.

In 1990 the industrial sector was inefficient and oligopolistic. Although small- and medium-sized firms accounted for 80 percent of manufacturing employment, they accounted for only 25 percent of the value added in manufacturing. Most industrial output was concentrated in a few, large establishments. For example, a six-month Senate inquiry determined in 1990 that eight of the country's seventeen cement manufacturing companies were under control of a single firm.

Mining

The 1980s were difficult for mining in the Philippines. In 1990 the mining and quarrying sector contributed 1.5 percent of GNP, approximately half the percentage it had accounted for ten years earlier. Mineral exports were 5.4 percent of merchandise trade in 1988, whereas in 1980 they constituted 17.8 percent. Rising operational costs and a depressed market severely affected the industry. In 1990 mining operations suffered from labor disputes, higher mandated wages, higher interest rates, typhoons, an earthquake, and power shortages.

In the early 1990s, the Philippines had large deposits of copper, chromium, gold, and nickel, plus smaller deposits of cadmium, iron, lead, manganese, mercury, molybdenum, and silver. Industrial minerals included asbestos, gypsum, limestone, marble, phosphate, salt, and sulfur. Mineral fuels included coal and petroleum.

In 1988 the Philippines was the sixth largest producer of chromium in the world and ranked ninth in gold production and tenth in copper production. The country's nickel-mining company, Nonoc Mining and Industrial Corporation, ceased operation in March 1986 because of financial and labor difficulties. The Asset Privatization Trust, a government entity in charge of selling firms acquired by the government through foreclosure proceedings, sold Nonoc in late 1990. The new owners expected to resume operations in the middle of 1991 and produce some 28,700 tons a year, which would again make nickel a major export earner for the Philippines.

Energy

During the 1970s and 1980s, the Philippines sought growth and self-sufficiency in energy production. In 1972 the government altered the legal arrangements for oil exploration from concessions to a service contracts, and serious oil exploration began in the mid- and late 1970s. As a result of exploration in the Palawan-Sulu seabed, oil was discovered in the Nido oil field in 1976. Commercial production began in 1979 and yielded 8.8 million barrels. Successful wells also were drilled in the Cadlao and Matinloc fields off Palawan in 1981 and 1982, but the fields were relatively small. The level of production varied during the 1980s but never exceeded 5 million barrels in any one year. In 1988 local production--2.2 million barrels--accounted for only 3 percent of domestic oil use (see table 11). A study released in early 1990, indicating that the geology of the Philippines was a favorable indicator of possible additional petroleum deposits, was used by the government to encourage oil exploration firms. Production-sharing arrangements allowed a firm first to recover the cost of its investment, after which 60 percent of profits would go to the government. In December 1990, there were new discoveries of oil and natural gas off the northwest coast of Palawan Island. Tests showed that the oil well could have a flow rate of 6,000 barrels per day, with potential reserves of about 1 billion barrels.

Between 1973 and 1983, power generation increased at an annual rate of 7.0 percent, two percentage points above the growth rate of real gross domestic product (GDP--see Glossary). In 1988 the National Power Corporation, which produced approximately 90 percent of the country's electricity, had a generating capacity of 5,772 megawatts. Of that, 42 percent was from oil-burning plants and 7 percent from dual oil-coal facilities. An additional 37 percent was from hydroelectric plants, and just under 15 percent was from geothermal plants.

**Table 11. Production, Exports, and Reserves of Major Minerals,
1985, 1987, and 1988 (in thousands of tons)**

Mineral	Production 1985	Production 1988	Exports 1987	Reserves 1987
Cement	3,080.0	4,300.0	38.6	6,507,569
Clay	381.4	418.3	---	1,121,163
Coal	1,257.9	1,330.0	---	369,000
Chromium	272.0	190.0	105.7	56,848
Copper	222.2	218.1	362.0	3,881,255
Gold	0.033	0.033	0.004	101,557
Nickel	28.2	10.8	483.4	1,566,101
Pyrite	232.5	300.0	0.054	988,482
Petroleum, crude*	3,285.0	2,170.0	---	16,300

--- means negligible.
*In thousands of barrels.
Source: Based on information from United States, Department of the Interior, Bureau of Mines, *Mineral Yearbook,* Washington, 1990, 446-50; Philippines, National Economic and Development Authority, *1989 Philippine Statistical Yearbook,* Manila, 1989, Table 4.14; and Edith Hodgkinson, *The Philippines to 1993,* London, 1988, 74.

The Philippines had a wealth of potential energy resources. It ranked second behind the United States in production of electricity from geothermal sources. Installed capacity in 1988 was 828 megawatts; estimated potential was 35,000 megawatts. Undeveloped hydroelectric potential of 3,771 megawatts also was identified. Coal resources, estimated to be 1.2 billion tons, also were plentiful, although of a rather poor grade for electrical generation. In addition to these sources, solar, animal waste, agriwaste, and other non-conventional sources were utilized for generating small amounts of electricity and other energy needs in rural areas. Together they accounted for about 15 percent of energy consumption.

In 1990 the Philippines was confronted with a crisis of insufficient electrical generating capacity. Metro Manila and the thirty-three provinces in the Luzon power grid experienced brownouts of up to four hours per day, with the grid averaging a daily deficiency of 262 megawatts. At the root of the problem was the decision by the Marcos regime to build a 620 megawatt nuclear-power plant on the Bataan Peninsula. The Aquino government decided not to use the facility because it was located on a seismic fault. As a result, a badly needed expansion of generating capacity in Luzon, which accounted for 75 percent of national electric consumption, did not come on line. The problem was compounded by inadequate planning and bureaucratic delays. There were delays in the building of a facility capable of generating 110 megawatts of geothermal power in Albay Province and a 300 megawatt coal-fired plant in Batangas Province. The short-term solution was to put up a series of gas-turbine plants with a combined rating of 500 megawatts. Only 245 megawatts came on stream between 1987 and 1989. Economists estimated that to achieve a 5.6 percent growth rate in real GNP, the country would need an additional 300 megawatts of generating capacity yearly.

Efforts also were being made to expand the country's rural electrification program. In 1985 it covered the franchise area of some 120 electrical cooperatives, reaching around 2.7 million households. The government planned to expand the coverage to some 4 million households by 1992.

The Service Sector

Finance

The Philippine financial system in the early 1990s was composed of banking institutions and non-bank financial intermediaries, including commercial banks, specialized government banks, thrift and rural banks, offshore banking units, building and loan associations, investment and brokerage houses, and finance companies. The Central Bank and the Securities and Exchange Commission maintained regulatory and supervisory control. The Philippines had a relatively sophisticated banking system; however, the level of financial intermediation was low relative to the size of the economy. In the late 1970s and early 1980s, a number of policy reforms were initiated to strengthen the system, but financial crises in 1981 and 1983 short-circuited their full effect. The financial community has undertaken recovery efforts since 1986.

Until the economic crisis of the mid-1980s, the largest commercial bank in the Philippines was the government-owned Philippine National Bank. Created in 1916 to provide agricultural credit for export crops, the Philippine National Bank accounted for 25 percent to 30 percent of commercial bank assets in the 1970s and early 1980s. As the result of the accumulation of non-performing assets, by 1987 the asset share of the Philippine National Bank had fallen by half. In 1988 there were twenty privately-owned domestic banks and four branches of foreign banks engaged in commercial banking. Since the passage of the General Banking Act of 1948, foreign investment in banking has been limited to 40 percent of domestic bank equity. Total assets of the commercial banking system in 1988 were about P330 billion.

The Philippine government controlled three specialized banks in 1991: the Development Bank of the Philippines, the Land Bank of the Philippines, and the Philippine Amanah Bank. The Development Bank of the Philippines, established in 1946 and initially designed to facilitate postwar rehabilitation, provided long-term finance. It supplied 47 percent of long-term loans and 15 percent of the medium-term loans. More than 70 percent of its loans were allocated to industry. The Land Bank of the Philippines, established in the early 1970s, financed the government land reform program. The Philippine Amanah Bank, organized in the mid-1970s, served Muslims in the southern Philippines. Offshore banking units have been allowed to do business in the Philippines since 1977. Also since 1977, certain domestic banks have been allowed to take foreign-currency deposits and engage in foreign-currency lending.

From its inception in 1948 until 1980, the Central Bank extensively regulated the commercial banking system and engaged in considerable rediscounting activity. Interest rates were set administratively, usually below the market clearing rate. Commercial bank lending tended to be short-term and granted to known, established borrowers. The system had periods of instability with several bank runs and a few failures. In 1980, at the instigation of the World Bank and the IMF, several measures were passed to increase competition in the financial sector, achieve greater efficiency, and increase borrowers' access to long-term funds. Large banks with a net worth of at least P500 million could engage in expanded commercial banking, or "unibanking," combining commercial and investment banking activities. In 1988 there were eight unibanks, including the Philippine National Bank. Further liberalization had occurred in 1983 when interest rates shifted from being administered to being market-determined.

Interest-rate ceilings had led to an excess demand for loans and credit rationing. The Malacañang Palace interfered in loan decisions regarding state-owned banks, weakening the quality of bank portfolios. It was argued that a market-determined interest rate would make such behavior less rewarding and more difficult. However, before the interest rate reform could be initiated and before the expanded commercial bank reform had an impact on the banking industry, a series of crises hit the Philippines, throwing the country's financial system into disarray.

The economic and political crisis that occurred in the aftermath of the assassination of Marcos's political rival, Benigno Aquino, resulted in a virtual collapse of much of the banking industry, particularly the smaller institutions. The larger banks suffered substantial losses from the drastic devaluations of the peso between 1983 and 1985. Commercial bank loans increased slightly in 1984, but then fell almost 30 percent in the following two years--from P116 billion to P83 billion--before turning upward again. Inflation during that three-year period was almost 80 percent. The two largest financial intermediaries, the Philippine National Bank and Development Bank of the Philippines, became insolvent, and a number of financial institutions failed, including the three largest investment houses, three commercial banks, the majority of the more than 1,000 rural banks, and the largest savings bank.

The Aquino government undertook a rehabilitation program for the Philippine National Bank and Development Bank of the Philippines. In 1986 non-performing assets of the two institutions were transferred to the government, reducing the value of the assets of the Philippine National Bank by 67 percent and that of the Development Bank of the Philippines by 87 percent. The relative importance of these two banks in the financial sector diminished dramatically. The domestically owned commercial banking sector, however, became more concentrated. From the mid-1950s to the early 1980s, the five largest private domestic commercial banks accounted for about 35 percent of total assets of the private domestic commercial banks. By 1988 that ratio had risen to around 55 percent. The combined assets of the five private domestic commercial banks, the Philippine National Bank, and the two largest foreign branch banks accounted for two-thirds of total commercial bank assets, up from 56 percent in 1980.

In 1990 the six largest commercial banks earned an estimated P7.9 billion in after-tax profits, an increase of 42 percent over 1989, which in turn was a 32 percent increase over 1988. A 1991 World Bank memorandum noted that the extent of bank profits indicated a "lack of competition" and a "market structure for financial services characterized by oligopoly." Philippine banks had the widest interest rate spread (loan rate minus deposit rate) in Southeast Asia.

Transportation

In 1988 there were 157,000 kilometers of roads, 26,000 of which were designated national (arterial) roads. Somewhat less than 50 percent of national roads were all-weather. The PanPhilippine Highway, also called the Maharlika Highway, running from Laoag City in Ilocos Norte to Zamboanga City at the southwest tip of Mindanao, was the country's main trunk road. The highway passed through twenty-one provinces. In the 1980s, the national road system increased by 10 percent, and the portion that was surfaced with asphalt or concrete increased by 20 percent. The planning target for 1992 called for 100 percent of arterial roads to be all-weather, and 95 percent to be paved. Local roads, however, were allowed to deteriorate. The condition of many roads was poor because of low design standards, substandard construction, inadequate maintenance, and damage from over-loaded vehicles. A program of rehabilitation and improvement of the local road system was part of the plan objectives.

In 1988, 1.3 million motor vehicles were registered with the Bureau of Land Transportation. About 22 percent were motorcycles; 30 percent were private automobiles, and 38 percent were utility vehicles. A large number of the utility vehicles were jeepneys, jeeps converted for hire to carry passengers. In the late 1980s, Metro Manila experienced a combination of heavy traffic congestion and a shortage of transportation, reflecting an increasing number of private automobiles and an insufficient number of public conveyance vehicles. A 1989 estimate indicated a shortage of 3,200 buses and 21,700 jeepneys in the Manila area, and many of the taxis and buses in Metro Manila were very old.

In 1991 there were two international airports: Manila's Ninoy Aquino International Airport and Mactan International Airport near Cebu City. Slightly over 1 million visitors arrived in the Philippines by air in 1988. About half of the national airports were served by the main domestic and international carrier, Philippine Air Lines. No additional airport construction was anticipated in the Medium-Term Development Plan, 1987-92. Thereafter, Manila's international airport, which is too small to handle expected increases in air traffic, would need to be relocated. During the talks between the United States and the Philippines in 1990, concerning the future of the two major United States military facilities in the Philippines, there was public discussion of relocating the international airport to the United States facility, Clark Air Base and making Ninoy Aquino a domestic airport.

There was a network of 622 public and 314 private seaports in the Philippine archipelago in the late 1980s. Six ports--Manila, Cebu, Iloilo, Cagayan de Oro, Zamboanga, and Davao handled approximately 80 percent of public port traffic. In 1988 a major construction project was underway at the Manila International Container Terminal. There was an ongoing series of port improvement projects, and plans for a fishing port program and a program to develop roll-on-roll-off capacity in order to link sea and road transportation systems.

In 1987 there were more than 3,000 passenger and cargo ships in the interisland shipping industry, with a total registered cargo tonnage of 417,500 tons. The ships accounted for about 85 percent of interisland cargo movements and nearly 10 percent of passenger-kilometers traveled nationwide. Somewhat less than one-third of the ships were liner vessels; the remainder were tramp ships. Liner ships were generally imported secondhand from Japan and in 1987 had an average age of about nineteen years. Although the industry was highly regulated, it was criticized for moving goods slowly and inefficiently and for safety violations, particularly overloading passengers during peak periods of travel.

The Philippines in 1990 had one main railroad line running north out of Manila 266 kilometers to San Fernando City in La Union Province and 474 kilometers south to Legaspi City in Albay Province. The system had deteriorated over the years, with utilization declining continuously to a tenth of the passenger traffic and a twentieth of the freight carried in 1960. In the first 10 months of 1990, the railroad carried 30,000 tons of freight, down from 48,000 in 1989. During the same period, passenger service turned around, however, climbing from 210 million passenger-kilometers in 1989 to 226 million in 1990.

The Philippine National Railroad began a project in 1990-91 to upgrade its southern track system, utilizing a P1.2 billion loan from Japan. When completed in 1993, travel time from Manila to Bicol would be cut substantially.

In 1984 a Light Rail Transit system began operation in Metro Manila running from Baclaran in the south to Monumento in the North. The fifteen-kilometer system provided some relief from Metro Manila's highly congested traffic network.

Telecommunications and Postal Services

The Philippine telecommunication system in 1989 consisted of some fifty-five telephone companies, seven domestic record carriers, four international record carriers, and two satellite ground stations. Approximately 70 percent of the country's telephone lines were located in Metro Manila. In 1989 there were 4.7 telephones per 100 persons in Metro Manila but only 0.8 telephones per 100 persons in the country as a whole. The country had approximately 380 radio stations broadcasting to 4 million receivers in English and all the major Philippine dialects, and 42 television stations transmitting to 6 million receivers, mainly in Pilipino and English. The mail volume handled by the more than 2,000 post offices in the Philippines doubled from approximately 400 million pieces in 1979 to approximately 800 million pieces in 1988.

Tourism

Tourism developed rapidly in the 1970s, with visitors numbering 1 million in 1980. Thereafter, the industry went into a slump, reaching the 1 million visitor mark again only in 1988. In that year, the average length of stay was 12.6 days, up from 8.9 days in 1987. Many of the visitors, however, were emigrant Filipinos returning for periodic visits with families and friends. In 1988 an average of 73 percent of Manila's 8,500 hotel rooms were occupied.

Estimates of tourist revenue varied considerably. In 1988 the Central Bank estimated it at US$405 million, 11 percent of the country's non-merchandise exports. Using a different formula, the Department of Tourism estimated tourism earnings at US$1.45 billion. Most tourists entered the country through Manila, but the city had relatively few amenities and suffered from congestion, pollution, and crime. Intramuros, the colonial Spanish walled city, had not been fully restored since its destruction at the end of World War II. Political instability in the country during the 1980s also was a deterrent to tourism. The Medium-Term Development Plan called for promotion of both domestic and international tourism.

Employment and Labor Relations

A high rate of population growth, lack of access to land, insufficient job creation in industry, and a history of inappropriate economic policies contributed to high unemployment and underemployment and a relatively high proportion of the labor force being in low-productivity, service sector jobs in the late 1980s. Real wages were low, having declined at about 3 percent per year since 1960, and relatively weak labor unions were unable to substantially affect the deterioration of workers' earning power.

Labor Force and Employment

Population growth averaged 2.9 percent from 1965 to 1980 and 2.5 percent in the late 1980s (see Population Growth). While more than 40 percent of the population was below fifteen years of age, the growth of the working-age population--those fifteen years of age and older--was even more rapid than total population growth. In the 1980s, the working-age population grew by 2.7 percent annually. In addition, the labor force participation rate--the proportion of working-age people who were in the labor force--rose approximately 5 percentage points during the 1980s, largely because of the increase in the proportion of women entering the work force. So the actual labor force grew by 750,000 people or approximately 4 percent each year during the 1980s.

Agriculture, which had provided most employment, employed only approximately 45 percent of the work force in 1990, down from 60 percent in 1960. Manufacturing industry was not able to make up the difference. Manufacturing's share of employed people remained stable at about 12 percent in 1990.

The service sector (commerce, finance, transportation, and a host of private and public services), perforce, became the residual employer, accounting for almost 40 percent of the work force in 1988 as contrasted with 25 percent in 1960. Much of this growth was in small-scale enterprises or self-employment activities such as hawking and vending, repair work, transportation, and personal services. Such endeavors are often referred to as the "informal sector," because of the lack of record keeping by its enterprises and a relative freedom from government regulation, monitoring, or reporting. Informal sector occupations were characterized by low productivity, modest fixed assets, long hours of work, and low wages. According to a 1988 study of urban poor in Metro Manila, Cebu, and Davao cities published in the *Philippine Economic Journal*, more than half of the respondents engaged in informal sector work as their primary income-generating activity.

Unemployment, which had averaged about 4.5 percent during the 1970s, increased drastically following the economic crises of the early 1980s, peaking in early 1989 at 11.4 percent. Urban areas fared worse; unemployment in mid-1990, for example, remained above 15 percent in Metro Manila.

Beyond the unemployment generated from economic mismanagement and crises was a more long-term, structural employment problem, a consequence of the highly concentrated control of productive assets and the inadequate number of work places created by investment in the industrial economy. The size and growth of the service sector was one indicator. Underemployment was another.

Underemployment has been predominantly a problem for poor, less educated, and older people. The unemployed have tended to be young, inexperienced entrants into the labor force, who were relatively well educated and not heads of households. In the first half of the 1980s, approximately 20 percent of male household heads and 35 percent of female household heads were unable to find more than forty days of work a quarter.

Overseas migration absorbed a significant amount of Philippine labor. From the late 1940s through the 1970s, migrants were largely Filipino members of the United States armed services, professionals, and relatives of those who had previously migrated. After liberalization of the United States Immigration and Nationality Act in October 1965, the number of United States immigrant visas issued to Filipinos increased dramatically from approximately 2,500 in 1965 to more than 25,000 in 1970. Most of those emigrating were professionals and their families. By 1990 Filipino-Americans numbered 1.4 million, making them the largest Asian community in the United States.

In the 1970s and 1980s, quite a different flow of migration developed: most emigrants were workers engaged in contract work in the Middle East and, to a lesser extent, elsewhere. Although some were professionals, the majority were production, construction, and transport and equipment workers or operators, as well as service workers. An increasing number also were merchant seamen. Inasmuch as wages paid for overseas contract work have been a multiple of what Filipinos could earn at home, such employment opportunities have been in great demand. Government statistics show that overseas placements of land-based workers increased from 12,500 in 1975 to 385,000 in 1988, a growth rate of about 30 percent per annum. The number of seamen also increased, from 23,500 in 1975, to almost 86,000 in 1988. The average stay abroad was 3.1 years for land-based workers and 6.3 years for seamen.

In 1982 the Philippine Overseas Employment Administration was established in the Ministry of Labor and Employment. The Philippine Overseas Employment Administration consolidated responsibility for regulating overseas land-based workers and seamen, supervising recruitment, as well as adjudicating complaints and conflicts. The agency also was tasked with promoting employment opportunities abroad for Filipinos. Overseas employment created two benefits for the economy: jobs and foreign exchange. The total number of placements abroad from 1980 through 1988, 3.2 million, was about one-half the growth in the country's labor supply during that period. Remittances through the banking system for the period 1983 to 1988 totaled approximately US$4.6 billion, an amount equal to 14 percent of merchandise exports during the same period. The Central Bank estimated that remittances passing through "informal channels" might be as much as twice the documented figure. If so, export of labor would be the largest single earner of foreign exchange.

Labor Relations
From independence in 1946 until martial law was declared in 1972, the government encouraged collective bargaining and, except for setting up a commission in 1970 to supervise the fixing of minimum wages, involved itself minimally in labor relations. For most of the martial law period (1972-81), strikes were forbidden or severely limited. The Marcos labor code of 1974 made arbitration compulsory. The right to strike was partially restored in 1976, but with considerable restrictions. The Aquino government took a somewhat more liberal approach to labor, but some of the structures of the Marcos period remained.

Organized labor in the Philippines has been relatively weak. In 1986 it was estimated that about 2.2 million Filipinos were part of the union movement, accounting for approximately 20 percent of the wage-and-salary work force or 10 percent of the total labor force. These workers were organized into some 2,000 unions, half of which were not connected to a national union or federation. In 1987 only 350,000 workers were covered by collective bargaining agreements.

The largest union body was the Trade Union Congress of the Philippines (TUCP). Formed in December 1974, it was designated the official labor center of the Philippines by the Marcos government. Another labor organization, the Kilusang Mayo Uno (KMU), or the May First Movement, was formed in July 1980, bringing together nine broadly based, more ideologically oriented unions. The two major union centers represented sharply different visions of the role of unions in society. Although TUCP supported Marcos, it represented itself as a proponent of nonpolitical unionism, concerned primarily with the collective bargaining process. The KMU was more openly political, projecting itself as a proponent of "genuine, militant, and nationalist unionism." Going beyond collective bargaining, the KMU called for the formation of worker solidarity movements and advocated a nationalist-oriented alternative to the prevailing economic and social policies of the government. The Labor Advisory and Consultative Council (LACC), formed at the onset of the Aquino administration in 1986 by then Labor Minister Agusto Sanchez, drew the various factions of the labor movement together to advise the Ministry of Labor and Employment. Membership in LACC included the KMU, the Federation of Free Workers, Lakas Ng Manggagawa Labor Center, and, for a short while, the TUCP.

When Aquino came into office in 1986, she had the backing of a wide spectrum of the population, including those affiliated with labor unions. In her May 1 speech that year, before a large and enthusiastic gathering of labor groups, Aquino presented a package of labor-law reforms, including extension of the right to strike, making it easier to petition for a union certification election, and abrogation of repressive labor legislation decreed by the Marcos government. Soon, however, the president began to shift ground as she received vigorous protests by both Filipino and foreign businessmen against her May Day promises. The pledges were rethought, modified in some cases, and not promulgated in others. This willingness to respond to the interests of the boardroom rather than the shop floor also extended to official appointments. In particular, her first minister of labor, Agusto Sanchez, was considered to be too prolabor and eased out within a year of his appointment.

The TUCP was generally supportive of the Aquino government, but the KMU and other progressive unions resisted the conservative drift of her administration through strikes, demonstrations, and antigovernment rallies. The KMU gained influence through its leadership of the national strike, or Welga ng Bayan, in 1987, 1989, and 1990. From September to December 1990, the KMU led a series of general strikes in response to dramatic increases in the prices of petroleum products. These labor actions were noteworthy both because of a heightened level of conflict between strikers and the authorities and because of the participation of professionals and other middle-class groups.

Repression of labor activists, widespread during the Marcos era, resurfaced early in the Aquino administration. In November 1986, the chairman of the KMU was murdered. The following January, the army opened fire on a march of the Peasant Movement of the Philippines (Kilusang Magbubukid ng Pilipinas--KMP) and their supporters who were protesting the lack of government action on land reform. Eighteen were killed and nearly 100 wounded. In 1990 the government charged two KMU labor leaders with sedition: Medardo Roda, the head of PISTON, a federation of drivers, and Crispin Beltran, the chairman of KMU. Old charges of slander and fraud dating back to 1967 and 1971 were revived against Beltran. The government also imprisoned the leader of the KMP, Jaime Tadeo, on ten-year-old fraud charges initiated against him by the Marcos government. After a 1990 violent strike, during which an estimated 500 participants were arrested, both the military and government officials suggested banning the KMU as a communist-front organization.

Economic Welfare

In 1990 the Philippines had not yet recovered from the economic and political crisis of the first half of the 1980s. At P18,419, or US$668, per capita GNP in 1990 remained, in real terms, below the level of 1978. A major thrust of Aquino's 1986 People Power Revolution was to address the needs of impoverished Filipinos. One of the four principles of her "Policy Agenda for People-Powered Development," was promotion of social justice and poverty alleviation. Government programs launched in 1986 and 1987 to generate employment met with some success, reversing the decline of the first half of the decade, but these efforts did little to alleviate the more chronic aspects of Philippine poverty.

Extent of Poverty

Individuals are said to be in absolute poverty when they are unable to obtain at least a specified minimum of the food, clothing, and shelter that are considered necessary for continued survival. In the Philippines, two such minimums have been established. The poverty line is defined in terms of a least-cost consumption basket of food that provides 2,016 calories and 50 grams of protein per day and of nonfood items consumed by families in the lowest quintile of the population. In 1988 the poverty line for a family of six was estimated to be P2,709 per month. The subsistence level is defined as the income level that allows purchase of the minimum food requirements only.

In 1985 slightly more than half the population lived below the poverty line, about the same proportion as in 1971. The proportion of the population below the subsistence level, however, declined from approximately 35 percent in 1971 to 28 percent in 1985. The economic turndown in the early 1980s and the economic and political crisis of 1983 had a devastating impact on living standards.

The countryside contained a disproportionate share of the poor. For example, more than 80 percent of the poorest 30 percent of families in the Philippines lived in rural areas in the mid-1980s. The majority were tenant farmers or landless agricultural workers. The landless, fishermen, and forestry workers were found to be the poorest of the poor. In some rural regions--the sugar-growing region on the island of Negros being the most egregious example--there was a period in which malnutrition and famine had been widespread.

Urban areas also were hard hit, with the incidence of urban poverty increasing between 1971 and 1985 by 13 percentage points to include half the urban population. The urban poor generally lived in crowded slum areas, often on land or in buildings without permission of the owner; hence, they were referred to as squatters (see Urban Social Patterns). These settlements often lacked basic necessities such as running water, sewerage, and electricity. According to a 1984 government study, 44 percent of all occupied dwellings in Metro Manila had less than thirty square meters of living area, and the average monthly expenditure of an urban poor family was P1,315. Of this, 62 percent was spent on food and another 9 percent on transportation, whereas only P57 was spent on rent or mortgage payments, no doubt because of the extent of squatting by poor families. About 55 percent of the poor surveyed who were in the labor force worked in the informal sector, generally as vendors or street hawkers. Other activities included service and repair work, construction, transport services, or petty production. Women and children under fifteen years of age constituted almost 60 percent of those employed. The majority of the individuals surveyed possessed a high school education, and 30 percent had a skill such as dressmaking, electrical repair, plumbing, or carpentry. Nevertheless, they were unable to secure permanent, full-time positions.

Causes of Poverty

From one perspective, poverty is a function of total output of an economy relative to its population--GNP per capita--and the distribution of that income among families. In the World Bank's *World Development Report, 1990*, the Philippines was ranked at the lower end of the grouping of lower middle-income economies. Given its relative position, the country should be able to limit the extent of poverty with a reasonably equitable sharing of the nation's income. In fact, the actual distribution of income was highly skewed (see table 12). Although considerable underreporting was thought to occur among upper-income families, and incorrect reporting from lack of information was common, particularly with respect to non-cash income, the data were adequate to provide a broad overview.

Table 12. Income Distribution by Decile, Selected Years, 1961-88 (in percentages)

Decile	1961	1971	1985	198 8
Top decile	41.0	37.1	36.4	35.7
Second decile	15.5	16.9	15.7	16.1
Third to sixth deciles	31.4	34.3	33.6	34.0
Seventh to tenth deciles	12.1	11.7	14.3	14.3
TOTAL	100.0	100.0	100.0	100.0

*Figures may not add to total because of rounding.
Source: Based on information from Philippines, National Economic and Development Authority, *1989 Philippine Statistical Yearbook,* Manila, 1989, Table 2.8.

In 1988 the most affluent 20 percent of families in the Philippines received more than 50 percent of total personal income, with most going to the top 10 percent. Below the richest 10 percent of the population, the share accruing to each decile diminished rather gradually. A 1988 World Bank poverty report suggested that there had been a small shift toward a more equal distribution of income since 1961. The beneficiaries appear to have been middle-income earners, however, rather than the poor.

The World Bank report concluded, and many economists associated with the Philippines concurred, that the country's high population growth rate was a major cause of the widespread poverty, particularly in the rural areas. Implementation of a government-sponsored family-planning program, however, was thwarted by stiff opposition from the hierarchy of the Roman Catholic Church (see Population Control). Church pronouncements in the late 1980s and early 1990s focused on injustice, graft and corruption, and mismanagement of resources as the fundamental causes of Philippine underdevelopment. These issues were in turn linked to the concentration of control of economic resources and the structure of the economy. Land ownership was highly unequal, but land reform initiatives had made little progress.

In urban areas also, the extent of poverty was related to the concentrated control of wealth. Considerable portions of both industry and finance were highly monopolized. Access to finance was severely limited to those who already possessed resources. The most profitable investment opportunities were often in areas in which tariff or other forms of government protection ensured high profits but did not necessarily result in rapidly expanding employment opportunities. In her election campaign President Aquino pledged to destroy the monopolies and structures of privilege aggravated by the Marcos regime. She looked to the private sector to revitalize the economy, create jobs for the masses of Filipinos, and lead the society to a higher standard of living. The state-protected monopolies were dismantled, but not the monopoly structure of the Philippine economy that existed long before Marcos assumed power. In their privileged positions, the business elite did not live up to the President's expectations. As a consequence, unemployment and, more importantly for the issue of poverty, underemployment remained widespread.

International Economic Relations

International Trade

At independence in 1946, the Philippines was an agricultural nation tied closely to its erstwhile colonizer, the United States. This was most clearly observed in trade relations between the two countries. In 1950 the value of the Philippines' ten principal exports--all but one being agricultural or mineral products in raw or minimally processed form--added up to 85 percent of the country's exports. For the first twenty-five years of independence, the structure of export trade remained relatively constant.

The direction of trade, however, did not remain constant. In 1949, 80 percent of total Philippine trade was with the United States. Thereafter, the United States portion declined as that of Japan rose. In 1970 the two countries' share was approximately 40 percent each, the United States slightly more, and Japan slightly less. The pattern of import trade was similar, if not as concentrated. The United States share of Philippine imports declined more rapidly than Japan's share rose, so that by 1970 the two countries accounted for about 60 percent of total Philippine imports. After 1970 Philippine exporters began to find new markets, and on the import side the dramatic increases in petroleum prices shifted shares in value terms, if not in volume. In 1988 the United States accounted for 27 percent of total Philippine trade, Japan for 19 percent.

At the time of independence and as a requirement for receiving war reconstruction assistance from the United States, the Philippine government agreed to a number of items that, in effect, kept the Philippines closely linked to the United States economy and protected American business interests in the Philippines. Manila promised not to change its (overvalued) exchange rate from the prewar parity of P2 to the dollar, or to impose tariffs on imports from the United States without the consent of the president of the United States. By 1949 the situation had become untenable. Imports greatly surpassed the sum of exports and the inflow of dollar aid, and a regime of import and foreign-exchange controls was initiated, which remained in place until the early 1960s.

The controls initially reduced the inflow of goods dramatically. Between 1949 and 1950, imports fell by almost 40 percent to US$342 million and surpassed the 1949 level in only one year during the 1950s. Being constrained, imports of goods and non-factor services as a proportion of GNP declined during the 1950s, ending the decade at 10.6 percent, about the same percentage as that of exports. By the late 1950s, however, exchange controls had begun to lose their effectiveness as most available foreign exchange was committed for required imports. A tariff law was passed in 1957, and, from 1960 to early 1962, import and exchange controls were phased out. Exports and imports increased rapidly. By 1965 the import to GNP ratio was more than 17 percent. Another acceleration of imports occurred in the early 1970s, this time raising the import to GNP ratio to around 25 percent, the level at which it remained into the 1990s. Imports in the 1970s were increasingly being financed by external debt rather than by exports.

The composition of imports evolved after independence as industrial development occurred and commercial policy was modified. In 1949, about 37 percent of imports were consumer goods. This proportion declined to around 20 percent during the exchange-and-import control period of the 1950s. By the late 1960s, consumer imports had been largely replaced by domestic production. Imports of machinery and equipment increased, however, as the country engaged in industrialization, from around 10 percent in the early 1950s to double that by the mid-1960s. As a result of the surge in petroleum prices in the 1970s, the import share of both consumer and capital goods fell somewhat, but their relative magnitudes remained the same.

No matter the trade regime, the Philippines had difficulty in generating sufficient exports to pay for its imports. In the forty years from 1950 through 1990, the trade balance was positive in only two years: 1963 and 1973. For a few years after major devaluations in 1962 and 1970, the current account was in surplus, but then it too turned negative. Excessive imports remained a problem in the late 1980s. Between 1986 and 1989, the negative trade balance increased tenfold from US$202 million to US$2.6 billion (see table 13).

Table 13. Balance of Payments, 1985- 89 (in millions of United States dollars)

	1985	1986	1987	1988	1989
Exports	4,629	4,842	5,720	7,074	7,821
Imports	-5,111	- 5,044	-6,737	- 8,159	-10,419
Trade balance	-482	-202	-1,017	- 1,085	-2,598
Invisibles and private transfers	447	1,156	573	695	1,133
Current account balance	-35	954	-444	- 390	-1,465
Direct investment and other long-term capital	3,094	1,249	601	605	1,449
Short-term capital	-2,741	-1,069	-246	- 34	-72
Capital account balance	353	180	355	571	1,377
Net errors and omissions	659	32	-209	480	389
Gold monetization, SDRs,* and valuation change*	160	209	202	339	161
Exceptional financing	-1,100	0	0	0	0
Changes in reserves	-37	-1,375	96	- 1,000	-462

*SDRs--Special Drawing Rights, a monetary unit of the International Monetary Fund (see Glossary) based on a basket of the United States dollar, the German deutsche mark, the Japanese yen, the British pound sterling, and the French franc.
Source: Based on information from International Monetary Fund, *Balance of Payments Statistics,* 41, Pt. 1, Washington, 1990, 536.

In 1990 weaker world prices for Philippine exports, higher production costs, and a slowdown in the economies of the Philippines' major trading partners restrained export growth to only slightly more than 4 percent. Increasing petroleum prices and heavy importation of capital goods, including power-generating equipment, helped push imports up almost 17 percent, resulting in a 50 percent jump in the trade deficit to more than US$4 billion. Reducing the drain on foreign exchange has became a major government priority.

A number of factors contributed to the rather dismal trade history of the Philippines. The country's terms of trade (see Glossary) have fallen for most of the period since 1950, so that in the late 1980s, a given quantity of exports could buy only 55 percent of the volume of imports that it could buy in the early 1950s. A second factor was the persistent overvaluation of the exchange rate. The peso was devalued a number of times falling from a pre-independence value of P2 to the dollar to P28 in May 1990. The adjustments, however, had not stimulated exports or curtailed imports sufficiently to bring the two in line with one another.

A third consideration was the country's trade and industrial policies, including tariff protection and investment incentives. Many economists have argued that these policies favorably affected import-substitution industries to the detriment of export industries. In the 1970s, the implementation of an export- incentives program and the opening of an export-processing zone at Mariveles on the Bataan Peninsula reduced the biases somewhat. The export of manufactures (e.g., electronic components, garments, handicrafts, chemicals, furniture, and footwear) increased rapidly. Additional export-processing zones were constructed in Baguio City and on Mactan Island near Cebu City. During the 1970s and early 1980s, nontraditional exports (i.e., commodities not among the ten largest traditional exports) grew at a rate twice that of total exports. Their share of total exports increased from 8.3 percent in 1970 to 61.7 percent in 1985. At the same time that nontraditional exports were booming, falling raw material prices adversely affected the value of traditional exports.

In 1988 the value of nontraditional exports was US$5.4 billion, 75 percent of the total. The most important, electrical and electronic equipment and garments, earned US$1.5 billion and US$1.3 billion, respectively. Both of these product groups, however, had high import content. Domestic value added was no more than 20 percent of the export value of electronic components and probably no more than twice that in the garment industry. Another rapidly growing export item was seafood, particularly shrimps and prawns, which earned US$307 million in 1988.

The World Bank and the IMF as well as many Philippine economists had long advocated reduction of the level of tariff protection and elimination of import controls. Those in the business community who were engaged in import-substitution manufacturing activities, however, opposed reductions. They feared that they could not successfully compete if tariff barriers were lowered.

In the early 1980s, the Philippine government reached agreement with the World Bank to reduce tariffs by about one-third and to lift import restrictions on some 3,000 items over a five- to six-year period. The bank, in turn, provided the Philippines with a financial sector loan of US$150 million and a structural adjustment loan for US$200 million, to provide balance-of-payments relief while the tariff wall was reduced. Approximately two-thirds of the changes had been enacted when the program ground to a halt in the wake of the economic and political crisis that followed the August 1983 assassination of former Senator Benigno Aquino.

In an October 1986 accord with the IMF, the Aquino government agreed to liberalize import controls and to eliminate quantitative barriers on 1,232 products by the end of 1986. The target was accomplished for all but 303 products, of which 180 were intermediate and capital goods. Agreement was reached to extend the deadline until May 1988 on those products. The liberalizing impact was reduced in some cases, however, by tariffs being erected as quantitative controls came down.

A tariff revision scheme was put forth again in June 1990 by Secretary of Finance Jesus Estanislao. After an intracabinet struggle, Aquino signed Executive Order 413 on July 19, 1990, implementing the policy. The tariff structure was to be simplified by reducing the number of rates to four, ranging from 3 percent to 30 percent. However, in August 1990, business groups successfully persuaded Aquino to delay the tariff reform package for six months.

Foreign Investment

Foreign participation in the Philippine economy was a controversial issue throughout much of the twentieth century. The 1935 Commonwealth Constitution contained several provisions limiting the areas of economic activity in which non-Filipinos could participate. Operation of public utilities, exploitation of natural resources, and ownership of public lands were limited to Filipinos or corporations controlled by Filipinos. Control of banking and credit was limited to Filipinos with the passage of the General Banking Act in 1948, and the Retail Nationalization Act of 1954 restricted ownership in retail trade to Filipinos. Except in specifically designated areas, foreigners could invest only through joint ventures with Filipino capitalists. Legal decisions altered the interpretation of various restrictive measures, as did Marcos decrees during the martial law era, but the basic restrictions remained and were reaffirmed in the 1987 constitution. Constraints on foreigners also were aimed at non-Filipino residents in the Philippines. The 1987 constitution, for example, includes a provision similar to one in the 1935 constitution defining as natural-born citizens only those individuals whose mother or father was a citizen. The Securities and Exchange Commission ruled in September 1990 that firms engaging in business in areas of the economy that had been at least partially nationalized could not employ non-Filipinos in management positions. Liberalization of rules limiting areas of foreign investment was being considered in the Philippine Congress in early 1991.

Despite legal restrictions, foreign investment has played a prominent role in Philippine economic development. In 1948 approximately 50 percent of the assets in manufacturing, commerce, and mining were foreign owned, as were 80 percent of electricity assets. By 1970, however, foreign ownership in manufacturing, commerce, and mining had declined to around 40 percent, and very little foreign investment remained in utilities. Incomplete data for the early 1980s indicated that foreigners controlled about 30 percent of the assets of the 1,000 largest corporations operating in the Philippines at that time. Central Bank statistics, reporting inflows without taking divestments into account, showed foreign investment inflows between 1970 and 1988 totaling US$2.9 billion. Half went to manufacturing, of which chemicals and food were the most important industries; 24 percent was invested in petroleum refining; and 12 percent was in banking and other financial institutions (see table 14).

United States corporations have been the largest foreign investors in the Philippines. Because of the colonial relationship between the United States and the Philippines, as well as a post-independence agreement protecting United States business interests, United States citizens were not bound by Philippine citizenship restrictions with respect to foreign investment until 1974. A government survey showed that 80 percent of foreign investment in 900 of the 1,000 largest firms in 1970 was American. In the late 1980s, the United States remained the largest foreign investor, but its dominant position had been eroded. According to Central Bank statistics, United States investment between 1970 and 1988 totaled US$1.6 billion, more than one-half the total of foreign-owned equity in the country (see table 15). Japan was second with US$396 million, almost 14 percent. The Central Bank reports for 1989 showed registration of US$310 million in foreign investment. The United States had the largest investment with US$68.8 million, followed by Japan with US$51.9 million. Also important were Hong Kong with US$16.9 million, the Netherlands with US$15.8 million, and Taiwan with US$14.7 million.

Table 14. Foreign Investment by Industry, 1970-88 (in millions of United States dollars)

Industry	Value	Percentage
Financial institutions		
Banks	224	7.7
Other	133	4.65
Total financial institutions	357	12.3
Manufacturing		
Chemicals and chemical products	394	13.6
Food	289	10.1
Basic metal products	169	5.8
Textiles	63	2.25
Transportation equipment	108	3.7
Petroleum and coal	82	2.8
Metal products except machinery	34	1.2
Other	262	8.9
Total manufacturing	1,401	48.3
Mining		
Petroleum and gas	697	24.05
Other	85	3.05
Total mining	782	27.0
Commerce	125	4.3
Services	129	4.5
Other	107	3.6
TOTAL	2,901	100.0

Source: Based on information from Central Bank of the Philippines, unpublished data.

Table 15. Foreign Investment by Country, 1970-88 (in millions of United States dollars)

Country	Value	Percentage
United States	1,649	56.9
Japan	396	13.7
Hong Kong	190	6.5
Netherlands	131	4.5
United Kingdom	103	3.5
Other	432	14.9
TOTAL	2,901	100.0

Source: Based on information from Central Bank of the Philippines, unpublished data.

Although foreign investors were forbidden by the Philippine constitution to either own or lease public agricultural lands, there were 124 transnational agribusiness firms operating in the Philippines in 1985, of which 58 were directly engaged in the cultivation of cash crops on the southern island of Mindanao. As early as the 1920s, Del Monte Corporation had established a pineapple plantation in Bukidnon in northern Mindanao. B.F. Goodrich and Goodyear Tire Corporation came in the 1950s, and Castle and Cooke entered in the 1960s, setting up a pineapple plantation in South Cotabato Province. The Philippine government facilitated investment of foreign enterprises in plantations through the government-owned National Development Corporation, which acquired land and leased it to the investors. Foreign-owned firms also were able to get around leasing prohibitions by entering into growers' agreements with landowners and subsequently changing the agreement to allow direct cultivation of the land. Such arrangements have generated considerable controversy.

In the late 1980s, pineapples were cultivated directly by Del Monte and the Castle and Cooke subsidiary, Dole Philippines. Together their plantations comprised 21,400 hectares in 1987. These two transnational corporations, along with a third, United Brands, also produced bananas, almost exclusively for sale in Japan. Production arrangements in the banana industry were more complicated than those in the pineapple industry, involving contract production-marketing arrangements with domestic agribusinesses and small growers, as well as direct cultivation. The three transnational corporations each controlled directly or through contract arrangements about 5,000 hectares of land planted in bananas in the late 1980s. In 1988 exports of bananas totaled US$146 million, and those of canned pineapples US$83 million.

External Debt

On October 17, 1983, it was announced that the Philippines was unable to meet debt-service obligations on its foreign-currency debt of US$24.4 billion and was asking for a ninety-day moratorium on its payments. Subsequent requests were made for moratorium extensions. The action was the climax of an increasingly difficult balance of payments situation. Philippine development during the decade of the 1970s had been facilitated by extensive borrowing on the international capital market. Between 1973 and 1982, the country's indebtedness increased an average of 27 percent per year. Although government-to-government loans and loans from multilateral institutions such as the World Bank and Asian Development Bank were granted at lower-than-market rates of interest, the debt-service charges on those and commercial loans continued to mount. In 1982 payments were US$3.5 billion, approximately the level of foreign borrowing that year and greater than the country's total debt in 1970. The next year, 1983, interest payments exceeded the net inflow of capital by about US$1.85 billion. In combination with the downturn in the world economy, increasing interest rates, a domestic financial scandal that occurred when a businessman fled the country with debts estimated at P700 million, escalating unrest at the excesses of the Marcos regime, and the political crisis that followed the Aquino assassination, the debt burden became unsustainable (see table 16).

The Philippines had turned to the IMF previously in 1962 and 1970 when it had run into balance of payments difficulties. It did so again in late 1982. An agreement was reached in February 1983 for an emergency loan, followed by other loans from the World Bank and transnational commercial banks. Negotiations began again almost immediately after the moratorium declaration between Philippine monetary officials and the IMF. The situation became complicated when it came to light that the Philippines had understated its debt by some US$7 billion to US$8 billion, overstated its foreign-exchange reserves by approximately US$1 billion, and contravened its February 1983 agreement with the IMF by allowing a rapid increase in the money supply. A new standby arrangement was finally reached with the IMF in December 1984, more than a year after the declaration of the moratorium. In the meantime, additional external funds became nearly impossible to obtain.

Table 16. External Debt, 1982- 90

Year	Outstanding Debt[1]	Debt Service[1]	Ratio of Debt to GNP[2]	Ratio of Debt Service to Exports[3]
1982	24.54	3.50	62.5	42.5
1983	24.36	3.02	71.5	36.3
1984	24.38	2.30	77.2	33.4
1985	26.92	2.57	83.5	32.0
1986	28.37	3.04	94.1	34.5
1987	30.03	3.61	87.8	38.5
1988	29.16	3.48	74.8	31.5
1989	28.92	3.38	65.2	26.3
1990	26.97[4]	2.35	57.9	n.a.

n.a.--not available.
[1]In billions of United States dollars.
[2]In percentages; GNP--gross national product.
[3]In percentages.
[4]As of June.

In each of these arrangements with the IMF, the Philippines agreed to certain conditions to obtain additional funding, generally including devaluation of the peso, liberalization of import restraints, and tightening of domestic credit (limiting the growth of the money supply and raising interest rates). The adjustment measures demanded by the IMF in the December 1984 agreement were harsh, and the economy reacted severely. Because of its financial straits, however, the government saw no option but to comply. Balance of payments targets were met for the following year, and the current account turned positive in FY (fiscal year-- see Glossary) 1986, the first time in more than a decade. But there was a cost; interest rates rose to as high as 40 percent, and real GNP declined 11 percent over 1984 and 1985. The dire economic situation contributed to Aquino's victory in the February 1986 presidential election.

When Marcos fled to the United States later that month, the Philippine external debt had grown to over US$27 billion. The country's most immediate concern was with meeting debt-service payments. Reduction in the size of the debt was a longer term issue. Debt servicing, US$3 billion in 1986, was a drain on both the country's foreign-exchange earnings and its investible surplus. Technocrats in the National Economic and Development Authority recommended declaring another moratorium, this time for two years, to allow the country a breathing space. Measures were introduced in Congress in 1986 and subsequent years to cap annual debt-service payments. The Aquino administration and the Central Bank, however, consistently resisted both tactics, opting instead for a cooperative approach with the country's creditors.

Some of the government and government-guaranteed debt was incurred under questionable circumstances, and there were persistent demands for repudiation of those loans that could be shown to be fraudulent. In November 1990, the Freedom from Debt Coalition, a non-governmental organization, presented findings from its investigation on six potentially fraudulent loans, together worth between US$4 billion and US$6 billion. The largest, a US$2.5 billion loan for the construction of the Bataan Nuclear Power Plant, involved allegations of irregularities in bidding procedures and design, overpricing, and kickbacks. The

Aquino government previously had filed a civil suit in the United States against Westinghouse Corporation, the corporation with which the Marcos government had contracted to build the nuclear power plant, but the Philippines continued to pay interest payments on the nuclear plant loans of US$300,000 per day while the case was under litigation. In response to the coalition's findings, however, the president said that the country would not pay fraudulent loans, a statement interpreted as a major policy change.

Government negotiators dealt mainly with three groups of creditors in their efforts to reduce the burden of debt servicing. The first, and in some ways the most important, was the IMF, because its imprimatur was considered necessary to conclude arrangements with other creditors. The second was the Paris Club, an informal organization of official creditors. The third group was the commercial bank creditors, numbering 330 as of 1990. Bank negotiations generally were with the twelve-member bank advisory committee, chaired by Manufacturers Hanover Trust.

The standby agreement that the Marcos government had negotiated with the IMF in 1985 was discontinued shortly after Aquino assumed office. The agreed-upon targets with respect to government spending and increases in the money supply had been wildly exceeded as Marcos dipped into government coffers in a desperate effort to win the 1986 election. In addition, the government wished to negotiate a more growth-oriented arrangement. An agreement on repayment terms for US$506 million of loans was concluded eight months later in October 1986. In January 1987, an agreement was reached with the Paris Club to stretch out over ten years, with a five-year grace period, US$870 million of loans that were to have been paid in 1987 and the first half of 1988. The IMF accord also triggered the release of US$350 million in new loans by commercial bank creditors that had been held up when the agreement with the IMF broke down in early 1986. In March 1987, the Philippines and the twelve-bank advisory committee came to terms on the rescheduling of the country's US$13.2 million debt to private banks and a reduction in the rate of interest. Signing of the agreement was delayed, however, by a group of creditor banks led by Barclays Bank of Britain, who demanded that the Philippine government guarantee the US$57 million debt of a private fertilizer firm, Planters Products, Inc. An accommodation was not reached until December 1987.

A second round of negotiations began in 1989. The Paris Club restructured US$2.2 million of debt coming due between September 1988 and June 1990. The IMF and commercial bank agreements allowed the Philippines to undertake, in early 1990, a three-pronged program under Brady Plan (see Glossary) guidelines. First, the government used funds from the World Bank, IMF, and other sources to repurchase US$1.31 billion of government debt from private banks at the 50 percent discount at which they were selling on the secondary market, which action reduced the country's debt by some US$650,000, and, in the process, the number of creditor banks fell from 483 to 330. Second, debt coming due between 1990 and 1994 was rescheduled. Last, some eighty banks subscribed to US$700 million in new loans.

In July 1990, it was reported that the IMF had reviewed Philippine economic performance and found it "favorable" for the period between October 1989, when the loan agreement was reached, and March 1990. By September, however, the situation had turned around. Agreed-upon targets had not been met with respect to the sizes of the government budgetary deficit, the trade balance, or the country's international reserves. As a consequence, the IMF had refused to release the September tranche (installment of funds) to the

Philippines. In turn, Manila canceled the 1989 standby agreement and reopened negotiations with the IMF. A new agreement was announced in early 1991. It involved a three-year credit package, totaling US$375 million, only one-third of the US$1.17 billion loan package suspended the previous September. Among other things, the agreement required the Philippines to implement new revenue-raising measures by the end of August 1991.

As a consequence of the country's failure to meet the September standby agreement targets, the commercial banks in February 1991 refused to disburse the last US$115 million of the US$706 million credit line agreed to in early 1990. At a meeting with Filipino officials, the bank advisory committee also declined to discuss providing some US$500 million in new funds. In February 1991, the Philippine government also said that it would ask the Paris Club for deferment of payment on US$1 billion in debts falling due from June 30, 1991 to July 31, 1992. In a measure to reduce the risk of lending to the government by commercial banks, in February 1991 the Philippines indicated that it would approach multilateral financial institutions such as the World Bank and the Asian Development Bank for cofinancing, in return for which the Philippine government would give up the possibility of rescheduling.

Efforts to reduce the external debt included encouraging direct investment in the economy. In August 1986, the Philippines initiated a debt-equity conversion program, which allowed potential investors who could acquire Philippine debt instruments to convert them into Philippine pesos for the purpose of investing in the Philippine economy. Because the value of the debt in the secondary market was substantially less than its face value (about half, at the time), the swap arrangement allowed investors to acquire pesos at a discount rate.

Most of the swapped debt was held by the Central Bank, which could provide the peso proceeds to retire the debt only through issuing new money, with obvious inflationary consequences. For this reason, the program was suspended in April 1988. At that time, US$917 million in debt reduction had taken place. Other issues were raised, however, about both the benefits to the Philippines and the fairness of the conversion program. Debt-equity swaps, it was argued, amounted to a considerable gain to investors, costing much less in dollars than was received in pesos. If an investment had taken place without the swap, a very large subsidy would not have been involved. Second, a considerable portion of the conversions appeared to have been by Filipinos bringing their wealth back into the country. Critics questioned whether those who engaged in capital flight should be awarded a premium for returning their wealth to the Philippines. There also was the question of the arbitrage possibilities of "round tripping," whereby investors with pesos engaged in capital flight to obtain foreign currency, which was used through the swap to achieve a much larger amount of pesos. Alternatively, an individual with dollars could engage in a swap and then convert pesos back into dollars through the exchange market. Although the government had some regulations concerning length of investment, the process was ripe for abuse. Nevertheless, the government resumed the program in December 1990 with an auction of US$7 million in debt paper. The new program was reported to have been altered to reduce inflationary pressures.

In March 1991, Philippine officials raised the issue of "condonation," or debt forgiveness, of Philippine debt with United States officials, requesting that the United States accord the Philippines similar treatment to that accorded Egypt and Poland. The United States resisted the entreaty, pointing out that whereas US$33 billion of Poland's US$48 billion debt was official, all but 20 percent of the Philippine debt was owed to commercial banks.

The Aquino administration spent an enormous amount of time and effort negotiating with various creditor groups to lower interest rates, reschedule the country's debt, and reduce the magnitude of the debt. A number of innovative schemes were undertaken; more were discussed. It was a process, however, that essentially meant running fast to stay in place. The size of the country's external debt in June 1990, US$26.97 billion, was about the same as the US$26.92 billion the country owed at the end of 1985, shortly before Aquino took office. Debt-service payments also changed very little: US$2.57 billion in 1985 as opposed to US$2.35 billion in 1990. The balance of payments pressures remained. The growth of the Philippine economy, however, caused the ratio of the country's debt to GNP to decline from 83.5 in 1985 to 65.2 in 1989, whereas that of debt service to exports fell from 32.0 to 26.3 over the same period. Projected debt servicing in September 1990 for the 1990s showed a rise from US$2.35 billion in 1990 to US$3.25 billion in 1995, falling off to US$2.08 billion in 1999.

Development Assistance

Official development assistance (ODA) includes grants and loans at concessional rates from official donors, both bilateral (individual country) and multilateral (e.g., the World Bank and the Asian Development Bank). In the early independence period, 90 percent of aid was bilateral grant aid, almost entirely from the United States. By the 1960s, however, there was growing assistance from multilateral organizations and Japan, 85 to 90 percent of which was in the form of loans (see table 17). During the 1970s and 1980s, concessionary loans became the dominant mode of assistance from all sources, averaging in excess of 80 percent of the total (see table 18).

**Table 17. Official Development Assistance by Source and Country,
1952-72 and 1978-88 (in millions of United States dollars)**

Source and Country	Grants	Loans	Total
1952-72			
Bilateral			
United States*	541	50	591
Japan	8	78	86
Other	14	11	25
Total bilateral	563	139	702
Multilateral	59	343	402
TOTAL	622	482	1,104
1978-88			
Bilateral			
United States	1,439	361	1,800
Japan	449	3,070	3,519
Other	448	590	1,038
Total bilateral	2,336	4,021	6,357
Multilateral	292	6,497	6,789
TOTAL	2,628	10,518	13,146

*Includes US$48 million from the Asia, Ford, and Rockefeller foundations.
Source: Based on information from Mila Bulan, "A Study of Official Development Assistance to the Philippines FY 1952-72," *Philippine Economic Journal* [Manila], 8, No. 3, 267; Rigoberto Tiglao, "Manna for Manila," *Far Eastern Economic Review* [Hong Kong], 151, No. 10, March 7, 1991, 53; and Central Bank of the Philippines, unpublished data.

Table 18. Official Development Assistance by Source and Type,
Selected Years, 1952-90 (in millions of United States dollars)

Year	Source Bilateral	Multilateral	Grants	Loans	Total
1952-61	238	28	228	38	266
1962-72	464	374	394	444	838
1978-85	3,060	4,930	1,169	6,821	7,990
1988	1,385	955	416	1,924	2,340
1989	1,445	1,389	745	2,089	2,834
1990	1,360	1,334	444	2,250	2,694

Source: Based on information from Mila Bulan, "A Study of Official Development Assistance to the Philippines FY 1952-72," *Philippine Economic Journal* [Manila], 8, No. 3, 267; Rigoberto Tiglao, "Manna for Manila," *Far Eastern Economic Review* [Hong Kong], 151, No. 10, March 7, 1991, 53; and Central Bank of the Philippines, unpublished data.

Following Aquino's accession to the presidency in 1986, ODA increased, primarily from the United States, Japan, the World Bank, and the Asian Development Bank. In the first three years of the Aquino government, 1986 to 1988, concessionary loan commitments increased 60 percent above the last three years of the Marcos regime, 1983-85, from an average of US$764 million to US$1,233 million per year. Grant-aid commitments increased even more, jumping 150 percent from an average of US$195 million to an average of US$486 million.

In November 1987, a bipartisan group of four members of the United States Congress proposed a major multinational aid initiative--a "mini Marshall Plan"--to help the Philippines address the manifold economic problems that were the legacy of the Marcos regime, support economic reform in that country, and help ensure the return of the Philippines to democracy. The initial proposal suggested US$5 billion in additional aid over a five-year period, along with a substantial increase in private foreign investment. By the time the program was announced, the goal of the Multilateral Aid Initiative had risen to $10 billion, mainly, but not always, divided equally between ODA and private investment.

At the request of Japan, the Multilateral Aid Initiative-- also referred to as the Philippine Assistance Plan--was set up under the Consultative Group, a group of international agencies and countries established in 1971 at the request of the Marcos government to coordinate assistance programs to the Philippines and chaired by the World Bank. The Multilateral Aid Initiative was clearly meant to precipitate a substantially larger flow of aid than had been committed to the Philippines in the two years since Marcos had fled the country.

The first Multilateral Aid Initiative pledging session, held in Tokyo, July 3-5, 1989, resulted in aid commitments of US$2.8 billion, plus US$600 million in debt relief by the Japanese. In the Philippines, the extent of "additional" aid was cast as a measure of international support for the Aquino regime. The country had received official development assistance commitments of about US$2.4 billion in 1988. Given that figure and estimates of the size of aid projects that were then under discussion between the Philippines and potential donors, estimates of new funds generated at the Tokyo pledge session ranged from US$250 million to US$1.5 billion to the full US$3.4 billion. The government, accordingly, received criticisms or plaudits as one judged the extent of success in generating new funds.

In 1990 there was no pledging session, reportedly because of the suspension of the IMF agreement in March 1990. A second session was held in Hong Kong on February 25 and 26, 1991, with a total of US$3.3 billion pledged. The Philippine government reported that by the end of 1990, the full amount pledged at the Tokyo session had been committed; however, actual disbursements were only US$839 million. Donor government representatives at the Hong Kong session expressed support publicly for the enactment of economic policies that Aquino advisers had worked out with the IMF, as well as concern over the resistance of the Philippine Congress to their implementation. The size of pledges and the willingness to comment on internal Philippine policy issues indicated that the donor nations hoped that the Philippines would be able to undertake a viable economic program but were concerned that it would be unable to do so.

Political Economy of United States Military Bases

In early 1991, the Philippine government was in ongoing negotiations with the United States on the future status of United States naval and air facilities at Subic Bay and Clark Air Base (see Relations With the United States; Foreign Military Relations). What would normally be an issue of foreign policy and national security became a major domestic political issue and took on an economic dimension of considerable importance. At the domestic level, the conflict was between those who argued that the continuing presence of the United States bases was an infringement on Philippine sovereignty and a continuation of a neocolonial relationship and those who, for a combination of internal security, foreign relations, and economic reasons, saw the need for maintaining the presence of the bases. President Aquino, through 1990, refused to publicly commit herself to a position; however, it was clear that her government was working to reach accommodation with the United States. As negotiations progressed, the economic issue became prominent.

There were three economic considerations from the point of view of the Philippine government. First, the proportion of the Philippine budget allocated for its armed forces was the smallest in the region, a fact linked to the presence of United States air and naval forces in the Philippines, as well as direct military assistance. Second, in the latter half of the 1980s, the bases directly employed between 42,000 and 68,000 Filipinos and contracted for goods and services from Filipino businesses. During this period, yearly base purchases of goods and services in the Philippine economy (when corrected for the estimated import content of the goods purchased) was in the range of P6.0 billion to P8.3 billion.

A third and politically very important consideration, was the sum given to the Philippines by the United States in connection with the presence of the bases, referred to as aid by United States officials and as rent by the Filipinos. Base-related payments were first agreed to in 1979 when United States president Jimmy Carter made a "best effort" pledge to secure US$500 million for the Philippines from the United States Congress over a five-year period. In 1983 another five-year commitment was made, this time for US$900 million. In October 1988, the Philippines' Secretary of Foreign Affairs Raul Manglapus and United States' Secretary of State George Schultz signed a two-year agreement for US$962 million, an amount double the previous compensation but substantially less than the US$2.4 billion that the Philippines initially demanded. In 1991 talks over the future of the bases and the size and terms of the aid or rent that would be given in consideration for continued United States access to military facilities in the Philippines was the most important unresolved issue. The decision of the Philippine administration to bring Secretary of Finance Jesus Estanislao into the negotiations in March 1991 was a further indication of the economic importance of the bases to the Philippine government.

* * *

Vicente B. Valdepeñas, Jr. and Gemelino M. Bautista's *The Emergence of the Philippine Economy* is a concise history of the Philippine economy from the pre-Hispanic period until the 1960s, and Frank H. Golay's *The Philippines* is an excellent overview of the 1945-59 period. Romeo M. Bautista, John H. Power, and others offer a major critique of Philippine industrialization policy and an argument for liberalizing the economy in *Industrial Promotion Policies in the Philippines*. The argument in favor of continued protectionism is put forth in Alejandro Lichauco's *Nationalist Economics*, and Alichir Ishii's *National Development Policies and the Business Sector in the Philippines* explores several aspects of the interaction between the business sector and the government. Yujiro Hayami, Ma. Agnes R. Quisumbing, and Lourdes S. Adriano's *Toward an Alternative Land Reform Paradigm* reviews the history of land reform and current reform efforts, and suggests an alternative policy. The monopolization and control of export agriculture industries during the martial law period is examined by Gary Hawes in *The Philippine State and the Marcos Regime*. Elias T. Ramos's *Dualistic Unionism and Industrial Relations* has the only extensive discussion of the development of unions in the Philippines.

An Analysis of the Philippine Economic Crisis, a collective work of University of the Philippines economists edited by Emmanuel S. De Dios, provides insight into the 1983 economic crisis. Walden Bello, David Kinley, and Elaine Elinson's *Development Debacle* and Robin Broad's *Unequal Alliance* criticize World Bank activities in the Philippines. The Philippine Institute for Development Studies has produced a number of studies of specific aspects of the economy. Its *Survey of Philippine Development Research* series contains articles that survey research on specific areas of the economy. Specialized studies include Rosa Linda P. Tidalgo and Emmanuel F. Esguerra's *Philippine Employment in the Seventies*, and James K. Boyce's *The Political Economy of External Indebtedness*, which examines the extent of capital flight from the Philippines.

A Guide to Philippine Economic and Business Information Sources, edited by David G. Timberman, provides a good bibliography of newsletters, government documents, and other material of interest to Philippines businesses. (For further information and complete citations, see Bibliography).

GOVERNMENT AND POLITICS

As President Corazon C. Aquino entered the final year of her six-year term in 1991, she presided over a demoralized nation reeling from the effects of natural calamities and economic malaise. The country had slid into dictatorship and gross economic mismanagement during Ferdinand E. Marcos's twenty-year presidency. When Aquino was elevated to the presidency in an inspiring People's Power Revolution in 1986, Filipinos' hopes rose. Inevitably, the stark realities of the nation's economic and political predicaments tarnished Aquino's image.

Aquino's achievements, however, were significant. She helped topple a dictator who had unlimited reserves of wealth, force, and cunning. She replaced a disjointed constitution that was little more than a fig leaf for Marcos's personalistic rule with a democratic, progressive document that won overwhelming popular approval in a nationwide plebiscite. She renounced the dictatorial powers she inherited from Marcos and returned the Philippines to the rule of law; she lived with the checks on her own power inherent in three-branch government; and she scheduled national elections to create a two-chamber legislature and local elections to complete the country's redemocratization.

The 1987 constitution returned the Philippines to a presidential system. The national government is in theory highly centralized, with few powers devolving to provincial and municipal governments. In fact, local potentates often reserve powers to themselves that the national government is not even aware of. The national government consists of three branches: the executive, headed by the president; two houses of Congress, the Senate and the House of Representatives; and the Supreme Court, which heads an independent judiciary. A bill of rights guarantees political freedoms, and the constitution provides for regular elections.

The performance of these institutions was, of course, conditioned by Philippine history and culture, and by poverty. For example, the twenty-four members of the Senate, elected by nationwide ballot, in the 1980s were drawn almost entirely from old, prominent families. Senators staked out liberal, nationalist positions on symbolic issues, such as military base rights for the United States, but were exceedingly cautious about any structural changes, such as land reform, that could jeopardize their families' economic positions.

Political parties grew in profusion after the Marcos martial law regime (1972-81) was ended. There were 105 political parties registered in 1988. As in the pre-Marcos era, most legal political parties were coalitions, built around prominent individuals, which focused entirely on winning elections, not on what to do with the power achieved. There was little to distinguish one party from another ideologically, which was why many Filipinos regarded the political system as irrelevant.

President Aquino's early years in office were punctuated by a series of coup attempts. Her greatest frustration, and a most serious impediment to economic development, was a fractious, politicized army. Some officers wanted to regain the privileges they enjoyed under Marcos; others dreamed of saving the nation (see Proclamation 1081 and Martial Law; Political Role). Although all coup attempts failed, they frightened away foreign investors, forced Aquino to fire cabinet members of whom the army did not approve, pushed her policies rightward, and lent an air of impermanence to her achievements.

Criticism of the Aquino administration came from all parts of the political spectrum. Filipino communists refused to participate in a government they saw as a thin cover for oligarchy. The democratic left criticized Aquino for abandoning sweeping reform and for her pro-business and pro-American policies. Her own vice president, Salvador H. Laurel, castigated her mercilessly from the beginning and even encouraged the army to overthrow her. The far right (sugar barons, military malcontents, and ex-Marcos cronies) characterized her as naive and ineffective and ridiculed her for being what she always said she was, a "simple housewife." In reality she was far more than that. Amidst this cacophony, Aquino seemed to have calmly accepted that she would not be able to resolve the Philippines' deeply rooted structural problems and that it would be enough to have restored political democracy. She prepared the ground for her successor.

The Roman Catholic Church also was a major political factor. It had reverted to a less visible (but no less influential) role than in the declining years of Marcos's rule, when its relative invulnerability to harassment spurred priests and nuns to become political activists. Most church leaders criticized human rights abuses by military units or vigilantes, but they supported constitutional government. Cardinal Jaime Sin, who played such a pivotal role in Aquino's triumph over Marcos, recognized her personal virtue but denounced the corruption that stained her administration. Some parish priests, disgusted by the country's extreme polarization of wealth and power, cooperated with the New People's Army (see The Communist Insurgency).

The communist insurgency had not been eradicated, although guerrillas posed less of a threat than they did before 1986. They conducted murderous internal purges. Still, if a guerrilla army wins by not losing, the New People's Army was a real alternative to the elected government. It fought for more than twenty years, and the class inequities it condemned continued to grow in the early 1990s. The fight against Filipino Muslim separatists in Mindanao likewise continued, also at a diminished level.

Philippine foreign relations in the late 1980s and early 1990s were colored by the contradiction between subjective nationalism and objective dependency. After nearly fifty years of independence, Filipinos still viewed their national identity as undefined and saw international respect as elusive. They chafed at perceived constraints on their sovereign prerogatives and resented the power of foreign business owners and military advisers. Yet, as a poor nation deeply in debt to private banks, multilateral lending institutions, and foreign governments, the Philippines had to meet conditions imposed by its creditors. This situation was galling to nationalists, especially because the previous regime had squandered its borrowed money. Filipinos also sought to achieve a more balanced foreign policy to replace the uncomfortably close economic, cultural, military, and personal ties that bound them to the United States, but this was unlikely to happen soon.

Government Structure

In 1991 the government was led by President Corazon C. Aquino, who was head of state, chief executive, and commander in chief of the armed forces. The vice president, who under the Philippine Constitution need not belong to the same party as the president, was Salvador H. Laurel. Aquino did not seek to create a political party to perpetuate her rule, preferring instead to rely on her personal popularity, which initially was strong but diminished throughout her term.

Constitutional Framework
The Philippines has a long history of democratic constitutional development. The Malolos Constitution of 1898-99 reflected the aspirations of educated Filipinos to create a polity as enlightened as any in the world (see The Malolos Constitution and the Treaty of Paris). That first constitution was modeled on those of France, Belgium, and some of the South American republics. Powers were divided, but the legislature was supreme. A bill of rights guaranteed individual liberties. The church was separated from the state, but this provision was included only after a long debate and passed only by a single vote. The Malolos Constitution was in effect only briefly; United States troops soon installed a colonial

government, which remained in effect until the establishment of the Philippine Commonwealth in 1935 (see Commonwealth Politics, 1935-41).

The 1935 constitution, drawn up under the terms of the Tydings-McDuffie Act, which created the Philippine Commonwealth, also served as a basis for an independent Philippine government from 1946 until 1973 (see Independence and Constitutional Government, 1945-72). The framers of the Commonwealth Constitution were not completely free to choose any type of government they wanted, since their work had to be approved by United States president Franklin D. Roosevelt, but as many were legal scholars familiar with American constitutional law, they produced a document strongly modeled on the United States Constitution. In fact, the 1935 constitution differed from the United States document in only two important respects: Government was unitary rather than federal, local governments being subject to general supervision by the president, and the president could declare an emergency and temporarily exercise near-dictatorial power. This latter provision was used by Marcos after September 1972, when he declared martial law.

The 1935 constitution seemed to serve the nation well. It gave the Philippines twenty-six years of stable, constitutional government during a period when a number of other Asian states were succumbing to military dictatorship or communist revolution. By the late 1960s, however, many Filipinos came to believe that the constitution only provided a democratic political cloak for a profoundly oligarchic society. A constitutional convention was called to rewrite the basic law of the land.

The delegates selected to rewrite the constitution hoped to retain its democratic essence while deleting parts deemed to be unsuitable relics of the colonial past. They hoped to produce a genuinely Filipino document. But before their work could be completed, Marcos declared martial law and manipulated the constitutional convention to serve his purposes. The 1973 constitution was a deviation from the Philippines' commitment to democratic ideals. Marcos abolished Congress and ruled by presidential decree from September 1972 until 1978, when a parliamentary government with a legislature called the National Assembly replaced the presidential system. But Marcos exercised all the powers of president under the old system plus the powers of prime minister under the new system. When Marcos was driven from office in 1986, the 1973 constitution also was jettisoned.

After Aquino came to power, on March 25, 1986, she issued Presidential Proclamation No. 3, which promulgated an interim "Freedom Constitution" that gave Aquino sweeping powers theoretically even greater than those Marcos had enjoyed, although she promised to use her emergency powers only to restore democracy, not to perpetuate herself in power. She claimed that she needed a free hand to restore democracy, revive the economy, gain control of the military, and repatriate some of the national wealth that Marcos and his partners had purloined. Minister of Justice Neptali Gonzales described the Freedom Constitution as "civilian in character, revolutionary in origin, democratic in essence, and transitory in character." The Freedom Constitution was to remain in effect until a new legislature was convened and a constitutional convention could write a new, democratic constitution to be ratified by national plebiscite. The process took sixteen months.

Although many Filipinos thought delegates to the Constitutional Commission should be elected, Aquino appointed them, saying that the Philippines could not afford the time or expense of an election. On May 25, 1986, she selected forty-four names from hundreds suggested by her cabinet and the public. She appointed respected, prominent citizens and, to be on the safe side, prohibited them from running for office for one year after the constitution's ratification. Delegates had the same profile as those who had drawn up the constitutions of 1898 and 1935: they were wealthy and well educated. They represented a range of political stances: some were leftists and some were ardent nationalists, but moderate conservatives held a majority. There were thirty lawyers, including two former Supreme Court justices. A nun, a priest, and a bishop represented the interests of the Catholic Church. Eight commissioners had also served in the aborted constitutional convention of 1972. Five seats on the fifty-member commission were reserved for Marcos supporters, defined as members of Marcos's New Society Movement, and were filled by former Minister of Labor Blas Ople and four associates. One seat was reserved for the Iglesia ni Kristo (Church of Christ), which, however, declined to participate. One of Aquino's appointees, leftist movie producer Lino Brocka, resigned, so the final number of commissioners was forty-eight.

The commission divided itself into fourteen committees and began work amidst great public interest, which, however, soon waned. Long, legalistic hearings were sometimes poorly attended. Aquino is known to have intervened to influence only one decision of the commission. She voiced her support of a loophole in the constitution's antinuclear weapons provision that allowed the president to declare that nuclear weapons, if present on United States bases, were "in the national interest."

The commissioners quickly abandoned the parliamentary government that Marcos had fancied, and arguments for a unicameral legislature also were given short shrift. Most delegates favored a return to something very much like the 1935 constitution, with numerous symbolic clauses to appease "cause-oriented" groups. The most controversial proposals were those pertaining to the Philippine claim to Sabah, presidential emergency powers, land reform, the rights of labor, the role of foreign investment, and United States military base rights. Special attention focused on proposals to declare Philippine territory a nuclear-free zone.

Aquino had asked the Constitutional Commission to complete its work within ninety days, by September 2, 1986. Lengthy public hearings (some in the provinces) and contentious floor debates, however, caused this deadline to be missed. The final version of the Constitution, similar to a "draft proposal" drawn up in June by the University of the Philippines Law School, was presented to Aquino on October 15. The commission had approved it by a vote of forty-four to two.

The constitution, one of the longest in the world, establishes three separate branches of government called departments: executive, legislative, and judicial. A number of independent commissions are mandated: the Commission on Elections and the Commission on Audit are continued from the old constitution, and two others, the Commission on Human Rights and the Commission on Good Government, were formed in reaction to Marcos's abuses. The Commission on Good Government is charged with the task of repossessing ill-gotten wealth acquired during the Marcos regime.

Some ambitious Filipino politicians hoped that the new Constitution would invalidate the 1986 presidential election and require that a new election be held. Their hopes were dashed by the "transitory provisions" in Article 17 of the new constitution that confirmed Aquino in office until June 30, 1992. Other officials first elected under the new constitution also were to serve until 1992.

Article 3, the bill of rights, contains the same rights found in the United States Constitution (often in identical wording), as well as some additional rights. The exclusionary rule, for example, prohibits illegally gathered evidence from being used at a trial. Other rights include a freedom-of-information clause, the right to form unions, and the requirement that suspects be informed of their right to remain silent.

The church and state are separated, but Catholic influence can be seen in parts of the Constitution. An article on the family downplays birth control; another clause directs the state to protect the life of the unborn beginning with conception; and still another clause abolishes the death penalty. Church-owned land also is tax-exempt.

The explosive issue of agrarian reform is treated gingerly. The state is explicitly directed to undertake the redistribution of land to those who till it, but "just compensation" must be paid to present owners, and Congress (expected to be dominated by landowners) is given the power to prescribe limits on the amount of land that can be retained. To resolve the controversial issue of United States military bases, the Constitution requires that any future agreement must be in the form of a treaty that is ratified by two-thirds of the Senate and, if the Congress requires, ratified by a majority of the votes cast in a national referendum.

Many provisions lend a progressive spirit to the Constitution, but these provisions are symbolic declarations of the framers' hopes and are unenforceable. For example, the state is to make decent housing available to underprivileged citizens. Priority is to be given to the sick, elderly, disabled, women, and children. Wealth and political power are to be diffused for the common good. The state shall maintain honesty and integrity in the public service. To be implemented, all of these declarations of intent required legislation.

Aquino scheduled a plebiscite on the new constitution for February 2, 1987. Ratification of the constitution was supported by a loose coalition of centrist parties and by the Catholic Church. The constitution was opposed by both the Communist Party of the Philippines-- Marxist Leninist (referred to as the CPP) and the leftist May First Movement (Kilusang Mayo Uno) for three reasons: It was tepid on land reform, it did not absolutely ban nuclear weapons from Philippine territory, and it offered incentives to foreign investors. But the communists were in disarray after their colossal mistake of boycotting the election that overthrew Marcos, and their objections carried little weight. The constitution faced more serious opposition from the right, led by President Aquino's discontented, now ex-defense minister, Juan Ponce Enrile, who reassembled elements of the old Nacionalista Party to campaign for a no vote to protest what he called the "Aquino dictatorship."

Aquino toured the country campaigning for a yes vote, trading heavily on her enormous personal prestige. The referendum was judged by most observers to turn more on Aquino's popularity than on the actual merits of the Constitution, which few people had read. Her slogan was "Yes to Cory, Yes to Country, Yes to Democracy, and Yes to the Constitution." Aquino also showed that she was familiar with traditional Filipino pork-barrel politics, promising voters in Bicol 1,061 new classrooms "as a sign of my gratitude" if they voted yes.

The plebiscite was fairly conducted and orderly. An overwhelming three-to-one vote approved of the Constitution, confirmed Aquino in office until 1992, and dealt a stunning defeat to her critics. Above all else the victory indicated a vote for stability in the midst of turmoil. There was only one ominous note--a majority of the military voted against the referendum. Aquino proclaimed the new Constitution in effect on February 11, 1987, and made all members of the military swear loyalty to it.

National Government
Under the Constitution, the government is divided into executive, legislative, and judicial departments. The separation of powers is based on the theory of checks and balances. The

presidency is not as strong as it was under the 1973 constitution. Local governments are subordinated to the national government.

Executive Department

Article 6 of the 1987 Constitution restores the presidential system with certain modifications. The president is elected by a direct vote of the people for a term of six years and is not eligible for reelection. The president must be a natural-born citizen of the Philippines, at least forty years of age, and a resident of the Philippines for at least ten years immediately preceding the election.

The president is empowered to control all the executive departments, bureaus, and offices, and to ensure that the laws are faithfully executed. Presidential nominations of heads of executive departments and ambassadors are confirmed by a Commission on Appointments, consisting of twelve senators and twelve representatives. The president may grant amnesty (for example, to former communists, Muslim rebels, or military mutineers) with the concurrence of a majority of all the members of Congress and, as chief diplomat, negotiate treaties, which must be ratified by two-thirds of the Senate.

The constitution contains many clauses intended to preclude repetition of abuses such as those committed by Marcos. The president's spouse cannot be appointed to any government post (a reaction to Imelda Marcos's immoderate accumulation of titles and powers). The public must be informed if the president becomes seriously ill (a reaction to the belated discovery of numerous kidney-dialysis machines in Marcos's bedroom in Malacañang). The president is prohibited from owning any company that does business with the government. And the armed forces must be recruited proportionately from all provinces and cities as far as is practicable, in order to prevent a future president from repeating Marcos's ploy of padding the officer corps with people from his home province.

Constitutional safeguards also prevent the president from ruling indefinitely under emergency powers. Martial law may be proclaimed, but only for sixty days. The president must notify Congress of the institution of martial law within forty-eight hours, and Congress can revoke martial law by a simple majority vote. The president may not abolish Congress. The Supreme Court may review and invalidate a presidential proclamation of martial law. Of course, Congress can grant the president emergency powers at any time.

The vice president has the same term of office as the president and is elected in the same manner. The vice president also may serve as a member of the cabinet. No vice president may serve for more than two successive terms. The president and vice president are not elected as a team. Thus, they may be ideologically opposed, or even personal rivals.

In 1991 the president's cabinet consisted of the executive secretary (who controlled the flow of paper and visitors reaching the president), the press secretary, the cabinet secretary, and the national security adviser, and the secretaries of the following departments: agrarian reform; agriculture; budget and management; economic planning; education, culture, and sports; environment and natural resources; finance; foreign affairs; health; interior and local governments; justice; labor and employment; national defense; public works and highways; science and technology; social welfare and development; tourism; trade and industry; and transportation and communications. Cabinet members directed a vast bureaucracy--2.6 million Filipinos were on the government payroll in 1988.

The bureaucracy in the late 1980s was overseen by a constitutionally independent Civil Service Commission, the members of which were appointed by the president to a single nonrenewable term of seven years. Because the Constitution prohibits defeated political candidates from becoming civil servants, bureaucratic positions cannot be used as consolation prizes.

Two problems, in particular, have plagued the civil service: corruption (especially in the Bureau of Customs and the Bureau of Internal Revenue) and the natural tendency, in the absence of a forceful chief executive, of cabinet secretaries to run their departments as independent fiefdoms. Bribes, payoffs, and shakedowns characterized Philippine government and society at all levels. The Philippine Chamber of Commerce and Industry estimated in 1988 that one-third of the annual national budget was lost to corruption. Corruption also occurred because of cultural values. The Filipino bureaucrat who did not help a friend or relative in need was regarded as lacking a sense of *utang na loob*, or repayment of debts (see Social Values and Organization). Many Filipinos recognize this old-fashioned value as being detrimental to economic development. A 1988 congressional study concluded that because of their "personalistic world view," Filipinos were "uncomfortable with bureaucracy, with rules and regulations, and with standard procedures, all of which tend to be impersonal." When faced with such rules they often "ignore them or ask for exceptions."

Legislative Department

The Philippines is unusual among developing countries in having a strong, bicameral legislature. The constitution establishes a 24-seat Senate and a House of Representatives with 200 elected representatives and up to 50 more appointed by the president. Senators are chosen at large, and the twenty-four highest vote-winners nationwide are elected. Senators must be native-born Filipinos at least thirty-five years old. The term of office is six years, and senators cannot serve more than two consecutive terms.

House of Representatives members are elected in single-member districts (200 in 1991), reapportioned within three years of each census. Representatives must be native-born Filipinos and at least twenty-five years of age. Their term of office is three years, except that those elected in May 1987 did not have to face the electorate until 1992. They may not serve for more than three consecutive terms. In addition, President Aquino was to be empowered to appoint to the House of Representatives up to twenty-five people from "party lists." This stipulation was intended to provide a kind of proportional representation for small parties unable to win any single-member district seats. However, Congress did not pass the necessary enabling legislation. The president also is allowed to appoint up to twenty-five members from so-called sectoral groups, such as women, labor, farmers, the urban poor, mountain tribes, and other groups not normally well-represented in Congress, "except the religious sector." Making these appointments would have provided an opportunity for Aquino to reward her supporters and influence Congress, but she has left most such positions unfilled. All members of both houses of Congress are required to make a full disclosure of their financial and business interests.

The constitution authorizes Congress to conduct inquiries, to declare war (by a two-thirds vote of both houses in joint session), and to override a presidential veto with a two-thirds vote of both houses. All appropriations bills must originate in the House, but the president is given a line-item veto over them. The Senate ratifies treaties by a two-thirds vote.

The first free congressional elections in nearly two decades were held on May 11, 1987. The pre-martial law Philippine Congress, famous for logrolling and satisfying individual demands, was shut down by Marcos in 1972. The 1973 constitution created a rubber-stamp parliament, or National Assembly, which only began functioning in 1978 and which was timid in confronting Marcos until some opposition members were elected in May 1984. In the 1987 elections, more than 26 million Filipinos, or 83 percent of eligible voters, cast their ballots at 104,000 polling stations. Twenty-three of twenty-four Aquino-endorsed Senate candidates won. The lone senator opposed to Aquino was former Minister of Defense Juan Ponce Enrile, her husband's former jailer and her one-time defender. Enrile was seated as the twenty-fourth and final member of the Senate, after the Supreme Court ordered the Commission on Elections to abandon plans for a recount. The new legislature was formally convened on July 27, 1987. The leader of the Senate is the Senate president, who stands next in the line of succession for the presidency after the country's vice president. Generally, the Senate had a reputation as a prestigious body with a truly national outlook, in contrast to the House of Representatives, which had more parochial concerns.

At least three-quarters of those elected to the House were endorsed by Aquino, but her influence was less than these results might seem to indicate. She never formed her own political party but merely endorsed men and women with various ideologies who, because of their illustrious family names and long political experience, were probably going to win anyway. Out of 200 elected House members, 169 either belonged to or were related to old-line political families. Philippine politics still was the art of assembling a winning coalition of clans.

Congress did not hesitate to challenge the president. For example, in September 1987, less than two months after the new Congress convened, it summoned the presidential executive secretary to testify about the conduct of his office. The following year, Congress also rejected Aquino's proposed administrative code, which would have conferred greater power on the secretary of national defense.

The internal operation of Congress has been slowed by inefficiency and a lack of party discipline. Legislation often has been detained in the forty-three House and thirty-six Senate committees staffed with friends and relatives of members of Congress. Indicative of the public frustration with Congress, in 1991 the National Movement for Free Elections (NAMFREL) and the Makati Business Club formed a group called Congresswatch to monitor the activities of sitting congress members and promote accountability and honesty.

Judicial Department

The legal system used in the early 1990s was derived for the most part from those of Spain and the United States. Civil code procedures on family and property and the absence of jury trial were attributable to Spanish influences, but most important statutes governing trade and commerce, labor relations, taxation, banking and currency, and governmental operations were of United States derivation, introduced at the beginning of the twentieth century.

Judicial power is vested in a Supreme Court and in such lower courts as may be established by law. The 1981 Judicial Reorganization Act provides for four main levels of courts and several special courts. At the local level are metropolitan trial courts, municipal trial courts, and municipal circuit trial courts. The next level consists of regional trial courts, one for each of the nation's thirteen political regions, including Manila. Courts at the local level have original jurisdiction over less serious criminal cases while more serious offenses are heard by the regional level courts, which also have appellate jurisdiction. At the national level is the Intermediate Appellate Court, also called the court of appeals. Special courts include Muslim circuit and district courts in Moro (Muslim Filipino) areas, the court of tax appeals, and the Sandiganbayan. The Sandiganbayan tries government officers and employees charged with violation of the Anti-Graft and Corrupt Practices Act.

The Supreme Court, at the apex of the judicial system, consists of a chief justice and fourteen associate justices. It has original jurisdiction over cases affecting ambassadors, other public ministers, and consuls, and over petitions for injunctions and writs of habeas corpus; it has appellate jurisdiction over all cases in which the constitutionality of any treaty, law, presidential decree, proclamation, order, or regulation is questioned. The Supreme Court also may hear appeals in criminal cases involving a sentence of life in prison. Article 3 of the Constitution forbids the death penalty "unless, for compelling reasons involving heinous crimes, the Congress hereafter provides for it."

The Supreme Court also regulates the practice of law in the Philippines, promulgates rules on admission to the bar, and disciplines lawyers. To be admitted to the Integrated Bar of the Philippines, candidates must pass an examination that is administered once annually. Professional standards are similar to those of the United States; the Integrated Bar Association's code borrows heavily from the American Bar Association's rules. Some 30,000 attorneys practiced law in the Philippines in the mid1980s, more than one-third of them in Manila. Counsel for the indigent, while not always available, is provided by government legal aid offices and various private organizations. Many of the private groups are active in representing "social justice" causes and are staffed by volunteers.

Members of the Supreme Court and judges of lower courts are appointed by the president from a list of at least three nominees prepared by the Judicial and Bar Council for every vacancy. The Judicial and Bar Council consists of a representative of the Integrated Bar, a law professor, a retired member of the Supreme Court, and a representative of the private sector. Presidential appointments do not require confirmation. Supreme Court justices must be at least forty years of age when appointed and must retire at age seventy. According to Article 11 of the constitution, members of the Supreme Court "may be removed from office on impeachment for, and conviction of, culpable violation of the Constitution, treason, bribery, graft and corruption, other high crimes, or betrayal of public trust." The House has exclusive power to initiate cases of impeachment. The Senate tries such cases, and two-thirds of the Senate must concur to convict someone. The judiciary is guaranteed fiscal autonomy.

The armed forces maintain an autonomous military justice system. Military courts are under the authority of the judge advocate general of the armed forces, who is also responsible for the prosecutorial function in the military courts. Military courts operate under their own procedures but are required to accord the accused the same constitutional safeguards received by civilians. Military tribunals have jurisdiction over all active duty members of the Armed Forces of the Philippines.

The traditional independence of the courts had been heavily compromised in the Marcos era. Because the 1973 constitution allowed Marcos to fire members of the judiciary, including members of the Supreme Court, at any time, anyone inclined to oppose him was intimidated into either complying or resigning. None of his acts or decrees was declared unconstitutional. The thirteen Marcos-appointed Supreme Court justices resigned after he fled, and Aquino immediately appointed ten new justices.

The Philippines has always been a highly litigious society, and the courts often were used to carry on personal vendettas and family feuds. There was widespread public perception that at least some judges could be bought. Public confidence in the judicial system was dealt a particular blow in 1988 when a special prosecutor alleged that six Supreme Court justices had pressured him to "go easy" on their friends. The offended justices threatened to cite the prosecutor for contempt. Aquino did not take sides in this dispute. The net effect was to confirm many Filipinos' cynicism about the impartiality of justice.

Justice was endlessly delayed in the late 1980s. Court calendars were jammed. Most lower courts lacked stenographers. A former judge reported in 1988 that judges routinely scheduled as many as twenty hearings at the same time in the knowledge that lawyers would show up only to ask for a postponement. One tax case heard in 1988 had been filed 50 years before, and a study of the tax court showed that even if the judges were to work 50 percent faster, it would take them 476 years to catch up. Even in the spectacular case of the 1983 murder of Senator Benigno Aquino, the judicial system did not function speedily or reliably. It took five years to convict some middle-ranking officers, and although the verdict obliquely hinted at then-Chief of Staff General Fabian Ver's ultimate responsibility, the court never directly addressed that question.

The indictment of former Minister of Defense Enrile on the charge of "rebellion with murder" shows that the courts can be independent of the president, but also that powerful people are handled gently. Enrile was arrested on February 27, 1990, for his alleged role in the December 1989 coup attempt in which more than 100 people died. Because Enrile was powerful, he was given an air-conditioned suite in jail, a telephone, and a computer, and a week later he was released on 100,000 pesos (for value of the péso--see Glossary) bail. In June 1990, the Supreme Court invalidated the charges against him. A further test of the court system was expected in the 1990s when criminal and civil charges were to be brought against Imelda Marcos. In 1991 Aquino agreed to allow the former first lady, who could not leave New York City without the permission of the United States Department of Justice, to return to the Philippines to face charges of graft and corruption. Swiss banking authorities agreed to return approximately US$350 million to the Philippine government only if Marcos were tried and convicted. Marcos did not seem to be reluctant to face the Philippine courts.

Local Government

The national government in the 1990s sought to upgrade local government by delegating some limited powers to local subdivisions and by encouraging people to participate in community affairs. Local autonomy was balanced, however, against the need to ensure effective political and administrative control from Manila, especially in those areas where communist or Muslim insurgents were active. In practice, provincial governors gained considerable leverage if they could deliver a bloc of votes to presidential or senatorial candidates. Control over provinces generally alternated between two rival aristocratic families.

During Marcos's authoritarian years (1972-86), a Ministry of Local Government was instituted to invigorate provincial, municipal, and *barangay* (see Glossary) governments. But, Marcos's real purpose was to establish lines of authority that bypassed provincial governments and ran straight to Malacañang. All local officials were beholden to Marcos, who could appoint or remove any provincial governor or town mayor. Those administrators who delivered the votes Marcos asked for were rewarded with community development funds to spend any way they liked.

After the People's Power Revolution, the new Aquino government decided to replace all the local officials who had served Marcos. Corazon Aquino delegated this task to her political ally, Aquilino Pimentel. Pimentel named officers in charge of local governments all across the nation. They served until the first local elections were held under the new constitution on January 18, 1988. Local officials elected in 1988 were to serve until June 1992, under the transitory clauses of the new constitution. Thereafter, terms of office were to be three years, with a three-term limit.

Organization

The 1987 Constitution retains the three-tiered structure of local government. There were seventy-three provinces in 1991 (see fig. 9). The province was the largest local administrative unit, headed by the elected governor and aided by a vice governor, also elected. Other officials were appointed to head offices concerned with finance, tax collection, audit, public works, agricultural services, health, and schools. These functionaries were technically subordinate to the governor but also answered to their respective central government ministries. Lower ranking functionaries, appointed by the governor, were on the provincial payroll.

Chartered cities stood on their own, were not part of any province, did not elect provincial officials, and were not subject to any provincial taxation, but they did have the power to levy their own taxes. As of 1991, there were sixty-one chartered cities headed by a mayor and a vice mayor. The mayor had some discretionary power of local appointment.

Municipalities were subordinate to the provinces. In 1991 there were approximately 1,500 municipalities. At the lowest level, with the least autonomy, were barangays, rural villages and urban neighborhoods that were called barrios until 1973. In 1991 there were about 42,000 barangays.

Various reorganization schemes have been undertaken to invigorate local government. One of the most far-reaching and effective was the creation of a Metro Manila (see Glossary) government in the mid-1970s to bring the four cities and thirteen municipalities of the capital region under a single umbrella. Metro Manila is an example of what geographers call the Southeast Asian primate city, a single very large city that is the center of industry, government, education, culture, trade, the media, and finance (see Urban Social Patterns). No other Philippine city rivaled Manila; all others were in a distinctly lesser league. Continued rapid population growth meant that the boundaries of Metro Manila were expected to expand in the 1990s.

During martial law, the provinces were grouped into twelve regions, and that arrangement was continued in the Apportionment Ordinance appended to the 1987 Constitution. Because these regions did not have taxing powers or elected officials of their own, however, they were more an administrative convenience for the departments of the national government than a unit of genuine local importance. In 1991 approximately 90 percent of government services were provided by the national government. Attempts by Aquino to decentralize delivery of some services were resisted by members of Congress because such moves deprived them of patronage.

The single biggest problem for local government has been inadequate funds. Article 10 of the Constitution grants each local government unit the power to create its own sources of revenue and to levy taxes, but this power is "subject to such guidelines and limitations as the Congress may provide." In practice, taxes were very hard to collect, particularly at the local level where officials, who must run for reelection every three years, were concerned about alienating voters. Most local government funding came from Manila. There is a contradiction in the Constitution between local autonomy and accountability to Manila. The Constitution mandates that the state "shall ensure the autonomy of local governments," but it also says that the president "shall exercise general supervision over local governments." The contradiction was usually resolved in favor of the center.

Regional Autonomy

By the 1990s, Philippine nationalism had not fully penetrated two regions of the country inhabited by national minorities: the Muslim parts of Mindanao and the tribal highlands of northern Luzon. Some Muslims and hill tribespeople did not consider themselves Filipinos, although they were citizens. Muslim separatism has a very long history. The Spaniards, Americans, and Japanese all had difficulty integrating the fiercely independent Moros into the national polity, and independent governments in Manila since 1946 have fared little better (see Marcos and the Road to Martial Law, 1965-72). The Moro insurgency has waxed and waned but never gone away. Enough Muslims participated in the 1987 elections to elect two of the twenty-four senators, but continuing land disputes were major factors preventing reconciliation between Christians and Muslims in Mindanao. The grievances of tribal groups, such as the Ifugao and Igorot, in northern Luzon were of more recent origin, having been stoked by ill-considered Marcos administration dam-building schemes that entailed flooding valleys in the northern Luzon cordillera where the tribal groups lived. When Aquino came to power, she was confronted with a Moro National Liberation Front demand for separation from the Philippines, and a Cordillera People's Liberation Army allied with the New People's Army. Aquino boldly negotiated a cease-fire with the Moro National Liberation Front, and her constitutional commissioners provided for the creation of autonomous regions in Muslim parts of Mindanao and tribal regions of northern Luzon (see The Moros).

Article 10 of the Constitution directed Congress to pass within eighteen months organic acts creating autonomous regions, providing that those regions would be composed only of provinces, cities, and geographic areas voting to be included in an autonomous region. Congress passed a bill establishing the Autonomous Region in Muslim Mindanao with Cotabato City designated as the seat of government, and Aquino signed it into law on August 1, 1989. The required plebiscite was set for November 19, 1989, in thirteen provinces in Mindanao and the island groups stretching toward Borneo. The plebiscite campaign was marred by violence, including bombings and attacks by rebels. Aquino flew to Cotabato on November 6, 1990, to formally inaugurate the Autonomous Region in Muslim Mindanao. She had already signed executive orders devolving to the Autonomous Region in Muslim Mindanao the powers of seven cabinet departments: local government; labor and employment; science and technology; public works and highways; social welfare and development; tourism; and environment and natural resources. Control of national security, foreign relations, and other significant matters remained with the national government. Because many of the provinces to be included actually had Christian majorities, and because the Moro National Liberation Front, dissatisfied with what it perceived to be the limitations of the new law, urged a boycott, only four provinces (Tawitawi, Sulu, Maguindanao, and Lanao del Sur) elected to join the Autonomous Region in Muslim Mindanao. Cotabato City itself voted not to join. So, a new capital had to be identified. In 1991 Maranaos, Maguindanaos, and Tausugs were disputing where the capital should be. Indications were that the government of the autonomous region would not have supervisory power over local government officials.

Congress passed a similar law creating a Cordillera Autonomous Region, but in a referendum held in five provinces (Abra, Benguet, Mountain, Kalinga-Apayao, and Ifugao) on January 29, 1990, autonomy failed in all provinces except Ifugao. The reasons for rejection were thought to be fear of the unknown and campaigning for a no vote by mining companies that feared higher taxation. In 1991 the Supreme Court voided the Cordillera Autonomous Region, saying that Congress never intended that a single province could constitute an autonomous region.

Politics

In 1991 Philippine politics resembled nothing so much as the "good old days" of the pre-martial law period--wide-open, sometimes irresponsible, but undeniably free. Pre-martial law politics, however, essentially were a distraction from the nation's serious problems. The parties were completely non-ideological. Therefore, politicians and office-holders switched parties whenever it seemed advantageous to do so. Almost all politicians were wealthy, and many were landlords with large holdings. They blocked moves for social reform; indeed, they seemed not to have even imagined that society required serious reform. Congress acquired a reputation for corruption that made the few honest members stand out. When Marcos closed down Congress in 1972, hardly anyone was disappointed except the members themselves.

The February 1986 People's Power Revolution, also called the EDSA Revolution (see Glossary) had restored all the prerequisites of democratic politics: freedom of speech and press, civil liberties, regularly scheduled elections for genuine legislatures, plebiscites, and ways to ensure honest ballot counting. But by 1991 the return to irrelevant politics had caused a sense of hopelessness to creep back into the nation that five years before had been riding the euphoric crest of a nonviolent democratic revolution. In 1986 it seemed that democracy would have one last chance to solve the Philippines' deep-rooted social and economic problems. Within five years, it began to seem to many observers that the net result of democracy was to put the country back where it had been before Marcos: a democratic political system disguising an oligarchic society.

The Inheritance from Marcos

Democratic institutions were introduced to the Philippines by the United States at the beginning of the twentieth century. The apparent success of these imported practices gave the Philippines its reputation as "the showcase of democracy in Asia." Before 1972 the constitutional separation of powers was generally maintained. Political power was centralized in Manila, but it was shared by two equally influential institutions, the presidency and Congress. The checks and balances between them, coupled with the openness of bipartisan competition between the Nacionalista and Liberal parties, precluded the emergence of one-person or one-party rule. Power was transferred peacefully from one party to another through elections. The mass media, sensational at times, fiercely criticized public officials and checked government excess.

Marcos inflicted immeasurable damage on democratic values. He offered the Filipino people economic progress and national dignity, but the results were dictatorship, poverty, militarized politics and a politicized military, and greatly increased dependence on foreign governments and banks. His New Society was supposed to eliminate corruption, but when

Marcos fled the country in 1986, his suitcases contained, according to a United States customs agent, jewels, luxury items, and twenty-four gold bricks. Estimates of Marcos's wealth ran from a low of US$3 billion to a high of US$30 billion, and even after his death in 1989, no one knew the true value of his estate, perhaps not even his widow.

If Marcos had been merely corrupt, his legacy would have been bad enough, but he broke the spell of democracy. The long evolution of democratic institutions, unsatisfactory though it may have been in some ways, was interrupted. The political culture of democracy was violated. Ordinary Filipinos knew fear in the night. An entire generation came of age never once witnessing a genuine election or reading a free newspaper. Classes that graduated from the Philippine Military Academy were contemptuous of civilians and anticipated opportunities for influence and perhaps even wealth. Marcos's worst nightmare came true when Corazon Aquino used the power of popular opinion to bring him down.

Aquino inherited a very distorted economy. The Philippines owed about US$28 billion to foreign creditors. Borrowed money had not promoted development, and most of it had been wasted on showcase projects along Manila Bay, or had disappeared into the pockets and offshore accounts of the Marcos and Romualdez families and their friends and partners. Many Filipinos believed that they would be morally justified in renouncing the foreign debt on grounds that the banks should have known what the Marcoses were doing with the money. Even Cardinal Jaime Sin declared it "morally wrong" to pay foreign creditors when Filipino children were hungry. Aquino, however, resolutely pledged to pay the debt. Otherwise, the nation would be cut off from the credit it needed. Although the Philippines could pay the interest on the debt every year, it could not pay the principal. This never-ending debt naturally inflamed Filipino nationalism. A Freedom From Debt Coalition advocated using the money to help the unemployed instead of sending the hard currency abroad.

The Rise of Corazon Aquino

Corazon Cojuangco Aquino, universally and affectionately known as "Cory," was a Philippine president quite unlike those who preceded her. Observers have groped for the right word to characterize the Aquino presidency. She was first called a "revolutionary," but later a mere "reformer." When the old landed families recaptured the political system, she was called a "restorationist."

She was born in 1933 into one of the richest clans in the Philippines, the powerful Cojuangcos of Tarlac Province. Her maiden name indicates Chinese mestizo ancestry; her Chinese great-grandfather's name could have been romanized to Ko Hwan-ko, but, following the normal practice of assimilationist Catholic Chinese-Filipinos, all the Chinese names were collapsed into one, and a Spanish first name was taken. Aquino neither sought power nor expected it would come to her. Her life was that of a privileged, well-educated girl sent abroad to the Ravenhill Academy in Philadelphia, the Notre Dame Convent School in New York, and Mount St. Vincent College, also in New York. She studied mathematics and graduated with a degree in French in 1953, then returned to the Philippines to study law, but soon married the restless, rich scion of another prominent Tarlac family, Benigno ("Ninoy") Aquino, Jr. Benigno Aquino became a mayor, a governor, and a flamboyant senator, and he probably would have been elected president of the Philippines in 1973 had Marcos not suspended elections. On the same night in 1972 when Marcos declared martial law, he sent troops to arrest Benigno Aquino. Senator Aquino was incarcerated for some seven years, after which Marcos allowed him to go to the United States. In August 1983, believing that Marcos was dying, Aquino ventured back to Manila and was gunned down just seconds after being escorted from the airplane (see From Aquino's Assassination to People's Power). Aquino's murder galvanized the Filipino people and was the beginning of the end for Marcos.

The Coalition Comes Undone (1986-87)

Ferdinand Marcos had perfected the art of ruling by dividing his enemies: scaring some, chasing others out of the country, playing one clan against another, and co-opting a few members of each prominent provincial family. The "oppositionists," as the controlled Manila press called them, were never united while Marcos was in Malacañang, and only through the intervention of Cardinal Jaime Sin did they agree on a unified ticket to oppose Marcos in the "snap election" that the ailing dictator suddenly called for February 1986. The widow Aquino had public support but no political organization, whereas the old-line politico Salvador H. "Doy" Laurel had an organization but little popular support. After difficult negotiations, Laurel agreed to run for vice president on a ticket with Aquino. Aquino won on February 7, 1986, but the margin of victory will never be known, for the election was marred by gross fraud, intimidation, ballot box stuffing, and falsified tabulation.

Aquino had to perform a delicate balancing act between left and right, within society at large and later within her own cabinet. Aquino and Laurel triumphed in good part because of the defection of Enrile, who was then minister of defense, and Fidel V. Ramos, the acting Armed Forces of the Philippines chief of staff. Both men had served Marcos loyally for many years but now found themselves pushed aside by General Fabian Ver, Marcos's personal bodyguard and commander of the Presidential Security Command. They risked their lives defying Marcos and Ver at the crucial moment. Enrile and Ramos conceived of the new government as a coalition in which they would have important roles to play. Laurel saw it the same way.

In one sense, the Aquino government initially was a coalition--it drew support from all parts of the political spectrum. The middle class was overwhelmingly behind "Cory," the democratic alternative to Marcos. Most leftists saw her as "subjectively" progressive even if she was "objectively" bourgeois. They hoped she could reform Philippine politics. On the right, only those actually in league with Marcos supported him. Aquino's support was very wide and diverse.

The coalition, however, began unraveling almost immediately. Enrile thought that Aquino should declare her government "revolutionary," because that would mean that the 1986 elections were illegitimate and that new presidential elections would be held soon. When Aquino made it clear that she intended to serve out her entire six-year term, Enrile and Laurel set out to undermine her. Ramos took a cautiously ambivalent position but ultimately supported Aquino. Without his loyalty, Aquino would not have survived the many coup attempts she successfully put down.

Aquino's political honeymoon was brief. Arturo Tolentino, Marcos's running mate in the February election, proclaimed himself acting president on July 6, 1986, but that attempt to unseat Aquino was short-lived. By October 1986, Enrile was refusing to attend cabinet meetings on the grounds that they were "a waste of the people's money." Aquino fired him the next month, after he was implicated in a coup plan code-named "God Save the Queen" (presumably because the conspirators hoped to keep Aquino on as a figurehead). The plotters were suppressed, and on the morning of November 23, Aquino met with her entire cabinet, except for Laurel, who was playing golf. She asked for the resignations of all other members of her cabinet and then jettisoned those leftists who most irritated the army and replaced Enrile with Rafael Ileto as the new minister of national defense. Aquino started a pattern, repeated many times since, of tactically shifting rightward to head off a rightist coup.

Enrile was out of the government, but Laurel remained in, despite his vocal, public criticism of Aquino. She relieved him of his duties as minister of foreign affairs on September 16, 1987, but could not remove him from the vice presidency. A month later, Laurel publicly declared his willingness to lead the country if a coup succeeded in ousting Aquino. The next year, he told the press that the presidency "requires a higher level of competence" than that shown by Aquino.

The disintegration of the original Aquino-Laurel-Enrile coalition was only part of a bigger problem: The entire cabinet, government, and, some would say, even the entire nation, were permeated with factionalism. Aquino also had difficulty dealing with the military. The first serious dispute between Aquino and the military concerned the wisdom of a cease-fire with the New People's Army. Aquino held high hopes that the communists could be coaxed down from the hills and reconciled to democratic participation if their legitimate grievances were addressed. She believed that Marcos had driven many people to support the New People's Army.

The Philippine military, which had been fighting the guerrillas for seventeen years, was hostile to her policy initiative. When talks began in September 1986, military plotters began work on the "God Save the Queen" uprising that was aborted two months later. Aquino tried reconciliation with the Moro National Liberation Front and sent her brother-in-law to Saudi Arabia, where he signed the Jiddah Accord with the Moro National Liberation Front on January 4, 1987. A coup attempt followed three weeks later. In the wake of these coup attempts, Aquino reformed her cabinet but she also submitted to military demands that she oust Executive Secretary Joker Arroyo, a political activist and her longtime confidant. Her legal counsel, Teodoro Locsin, whom the military considered a leftist, and her finance secretary, Jaime Ongpin, also had to go. (Ongpin was later found dead; the coroner's verdict was suicide, although he was lefthanded and the gun was in his right hand.)

Aquino had been swept into office on a wave of high expectations that she would be able to right all of the wrongs done to the Philippines under Marcos. When she could not do this and when the same problems recurred, Filipinos grew disillusioned. Many of Aquino's idealistic followers were dismayed at the "Mendiola Massacre" in 1987 in which troops fired into a crowd of protesting farmers right outside Malacañang. The military was simply beyond her control. The entire staff of the Commission on Human Rights resigned in protest even though Aquino herself joined the protestors the next day. Those people who hoped that Aquino would liberally use emergency power to implement needed social changes were further dismayed by the fate of her promised land reform program. Instead of taking immediate action, she waited until the new Congress was seated, and turned the matter over to them. That Congress, like all previous Philippine legislatures, was dominated by landowners, and there was very little likelihood that these people would dispossess themselves.

Aquino's declining political fortunes were revealed in public opinion polls in early 1991 that showed her popularity at an all-time low, as protesters marched on Malacañang, accusing her of betraying her promises to ease poverty, stamp out corruption, and widen democracy. Nevertheless, Aquino's greatest achievement in the first five years of her term was to begin the healing process.

The President and the Coup Plotters

Philippine politics between 1986 and 1991 was punctuated by President Aquino's desperate struggle to survive physically and politically a succession of coup attempts, culminating in a large, bloody, and well-financed attempt in December 1989. This attempt, led by renegade Colonel Gregorio Honasan, involved upwards of 3,000 troops, including elite Scout Rangers and marines, in a coordinated series of attacks on Camp Crame and Camp Aquinaldo, Fort Bonifacio, Cavite Naval Base, Villamor Air Base, and on Malacañang itself, which was dive-bombed by vintage T-28 aircraft. Although Aquino was not hurt in this raid, the situation appeared desperate, for not only were military commanders around the country waiting to see which side would triumph in Manila, but the people of Manila, who had poured into the streets to protect Aquino in February 1986, stayed home this time. Furthermore, Aquino found it necessary to request United States air support to put down this uprising.

Politically this coup was a disaster for Aquino. Her vice president openly allied himself with the coup plotters and called for her to resign. Even Aquino's staunchest supporters saw her need for United States air support as a devastating sign of weakness. Most damaging of all, when the last rebels finally surrendered, they did so in triumph and with a promise from the government that they would be treated "humanely, justly, and fairly."

A fact-finding commission was appointed to draw lessons from this coup attempt. The commission bluntly advised Aquino to exercise firmer leadership, replace inefficient officials, and retire military officers of dubious loyalty. On December 14, 1989, the Senate granted Aquino emergency powers for six months.

One of the devastating results of this insurrection was that just when the economy had finally seemed to turn around, investors were frightened off, especially since much of the combat took place in the business haven of Makati. Tourism, a major foreign-exchange earner, came to a halt. Business leaders estimated that the mutiny cost the economy US$1.5 billion (see Tourism).

Political Parties

Philippine political parties are essentially non-ideological vehicles for personal and factional political ambition. The party system in the early 1990s closely resembled that of the premartial law years when the Nacionalista and Liberal parties alternated in power. Although they lacked coherent political programs, they generally championed conservative social positions and avoided taking any position that might divide the electorate. Each party tried to appeal to all regions, all ethnic groups, and all social classes and fostered national unity by never championing one group or region. Neither party had any way to enforce party discipline, so politicians switched capriciously back and forth. The parties were essentially pyramids of patron client relationships stretching from the remotest villages to Manila. They existed to satisfy particular demands, not to promote general programs. Because nearly all senators and representatives were provincial aristocrats, the parties never tackled the fundamental national problem--the vastly inequitable distribution of land, power, and wealth.

Ferdinand Marcos mastered that party system, then altered it by establishing an all-embracing ruling party to be the sole vehicle for those who wished to engage in political activity. He called it the New Society Movement (Kilusang Bagong Lipunan). The New Society Movement sought to extend Marcos's reach to far corners of the country. Bureaucrats at all levels were well advised to join. The New Society Movement offered unlimited patronage. The party won 163 of 178 seats in the National Assembly in 1978 and easily won the 1980 local elections. In 1981 Marcos actually had to create his own opposition, because no one was willing to run against him.

Opposition Parties

The New Society Movement fell apart when Marcos fled the country. A former National Assembly speaker, Nicanor Yniguez, tried to "reorganize" it, but others scrambled to start new parties with new names. Blas Ople, Marcos's minister of labor, formed the Nationalist Party of the Philippines (Partido Nationalista ng Pilipinas) in March 1986. Enrile sought political refuge in a revival of the country's oldest party, the Nacionalista Party, first formed in 1907 (see A Collaborative Philippine Leadership). Enrile used the rusty Nacionalista machinery and an ethnic network of Ilocanos to campaign for a no vote on the Constitution, and when that failed, for his election to the Senate. Lengthy negotiations with mistrustful political "allies" such as Ople and Laurel delayed the formal reestablishment of the Nacionalista Party until May 1989. Enrile also experimented with a short-lived Grand Alliance for Democracy with Francisco "Kit" Tatad, the erstwhile minister of information for Marcos, and the popular movie-star senator, Joseph Estrada. In 1991 Enrile remained a very powerful political figure, with landholdings all over the Philippines and a clandestine network of dissident military officers.

Vice President Laurel had few supporters in the military but long-term experience in political organizing. From his family base in Batangas Province, Laurel had cautiously distanced himself from Marcos in the early 1980s, then moved into open opposition under the banner of a loose alliance named the United Nationalist Democratic Organization (UNIDO). Eventually, the UNIDO became Laurel's personal party. Aquino used the party's organization in February 1986, although her alliance with Laurel was never more than tactical. UNIDO might have endured had Aquino's allies granted Laurel more patronage when local governments were reorganized. As it was, Laurel could reward his supporters only with positions in the foreign service, and even there the opportunities were severely limited. The party soon fell by the wayside. Laurel and Enrile formed the United Nationalist Alliance, also called the Union for National Action, in 1988. The United Nationalist Alliance proposed a contradictory assortment of ideas including switching from a presidential to a parliamentary form of government, legalizing the Communist Party of the Philippines, and extending the United States bases treaty. By 1991 Laurel had abandoned these ad hoc creations and gone back to the revived Nacionalista Party, in a tentative alliance with Enrile.

In 1991 a new opposition party, the Filipino Party (Partido Pilipino), was organized as a vehicle for the presidential campaign of Aquino's estranged cousin Eduardo "Danding" Cojuangco. Despite the political baggage of a long association with Marcos, Cojuangco had the resources to assemble a powerful coalition of clans.

The Liberal Party, a democratic-elitist party founded in 1946, survived fourteen years of dormancy (1972 to 1986), largely through the staunch integrity of its central figure, Senate president Jovito Salonga, a survivor of the Plaza Miranda grenade attack of September 1971. In 1991 Salonga also was interested in the presidency, despite poor health and the fact that he is a Protestant in a largely Catholic country.

In September 1986 the revolutionary left, stung by its shortsighted boycott of the February election, formed a legal political party to contest the congressional elections. The Partido ng Bayan (Party of the Nation) allied with other leftleaning groups in an Alliance for New Politics that fielded 7 candidates for the Senate and 103 for the House of

Representatives, but it gained absolutely nothing from this exercise. The communists quickly dropped out of the electoral arena and reverted to guerrilla warfare. As of 1991, no Philippine party actively engaged in politics espoused a radical agenda.

Progovernment Parties

In 1978 the imprisoned former senators Benigno Aquino and Lorenzo Tañada organized a political party named Lakas ng Bayan (Strength of the Nation; also known by its abbreviated form, LABAN, meaning fight). LABAN won 40 percent of the Manila vote in parliamentary elections that year but was not given a single seat in Marcos's New Society Movement-dominated parliament. After Aquino went into exile in the United States, his wife's brother, former Congressman Jose Cojuangco, managed LABAN. Cojuangco forged an alliance with the Pilipino Democratic Party (PDP), a regional party with strength in the Visayas and Mindanao, that had been organized by Aquilino Pimentel, the mayor of Cagayan de Oro City. The unified party was thereafter known as PDP-LABAN, and it--along with UNIDO conducted Corazon Aquino's presidential campaign against Marcos.

In its early years, PDP-LABAN espoused a strongly nationalist position on economic matters and United States base rights, aspiring to "democratize power and socialize wealth." Later, after Aquino became president, its rhetorical socialism evaporated. In the late 1980s and early 1990s, PDP-LABAN had the distinct advantage of patronage. Aquino named Pimentel her first minister of local government, then summarily dismissed every governor and mayor in the Philippines. Pimentel replaced them with officers in charge known personally to him, thereby creating an instant pyramid of allies throughout the country. Some, but not all, of these officers in charge won election on their own in the January 1988 local elections.

PDP-LABAN was not immune from the problems that generally plagued Philippine political parties. What mainly kept the party together was the need to keep Aquino in power for her full six-year term. In June 1988 the party was reorganized as the Struggle of Filipino Democrats (Laban ng Demokratikong Pilipino). Speaker of the House Ramon Mitra was its first president, but he resigned the presidency of the party in 1989 in favor of Neptali Gonzales.

In 1990 Aquino announced the formation of a movement called Kabisig (Arm-in-Arm), conceived as a non-governmental organization to revive the spirit of People's Power and get around an obstinate bureaucracy and a conservative Congress. By 1991 its resemblance to a nascent political party worried the more traditional leadership, particularly Mitra. Part of Aquino's governing style was to maintain a stance of being "above politics." Although she endorsed political candidates, she refused to form a political party of her own, relying instead on her personal probity, spirituality, and simple living to maintain popular support.

Voting and Elections

Elections in the Philippines are the arena in which the country's elite families compete for political power. The wealthiest clans contest national and provincial offices. Families of lesser wealth compete for municipal offices. In the barangays, where most people are equally poor, election confers social prestige but no real power or money.

Voting rates have generally been high (approximately 80 to 85 percent in national elections), despite obstacles such as difficult transportation, the need to write out the names of all candidates in longhand, and, occasionally, the threat of violence. Filipinos enjoy and expect elections so much that even Ferdinand Marcos dared not completely deny them this outlet. Instead, he changed the rules to rig the elections in his favor.

Until 1972 Philippine elections were comparable to those in United States cities during early industrialization: flawed, perhaps, by instances of vote-buying, ballot-box stuffing, or miscounts, but generally transmitting the will of the people. A certain amount of election-related violence was considered normal. Marcos overturned this system with innovations such as asking voters to indicate by a show of hands if they wanted him to remain in office. In the snap election of 1986, Marcos supporters tried every trick they knew but lost anyway. The heroism of the democratic forces at that time inspired many Filipinos.

The 1987 constitution establishes a new system of elections. The terms of representatives are reduced from four years to three, and the presidential term is lengthened from four years to six. Senators also serve a six-year term. The Constitution's transitory provisions are scheduled to expire in 1992, after which there is to be a three-year election cycle. Suffrage is universal at age eighteen. The constitution established a Commission on Elections that is empowered to supervise every aspect of campaigns and elections. It is composed of a chairperson and six commissioners, who cannot have been candidates for any position in the immediately preceding elections. A majority of the commissioners must be lawyers, and all must be college-educated. They are appointed by the president with the consent of the Commission on Appointments and serve a single seven-year term. The Commission on Elections enforces and administers all election laws and regulations and has original jurisdiction over all legal disputes arising from disputed results. To counter the unwholesome influence occasionally exercised by soldiers and other armed groups, the commission may depute law enforcement agencies, including the Armed Forces of the Philippines. In dire situations, the commission can take entire municipalities and provinces under its control, or order new elections.

The constitution also empowers the commission to "accredit citizens' arms of the Commission on Elections." This refers to the National Movement for Free Elections (NAMFREL), a private group established in the 1950s, with advice and assistance from the United States, to keep elections honest. NAMFREL was instrumental in the election of President Ramon Magsaysay in 1953, and played a minor role in subsequent presidential elections. It lapsed into inactivity during the martial law years, then played an important role in Aquino's 1986 victory. NAMFREL recruited public-spirited citizens (320,000 volunteers in 104,000 precincts in the 1987 congressional elections) to watch the voting and monitor ballot-counting, and it prepared a "quick count," based mostly on urban returns, to publicize the results immediately. Because the Commission on Elections can take weeks or even months to certify official returns, the National Movement for Free Elections makes it harder for unscrupulous politicians to distort the results. NAMFREL itself has sometimes been denounced by election losers as being a tool of United States intervention and has not always been impartial. In 1986 it favored Aquino, and its chairman, Jose Concepcion, was subsequently named Aquino's minister of trade and industry.

The final decision on all legislative elections rests with the electoral tribunals of the Senate and House of Representatives. Each electoral tribunal is composed of nine members, three of whom are members of the Supreme Court designated by the chief justice. The remaining six are members of the Senate or the House, chosen on the basis of proportional representation from parties in the chamber.

The first congressional elections under the 1987 constitution were held on May 11, 1987. Political parties had not really coalesced. Seventy-nine separate parties registered with the Commission on Elections, and voters had a wide range of candidates to choose from: 84 candidates ran for 24 Senate seats, and 1,899 candidates ran for 200 House seats. The elections were considered relatively clean, even though the secretary of local government ordered all governors and mayors to campaign for Aquino-endorsed candidates. There were sixty-three election related killings. Some of these deaths were attributable to small-town family vendettas, whereas others may have had ideological motives. The armed forces charged that communists used strong-arm tactics in areas they controlled, and the communists in turn claimed that nineteen of their election workers had been murdered. Election results showed a virtual clean sweep for candidates endorsed by Aquino.

The next step in redemocratization was to hold local elections for the first time since 1980. When Aquino took office, she dismissed all previously elected officials and replaced them with people she believed to be loyal to her. Local elections were originally scheduled for August 1987, but because many May 1987 congressional results were disputed and defeated candidates wanted a chance to run for local positions, the Commission on Elections postponed local elections first to November 1987 and then to January 18, 1988. More than 150,000 candidates ran for 16,000 positions as governor, vice governor, provincial board member, mayor, vice mayor, and town council member, nationwide.

More than a hundred people were killed in election-related violence in 1988. Elections had to be postponed in six Muslim provinces, two Ilocano provinces, two New People's Army-dominated provinces, and Ifugao because of unsettled conditions. The Commission on Elections assumed direct control of many towns, including some parts of Manila. The formerly unwritten rule of Filipino politics that political killings be confined to followers and henchmen and not to the candidates themselves now seemed to have been broken: Thirty-nine local candidates were killed in the 1988 campaign. Aquino remained aloof from the 1988 local elections, but many candidates claimed her backing. Personalities and clan rivalries seemed to take precedence over ideological issues.

The final step in redemocratization was the thrice-postponed March 1989 election for barangay officials. Some 42,000 barangay captains were elected. At this level of neighborhood politics, no real money or power was involved, the stakes were small, and election violence was rare. The Commission on Elections prohibited political parties from becoming involved.

The Return of Old-Style Politics in the Countryside

Philippine politics, along with other aspects of society, rely heavily on kinship and other personal relationships. To win a local election, one must assemble a coalition of families. To win a provincial election, the important families in each town must be drawn into a wider structure. To win a national election, the most prominent aristocratic clans from each region must temporarily come together. A family's power is not necessarily precisely correlated with wealth--numbers of followers matters more--but the middle class and the poor are sought mainly for the votes that they can deliver. Rarely will they be candidates themselves.

The suspension of elections during martial law seemed at first to herald a radical centralization of power in Manila, specifically in the Marcos and Romualdez clans, but traditional provincial oligarchs resurfaced when Aquino restored elections. To the dismay of her more idealistic followers, Aquino followed her brother's advice and concluded agreements with many former Marcos supporters who were probably going to win elections anyway. About 70 percent of the candidates elected to the House of Representatives in 1987 were scions of political dynasties. They included five relatives of Aquino: a brother, an uncle, a sister-in-law, a brother-in-law, and a cousin. Another brother in-law was elected to the Senate. The newly elected Congress passed a bill prohibiting close relatives of government officials from becoming candidates, but it did not take effect until after the 1988 local elections. Many of the same prominent families who had dominated Philippine society from the Spanish colonial period returned to power. Commonly, the same two families vie for control of provinces. The specific reason for social and political bi-polarity is not known, but it nourishes feuds between rival clans that are renewed generation after generation.

Coercion is an alternative to buying votes. Because the population of the Philippines has multiplied by a factor of nine in the twentieth century, there is not enough land to go around (see Migration). As a result, tenant-landlord relationships have become more businesslike and less personal, and some old elite families now rely on force to protect their interests. Article 18 of the constitution directs the dismantling of all "private armies," but it seemed unlikely that it could be enforced.

Church-State Relations

During the Spanish colonial period, the Catholic Church was extensively involved in colonial administration, especially in rural areas (see The Friarocracy). With the advent of United States control, the Catholic Church relinquished its great estates. Church and state officially were separated, although the church, counting more than 80 percent of the population as members, continued to have influence when it wanted to exert it. For much of the Marcos administration, the official church, led by archbishop of Manila, Cardinal Jaime Sin, adopted a stance of "critical collaboration." This meant that although Sin did not flatly condemn Marcos, he reserved the right to criticize. Below the cardinal, the church was split between conservative and progressive elements, and some priests joined the communist dominated National Democratic Front through a group named Christians for National Liberation (see Church and State). Cardinal Sin was instrumental in the downfall of Marcos. He brokered the critical, if temporary, reconciliation between Aquino and Laurel and warned the Marcoses that vote fraud was "unforgivable." In radio broadcasts, he urged Manileños to come into the streets to help the forces led by Enrile and Ramos when they mutinied in February 1986. The church, therefore, could legitimately claim to be part of the revolutionary coalition.

Aquino is a deeply religious woman who has opened cabinet meetings with prayers and sought spiritual guidance in troubled times. Although there were reports that the Vatican in late 1986 had instructed Cardinal Sin to reduce his involvement in politics, Aquino continued to depend on him. The Catholic Bishops Conference of the Philippines issued a pastoral letter urging people to vote yes in the 1987 constitutional plebiscite. In March 1987, Sin announced that he was bowing out of politics, but two months later he broadcast his support for ten Aquino-backed candidates for the Senate and recommended that voters shun candidates of the left. In 1990 Sin defined his attitude toward the government as one of "critical solidarity."

The church was very pleased with provisions of the 1987 Constitution that ban abortion and restore a limited role for religion in public education. The Constitution is essentially silent on the matter of family planning. The church used its very substantial influence to hinder government family-planning programs. Despite the fact that the population grew by

100,000 people per month in the late 1980s, Cardinal Sin believed that the Marcos government had gone too far in promoting contraception. He urged Aquino to "repeal, or at least revise" government family-planning programs. In August 1988, the bishops conference denounced contraception as "dehumanizing and ethically objectionable." For churchmen, this was an issue not to be taken lightly. One bishop called for the church to "protect our people from the contraceptive onslaught" and the bishops conference labeled rapid population growth a "non-problem." In 1989 the United States Department of Commerce projected the Philippine population at 130 million by the year 2020--in a country the size of California (see Population Control).

Civil-Military Relations
The Philippines had an unbroken tradition of civilian control of the military until martial law was imposed in 1972. Under Article 2 of the 1987 Constitution, civilian authority is again, "at all times, supreme over the military." Many military leaders found this difficult to accept. Under Marcos, they could count on authorization to take a hard line against communists and Muslim separatists, on opportunities to run civilian businesses and industries, and on being consulted on most matters.

Under Aquino, the officers could feel a chill coming from Malacañang. Aquino retired all "overstaying generals," signed cease-fires with the communists and the Moro National Liberation Front, harbored "leftist" advisers in her presidential office, released political prisoners (including New People's Army founder Jose M. Sison), and only grudgingly improved military pay. Aquino also established a Commission on Human Rights to investigate and publicize instances of military abuse and only later broadened the commission's mandate to include atrocities committed by the New People's Army.

Military Factions
In 1983, the year of crisis resulting from the Benigno Aquino assassination, members of the Philippine Military Academy class of 1971 formed the Reform the Armed Forces Movement (RAM). Notable among its leaders was the chief of Enrile's security detail, Colonel Gregorio "Gringo" Honasan. RAM first demonstrated against corruption in the armed forces in 1985, while Marcos was president. Most RAM officers, including Honasan, have not supported a political idealogy. They viewed themselves as protectors of the people against corrupt, incompetent civilians. Others espoused an agenda with a populist, or even leftist tone. By 1990 RAM was said to no longer stand for Reform the Armed Forces Movement but rather for Rebolusyonariong Alyansang Makabayan, or Revolutionary Nationalist Alliance.

The military in 1991 contained many factions based on loyalties to military and civilian patrons, military academy class ties, linguistic differences, and generational differences. One faction consisted of those still loyal to Marcos; others consisted of those loyal to Enrile or to Ramos. Discord existed between Tagalogs and Ilocanos. Graduates of the Philippine Military Academy in Baguio were at odds with reserve and noncommissioned officers. Within the Philippine Military Academy faction, loyalties ran according to year of graduation. Another faction, the Young Officers' Union (YOU), was made up of a younger group of officers, distinct from RAM. YOU leaders were well educated; some were intelligence officers who had penetrated the communist underground and might have gained some respect for communist organizing principles, revolutionary puritanism, and dedication to ideology. They studied the writings of the late Filipino nationalist Claro M. Recto, espoused a doctrine they called Philippine nationalism, and were reported to believe that a social revolution could be sparked by a military uprising. By 1991 politicized military officers began to focus less on Aquino than on her possible successors. Whatever political leaders it supported, the Philippine military in the 1990s was expected by some observers to remain fractured, factionalized, and frustrated, and civilian control was by no means guaranteed.

Vigilantes

Starting in 1987 a new, unsettling element clouded civil military relations: vigilante groups that hunted down suspected communists and other leftists. The first and most famous such group was Alsa Masa (Masses Arise), which virtually eliminated communist influence from the Agdao slum area of Davao City. The potential for civilians to accomplish what the military could not aroused official interest. Soon there were more than 200 such groups across the country, with names that hinted at their violent, cult-like nature: Remnants of God; Guerrero of Jesus; Sin, Salvation, Life, and Property; Rock Christ; and, the frightening Tadtad (Chop-Chop), which liked to pose its members for photographs with the severed heads of their victims. Vigilantes often carried magical amulets to ward off bullets, and their rituals were sometimes performed to loud rock music.

Domestic human rights groups, such as Task Force Detainees, and international monitors, such as Amnesty International, publicized incidents of torture. Amnesty International asserted that torture of communist rebels and sympathizers had become a common practice. One paramilitary group in 1988 responded to such criticism by shooting the Filipino regional chairman of Amnesty International. Six human rights lawyers were killed in the first three years of the Aquino government. More than 200 critics of the government were victims of extrajudicial executions. Many vigilantes carried pistols; others were skilled with long, heavy knives called bolos.

Despite many documented abuses, United States and Philippine government officials have spoken in support of some vigilante groups. Aquino cited Alsa Masa's success in Davao as a legitimate exercise of People's Power. Her secretary of local government, Jaime Ferrer, ordered all local officials to set up civilian volunteer organizations or face dismissal. Ferrer was gunned down on August 2, 1987, for this and other anticommunist activities. The government made a distinction between ad hoc vigilante groups and the civilian volunteer organizations. The latter, which included Nation Watch (Bantay Bayan), were to conform to the following guidelines set forth on October 30, 1987, by the Department of National Defense: membership in the organizations was to be voluntary, members would be screened by the police, the organizations were to be defensive, and they were to eschew identification with individual landowners or politicians. Ramos fully supported the civilian volunteer organizations. He described their relationship to the uniformed military as "synergistic" and in 1989 grouped all 20,000 civilian volunteer organizations together under an umbrella organization called the National Alliance for Democracy. In reality, the lines between official and unofficial vigilante groups are often blurred. Large businesses have donated money to the National Alliance for Democracy and used its members as strikebreakers to counter leftist unions.

The Media

The Constitution guarantees freedom of the press and also provides free access to records, documents, and papers pertaining to official acts. Government officials, however, tended to be leery of reporters, who sometimes ran stories gathered from a single source or based on hearsay. Libel suits were frequent in the 1980s.

Traditionally, major newspapers published in Manila have been owned by elite families. Prior to 1972 Philippine newspapers were freewheeling, often publishing unsubstantiated stories, but willing to expose wrongdoing in high places. When Marcos declared martial law in 1972, he confiscated the assets of newspapers owned by families not part of his coalition. From 1972 to 1986, although newspapers were not officially government-owned or government-supported, they were controlled by Marcos's relatives, friends, and cronies. After the August 1983 Aquino assassination, newspapers gradually became more politically independent. When Marcos fled in 1986, the Commission on Good Government confiscated the assets of crony-owned newspapers and the exuberant Philippine press revived quickly; in many cases newspapers were operated by the families that had controlled them prior to martial law. In 1991 there were approximately thirty daily newspapers in the Philippines. Twelve mainly English language broadsheets provided serious news. Fourteen tabloids, mostly Tagalog and Cebuano, offered sensationalism. Four newspapers were printed in Chinese. Only one newspaper, the Manila Bulletin, had consistently shown a profit. Another, the Inquirer, began to show a profit in 1990. Most other newspapers were losing concerns used by the businesspeople who owned them to influence government policy and officials.

Television stations in Manila were very profitable to the wealthy investors who owned them. They also emerged as a significant political factor, and coup attempts often featured assaults on television stations. There were very few television stations outside Manila. Radio reached people in remote areas, even villages without electricity. Radio stations in the provinces tended to be owned by wealthy local families involved in politics.

Unsolved Political Problems

In 1991, after five years of democracy, many systemic political problems remained. These included the twin insurgencies, the sputtering economy, the skewed distribution of wealth and land, and widespread human rights abuses.

As of 1991, the New People's Army had been in the field for twenty-two years and was further from being able to seize power than it had been a decade before. Many trends were unfavorable. More than a hundred communist leaders had been captured, armed troop strength was down, weapons were in short supply, and morale was low. Still, the government could not eliminate the New People's Army (see The Counterinsurgency Campaign). The stalemate made the government seem ineffective. Despite the decline in the late 1980s in the fortunes of the international communist movement and the Communist Party of the Philippines, the communists, as the only Philippine political party addressing the problems of the very poor, could not be discounted.

The Moro National Liberation Front and other rebellious Muslim armies on Mindanao remained in a state of discontent in the early 1990s. As had been the case under four regimes (Spanish, American, Japanese, and Filipino), there were scant prospects that the Muslims could be fully integrated into Philippine society. They were unlikely to be satisfied with the limited autonomy over a limited region embodied in the Autonomous Region in Muslim Mindanao. Neither the government nor the Moro National Liberation Front could win a final victory. Consequently, the problem was likely to continue to fester.

The Philippine economy has exemplified the "revolution of rising expectations." In the early 1990s, Manileños watched American movies and *provincianos* watched films made in

Manila. Even rural villagers dreamed of cars, cities, excitement, and an end to the grinding poverty that condemned them to hunger and their children to malnutrition. Filipinos had high aspirations, as shown by the sacrifices they made to send their children to college, but most were doomed to bitter disappointment. The Philippine economy, strapped with a US$28 billion debt inherited from the Marcos administration, offered only limited opportunities (see External Debt).

One of the greatest disappointments of the Aquino years was the lack of progress in the agrarian reform program. Aquino could have used her political honeymoon and her inherited dictatorial powers to divest the old aristocrats of their estates and pass out land to the farmers who actually tilled it, but she waited until the new Congress was elected and gave the job to them. About 90 percent of Congress members were landowners. The version of the Comprehensive Agrarian Reform Program passed by the Congress was signed as the Comprehensive Agrarian Reform Law by President Aquino on June 10, 1988. It included many loopholes deliberately added by members of Congress to enable landowners (including themselves) to evade the intent of the law. A bloc of landowning legislators led by Aquino's brother, Jose Cojuangco, resisted efforts to pass more effective agrarian reform measures.

The Commission on Human Rights, established under the 1987 constitution, had not been effective, at least in its first four years. The Constitution grants the commission broad powers to monitor the government's compliance with international treaty obligations on human rights. The commission, however, claiming that it cannot investigate abuses that occur "in an environment of war," as of the end of 1989 had resolved only about 10 percent of the cases brought before it and reverted to investigating ordinary civil police matters. Even notorious cases, such as the 1987 Lupao Massacre, in which seventeen villagers, including six children and two octogenarians, were lined up and shot after an engagement between the army and guerrillas, did not result in any military or civilian convictions. In 1990 the Supreme Court decided that warrantless arrests of suspected subversives were constitutional.

Foreign Affairs

Philippine foreign policy in the early 1990s was broadly pro-democratic and pro-Western in orientation. Philippine international prestige was at an all-time high when Marcos was overthrown. During the Aquino administration, the Philippines pursued active, nationalist policies aimed at promoting "genuine independence" and economic development. As a charter member of the United Nations, the Philippines participated in all its functional groups, such as the Food and Agriculture Organization; the World Health Organization; the United Nations Educational, Scientific and Cultural Organization; and the Economic and Social Commission for Asia and the Pacific. In addition, the Philippines has been a member of the Association of Southeast Asian Nations (ASEAN), the International Monetary Fund (see Glossary), the World Bank (see Glossary), and the General Agreement on Tariffs and Trade. The Philippines was a founding member of the Asian Development Bank, which is headquartered in Manila.

Article 2 of the Constitution states that "the State shall pursue an independent foreign policy." For historical, economic, cultural, and strategic reasons, the Philippines has been tied most closely to the United States. Economic necessity dictated maintaining a smooth working relationship with Japan. Filipinos wanted a foreign policy oriented more toward their

Southeast Asian neighbors, but for most purposes implementing such a policy was not high on their agenda. The proximity and large population of China, plus the presence of Chinese in the Philippines, required amicable relations with Beijing. Because of the Muslim separatist movement, and also for economic reasons, relations with Middle Eastern countries became more important in the 1970s and 1980s.

Filipino Nationalism

Filipino nationalism, which is an important element of foreign policy, showed every sign of intensifying in the early 1990s. Diverse elements in Philippine society have been united in opposition to their common history of foreign subjugation, and this opposition often carried an anti-American undertone.

Leftists have long held that Philippine history is a story of failed or betrayed revolutions, with native compradors selling out to foreign invaders. In the post-Marcos years, this thesis received wide acceptance across the political spectrum. The middle class was deeply disillusioned because five successive United States administrations had acquiesced to Marcos's dictatorship, and Filipino conservatives nursed grievances long held by the left.

Relations with the United States

Precisely because the "special relationship" between the United States and the Philippines has been lengthy and intimate, it sometimes has resembled a family feud. Aquino enjoyed great prestige and popularity in the United States and was named *Time* magazine's "Woman of the Year" for 1986. Aquino had spent much of her early life in the United States and returned in September 1986 for a triumphant tour of Washington, New York, Boston, and San Francisco, culminating in an address to an emotion-filled joint session of the United States Congress and a congressional pledge of strong support for her government. Soon after, however, Philippine and United States government leaders faced substantial differences on economic and military issues.

United States officials frequently expressed concern that Aquino was not reforming her government quickly enough to preempt the New People's Army's appeal. And, although United States officials repeatedly warned coup plotters that the United States would cut military aid if they overthrew Aquino, many Filipinos worried that what they perceived as the United States government's obsession with national security might tempt the United States to support a military coup. To allay these fears, the United States dispatched two fighter planes to protect Aquino during the December 1989 coup attempt. Nevertheless, recriminations resumed within months. Irritated by US$96 million in aid cuts, Aquino refused to meet Secretary of Defense Richard Cheney when he visited Manila in February 1990.

In the late 1980s, Philippine-United States relations were bedeviled by a new problem: heightened concern for the safety of United States military and civilian personnel in the Philippines. Two United States airmen were shot and killed in Angeles City in 1987. In 1989 Colonel James N. Rowe, who was serving with the United States Joint Military Advisory Group, was assassinated near the United States military compound in Quezon City. (In February 1991, two communists were sentenced to life imprisonment for the murder of Rowe.) At least ten other United States citizens were killed by communists in the Philippines between 1986 and 1991. United States Peace Corps volunteers were withdrawn in 1990, when intelligence sources claimed to have uncovered plans for mass abductions. One volunteer was said to have been kidnapped by the New People's Army, but he emerged unharmed. Finally, in 1990 the United States government authorized hazardous duty pay for diplomats, troops, and other federal employees in the Philippines.

United States access to air and naval bases in the Philippines dominated Philippine-United States relations in 1991, with emotional issues of Philippine nationalism often weighing more heavily than economic or strategic arguments. The Military Bases Agreement of 1947, as amended in 1979 and updated in 1983 and 1988, was set to expire in September 1991 (see Foreign Military Relations). Clark Air Base, located north of Manila in the plain of Central Luzon, was a logistical hub for the United States Thirteenth Air Force, and Subic Bay Naval Base was an extremely valuable repair and resupply facility for the United States Seventh Fleet. Approximately 15,000 United States military personnel (exclusive of sailors temporarily ashore at Subic), 1,000 defense civilians, and 24,000 military dependents were assigned to the bases. The United States maintained that both bases were vital for power projection in the western Pacific, Indian Ocean, and Middle Eastern theaters and wanted indefinite access to both facilities, along with the Crow Valley gunnery range north of Subic Bay and some smaller communications installations.

Extension of United States base rights became a pivotal issue in Manila politics. The need for some sort of military alliance with the United States was rarely questioned, but the physical presence of the bases has irritated nationalists beyond endurance. The socially deformed communities outside their gates were seen as a national disgrace. Angeles City (near Clark) and Olongapo City (near Subic) had innumerable bars and thousands of prostitutes, which caused Filipinos to be concerned about acquired immune deficiency syndrome (AIDS; see Health and Living Standards). There were numerous criminal gangs and smugglers and criminal jurisdiction was a perennial problem.

The nuclear issue complicated matters. Article 2 of the Constitution says that the Philippines, "consistent with national interest, adopts and pursues a policy of freedom from nuclear weapons in its territory." Interpreted strictly, this article challenged the United States policy of never confirming or denying the presence of nuclear weapons at any specific location. Aquino finessed the issue, apparently determining that it was in the national interest not to do anything to make the United States leave the bases. But the Philippine Senate in June 1988 passed by a vote of nineteen to three a bill that would have banned from the Philippines the "development, manufacture, acquisition, testing, use, introduction, installation, or storage" of nuclear weapons. The bill was defeated in the House, but its margin of passage in the Senate indicated potential difficulty in obtaining the votes of the two-thirds of the Senate required to ratify any future base agreement.

Despite negative developments in Philippine-United States relations, congruent interests in the early 1990s bound the two countries. United States foreign aid to the Philippines in 1990 reached nearly US$500 million; United States private investment stood at more than US$1 billion; and the United States and Japan were key donors to the Multilateral Aid Initiative, also known as the Philippine Assistance Plan, which offered some debt relief and new credit in return for desired structural reforms (see Development Assistance). Political activity in Filipino-American communities in the United States added another dimension to Philippine-United States relations. Early maneuvering for the 1992 Philippine presidential election was as feverish among these communities on the United States west coast as it was in Manila.

Relations with Asian Neighbors

For decades the Philippines was an active proponent of regionalism. In 1954 it joined Australia, Britain, France, New Zealand, Pakistan, Thailand, and the United States in the Southeast Asia Treaty Organization against the perceived threat from the Chinese and Indochinese communist regimes. This alliance was phased out in 1977.

Manila's quest for regional cooperation received a significant boost in the 1965-66 period, when bilateral problems between Indonesia and Malaysia that had been known as the confrontation--until then the main obstacle to regionalism in Southeast Asia--gave way to neighborliness. In August 1967 the Association of Southeast Asian Nations was formed by Indonesia, Malaysia, the Philippines, Singapore, and Thailand to pursue economic, social, cultural, and technical cooperation.

The Philippines was also party to a multilateral dispute over ownership of the Kalayaan Islands, as Filipinos call some of the Spratlys, a scattered group of atolls west of the Philippine island of Palawan and east of Vietnam, also claimed in toto or partially by China, Malaysia, Taiwan, and Vietnam (see External Defense). Tomas Clomas, a Manila lawyer, visited the islands in 1956, claimed them for himself, named them Kalayaan (Freedomland), then asked the Philippine government to make them a protectorate. Philippine troops were sent to the Kalayaans in 1968. All parties to the dispute were interested in possible offshore oil around the islands. The law of the sea grants to any country that receives international recognition of a claim to even a rock sticking out of the water exclusive economic rights to all resources, including oil, within a 200-nautical-mile radius of that point. Manila regularly tried to extract from the United States a declaration that it would defend the Philippines' claim to the Kalayaans as part of the Mutual Defense Treaty between the Republic of the Philippines and the United States of America, but the United States just as regularly refused so to interpret that treaty.

Aquino broke the tradition that a Philippine president's first overseas trip was to Washington. She visited Jakarta and Singapore in August 1986. Indonesian president Soeharto promised not to aid Muslim separatists in Mindanao but cautioned Aquino not to attempt reconciliation with communist insurgents. Singapore's Prime Minister Lee Kuan Yew echoed Soeharto's warning. Both leaders encouraged the Philippines to find a way to extend United States base rights. Although the governments espoused differing world views, the Philippines has had few disputes with Indonesia or Singapore, and relations remained neighborly in the early 1990s. The Philippines enjoyed a cooperative relationship with Thailand. The two countries in 1991 had no disputes and many common interests, including a history of security cooperation with the United States.

Malaysia

Philippine relations with Malaysia have been bedeviled by a lingering dispute over the status of Sabah, the northeast corner of Borneo. The Philippines based its case on a claim to territories that were part of the former Sultanate of Sulu, a nineteenth-century entity whose territory straddled the present maritime boundary between Malaysia and the Philippines. In 1991 one descendent of the sultan, a Filipino citizen, still received a stipend stemming from cession of the sultanate to a British company. Philippine presidents have revived this claim occasionally. It was revealed in 1968 that Marcos was training a team of saboteurs on Corregidor for infiltration into Sabah. Marcos later decided to drop the claim, but the aggrieved Malaysians insisted on such an explicit, humiliating public renunciation that no

Philippine president could meet their conditions. The Philippine constitution, by not mentioning Sabah, seems to have dropped the claim. Aquino rushed a bill to Congress in November 1987 to renounce the claim once and for all, hoping to get the issue out of the way before Malaysia's Prime Minister Mahathir bin Mohamad arrived for the ASEAN summit in December, but Congress did not act.

Vietnam

There was little diplomatic or cultural intercourse between the Philippines and Vietnam until the 1960s. The Philippines contributed a small civic action unit to the United States effort during the Vietnam War but refused to allow the United States to mount B-52 bombing runs from Clark Air Base. (The aircraft flew from Guam, and were refueled from Clark.) Beginning in 1975, tens of thousands of Vietnamese and Cambodian refugees entered the model refugee camp set up by the United Nations at Morong on the Bataan Peninsula. A clean, well-run place, it provided Vietnamese and Cambodians bound for the United States with training in English, American history, and vocational skills. The Philippines joined other ASEAN states in opposing Vietnam's occupation of Cambodia, even indicating a willingness to support the Khmer Rouge, if necessary, to rid Cambodia of Vietnamese forces.

Japan

Philippine-Japanese relations were smooth and successful in the early 1990s, despite bitter memories of the cruelty of the Japanese during their occupation of the Philippines in World War II. In mid-1986 the Philippines, concerned about Japan's possible remilitarization, joined with other Asian nations to protest the adoption of revisionist history textbooks by the Japanese education ministry. For the majority of Filipinos, however, World War II memories have faded or are nonexistent. Japan was a major source of development funds, trade, investment, and tourism in the 1980s, and there have been few foreign policy disputes between the two nations.

Aquino visited Japan in November 1986 and met with Emperor Hirohito, who offered his apologies for the wrongs committed by Japan during World War II. New aid agreements also were concluded during this visit. Aquino returned to Japan in 1989 for Hirohito's funeral and in 1990 for the enthronement of Emperor Akihito.

China

Philippine relations with China and Taiwan were cautious in the 1990s. Manila's relations with Beijing were hostile in the 1950s and 1960s. The unspoken threat of Chinese aid to the New People's Army was ever present but never materialized. By contrast, the Filipino-Chinese business community had many connections with relatives and partners in Taiwan. Diplomatic relations between Manila and Beijing were opened in 1973. Since that time, the relationship has been correct but not warm.

In 1988 Aquino visited China, met with elder statesman Deng Xiaoping, and made a ceremonial pilgrimage to her ancestral home and temple in Fujian Province. The closer relationship fostered by that trip later dissipated because of Beijing's sensitivity to what was perceived as a Philippine bias in favor of Taiwan. A Philippine government spokesperson had inadvertently referred to a visiting delegation from Taiwan as representatives of "the Republic of China." The disclosure of a secret visit to Taiwan, made by the Philippine secretary of foreign affairs, Raul Manglapus, in October 1989, upset Beijing even more. In 1990 Aquino reaffirmed the Philippines' one-China policy, but she reserved the right to develop trade and economic ties with Taiwan. China, for its parts, has sought with limited success to conduct an "oil diplomacy" with the Philippines, a country completely dependent on imported oil. In December 1990 Aquino welcomed the Chinese premier, Li Peng, to Manila after earlier having suspended official contacts in the wake of the June 1989 violence around Beijing's Tiananmen Square.

Relations with the Soviet Union

The Philippine government was always deeply suspicious of the Soviet Union because of Moscow's ideological support for communist insurgents. Marcos sometimes dispatched his wife to Moscow, but only for the purpose of reminding Washington that there were alternatives to exclusive reliance on the West for aid. Soviet Communist Party general secretary Leonid Brezhnev reciprocated by voicing support of Manila in opposition to the Communist Party of the Philippines and the New People's Army. The government of Mikhail Gorbachev was embarrassed by its own diplomatic clumsiness in dispatching the sole foreign ambassador to attend Marcos's pitiful final inauguration on February 25, 1986, but it later opened cautious diplomatic dialogue with the Aquino government and promised to continue to refuse support to the Communist Party of the Philippines and its New People's Army. In 1988 Moscow played on the Philippine-United States bases controversy by offering to pull out from Cam Ranh Bay in Vietnam in return for United States withdrawal from Clark and Subic bases, an initiative that withered on the vine. In 1991 the Moscow hoped to acquire access to Philippine ports and dockyards for its fishing fleet as a result of warmer relations with Manila.

Relations with the Middle East

There are three dimensions to Philippine relations with Middle Eastern countries: oil dependence, Muslim separatism, and labor conditions for Filipino contract workers in Saudi Arabia and the Persian Gulf states. The Philippines required reasonably priced oil, and fluctuations in world oil prices caused serious problems for the Philippines, including politically incendiary strikes by the drivers of jeepneys, jeeps converted to carry passengers, which were a vital from of public transport in Manila. For this reason, the Philippine government was very conscious of the need to maintain amicable relations with Middle Eastern oil producers and of the effect that its treatment of the Muslim minority could have on those relations. Furthermore, although Moro National Liberation Force leader Nur Misuari lived and worked in Libya and Saudi Arabia, Arab leaders were reticent in their support for Misuari. In addition, as of January 1991, there were an estimated 495,300 Filipinos working in the Middle East, including 390,000 in Saudi Arabia, 2,000 in Kuwait, and 50 in Iraq. Those workers were a major source of Philippine hard currency earnings, but their presence also made the Philippines vulnerable to volatile changes in Middle Eastern politics.

As her administration entered its final year, Aquino could look with some satisfaction on her great achievements of restoring democracy and returning the Philippines to normalcy. The political system appeared to be stabilizing, as citizens and soldiers impatient for change pinned their hopes on national and local elections scheduled for 1992. The great unanswered question was whether normalcy was enough for a country with an under-performing economy, a semifeudal social system, and a rapidly growing population. Democracy faced one of its toughest challenges in the Philippines.

* * *

The single best source for understanding Philippine politics and society is the new edition of David J. Steinberg's concise, insightful *The Philippines: A Singular and a Plural Place*. Bryan Johnson's *The Four Days of Courage* is a gripping account of the February Revolution of 1986. Raymond Bonner's controversial *Waltzing With a Dictator* provides a highly detailed account of what he sees as a symbiotic relationship between Marcos and various United States administrations. Articles by Benjamin Muego, David Rosenberg, and Gareth Porter in Steven Dorr and Deborah Mitchell's *The Philippines in a Changing Southeast Asia* offer valuable information on the Philippines' relationships with its Southeast Asian neighbors. *The Aquinos of Tarlac*, by Filipino writer Nick Joaquin, supplies excellent background material on President Aquino and her family, and an article by Stanley Karnow in the *New York Times Magazine*, "Cory Aquino's Downhill Slide," reports sympathetically but disappointedly on the Aquino presidency.

Gregg R. Jones, an American who spent time in the hills with communist rebels, reveals much about the guerrilla movement in his *Red Revolution*. Two detailed reports on human rights in the Philippines are Amnesty International's *Philippines* and Asia Watch's, "The Philippines." *Everyday Politics in the Philippines*, by Benedict J. Kerkvliet, gives villagers' views of political and social life, and a detailed, probing series of articles by John McBeth about the resurgence of provincial dynasties is found in the *Far Eastern Economic Review*. An insightful analysis of Filipino nationalism and how it is interwoven with religious imagery is contained in three essays by Ian Buruma published in *The New York Review of Books*.

For a year-to-year summary of political developments, the best sources are the annual survey articles appearing in the February issues of *Asian Survey* and in the Far Eastern Economic Review's *Asia Yearbook*. (For further information and complete citations, see Bibliography.)

NATIONAL SECURITY

Geographically insulated from the turmoil and conflict which plagued the Southeast Asian mainland during the decades after World War II, Filipinos perceived no direct external threat to their island nation. Challenges came from within. A series of rural insurgencies plagued the Philippines. In 1990 the government faced three major challenges--Muslim separatists, the communist New People's Army (NPA), and, ironically, the Philippine military, traditionally the government's protector. The rebellion by Filipino Muslims in Mindanao and the Sulu Archipelago seemed least menacing of the three major challenges to the government. Commonly known as Moros, the Muslims had waged guerrilla warfare since 1972, alternately pressing for either secession or increased autonomy. The intensity of the Moro insurgency, however, had significantly declined since its violent peak in the mid-1970s. Divisions over leadership and goals among the three main Moro factions, reduced external support, pressure by the armed forces, and government political accommodations-- including the creation in 1990 of a Muslim autonomous region-- contained periodic threats of a resurgent Moro rebellion in the 1990s. Although government forces and Muslim rebels clashed only occasionally by 1991, the government still respected the Moros' political and military power and guarded against escalating violence in the south.

The Communist Party of the Philippines (CPP) and its military arm, the NPA, presented a greater challenge to the government. Using the Maoist strategy of protracted people's war, the communists had pursued a "national democratic revolution" since the late 1960s. After slow but steady expansion through the 1970s and early 1980s, the communist rebellion grew rapidly during President Ferdinand E. Marcos's last years. By 1985 the NPA operated in a considerable majority of the country's seventy three provinces, and exercised substantial control in some 20 percent of Philippine villages.

Following Corazon C. Aquino's rise to power in 1986, the strength of the NPA peaked, then began to decline. The advent of a popular president was only the first of several significant setbacks for the communists; some were caused by the communists themselves. The CPP's failure to participate in the downfall of Marcos and the subsequent reversal of the rebels' fortunes sparked unprecedented debate within the party over how to pursue the struggle. Repeated arrests of top insurgent cadres also prompted a bloody purge of the rebels' ranks as the communists attempted to weed out suspected government informants. Frustrated with the party's inability to raise more funds domestically through "revolutionary taxes," combined voluntary and coerced donations, the CPP turned to foreign sources increasingly in the late 1980s. Most funds came from sympathetic western political, labor, and charitable groups. Breaking with a longstanding policy of "self-sufficiency," the communists also pursued foreign government support. As of 1991, however, there was no evidence that any nation had responded to the CPP's appeal. With an estimated 18,000 to 23,000 full-time guerrillas in 1991, the CPP and the NPA remained a potent, though not immediate, threat to the government.

Ironically, the Philippine military, long the state's defender against insurgency, posed the most serious threat to the democratically elected government of President Aquino. Most observers traced the military's unprecedented rebelliousness to the Marcos martial law era (1972-81). As the Armed Forces of the Philippines (AFP) grew rapidly in size during the 1970s, so did its leaders' involvement in the nation's political life. Professionalism eroded as Marcos loyalists were rewarded with key positions in the military, government, and civilian corporations. By February 1986, the military was deeply factionalized and widely criticized by human rights groups for abuses and corruption. In the wake of a fraudulent tally of the presidential election and Marcos's refusal to step aside, led by the commander of the Philippine Constabulary Lieutenant General Fidel V. Ramos and Minister of National Defense Juan Ponce Enrile, a group of reform-minded officers mutinied and sparked a popular revolt that unseated Marcos and allowed Corazon Aquino to assume the presidency.

Military rebellions continued under Aquino. Three, in July 1986 and January and April 1987, were relatively small affairs led by disgruntled former Marcos loyalists. A potentially serious plot in October to November 1986 was stillborn and resulted in the removal of the minister of national defense, Juan Ponce Enrile. The rebellions of August 1987 and December 1989, however, were credible coup attempts that, by most accounts, almost toppled the president. They were led by many of the same reformist officers that had helped bring Aquino to power. Although only a fraction of the AFP actively supported the coup attempts, many personnel were said to be sympathetic to the mutineers' complaints about the government. The threat of yet another military rebellion persisted in 1991 but had diminished considerably as rebel leaders surrendered to the government and talks began between military leaders and rebels.

When not distracted by coup attempts, the 153,500-strong armed forces focused on combating the communist insurgency and, to a lesser extent, the threat of a rejuvenated Moro rebellion. The ground forces dominated the counterinsurgency effort. The smaller navy and air force provided support and a limited patrol capability. Improvements in the military's image, discipline, and performance during the late 1980s contributed to reversing CPP growth.

With nearly all available resources committed to internal security functions, the AFP's conventional capabilities were modest. The nation had faced no threat of direct foreign aggression since Japan's invasion during World War II. The United States and the Philippines were parties to a mutual defense treaty, and should a credible external threat emerge, the military would be likely to rely on support from the United States. A separate treaty, which was to expire in 1991, provided for the maintenance of several United States military installations in the Philippines. Negotiations on the future of the American bases beyond September 1991 were ongoing in mid1991.

The Armed Forces in National Life

Historical Background

Philippine military tradition traces the formal beginnings of the national armed forces to the military force established under the revolutionary government in 1897 by Emilio Aguinaldo. The revolutionary army fought successively for independence from Spain and the United States (see The 1896 Uprising and Rizal's Execution). Although this revolutionary army was disbanded in late 1899 after Aguinaldo recognized the futility of meeting the numerically superior and better armed United States forces in frontal engagements, a guerrilla war against the United States continued until 1903. According to their own ethos, the armed forces of the late twentieth century had inherited the people's mandate to defend the sovereignty of the Philippine nation.

The United States colonial government, installed in 1899, made no attempt to resurrect the defeated Philippine army, but military and paramilitary forces still played an important role in national life. For example, the Philippine Scouts were an indigenous military force integrated with the United States forces maintained in the Philippines for external defense.

The Philippine Constabulary, established by the United States administration in 1901, played an important and enduring role. Although originally staffed by Filipinos and led by Americans, the Philippine Constabulary acquired a Filipino chief in 1917, and by 1933 nearly all its officers were Filipino. Constables performed a wide variety of public service roles, acting as jail guards, postmasters, game wardens, and telegraph repairmen, and the Philippine Constabulary's melding of police, paramilitary, and civilian functions provided a model for the later establishment of the armed forces.

The Philippine Constabulary's role in national life waned in the 1920s as civilian institutions began to develop, but military influence rose again with the establishment of the army in 1936, the year after the Philippines achieved commonwealth status. The new army was closely patterned after the United States model. It was envisioned as a small, professional force of some 10,000 regulars, who were to be augmented by a reserve force with an eventual strength of 400,000 by independence--promised for 1946. Although the army's relatively small size seemed to ensure that it would play only a small part in national life, its role in putting down a number of peasant revolts, as well as the growing Japanese threat, forced the army into a more prominent position in the late 1930s. At the beginning of World War II, the Philippine army supported United States forces; when the latter withdrew, it continued protracted guerrilla warfare to combat the Japanese occupation.

Following World War II, the military's influence waxed and waned, based on internal security threats and the inclinations of the national administration. The armed forces became involved in partisan politics in the late 1940s and early 1950s and influenced the 1946 and 1949 elections. In the early 1950s, career officers filled high government posts in the administration of Ramon Magsaysay (1953-57). The drive to defeat the Huk (see Glossary) rebellion in the mid- to late 1940s also involved the military in Central Luzon's local government and led to a great expansion of the armed forces' civic action mission (see The Magsaysay, Garcia, and Macapagal Administrations, 1953- 65). During the late 1950s and early 1960s, the military's influence declined. Under the administrations of presidents Carlos P. Garcia (1957-61) and Diosdado Macapagal (1961-65), military budgets were reduced, civic action was trimmed, and the armed forces were kept relatively subordinate to civilian control.

The ascent of Ferdinand Marcos to power in 1965 reversed the trend toward professionalism in the AFP. During the twenty years of his rule, he granted unprecedented power to the Philippine military, which became more deeply involved than ever before in the country's political life. On taking office, he reorganized the AFP and shuffled personnel to increase his personal control over the military. A former army officer himself, Marcos was comfortable with military men and developed the armed forces into his principal power base.

The declaration of martial law by Marcos in 1972 set the stage for enlarging the role of the military in society. The armed forces became the government's principal tool to combat the fledgling communist insurgency and, during the mid-1970s, the violent Muslim rebellion. The AFP budget grew rapidly and its strength increased threefold. Civic action operations expanded as part of the military's program to aid rural development, increase support for the government, and undercut the insurgents. The military was involved in administering the national criminal justice system, particularly in insurgent-affected areas. The military also was directly involved in the management of the economy as AFP officers took charge of many major companies, moving far from the original model of a small, apolitical military that performed functions strictly limited to conventional defense against outside aggression.

Although the AFP's influence diminished somewhat following the end of martial law in 1981, Marcos continued to control the military closely through his close friend General Fabian Ver, whom he had installed as AFP chief of staff in 1981. The president directed promotions and assignments and delayed retirements, ensuring that officers personally loyal to him filled key positions.

Filipinos increasingly criticized the personalization and manipulation of the military by Marcos, especially following the military's alleged involvement in the 1983 assassination of his political rival, Benigno Aquino. Discontent also emerged in the military and played a decisive role in Marcos's overthrow. Critical of Marcos's domination of the military and of senior officers' alleged corruption and incompetence, a group of midlevel AFP officers founded a reform movement--the Reform the Armed Forces Movement (RAM) in 1982. These officers, led by then Minister of National Defence Juan Ponce Enrile and Vice Chief of

Staff Fidel V. Ramos spearheaded the February 1986 military leadership of the popular revolt that ultimately toppled Marcos.

Despite the Aquino government's attempts to de-politicize the Philippine military, the February 1986 rebellion against Marcos was not the last uprising. Units loyal to the deposed president mutinied in Manila only months after Aquino took office, and by 1991 there had been six open rebellions against her rule. The two most serious, in August 1987 and December 1989, were led by the RAM officers that had helped bring her to power. In 1991 discontented elements of the AFP, led by fugitive RAM founders, still threatened to unseat the president.

External Defense

The Philippines perceived no serious threat of external aggression in 1991. The reduction in the Soviet naval and air presence in Vietnam and a more benign Soviet foreign policy had eased fears of involvement in superpower contention. Although some Filipinos were wary of the growth of Japanese military capabilities, Japan was not seen as a near-term threat.

The Philippines had two territorial disputes in 1991 that had national security implications. The first concerned a shallow section of the South China Sea west of the Philippine archipelago containing some small islands that were part of the larger group of Spratly Islands. Referred to as Kalayaan by the Philippines, it is a rich fishing area that had been identified as a potential source of petroleum deposits (see Relations with Asian Neighbors). The Spratlys, however, were claimed in toto by China, Vietnam, and Taiwan, whereas Malaysia laid claim to parts of the continental shelf underlying the southernmost islands in the chain.

The Philippine government first put forth informal claims to Kalayaan in the mid-1950s. In 1978 Marcos made formal claims by declaring that fifty-seven of the islands were part of Palawan Province by virtue of their presence on the continental margin of the archipelago. The Philippine military, which first occupied three of the islands in 1968, continued to garrison marines on several islands. China, Vietnam, and Taiwan also occupied several islands. Although the Chinese and Vietnamese navies clashed in the Spratlys in March 1988, as of 1991, the Philippines had not been involved in any military confrontations over the islands.

The other territorial dispute involved the Malaysian state of Sabah on northern Borneo. In 1962, when the British-administered territories of Sarawak and Sabah were incorporated into Malaysia, the Philippines notified Britain of its claim to Sabah on the grounds that it formed part of the Sultanate of Sulu and had only been leased to British traders beginning in 1878. When Malaysia was formed in 1963, the Philippines established diplomatic relations but then immediately broke relations over the Sabah issue and did not reestablish them until 1969. Marcos publicly renounced the claim to Sabah in 1977, but Malaysia insisted that total renunciation required a constitutional amendment. The issue was clouded by ties between Muslims in the southern Philippines and Sabah, and by Philippine allegations--denied by Malaysia-- that Sabah afforded sanctuary to Moro rebels.

Political Role

The military exerted a strong influence on political life during the early 1990s. Observers generally agreed that the armed forces' unprecedented rebelliousness was rooted in the AFP's political role in the Marcos era. Although the military historically had a symbiotic relationship with Philippine politicians, the martial law era (1972-81) produced tremendous growth in the AFP's political role. The growing insurgent challenge spurred rapid growth in the AFP and increased the military's involvement in politics as deployed units worked with local governments to combat the rebels and military tribunals dispensed justice in insurgent-affected areas. As a result, AFP officers became important power brokers at all levels of society, and favored officers were given key government positions or placed on the boards of state-run companies (see The Inheritance from Marcos).

As popular opposition to Marcos grew in the wake of the 1983 Aquino assassination, the president increasingly relied on the military as his principal power base. Marcos concentrated power in the hands of General Fabian Ver who, as military chief of staff and head of the National Intelligence and Security Authority, ensured that critical positions were filled by officers unquestionably loyal to the president. Ver's family and protégés and other ethnic Ilocanos were advanced, often at the expense of better qualified candidates. Lieutenant General Fidel V. Ramos, vice chief of staff and later Aquino's chief of staff and secretary of national defense, pointed to political manipulation of the armed forces as a key factor in his decision to break with Marcos in February 1986.

The RAM was openly critical of Marcos's politicizing of the AFP. Nominally led by Colonel Gregorio Honasan, RAM consisted mostly of graduates of the prestigious Philippine Military Academy, many from Honasan's class of 1971. RAM officers first gained wider public attention in 1985 when, at an academy alumni parade, they openly protested before Marcos and AFP leaders. The officers called for military reforms that would address the problems of favoritism, incompetence, and corruption in senior leadership. Later, these reformists played a key role, along with Ramos and Enrile, in initiating the People's Power (see Glossary) Revolution that brought Corazon Aquino to power (see From Aquino's Assassination to People's Power).

Following the change of government, Enrile, reappointed to head the Ministry of National Defense, and new Chief of Staff General Ramos undertook a series of internal reforms designed to professionalize the renamed New Armed Forces of the Philippines. (After one year, in 1987, the military reverted to its former name, Armed Forces of the Philippines.) Twenty-two generals, whose retirements Marcos had postponed, were quickly dismissed along with other senior officers perceived as Marcos loyalists. In an effort to reduce the armed forces' involvement in government, officers assigned to positions outside the armed forces were recalled. The 1987 Philippine constitution permanently bars retirement extensions, military service in civilian positions, and military personnel's involvement in politics. A widespread program of reeducation and retraining was initiated to instill professional values at all levels.

Despite government efforts, the military did not "return to the barracks," at least not for long. During Aquino's first four years, military elements repeatedly rebelled (see Civil-Military Relations). The first rebellion occurred in July 1986, only five months after the president took office. Several hundred Marcos supporters backed Arturo Tolentino, who had been Marcos's vice presidential running mate in the February election, in a takeover of the elegant Manila Hotel. Following calls for Marcos's return to the presidency, the mutineers surrendered and were punished with fifty push-ups. Later in 1986, RAM officers-- seen as heroes of the February revolution--again emerged as a political force. Rampant rumors of an imminent RAM coup in November led the president to dismiss Enrile, who was seen as the

RAM leaders' mentor. Aquino also dismissed several "leftists" from her cabinet in an apparent response to military critics.

Military rebellions continued in 1987, culminating in a coup attempt that seriously threatened Aquino's presidency. On January 27, Marcos loyalists struck again, seizing a Manila television station and some military targets. Although the government quickly contained the rebellion, holdouts did not surrender until four days later. During April, a smaller group of military rebels briefly occupied the Philippine army headquarters in what became known as the Black Saturday rebellion. The mutineers surrendered within hours.

On August 28, RAM launched the most serious coup attempt up to that time. In Manila Honasan led hundreds of troops in attacks on television stations, Villamor Air Base, and the Malacañang Palace. The palace assault failed, and rebel forces eventually rallied at Camp Aguinaldo where they seized the AFP General Headquarters. Military rebels also seized several military camps around the country in simultaneous revolts. The coup collapsed after the first day, and Honasan escaped with several hundred followers. Many believed the coup came perilously close to success.

Underlying the RAM move was deep-seated military dissatisfaction with the government and the belief among military officers that they sometimes had an obligation to intervene in the nation's political life. Reformist leaders complained that the Aquino government was critical of the military and unfairly lenient toward the communists. They called for further reform of the government and military and for a more effective counterinsurgency program. A poll of military officers prior to the August coup attempt showed broad support for RAM's grievances and substantial support for its tactics. More than 75 percent of those polled blamed political incompetence and corruption for NPA growth. Almost all supported a military role in national development, and almost half thought the AFP might have to seize political power to prevent a communist takeover. Following the revolt, the Aquino government responded to some military complaints by improving military pay and benefits.

More than two years passed before RAM acted again, this time with the support of several generals, some Marcos loyalists, and a shadowy new military group called the Young Officers' Union. This long and bloody coup attempt began on December 1, 1989, when rebels launched a series of attacks in Manila and seized a major air base in Cebu. Elite marine and army Scout Ranger units briefly held parts of the army and air force headquarters and Manila's Ninoy Aquino International Airport before moving against Camp Aguinaldo. Although the attack on the armed forces headquarters failed, rebels seized part of Manila's Makati financial district and bombed the presidential palace grounds. United States warplanes from Clark Air Base overflew rebel bases in a show of support for the president, but they did not fire on the mutineers. The Makati standoff ended on December 7 with the negotiated surrender of the Scout Rangers, and the Cebu rebellion collapsed two days later. Nearly 100 people died in the fighting, and more than 600 people were injured.

The shadow of the 1989 coup attempt and threat of further military unrest hung over much of 1990. Perceived political instability discouraged investors and contributed to an economic downturn, and frequent coup rumors and Manila bombings attributed to military rebels fueled several serious coup scares in the capital. Within the rebel movement, the Young Officers' Union's younger, more radical idealists emerged as a growing force. The group's public statements portrayed them as social revolutionaries. Meanwhile, a presidentially appointed panel investigated the 1989 coup and its causes. The Davide Commission concluded that, although many complaints of the military were legitimate, a hidden agenda--a desire for the power and privilege that the military enjoyed under Marcos--animated the rebel movement.

The Counterinsurgency Campaign

The armed forces' primary mission in the late 1980s was combating the communist insurgency. During Marcos's last years, the communist movement expanded rapidly in political influence and military strength. By 1986, when Aquino came to power, the armed forces estimated that there were some 22,500 regular NPA guerrillas active in sixty-three of the country's seventy-three provinces. Reported insurgent strength peaked the following year at about 26,000 people. The Muslim insurgency, meanwhile, was relatively quiet. Although the military maintained forces in Moro areas, clashes with government forces were infrequent and the threat of a full-scale resurgence was low (see The Communist Insurgency; The Moros).

Despite many well-publicized programs, the counterinsurgency effort in the early and mid-1980s was clearly failing to stem the rising tide of communist influence. Government estimates of NPA strength more than tripled between 1983 and 1986, from around 6,000 to more than 20,000. Recognizing the growing problem, Marcos escalated the counterinsurgency effort, emphasizing civic action. Under the aegis of the Home Defense Program, military units constructed roads and schools, provided disaster relief, assisted in maintaining security and public utilities, and performed law enforcement. Army engineer units, greatly expanded with United States assistance, played a key role in these development efforts. The armed forces also took part in literacy projects and the National Livelihood Program, which were designed to improve the standard of living in rural areas.

These programs notwithstanding, the government lost ground in its efforts to win hearts and minds. Part of the reason was the declining popularity of the Marcos government and increasing criticism of the armed forces. Many Filipinos felt that those in the military, particularly in the Philippine Constabulary and the militia, the Civilian Home Defense Force, had become increasingly abusive and corrupt. Human rights groups documented numerous petty crimes as well as more serious instances of unlawful arrest, torture, and "salvaging," the assassination of suspects and detainees. Most victims were suspected insurgents or their supporters. Public respect for the military eroded while relations between the armed forces and important groups, such as the Roman Catholic Church, deteriorated. Attempts to improve discipline within the armed forces through retraining, punishment, and dismissal appeared to do little to quell growing public fear and suspicion.

Initially, the Aquino government reversed the decline in human rights performance and made notable strides in restoring the tarnished image of the military. The 1987 constitution outlawed torture and all forms of "secret and incommunicado detention." It also established a permanent Commission on Human Rights and directed that the militia, constabulary, and police forces--frequent targets of abuse complaints--be disbanded. The armed forces were far less abusive in 1986 according to human rights groups. However, military discipline apparently worsened over the next two years. In 1987 military personnel were primary suspects in the assassination of a prominent leftist political activist and in two other incidents that resulted in the deaths of twelve Manila demonstrators and seventeen rural villagers. International human rights monitors alleged that abuses in 1988 were as bad as they were under Marcos. In an apparent reaction to mounting criticism, the military renewed efforts to improve civil-military relations, and reported abuse by the military declined over the next two years.

Human rights remained a concern in 1991. According to the United States Department of State's 1990 annual human rights report to Congress, abuses--including extra-judicial killings-- continued. The report also criticized the government's failure to prosecute those responsible for the crimes. Lapses in the administration of justice were attributed in part to the strong imperative of the military to protect its own members, who were tried in military courts. Convictions on human rights violations were rare. Still, by 1990 the overall armed forces human rights record under Aquino was much improved over the Marcos era.

Although the Aquino government scored other successes in its counterinsurgency campaign, initial efforts proved disappointing. The new administration hoped that many NPA personnel could be coaxed out of the hills following the overthrow of Marcos and took up the theme of reconciliation in 1986. One of Aquino's first acts was to release political detainees, including captured CPP chairman Jose Maria Sison. Later, following talks with senior representatives of the communists' National Democratic Front, the government agreed to a sixty-day cease-fire, which ended in February 1987. The president also issued an executive order establishing the National Reconciliation and Development Program. The revived rebel amnesty program was inaugurated in January 1987 to encourage NPA defections by offering land, job training, and assimilation into society. The reconciliation approach was a disappointment to the government, however, as few insurgents surrendered. As a result, Aquino altered government strategy in March 1987 when she announced the "unleashing" of the military.

Following the 1986 change of government, the military resumed full-scale counterinsurgency operations with a new strategy known as Mamamayan, meaning people. Mamamayan was similar in most respects to the previous counterinsurgency, or COIN, plan, Marcos's Katatagan (stability), but added President Aquino's theme of reconciliation to the original program of "clear, hold, consolidate, and develop." The revised COIN plan called for military units, with the cooperation of other government agencies, to systematically clear areas of insurgents, to hold the region against returning guerrillas, to consolidate support for the government, and to develop the area economically. The first task--clearing rebel-infested areas--was seen as the task of mobile forces--the army battalions and constabulary special action forces. The role of holding and consolidating liberated regions was assigned to territorial forces--the constabulary, police, and militia units.

The updated counterinsurgency strategy was complemented by revamped armed forces tactics that were generally credited with contributing to the insurgency's decline during the late 1980s. Under Aquino, the military continued its shift away from conventional methods such as food blockades, cordon and search operations and hamletting (the forced relocation of villages controlled or threatened by the NPA). These methods, employed during the 1970s war against the Moros, were too often ineffective and counterproductive because they frequently alienated the populace. In other respects, the military's approach to COIN efforts changed little. Most military units operated as they had under Marcos, in static positions protecting town halls, businesses, and major roads.

The deployment of special operations teams beginning in 1987 and the formation of new militia units in 1988 were touted by military leaders as important steps toward more effective COIN. Special operations teams were squad-sized military counterinsurgency teams dispatched to CPP-influenced villages to dismantle the communists' political infrastructure by conducting civic action and propaganda programs. These teams worked in conjunction with the newly revamped militia, now called the Citizens Armed Forces Geographic Units (CAFGUs), to provide security to each remote *barangay* (see Glossary). The CAFGUs replaced the Civilian Home Defense Force, which was frequently criticized as abusive by human rights groups. Local anticommunist vigilante groups, some associated with the military, also proved effective deterrents to communist organizing and NPA activity in certain areas (see Organization and Training).

Improved military intelligence also played an important role in undercutting the insurgency in the late 1980s. Military intelligence agents repeatedly captured top CPP and NPA cadres and gathered revealing CPP and NPA documents. Rodolfo Salas, the CPP's former chairman, was among numerous central committee members rounded up. The fear of government intelligence penetrations of communist ranks contributed to devastating purges of rebel ranks between 1985 and 1988.

Perhaps the biggest contribution to the counterinsurgency campaign in the late 1980s was political, not military. Communist leaders admitted that Aquino, by restoring popular government and democratic institutions, significantly set back the revolutionary movement. Further civilian contributions in the fight against the communists were encouraged by the creation in 1987 of Peace and Order Councils. Established at all levels of government, the councils consisted of political and military leaders as well as selected community representatives and were charged with fostering greater civilian involvement and cooperation in what traditionally had been a military counterinsurgency struggle. A 1989 United States military study, however, concluded that the COIN effort remained largely a military effort despite the communist insurgency's political character.

Foreign and Filipino critics of the government's COIN program further alleged that the communist insurgency had endured for more than twenty years because the Philippines had not effectively addressed the social and cultural roots of the rural rebellion. The communist rebellion, it was said, was fed by the same social and economic inequities that had prompted previous peasant uprisings. The disparity between the small, but very wealthy, elite and the many impoverished was fundamental to the appeal of the revolutionary movement. Issues such as land reform resonated strongly among poor farmers, who also complained of abuses by landlords and politicians. Until such grievances were resolved, observers noted, they would continue to fuel insurgent activity in the country.

Recruitment and Personnel

The combined strength of the four armed services at the end of 1990 was approximately 153,500. The army had some 68,000 troops, the constabulary 45,000, the air force 15,500, and the navy 25,000, including about 8,000 in the marines and 2,000 in the coast guard. After rapid growth during the 1970s, when armed forces strength trebled, total military strength remained relatively stable in the 1980s. (There were 155,000 personnel in the Philippine military in 1980.) With a relatively youthful population, maintaining the strength of the armed forces was not a drain on human resources. More than 8 million men were of military age, between eighteen and thirty-two. Military strength per capita was only 2.5 per 1,000 population, lower than nearly all the country's Asian neighbors.

Although universal service was mandatory, the Armed Forces of the Philippines was a de facto volunteer force. The 1980 National Service Law provided the legal basis for conscription and required all citizens--male and female--to perform service in the military, civic welfare, or law enforcement agencies. However, the law was never fully implemented. Conscription was not necessary during the 1980s because volunteers greatly outnumbered available slots. Despite the inherent danger of military service during the fight against the communist insurgency, limited employment opportunities for unskilled young adults ensured an abundant supply of volunteers. The armed forces had no recruiting apparatus; units instead recruited locally to fill vacancies. Potential recruits had to be eighteen years old, unmarried, and possess a high school diploma.

Officers were commissioned from three major sources. Regular officers were commissioned from the prestigious Philippine Military Academy, which produced 15 percent of all officers. Some 65 percent were graduates of Citizen Military Training, formerly the Reserve Officers Training Corps (ROTC). Most received reserve commissions, whereas some, called "integrees," were integrated into the regular officer corps. Enlisted personnel who completed Officer Candidate School accounted for some 18 percent of all officers. The other 2 percent of officers received direct commissions as medical or legal professionals or graduated from foreign military academies. Noncommissioned officers (NCOs) did not constitute the professional corps found in most Western armies and were only marginally involved in leadership and decision making.

Ethnic and linguistic differences were important in the military. Local recruiting ensured that personnel were drawn from all sections of the country, but certain regions were disproportionately represented. The majority of military personnel spoke Tagalog and were from the heartland of central and southern Luzon. Despite continuing efforts to increase the number of Muslims in the military, Moros from the southern Philippines were underrepresented. Traditionally, Ilocanos from northern Luzon comprised a disproportionate share of officer and enlisted ranks. This emphasis was especially true under Marcos, who tended to promote fellow Ilocanos to positions of power in the armed forces and police. Because of this tendency--shared by previous presidents--the 1987 constitution directs that the "armed forces shall be recruited proportionately from all provinces and cities as far as practicable." Although language and dialect compelled people from the same region to associate with one another, these groups were not so exclusive that they formed significant factions.

A variety of internal divisions plagued the officer corps in the late 1980s. The most significant rifts essentially were political--between those who supported the government and those who advocated its overthrow. The military-sparked popular revolt against Marcos and the subsequent series of uprisings against Aquino brought military leaders into direct, sometimes bloody, conflict. A variety of military factions and fraternal groups, including RAM, Young Officers' Union, and Marcos loyalists, emerged as important antigovernment players (see Political Role). In an effort to contain the influence of these groups, the government ordered military fraternal organizations disbanded in 1987. However, through clandestine contacts, RAM, the Young Officers' Union, and Marcos loyalists orchestrated the 1989 coup attempt with the support of three generals. These groups remained active in 1991, criticizing government and military leaders and threatening another coup attempt. Their activities continued to undermine the authority of the military chain of command.

Following the 1989 coup attempt, the president's military adviser, a retired army commander, attributed the involvement of so many junior leaders to a "generational gap" in the armed forces between mostly loyal senior officers and the more rebellions junior ranks. He credited younger officers' better education for the tendency of some, like those in the

Young Officers' Union, to become more involved in politics and to question the directives of their superiors.

Frictions created by perceived inequity in the military's personnel system also dogged the officer corps. Although the divisive Marcos-era practice of extending generals beyond their scheduled retirement was discontinued in 1986, other controversial practices continued under Aquino. Officers with reserve commissions--the majority of the officer corps-- complained that the personnel system favored regular officers, especially Philippine Military Academy (PMA) graduates. Although past regimes, such as Marcos's, had advanced ROTC graduates, nearly all top generals under Aquino were academy alumni. Bond between PMA graduates, especially classmates, tended to perpetuate this favoritism. In 1986 reservists formed an organization similar to the PMA alumni association to promote their interests. The presidentially appointed Davide Commission investigating the causes of the 1989 coup attempt identified another source of discontent--the role of personal ties in promotions and assignments. Observers noted that the patron client ties and personal loyalties that were typical of Philippine society were perhaps the biggest factor in officers' career prospects.

Women belonged to a separate Women's Auxiliary Corps in each of the services. Except for Officer Candidate School, they were trained separately. Women were assigned to a limited number of specified support positions and were a relatively small part of the total force.

Defense Spending and Industry

After steadily declining defense spending during the early 1980s, the defense budget grew in the latter half of the decade. Military spending in 1988 totaled 14.14 billion pesos (for value of the peso--see Glossary), or US$680 million, about 1.7 percent of the country's gross national product (GNP--see Glossary). The 1988 budget represented a greater than 50 percent increase in real spending for defense (adjusted for inflation) over 1985, the last full year Marcos was in office. Defense spending as a proportion of national government expenditures also grew during Aquino's tenure, from a 1985 low of 7.7 percent, to 9.1 percent in 1989. Still, the military's share of the national budget, like total military spending, did not approach the peaks reached during the Moro wars of the 1970s. In 1979 the Philippines spent more than P17 billion (US$806 million) in comparable 1988 pesos for defense, a figure that represented almost 17 percent of the government's budget.

Budget figures do not include United States security assistance, which represented a substantial portion of total spending on the Philippine military. United States military aid increased significantly after Aquino came to power, accounting for 80 percent of military spending on procurement, operations, and maintenance in 1989. United States military aid that year amounted to US$127.6 million. Most of the assistance--US$125 million--was provided as a grant under the Military Assistance Program whereas the US$2.6 million balance funded training for Filipinos under the United States International Military Education and Training Program. During the 1988 review of the Military Bases Agreement, the United States pledged its best efforts to increase grant aid to the Philippine military to US$200 million annually in 1990 and 1991.

The thrust of United States security assistance efforts in the late 1980s was to help the Philippine armed forces better combat the communist insurgency. Improved tactical mobility and communications and better equipped soldiers were top priorities. Between 1986 and 1989, the United States sent the Philippines almost 2,900 military vehicles, nearly 50 helicopters, more than 1,650 radios, approximately 225,000 military uniforms, and more than 150,000 pairs of combat boots. Other assistance items included assorted infantry weapons and ammunition and medical equipment.

The Self-Reliant Defense Posture (SRDP) program, initiated in 1974, took the development of a domestic defense industry as its objective. Defense officials contracted SRDP projects with the government arsenal and local manufacturers, encouraging the use of indigenous raw materials and production capacity. Projects included domestic production of small arms, radios, and assorted ammunition. One of the most significant SRDP operations was the manufacture of the M-16A1 rifle under license from Colt Industries, an American company. According to a 1988 statement by the Philippine armed forces chief of staff, the SRDP not only increased Philippine self-reliance, but also cut costs, provided jobs, and saved much-needed foreign-exchange funds.

Despite growing budgets and increased foreign military aid, the armed forces still was described in 1989 as one of the most poorly funded militaries in Asia. Philippine defense spending on a per capita and per soldier basis remained the lowest of the Association of Southeast Asian Nations (ASEAN) countries, despite an active communist insurgency. One study of the military concluded that the armed forces suffered from major resource problems. The author cited serious shortages of vehicles, helicopters, radios, basic infantry equipment, and spare parts. Food, medicine, and clothing also were said to be in chronically short supply. Shortages were compounded by an inefficient logistics system hobbled by red tape and corruption. Soldiers' poor living and working conditions often were mentioned as underlying factors in the military's discipline problems. Top AFP leaders acknowledged many of these shortcomings and were attempting to correct the mismanagement of resources.

Plans in 1990 called for modernizing the military, particularly the air force and navy-- services whose forces had received relatively little funding because of the army's extended counterinsurgency campaign. Many of the navy's major ships and craft were World War II-era, and the aging fleet was increasingly difficult to maintain. Modernization plans called for phasing out inefficient ships, refitting others, and acquiring more patrol craft. Using United States military aid, the navy contracted in 1989 for thirty-five fast patrol craft, thirty of which were to be assembled in the Philippines by 1997. The air force inventory, described as one of the most primitive in the region, likewise was to be enhanced by major purchases under a ten-year modernization scheme. The United States was scheduled to deliver twenty-nine MD-520 attack helicopters between 1990 and 1992. The air force also was hoping to add two squadrons of modern fighters such as the United States F-16 to its fleet of nine F-5s.

The Structure of the Armed Forces

Commonwealth Act 1, the National Defense Act of 1935, mandated the formation of the Army of the Philippines, comprising all eventual land, sea, air, and national police forces. The existing Philippine Constabulary was abolished and used as the nucleus of the new army. The Philippine Constabulary's air force became the army's air arm and a small maritime element, the Offshore Patrol, was added in 1939. Coincident with a reorganization of the government following independence, the military forces were redesignated the Armed Forces of the Philippines in 1947. That organization was essentially an army command in which air force, maritime, and police internal security units were constituted as subordinate commands. A more fundamental reorganization of the military establishment in 1950, which was brought about in part by the growing Huk insurgency (see The Huk Rebellion), established four separate services--army, navy, air force, and national police--under a joint headquarters. The national police was renamed the Philippine Constabulary in 1959. The army continued to dominate the command structure, however, until 1960 when the headquarters was converted to a truly joint command.

The Philippines deployed combat forces abroad on three occasions. Expeditionary forces served in the Republic of Korea (South Korea) under the United Nations Command between 1950 and 1955. Also under United Nations auspices, air force officers and enlisted personnel were sent to the Republic of the Congo (now Zaire) in 1963. From 1966 until the early 1970s, the 2,000-strong Philippine Civic Action Group, composed mainly of engineer, security, medical, and rural community development teams, was active in the Republic of Vietnam (South Vietnam).

The 1987 constitution mandated further changes in the structure of the armed forces. The existing militia, the Civilian Home Defense Force, was ordered disbanded and was replaced beginning in 1988 with a new auxiliary force under the direct control of military regulars. More significantly, the 1987 constitution calls for the government "to establish and maintain one police force, which shall be national in scope and civilian in character." Pursuant to that mandate, Aquino signed a law directing that the Philippine Constabulary, one of the four military services, be combined with the civilian Integrated National Police to form the Philippine National Police. The process of integrating the two organizations under a newly created Department of Interior and Local Government began on January 1, 1991.

Organization and Training

The 1987 constitution mandates civilian control of the military and establishes the president as commander in chief of the armed forces. The president also heads the National Security Council, ostensibly the policy-making and advisory body for matters connected with national defense. President Aquino reestablished the council in 1986 through an executive order that provided for a National Security Council director to advise the president on national security matters and for a National Security Council Secretariat. The council itself is composed of the president and at least nine others: the vice president; the AFP chief of staff; National Security Council director; the executive secretary; and the secretaries of foreign affairs, national defense, interior and local government, justice, and labor and employment (called ministers before 1987). By the end of 1990, however, the National Security Council had only convened twice.

Much of the real authority for policy development appeared to reside with a smaller cabinet group that met more frequently. A cabinet Cluster for Political and Security Affairs, known as Cluster E, routinely advised the president on national security matters. Cluster E membership was more limited, but included key members of the National Security Council, such as its director and the secretaries of national defense, foreign affairs, justice, and finance.

Responsibility for national security was vested in the Department of National Defense. The principal functions of the department in 1991 were to defend the state against internal and external threats and, through the Philippine National Police, to maintain law and order. A broad interpretation of these roles historically has involved the department in national development tasks, including civic action, to address the causes for internal unrest. The secretary of national defense, by law a civilian, was charged with advising the president on defense matters and developing defense policy.

Authority over the AFP's four services was vested in the chief of staff, a general. The chief of staff exercised command through the General Headquarters, which was located with the Department of National Defense in Manila's Camp Aguinaldo. Immediately subordinate to him was the vice chief of staff, a lieutenant general, and the deputy chief of staff, a major general who was the military's chief administrator. The General Headquarters was staffed with a coordinating staff, J-1 through J-9, and a special staff. Coordinating staff officers included deputies for personnel, intelligence, operations, logistics, plans, comptroller, civil-military operations, and education and training. Also subordinate to the chief of staff were the various specified and support commands and area unified commands (see fig. 10).

Throughout the country, the regionally based area unified commands exercised operational control over AFP units of all services deployed in their regions. AFP General Headquarters created six area commands in 1987 and 1988 by combining the thirteen regional unified commands that had been formed in 1983. Area command boundaries were defined by the country's numbered political regions (see fig. 9). Northern Luzon Command incorporated regions 1, 2 and 3; Southern Luzon Command encompassed region 4 (except Palawan) and region 5; Visayas Command covered the Visayan Islands in regions 6, 7, and 8; and Southern Command incorporated the island of Mindanao and the Sulu Archipelago, regions 9 through 12. The AFP's Western Command was responsible for the province of Palawan (part of region 4) and for Philippine claims in the Spratly Islands. The sixth area command, the National Capital Region Command, had operational control over military units in metropolitan Manila. Area commanders directed counterinsurgency operations in their respective areas, but support functions--such as training and logistics--were left to the military support services and joint commands such as the AFP's Logistics Command and Training Command.

The armed forces maintained several military training institutions in 1991. Foremost among these was the Philippine Military Academy, founded in 1905 to train Filipino officers for the Philippine Constabulary. Located at Fort del Pilar, Baguio, the academy trained future officers of all four services. Male cadets between the ages of seventeen and twenty-three were selected through a highly competitive examination for a four-year course, patterned on the United States Military Academy, leading to a bachelor of science degree and an officer's commission. Attrition took a heavy toll. Only about 100 of the 400 cadets admitted each year completed the course. Graduates were given their choice of service within established quota limits, with preference given to those with the highest class standing. The Philippine Constabulary was most often a cadet's first choice, reflecting the potential for developing supplementary income and local influence that came with the job. Officers assigned to the navy and air force usually attended orientation courses before being assigned to their units.

Reserve officers were trained under the Citizen Military Training system, formerly known as the Reserve Officer Training Corps. Basic military training under this system was mandatory for all high school students. Male college students were required to take additional basic training and had the option of advanced training leading to a reserve officer's commission. A small number of Citizen Military Training graduates were integrated into the regular officer corps. Women were commissioned into the Women's Auxiliary Corps of one of the services following training at selected universities.

Officer Candidate School was a third source of commissions. Candidates were required to have a bachelor's degree and were accepted from the enlisted ranks and the civilian sector.

In the late 1980s, women were admitted with men to this one-year program taught at the AFP's Training Command at Camp Capinpin, near Manila, in Rizal Province.

Career training for officers was patterned after that in the United States. The AFP's Command and General Staff College prepared officers of all services for command, staff, and managerial positions normally assigned to field-grade officers. Only 25 percent of mid-grade officers were chosen to attend the eight-month cause at Fort Bonifacio in Manila. The National Defense College, also at Fort Bonifacio, was the military's senior education institution. A select group of senior officers and government officials attended a course given each year at the college and received master's degrees in national security administration. The curriculum was designed to provide the broad perspective necessary for national policy making.

Acknowledging systemic weaknesses, the AFP undertook several programs to upgrade training in the late 1980s. To improve management of the training system, training staffs were established in the AFP's General Headquarters and added to service and unified command staffs in 1988. The Training Command was organized at Camp Capinpin. In addition to conducting a variety of training for enlisted personnel, noncommissioned officers (NCOs), and officers, the Training Command was charged with developing instruction and standardizing common training among the services.

Army

The Philippine army was formally organized in 1936 after the United States accorded the Philippines commonwealth status in 1935, but it traced its origins to the rebel forces established in 1896 to fight for national independence. The army was intended to be a small standing army modeled on the United States Army, but army strength varied widely over the years, depending on the internal threat. After dramatic growth during the 1970s, total army strength remained relatively stable during the 1980s. With some 68,000 troops in 1990, the army was by far the largest of the services. The commanding general, a major general, directly controlled the service's administrative, logistics, and training functions from headquarters at Fort Bonifacio in Manila, but area unified commands exercised operational control over nearly all combat units. Army units were actively involved in the fight against the communist insurgency and, to a lesser extent, monitored the mostly dormant Muslim rebellion.

The army's major tactical units were its eight light infantry divisions. Three divisions were headquartered on the northern Island of Luzon, two were based in the central Visayan Islands, and three operated on the southern island of Mindanao. All except one consisted of three brigades, and that one had two brigades. Although the army's overall strength did not change, during the late 1980s it was structurally expanded, from the four divisions that had existed since 1983 to eight in 1990. The basic maneuver unit was the infantry battalion. Although authorized to contain some 600 soldiers, battalions typically had 500 troops or fewer assigned.

In addition to these infantry formations, the army had a light armored brigade, eight artillery battalions, three engineer brigades, and a construction battalion. Support units included a service support brigade, a training command, a signal group, an intelligence and security group, a civil-military operations battalion, and a finance center. The elite army Scout Ranger regiment, a specialized counterinsurgency force, was disbanded following its participation in the 1989 coup attempt.

The army's weapons were appropriate to its light infantry force structure and counterinsurgency mission (see table 19). Major items included 41 light tanks, 85 armored infantry fighting vehicles, 285 armored personnel carriers, and assorted light and medium towed artillery. Most arms and equipment were of United States make or design, although sources of weapons and supplies had diversified since the 1970s. The standard infantry weapon was the United States M-16A1 rifle, manufactured in the Philippines under a license agreement.

Table 19. Major Army Equipment, 1990

Type and Description	Country of Origin	In Inventory
Tanks		
Scorpion (light) with 76mm gun	Britain	41
Armored personnel carriers		
M-113	United States	100
Chaimite	Portugal	20
V-150 Commando	United States	165
Armored infantry fighting vehicles (AIFV)	-do-	85
Howitzers		
105mm M-101 towed	United States	n.a.
105mm M-102	-do-	n.a.
105mm M-26	Spain	n.a.
105mm M-56 pack	Italy	n.a.
Total 105mm	230	
155mm M-68 towed	Israel	n.a.
155mm M-114	United States	n.a.
Total 155mm	12	
Mortars		
81mm M-29	-do-	n.a.
107mm M-30	-do-	40
Recoilless launchers		
75mm M-20	-do-	n.a.
90mm M-67	-do-	n.a.
106mm M-40A1	-do-	n.a.

n.a.--not available.
Source: Based on information from *The Military Balance, 1990- 1991,* London, 1990, 174-75; *Jane's Infantry Weapons, 1990-91,* London, 1990; and *Jane's Armour and Artillery, 1990-91,* London, 1990.

The army operated a variety of schools for its arms and branches. The Army Training Command was located at Fort Magsaysay in Nueva Ecija, north of Manila. The training command provided basic training for enlisted personnel and officers and advanced training in some specialties such as infantry and artillery. Specialized training in other areas, such as armor, intelligence, and engineering, was the responsibility of service extension schools operated by the commanders of those army units. Many soldiers, however, never attended centralized military schools, but instead were trained by army divisions at basic training centers throughout the country.

Navy

The navy, the newest of the services, traces its ancestry to the Offshore Patrol, which was formed as part of the army in February 1939. It became autonomous and was redesignated the Philippine Naval Patrol in 1947. After the armed forces reorganized in 1950, the force became known as the navy. Naval personnel strength of approximately 25,000 in 1990 included marine, coast guard, and naval air units. Naval headquarters was in Manila, close to its major base at Cavite, south of the city. Other major naval bases were located in Zamboanga City, Cebu City, and at Subic Bay on Luzon, west of Manila. The Subic Bay facility, probably without peer as a deep-water port in the region, was used almost exclusively by the United States Navy.

The navy's principal mission was to protect and police the nation's 7,100 islands with a combined coastline of 36,289 kilometers, double that of the United States, and the Philippines' claimed exclusive economic zone (EEZ--see Glossary) of 200 nautical miles. The navy also had important support missions for the other armed forces and agencies of the government, especially in transporting troops and equipment between islands. It occasionally joined with other services in conducting joint operations and amphibious assaults. Through its subordinate coast guard arm, the navy was responsible for enforcement of maritime laws and regulations and countering widespread smuggling, poaching, and pirating in Philippine waters, including interception of covert supply lines to insurgent groups. The navy was hard-pressed to fulfill its broad responsibilities; senior naval officers candidly admitted that the fleet was too small and ill-maintained to patrol its large coastline and EEZ effectively and protect the Philippine claim to Kalayaan.

The navy was commanded by a rear admiral, known as the flag officer in command, who was supported by vice and deputy flag officers in command. Major naval operating forces came under the commander of the fleet, who directed the naval air, special warfare, assault craft, amphibious, and patrol groups. The navy also maintained six naval districts that supervised deployed naval forces under the operational control of the area unified commanders. The naval headquarters controlled the training command, coast guard and marine commands, and the naval support group which provided supply and maintenance support to the fleet.

All major combatants in the fleet were former United States ships, most of World War II vintage. In late 1989, the navy maintained three frigates and eleven corvettes, none with missiles (see table 20). Consistent with the navy's mission, the mainstays of the fleet were patrol boats, including twelve coastal and thirty-nine inshore patrol craft. The navy also used eleven amphibious ships and some seventy-five landing craft for inter-island transport.

Many of the navy's ships, however, were in poor repair and of questionable operational capability. Roughly one-third of the ships were said to be serviceable, and only about twenty of them put to sea regularly. Because of these operational deficiencies, which the navy attributed to budget shortfalls, the navy embarked on a modernization program in 1990. Plans called for the overhaul of some ships and for the acquisition of thirty-five new patrol craft. Several older ships, including four frigates, had been decommissioned in the late 1980s, and more retirements of inoperable ships were planned.

Table 20. Major Naval Equipment, 1990

Type and Description	Country of Origin	In Inventory
Navy		
Frigates		
Cannon class	United States	1
Casco class	-do-	2
Corvettes		
Auk class	-do-	2
PCE-827 class	-do-	7
Admirable class	-do-	2
Patrol craft		
PC-461 class	-do-	2
Kagitingan class	Germany	4
PGM-39/71 class	United States	4
Patrol craft-fast (PCF)	Various	41[1]
Amphibious ships and craft		
Landing ship, tank (LST-511 class)	United States	11
Landing ship, medium (LSM)	-do-	2
Landing craft, utility (LCU)	-do-	9
Landing craft, medium (LCM)	-do-	60
Landing craft, vehicle and personnel (LCVP)	-do-	6
Naval Aviation		
Pilatus Britten-Norman BN-2B Islander (patrol and search and rescue)	Britain	12
MBB BO-105C utility helicopters (search and rescue)[2]	Philippines	10
Marines		
Armored vehicles		
Armored personnel carrier, V-150	United States	18
Armored personnel carrier, LAV-25[3]	- do-	36
Landing vehicle, LVTP-5	-do-	18
Landing vehicle, LVTH-6 (105mm howitzer)	-do-	20
Landing vehicle, LVTP-7	-do-	55
Artillery		
M-101 105mm, towed	-do-	150
Mortars		
M-30 107mm	-do-	n.a.
M-29 81mm	-do-	n.a.

n.a.--not available.

[1]Thirty-five on order.

[2]Produced under license agreement with Messerschmitt-Bölkow-Blom, Germany.

[3]The marines were scheduled to acquire thirty-six additional LAV- 25s and as many as thirty LVTP-7s.

Source: Based on information from *The Military Balance, 1990- 1991,* London, 1990, 174-75; "The Modernization of the Philippine Navy," *International Defence Review,* 23, January 1990, 88; and *Jane's Fighting Ships, 1990-91,* London, 1990.

The coast guard, established in 1967, was the navy's law enforcement arm. Its responsibilities included testing and licensing seamen and vessels, providing navigational aids, and protecting life and property at sea. To fulfill these missions, the coast guard operated nearly ninety small patrol boats and conducted search and rescue operations with two larger boats, a fixed-wing aircraft, and a helicopter. In 1990 the coast guard commander, a navy commodore, supervised some 2,000 personnel and 8 operational districts.

Although the marine corps mission was to conduct amphibious operations, in practice the marines generally were employed in assisting the army and constabulary in counterinsurgency operations against the Moros and communists. The service was commanded by the marine commandant, a brigadier general, and headquartered at Fort Bonifacio in Manila. The marine corps grew modestly during the 1980s; strength in 1990 was about 8,000 troops, up from 6,800 troops in 1983. The marine corps organization grew commensurately, from two brigades to four. The ten marine battalions were equipped with a variety of mostly United States-made equipment, including amphibious vehicles, armored personnel carriers, and howitzers. Their performance in counterinsurgency operations had earned marines the reputation for being a well-disciplined and well-respected force, but their support of Marcos in 1986 and involvement in a subsequent coup attempt against Aquino tarnished the marines' image.

Air Force

Traditionally, the air force's primary mission was air defense of the nation. In the mid-1980s, however, the air force shifted its principal effort to supporting the ground forces in counterinsurgency operations, using both fixed-wing aircraft and helicopters. The air force's other roles included search and rescue, transportation, and communications for all services. The Air Force Security Command (formerly the Aviation Security Command) was responsible for security of the nation's airports. The air force regularly took part in disaster relief and emergency operations in cooperation with civilian organizations and participated in national development programs.

The air force was headquartered at Villamor Air Base (formerly called Nichols Air Base) in Manila and was commanded by a two-star general. Other major bases included Basa and Clark air bases in Pampanga Province, Fernando Air Base in Batangas Province, Sangley Point Air Base in Cavite Province, and Mactan Air Base in Cebu Province. Flight training was conducted at the Air Force Flying School located at Fernando Air Base. Clark Air Base in Central Luzon was used primarily by United States forces based or training there. Although normally based at one of these facilities, aircraft, especially helicopters, routinely operated out of forward bases throughout the country in support of area commands' counterinsurgency operations. With approximately 15,500 officers and enlisted personnel, the air force was slightly smaller in 1990 than in the early 1980s, when personnel totaled 16,800.

The air force inventory in 1990 included fifteen combat aircraft and seventy-one armed helicopters, all United States made (see table 21). In 1987, the Philippines grounded its fleet of F-8 Crusaders, leaving only two squadrons of F-5 Freedom Fighters to provide air defense. The fighters were armed with United States-made AIM-9B Sidewinder missiles. Counterinsurgency operations were supported by a squadron of eight T-28D Trojan propeller-driven trainer/attack airplanes, and a wing equipped with fifty-five Bell UH-1H/Iroquois transport helicopters and sixteen AUH-76 attack helicopters.

Table 21. Major Air Force Equipment, 1990

Type and Description	Country of Origin	In Inventory
Fighter aircraft		
Northrop F-5A Freedom Fighter	United States	71
Counterinsurgency aircraft		
North American T-28D Trojan	-do-	8
Search and rescue reconnaissance aircraft		
Fokker F-27M Friendship/Maritime	Netherlands	2
Lockheed RT-33A Shooting Star	United States	3
Grumman HU-16B Albatross	-do-	4
Transport and utility aircraft		
Lockheed C-130H Hercules	-do-	3
Lockheed L-100-20 Hercules	-do-	3
Fokker F-27 Friendship [1]	Netherlands	8
Fokker F-28 Fellowship [1]	-do-	1
Douglas C-47	United States	3
N-22B Nomad	Australia	9
Britten-Norman BN-2 Islander	Britain	10
Cessna 180	United States	6
Cessna 210	-do-	2
Cessna 310	-do-	1
DHC-2	Canada	5
U-17A/B	n.a.	15
Trainer aircraft		
Northrop F-5B Freedom Fighter	United States	2
Lockheed T/RT-33A Shooting Star	-do-	8
Cessna T-41D Mescalero	-do-	20
SIAI-Marchetti SF-26OMP/WP	Italy	23
SIAI-Marchetti S-211	-do-	4
Helicopters		
Bell UH-1H/M Iroquois (counterinsurgency)	United States	55
Bell UH-1H Iroquois (transport)	-do-	17
Bell 205	-do-	15
Sikorsky AUH-76 (S-76 attack version)	-do-	16
McDonnell Douglas MD-520 (attack)	- do-	2
Sikorsky S-70A	-do-	2
Bell 212	-do-	1
PADC MBB BO-105C (search and rescue) [2]	Philippines	10
SA-330 Pumal	France [3]	2
Air-to-air missiles		
AIM-9B Sidewinder	United States	n.a.

n.a.--not available.

[1] Assigned to presidential airlift wing.

[2] Produced under license from Messerschmitt-Bölkow-Blom, Germany.

[3] Principally built in France, but also produced in Romania and Indonesia.

Source: Based on information from *The Military Balance, 1990- 1991,* London, 174-75; and *Jane's All the World's Aircraft, 1989-90,* London, 1989.

Support units included seven transport squadrons; three training squadrons; a presidential airlift wing; and assorted reconnaissance, search and rescue, and liaison aircraft. Aircraft assigned to these elements were obtained from many countries, including Britain, Australia, Italy, and the Netherlands as well as the United States. In 1990 the air force expanded its capabilities by acquiring a variety of new aircraft. The Philippines received four Italian S-211 jet trainers and contracted for delivery of fourteen more. In addition, the air force was to receive twenty-nine United States-made MD-520 attack helicopters and hoped to upgrade its fighter fleet with the purchase of two squadrons of more modern fighters.

Philippine Constabulary

The Philippine Constabulary, which was to be disbanded and absorbed into a civilian police force beginning in 1991, was the oldest of the nation's four armed forces. It was established by the United States colonial government in 1901 to preserve peace and order and provided the nucleus of the first regular division of the Commonwealth's army in 1936. It remained an element within the army (after 1946 as the Military Police Command) until 1950 when it was reestablished as a separate force. It was formally renamed the Philippine Constabulary in 1959.

After its renaming, the Philippine Constabulary officially constituted a national police force and essentially operated as a gendarmerie, holding primary authority for law enforcement and domestic security. It was responsible for dealing with large scale crime, conducting wide-area operations, and enforcing the peace and national laws, especially in remote areas where other forces were nonexistent or ineffective. The constabulary also played a prominent role in combating the Moro and communist insurgencies. Following the creation of the Integrated National Police in 1975, the constabulary operated with the new force under a joint command structure (see Law Enforcement).

Organized and equipped along military lines, the constabulary was headed in 1990 by a major general, who served concurrently as the director general of the Integrated National Police. He was assisted by deputies for the Philippine Constabulary and Integrated National Police, and by his Camp Crame, Manila, headquarters staff, which was similar to the AFP's General Headquarters staff. Constabulary forces throughout the country were supported and controlled through a system of regional commands, with one command in each of the country's twelve political regions. Under the operational control of the area commands, the regional commands controlled subordinate Philippine Constabulary and Integrated National Police provincial commands. These 73 provincial headquarters in turn supervised 234 constabulary companies, which were the constabulary's line units. Regional Special Action Companies provided backup to the line companies and acted as counterinsurgency strike forces. An additional area command, known both as Capital Command and the Metropolitan Police Force, directed Philippine Constabulary and Integrated National Police elements in Manila. Metropolitan District Commands performed a similar function in eight of the nation's other major urban areas.

The constabulary also had a variety of specialized units with nationwide responsibilities that operated independently of the regional command system. These included the Criminal Investigative Service, Highway Patrol Group, Security Group, Crime Lab, and Support Command. The Philippine Constabulary Training Command was responsible for instructing enlisted constables and their officers, whose training paralleled that of the army. In 1983 the constabulary created an elite national reaction force, the Philippine Constabulary Special

Action Force, with the capability to combat terrorism, hijacking, and insurgency. These additions contributed to the overall growth of members of the constabulary during the 1980s, from approximately 33,500 in 1980, to an estimated 45,000 members in 1990.

On January 1, 1991, the Philippine Constabulary and the Integrated National Police were combined to form the Philippine National Police. The Philippine National Police took immediate responsibility for most former Integrated National Police functions, including fire and jail services, and was to assume responsibility for the counterinsurgency effort from the AFP after two years, in 1993. Few details were available at the end of 1990 on how the military planned to effect the transfer of police and, ultimately, counterinsurgency responsibilities to civilian control.

Reserves and Auxiliaries

The Philippine reserve program was founded on the citizen army concept laid out in the National Defense Act of 1935, whereby defense would be provided by a limited professional cadre backed by citizen reservists rather than by a large conscript army. In 1989 the AFP claimed that active forces of about 153,500 people were backed by some 800,000 reservists. However, this number probably included all eligible former soldiers, many of whom might be difficult to recall. Other sources placed total reserve strength at 128,000--approximately 100,000 in the army, 12,000 in the navy, and 16,000 in the air force. Only a small fraction of these--less than 50,000--were thought to be active by involved in the reserve program.

The AFP reserve program was administered by an element of the General Headquarters staff, within the office of civil-military operations. Reserve forces fell into two major categories: Auxiliary Reserve Units and Citizens Armed Forces Geographic Units (CAFGUs). Reservists of the first category were predesignated civilians in critical public sector jobs, such as electric power and water service, who were subject to federal mobilization. They had no military training and were not intended to support military operations directly in the event of a callup.

The CAFGUs consisted of both inactive military reserve forces and militia units actively involved in counterinsurgency. Each service had its own inactive CAFGU reserve component. On paper, the army had thirteen divisions of CAFGU reservists, one in each political region, including Manila. These units, however, never trained nor even conducted organizational meetings. Instead, Regional Community Defense Units--which administered the Citizen Military Training program--maintained rosters of individual reservists. A few reserve officers participated at their own expense in annual training, but there was no individual training for enlisted reservists.

CAFGU active auxiliaries--essentially militia who provided for village self-defense-- were the heart of the reserve program. Under the direct control of the active military, they replaced the Marcos-era Civilian Home Defense Force, a poorly trained and equipped force widely criticized as being corrupt and abusive. Members of the active CAFGUs were full-time militia who were recruited and based in their home areas, where they were charged with defending against insurgent attacks. CAFGU companies were trained and commanded by active officers and NCOs of the army and constabulary. If mobilized, the militia were to become part of their sponsoring active army or constabulary unit. The 720 CAFGU active auxiliary companies had around 64,000 members in 1990.

Other armed groups, labeled vigilantes, were sometimes sponsored or endorsed by the military. Aquino initially praised some of these anticommunist citizens' groups--such as

Davao City's Alsa Masa (Masses Arise)--for their success at discouraging communist insurgent activity in their neighborhoods during the late 1980s. In 1988, however, an international human rights group charged that Philippine vigilantes had committed "grave violations on a wide scale." Armed forces-sponsored self-defense groups who were unarmed were not so controversial. These civilian volunteer organizations, including Bantay Bayan (Nation Watch), supported the military by reporting insurgent activity in their *barangays*.

Uniforms, Ranks, and Insignia

The rank structure of the armed forces in the early 1990s was very similar to that of counterpart services in the United States (see fig. 11). There were, however, no warrant officer ranks in any of the four armed forces, and all four services maintained seven enlisted grades rather than nine as in the United States system (see fig. 12). The army, air force, and constabulary used the same ranks and insignia. Officer ranks corresponded to their United States counterparts, except that naval flag officers were called commodores and admirals but were equivalent to United States Navy rear admirals. The single full general in the nation in 1990 was a constabulary officer who had received his fourth star by virtue of his position as the AFP chief of staff. Likewise, the AFP vice chief of staff was the only lieutenant general, and the four service chiefs were major generals. The military had some 100 general officers. AFP uniforms reflected the military's close ties to the United States and the Philippines' hot, humid climate. Field uniforms for all services were a mixture of American-style olive-drab and camouflage jungle fatigues. Because of chronic uniform shortages, military personnel often wore civilian clothes, making armed soldiers difficult to distinguish from militia, insurgents, vigilantes, or members of private security forces. Dress uniforms were similar to those worn by United States forces, made of summer-weight tan or white fabric.

Salary and Benefits

Pay was poor but fairly competitive with the civilian economy and the standard of living of the average Filipino, ensuring that the AFP never lacked sufficient volunteers. Still, many soldiers lived at or below the poverty line. The average private made the equivalent of about US$50 a month, and not even senior officers could afford to live lavishly on their salary alone. In apparent recognition of the impact of poor pay on military morale, Aquino authorized additional benefits and a pay increase that averaged 60 percent in the wake of the 1987 coup attempt. Benefits included housing, medical and dental care, commissary privileges, insurance, death benefits, and a retirement plan for service of twenty to thirty years.

Foreign Military Relations

The Philippines maintained its closest military relations with the United States. Close contacts were based on cooperative ventures, such as joint exercises, and on longstanding military links. Military relations were first established in the colonial era when the United States helped the Philippines to develop its military. The United States and the Philippines maintained their relationship as allies during World War II and the postwar period. Most Philippine military institutions were modeled after United States counterparts, and the United States remained the AFP's principal benefactor in 1990, providing substantial funds and training. Formal relations between the armed forces of the two countries were based on two agreements: the 1947 Military Bases Agreement, which provided for United States facilities in the Philippines, and the 1951 Mutual Defense Treaty, between the Republic of the Philippines and the United States of America.

Under the Mutual Defense Treaty, the Philippines and the United States each agreed that "an armed attack in the Pacific Area on either of the Parties would be dangerous to its own peace and safety." Both nations pledged that in such an event each "would act to meet the common danger in accordance with its constitutional processes." The United States government guaranteed to defend the security of the Philippines against external aggression but not necessarily against internal subversion. The treaty was the basis for an annual joint exercise, known as Balikatan, between the two nations.

Signed in 1947 by the government of the newly independent Philippines, the Military Bases Agreement originally provided the United States with ninety-nine years of access. Almost from the beginning, however, several Military Bases Agreement-related issues were the subject of controversy in the Philippines, arousing sometimes strident opposition to the presence of United States bases. Some Filipinos saw the facilities as an infringement on Philippine sovereignty and a vestige of the country's colonial past. Some also charged that the agreement's rules on criminal jurisdiction shielded United States military personnel from Philippine law and that the economic and military aid provided by the United States as compensation was inadequate. Finally, opponents blamed the United States military for conditions in towns around the facilities, which were notorious for their red-light districts and consequent social problems.

Amendments to the text of the Military Bases Agreement addressed some Philippine concerns but did not quell opposition altogether. A 1959 amendment shortened the duration of the agreement with a proviso that either party could terminate the agreement with one year's notice after 1991. Amendments in 1965 revised legal jurisdiction in criminal and civil matters. After long and difficult negotiations in the late 1970s, the agreement again was amended in 1979 to reaffirm Philippine sovereignty over the bases, ensure the United States unhampered access to the facilities, and provide for a thorough review of the agreement every five years. The first review, in 1983, resulted in several further concessions to Philippine demands for increased sovereignty. The United States also pledged its best efforts to provide the Philippines with US$900 million in economic and military aid over the next five years (1984-88), up from US$500 million over the previous five years. The seven months of negotiation during the 1988 Military Bases Agreement review were highly contentious. The United States agreed to increase efforts to provide the Philippines with US$481 million in aid annually over the two remaining years of the agreement's fixed term.

In 1990 Philippine and United States representatives began a new round of negotiations on the future of United States bases. The 1987 constitution states that a treaty approved by the Philippine Senate is necessary for foreign bases to remain in the country after 1991. Only a few of the twenty-two original United States military facilities established in 1947 remained in the Philippines in 1990. The two most important were the Subic Bay Naval Base, in Zambales Province (and the adjacent naval air station at Cubi Point), and Clark Air Base, a large facility in Pampanga Province, northwest of Manila. Other ancillary facilities included John Hay Air Station in Benguet Province, San Miguel Naval Communications Station in Zambales Province, and Wallace Air Station in La Union Province.

After preliminary talks in May 1990, negotiations began in earnest in September and were continued into 1991. Citing constitutional requirements and the amended Military Bases Agreement, Philippine negotiators notified United States officials early in the talks that, without a new treaty, United States access to the bases would be terminated in 1991. Philippine officials further stated that their goal was to reach agreement on United States military phase-out, a move that would satisfy Philippine sensitivities over sovereignty. At the same time, Philippine officials were anxious to minimize the adverse impact of a United States withdrawal on the bases' 22,000 workers and on the surrounding communities. Before the talks began, a joint Philippine executive-legislative commission drafted a plan for the conversion of the bases to Philippine military and commercial uses. The chief United States negotiator, meanwhile, announced United States plans to withdraw its air fighter wing at Clark Air Base as part of an overall plan to reduce forces in the region.

As part of bases-related compensation, the United States continued to provide financial, equipment, and logistical support to the Philippine military throughout the 1980s. The effect of United States-supplied equipment, training, and logistical support on the AFP would be difficult to overstate. Most Philippine military equipment was of United States design or manufacture, and, despite growing self-reliance and more Philippine purchases from other countries, United States assistance provided for most AFP capital procurement. Also, the United States funded the military education of more than 20,000 Filipinos between 1950 and 1990. In the late 1980s, approximately seventy officers and senior enlisted personnel studied at United States military schools each year. Some Filipinos attended the United States Military Academy at West Point, and a smaller number graduated from United States naval, air force, and coast guard academies.

Military relations with regional neighbors were conducted primarily within the framework of ASEAN. ASEAN had no defense function, however, and its members were committed to establishing a "zone of peace, freedom, and neutrality" in the region. Outside the ASEAN framework, the Philippines conducted joint military training exercises on a bilateral basis with some regional neighbors. In addition, members of the Philippine armed forces trained in Australia, Malaysia, Thailand, and Singapore, as well as in Britain, Germany, and Belgium.

Intelligence and Security Agencies

The period following the overthrow of the Marcos regime brought important changes to the Philippines' intelligence and security structure. During the martial law era (1972-81), the volume and scope of government intelligence activity had greatly expanded. The preeminent intelligence agency was the National Intelligence and Security Authority, headed by General Fabian Ver, a close Marcos confidant and chief of staff of the Philippine armed forces. By the end of Marcos's tenure, the National Intelligence and Security Authority and the rest of the country's intelligence apparatus were heavily focused on tracking the president's political opponents. Security agents were suspected of numerous human rights abuses.

The revamp of the nation's intelligence system commenced with Aquino's rise to power. The new government significantly curtailed intelligence operations and purged many of General Ver's operatives. Drafters of the 1987 constitution installed legal safeguards against the kind of abuses committed by the Marcos intelligence and security apparatus. The National Intelligence and Security Authority, tainted by its close association with the deposed president, was renamed the National Intelligence Coordinating Agency and refocused its efforts away from political opposition leaders to internal security threats, especially the communist insurgency. Notable intelligence successes against the communist rebels during the late 1980s were an apparent result of this reorientation. Government operatives repeatedly captured top CPP and NPA cadres, prompting devastating purges within the insurgent ranks as guerrillas attempted to ferret out the sources of intelligence penetrations.

In 1990 Aquino issued an executive order authorizing her national security adviser to oversee the National Intelligence Coordinating Agency and other elements of the intelligence community. The adviser was empowered to audit the agencies and was charged with ensuring that they were responsive to the needs of the president and the National Security Council. The secretaries of national defense and justice, whose departments performed intelligence functions, were directed to work with the national security adviser to fulfill the president's mandate.

The Department of Justice's principal intelligence-gathering organ, the National Bureau of Investigation, was formed in 1936 as the Division of Investigation and patterned after the United States Federal Bureau of Investigation. The bureau's principal mission was to assist the Philippine Constabulary and police in crime detection and investigation, freeing them to concentrate on maintaining peace and order. Collection of intelligence on internal security threats was considered a related function.

The Department of National Defense, meanwhile, maintained an extensive intelligence apparatus. Although little was publicly revealed about its organization or operation, it was known that the military's principal intelligence organ was the Intelligence Service of the AFP. Headed by a brigadier general, Intelligence Service units operated throughout the country. Their mission in 1990 included not only pursuing insurgents, but also gathering information on military coup plotters and participants. The military services, too, maintained their own intelligence arms. The regimental-size Intelligence and Security Group supported the army while the Constabulary Security Group served Philippine Constabulary leaders. The division of responsibilities among these military intelligence agencies, as well as the institutional mechanisms, if any, that were set up to coordinate their activities, were unclear.

Public Order and Internal Security

When Aquino assumed office in February 1986, she immediately began dismantling repressive restrictions on civil and public liberties. Political prisoners, including top communist leaders, were released. Restrictions on the media's ability to report freely and to criticize the nation's leaders were removed. Aquino also allowed far greater freedom of political expression.

Although she enjoyed broad public support, Aquino inherited a variety of internal security threats from her predecessor. Chief among them was the insurgency inspired by the CPP and its military arm, the NPA. After modest growth during the first two years of Aquino's tenure, insurgent strength waned in the late 1980s. Although communist guerrillas remained active throughout most of the country, internal dissension and improved AFP tactics had reduced their threat. Meanwhile, Muslim insurgents in the south threatened to resume their armed struggle for independence or autonomy. A combination of political maneuvering within the government, continued Moro factionalism, and decreased foreign support, however, reduced prospects for open rebellion. By 1990 the Muslims, although locally active and still a potent military force, showed little inclination to resume full-scale conflict.

Repeated military rebellions and coup attempts constituted the most pressing challenge to Aquino's authority. The highly politicized military generally was seen as another legacy of the Marcos regime. Military dissidents exploited widely shared grievances in order to recruit supporters for their rebellions. These grievances were at the root of military restiveness. Many officers complained that the Aquino government was insensitive to the military's concerns and that her administration was corrupt and unable to lead.

Aquino also faced a serious crime problem within the Philippines. A variety of social and cultural factors contributed to the problem. Widespread poverty and the growing urbanization of the nation's traditionally rural society often were cited as contributors. The crime rate generally paralleled the state of the economy, dramatically worsening during the mid-1980s before improving at decade's end. Violence, long common in Philippine society, was aggravated by insurgency and the prevalence of high-powered firearms. Drugs were a modest but growing problem, and CPP-inspired terrorism against Philippine officials, and sometimes Americans, escalated in the late-1980s.

To deal with criminal activity, the government focused on improving the performance of the police and the courts. Aquino took several steps to remedy widespread skepticism about the fairness and effectiveness of the judicial system. She ended presidential political interference in judicial affairs and took steps to speed the sluggish legal process and reduce the logjam of court cases. Efforts to improve Integrated National Police discipline and professionalism continued, with special attention given to the perception that police were excessively corrupt and abusive.

The Communist Insurgency

The Philippine communist insurgency of the 1990s was rooted in the nation's history of peasant rebellion. Rural revolts-- isolated and unsuccessful--were common during the early part of the twentieth century and before. Discontent among peasants over land tenancy and growing population pressures inspired increasing violence in the 1930s, especially in Central Luzon where isolated peasant rebellions gave way to better organized, sometimes revolutionary movements. After World War II, tensions between peasants and the government-backed landlords grew, leading to the Huk rebellion. Formerly anti-Japanese guerrillas, the Huk (see Glossary) fighters were associated with the Communist Party of the Philippines (Partido Kommunista ng Pilipinas--PKP), which had been established in 1930. The rebellion waned during the early 1950s, but Huk supporters and the remnants of the Huk army later played important roles in the founding of the NPA in the late 1960s.

The CPP guerrilla movement, the NPA, was a successor to the PKP-Huk actions. Jose Maria Sison and a handful of young revolutionaries founded the CPP--Marxist Leninist, now usually referred to as the CPP, in Central Luzon on December 26, 1968. It soon became the core communist political organization, leaving just a small remnant of the original PKP. The NPA was formed the following March with sixty former Huk fighters. The new party has been a result of an internal schism in the parent PKP, created by ideological differences and by personal animosity between Sison and PKP leaders. The CPP pursued a Maoist-inspired program unlike the Soviet-sponsored PKP. The PKP eventually renounced armed insurrection and, in 1990, was an inconsequential, quasi-legal political party with about 5,000 members. The outlawed CPP, meanwhile, aggressively pursued its guerrilla war, and in 1990 fielded some 18,000 to 23,000 full-time insurgents.

Ideology and Strategy

The CPP's ideology was taken largely from Chinese communism and adapted to circumstances in the Philippines. CPP chairman Sison's writings, which drew heavily on Mao Zedong's philosophy, provided the theoretical basis for the movement. Chief among them was *Philippine Society and Revolution*, published in 1970 under the pseudonym Amado Guerrero and often referred to as the CPP's bible. Sison characterized the Philippines as a semi-feudal, semi-colonial society "ruthlessly exploited" by United States imperialists, the "comprador big bourgeoisie," landlords, and bureaucratic capitalists. Armed revolution was viewed as the only way to overthrow the "United States-Marcos regime" (later the "United States-Aquino regime"), free the people from their oppression, and institute a people's democratic revolution. This proletarian revolution to overthrow the exploiting classes was to be propelled by an alliance between peasants and workers.

Sison's works outlined several important strategic maxims. The revolution had to be flexible, adapt itself to local situations, and employ self-criticism. CPP strategy emphasized political over military struggle. The key was to create a broad national alliance, establish front groups, and employ coalitions to broaden support for the CPP's revolutionary struggle. On the military front, the party adopted the Maoist principle of protracted people's war, attempting to establish a strong rural base and encircle the cities from the countryside. Finally, the CPP's chairman emphasized that the revolution must exploit the country's fractured geography by spreading throughout the mountainous island nation.

Development of the Revolutionary Movement

Sison's dictums were evident in the party's early development. On the theory that the Huks were defeated because their uprising was localized, the CPP emphasized expansion to other regions of Luzon, and to other islands. After several devastating routs by concentrated AFP attacks, in 1974 the NPA abandoned its early attempts to form Chinese-style base areas. From the CPP's birthplace in Central Luzon, guerrilla cadres established operations in remote areas of Northern Luzon, the Bicol Peninsula, Samar Island, and on the southern island of Mindanao. In each of these impoverished areas, the NPA undertook to support local residents in disputes with the central government, local military and civilian officials, and landlords. In most areas, the communists were able to take advantage of peasant unrest over land issues by embracing the theme of land reform.

Government initiatives did little to check the slow, steady growth of the NPA in the 1970s. Sison and NPA chief Bernabe Buscayno, alias Commander Dante, were arrested, and more than a dozen CPP and NPA leaders were captured or killed during 1976 and 1977. The government also mounted major anti-insurgency campaigns in Northern Luzon and elsewhere. Still, the communists continued to broaden their base of popular support, expand the geographical reach of the movement, and escalate their attacks on military and government targets. Several factors helped the communists gain support: the NPA's decentralized organization, which granted local commanders wide autonomy; Philippine geography, which prevented easy access to remote rebel-dominated areas; the armed forces' preoccupation with the Moro insurgency; and the continued appeal of the insurgents' pledges to solve specific grievances against the government and provide a better life for discontented Filipinos.

In 1983 Philippine officials estimated that the communists exercised substantial control over 2 to 3 percent of the nation's villages and that the NPA fielded some 6,000 full-time guerrillas. The insurgency grew rapidly after that year, largely as a result of growing political turmoil and increasing discontent with the Marcos government. By 1986, when Aquino came to power, approximately 22,500 NPA fighters were operating throughout nearly all the country's provinces. Equally important, some 20 percent of the Philippines' 40,000 villages were influenced by the communists. Although they admitted that they were not yet in a position to bring down the government, CPP leaders calculated that they were in the final phase of the "strategic defensive" and would soon be able to fight the government to a draw and take the offensive.

The overthrow of Marcos, however, threw the communist movement into disarray. The former president's unpopularity was the party's best recruiting theme. Strategic errors added to the communists' woes. The CPP's call for a boycott of the 1986 presidential election was overwhelmingly rejected by Filipinos and by many of the communists' local political organs. Party leaders later confessed that the strategy was a major blunder that left the insurgents with no role in the change of government. The CPP's chairman, Rodolfo Salas, resigned in 1986 in the midst of an unprecedented strategic debate within the communist ranks. Many party cadres called for a conciliatory policy toward the new and popular Aquino government, and for open political participation. Initially the CPP adopted a policy of "critical collaboration" with the Aquino administration, but after the lapse of the sixty-day cease-fire in February 1987, the NPA resumed all-out armed attacks. In 1987, after intense and prolonged debate, the party's executive committee confirmed the primacy of the armed struggle and renewed the CPP's commitment to a protracted people's war.

A series of setbacks challenged the communists through the end of the 1980s. The advent of a popular president especially hurt CPP support among the Philippine middle class, students, labor, and other mostly urban segments of society. Recruiting suffered, as did domestic financial support for the guerrillas. Villages in areas largely controlled by the NPA failed to support CPP-backed candidates in the May 1987 congressional elections. The government also succeeded in capturing a number of top CPP and NPA leaders, particularly in 1987 and 1988. Among them were Rodolfo Salas, the former party chairman, and Romulo Kintanar, the NPA chief. Kintanar, however, escaped from prison only months after his 1988 arrest. One result of the repeated roundups of key leaders was a series of bloody internal party purges during 1987 and 1988; rebels suspected of being government informers were executed or expelled. Philippine military leaders publicized widely the mass graves of suspected penetration agents. Popular support for the insurgents waned, and rebel morale was devastated. Mindanao, long an NPA stronghold, was especially hard hit by the loss of up to one-half of insurgent cadres.

By the end of the 1980s, NPA strength had begun to decline. According to government figures, full-time guerrilla strength was 24,000 to 26,000 in 1988, the year that Aquino said would be seen as the turning point in the government's counterinsurgency effort. The NPA was then operating in sixty of the nation's seventy-three provinces and claimed a following of some 500,000 Filipinos. By 1991, the government estimated that insurgent strength had fallen to 18,000 to 23,000 guerrillas. Still, the military believed that the rebels exercised considerable control over more than 18 percent of the Philippines' roughly 42,000 villages, and around 30,000 Filipinos were thought to be CPP members. (Other estimates of rebel strength and influence varied widely; one unofficial source placed NPA strength at 34,000.)

Leadership and Organization

The CPP was nominally led by its Central Committee, which in 1989 had some thirty full and nine alternate members. In the party's decentralized structure, the Central Committee acted as the highest policy-making body and provided theoretical guidance to lower echelons. The Central Committee met infrequently, however, and real power was vested in members of its Political Bureau. The Political Bureau was thought to have at least nine members in 1989, but it attempted to meet only once every six months. Day-to-day decisions were made by a five-member Executive Committee. In late 1989, the committee included the party's acting chairman, Benito Tiamzon; Wilma Austria-Tiamzon, his wife; Ricardo Reyes; Romulo Kintanar; and Jose Maria Sison. Sison, the CPP's founder, was actively speaking and writing in support of the revolution while living in self-imposed exile in the Netherlands. Despite Sison's denials, the military maintained that he continued to direct the CPP from abroad as its chairman in absentia.

CPP political and military operations were monitored and controlled through a system of territorial and functional organs. Six territorial commissions directed the basic work of party political cadres and military commanders: Northern Luzon, Central Luzon, Southern Luzon, Visayas, Mindanao, and Manila-Rizal (see fig. 13). In keeping with the CPP's policy of "democratic centralism," party affairs were managed by committees at echelons down to village level. Beneath the territorial commissions were sixteen regional and island party committees, which oversaw front, district, and section committees. At the bottom of the CPP's organizational hierarchy were local party branches and barrio revolutionary committees. In a parallel organization, the NPA maintained operational commands at each level of the CPP structure to coordinate the movements' political and military struggle.

Less was known about the organization and function of the party's national-level functional commissions, but the existence of at least three--the National United Front Commission, the Finance Commission, and the Military Commission--seemed certain in 1990. The Military Commission, whose apparent role was to direct and coordinate NPA activity, was directed by Executive Committee member Romulo Kintanar, who was often described as the NPA's commander. Establishing, directing, and sustaining party front groups was the function of the United Front Commission, which guided the CPP-dominated National Democratic Front and other political fronts and, through the Middle Forces Department, the activities involved in pursuing the party's interests in other areas, such as relations with the Catholic Church. The CPP's Finance Commission presumably managed taxation, fundraising, and spending. Another organ, the National Organization Commission, reportedly was to be dissolved, along with the Manila-Rizal Commission, to form the National Urban Center Commission in mid-1990.

Political Organizing and Front Groups

The CPP's efforts to broaden its grass-roots political support were based on the party cadres' systematic organization of support at the village level. The communists' network of *barangay* cells provided for the NPA's physical support and made the communists a potent political movement. Typically, a small band of CPP and NPA organizers first conducted a "social investigation" of a targeted *barangay* and identified key leaders and major sources of discontent. The cadres mixed with the people and gained their confidence by lending assistance, such as help in harvesting crops or in providing rudimentary medical care. Later, in a series of well-established steps, they set up an organizing committee and front groups representing peasants, youth, and others. Eventually, the organizing committee became the barrio revolutionary committee, the fundamental element of the communists' shadow government. The CPP's methodology for organizing *barangays* clearly had been successful.

Through the country, the communists' National United Front Commission operated a wide variety of front groups designed to draw legal left-wing organizations and sympathetic individuals into collaboration with the CPP. As part of this alliance building program directed mainly at the "middle forces," the CPP maintained fronts targeted at labor, students, intellectuals, church workers, human rights groups, women, businessmen, and peasants, as well as umbrella political fronts. In some cases, these fronts were widely recognized as communist-controlled, and the party had difficulty attracting and keeping partners because of its dominance. In other instances, the CPP's influence was not as obvious, and fronts operated with greater outside participation and some autonomy. In general, the front groups prospered in the mid-1980s as a result of growing opposition to the Marcos government. Aquino's more popular presidency, however, frustrated the CPP's efforts to sustain and build on its legal and quasi-legal partnerships with "cause-oriented" groups.

The CPP's principal political front was the National Democratic Front. Many of the party's other fronts--such as those aimed at the students and the church--operated under the broad National Democratic Front umbrella. Founded in April 1973, the front emphasized nationalist themes over communist ideology in order to attract broader participation. Because its strong links to the CPP were recognized, however, the National Democratic Front remained underground. As a result, the CPP moved in May 1985 to establish another, even broader front, the New Nationalist Alliance (Bagong Alyansang Makabayan--BAYAN). Many of the CPP's other fronts quickly affiliated with the new political umbrella group. Although Bayan's founders included many well known non-communists, the CPP's early move to take control of BAYAN's council and agenda resulted in numerous defections.

The radicalization of elements in the Catholic Church beginning in the late 1960s provided another avenue for the expansion of CPP front operations. Recognizing how the church's unparalleled credibility and extensive infrastructure could benefit the revolution, the communists made the Catholic Church a primary target. The party established a front, Christians for National Liberation, in 1972 with the express purpose of penetrating the church. In 1986 an activist claimed that Christians for National Liberation had a clandestine membership of over 3,000 clergy and layworkers. Radical clergy and church activists, many adopting liberation theology (see Glossary), supported the insurgency in a variety of ways. Some church activities even provided facilities and financial and logistical support to the guerrillas. Other church activists joined the NPA, and several well-known priests led guerrilla bands. As a result, the armed forces became deeply distrustful of the church's role, especially in remote rural areas where the NPA was most active. There, some of the Church's Basic Christian Communities--support groups for poor peasants--fell under communist control.

Another prominent target of CPP front operations was the workers' movement (see Employment and Labor Relations). The communists' flagship labor front was the Kilusang Mayo Uno (May First Movement--KMU). An umbrella organization formed in 1980, the KMU claimed 19 affiliated labor federations, hundreds of unions, and 650,000 workers in 1989. Although it denied its ties to the CPP, the movement had an openly political and revolutionary agenda. As one of the country's largest labor groups, it played a prominent role in the anti-Marcos movement. However, the KMU-led general strikes during the Aquino administration sometimes turned violent. Peasant farmers were the target of another CPP-sponsored front, the Peasant Movement of the Philippines (Kilusang Magbubukid ng Pilipinas). Established in 1985, this movement claimed 500,000 members and 2 million supporters for its agenda, which revolved around land reform.

Military Operations and Tactics

The NPA's armed insurrection followed the traditional pattern of guerrilla warfare. NPA units were formed at the regional and front levels and were normally company-sized or smaller. Main regional guerrilla units usually had 80 to 150 fighters, whereas secondary units had 30 to 60 fighters. NPA operations were, by design, extremely decentralized, with local commanders having wide latitude to conduct attacks as they chose. Typically, NPA elements avoided contact with AFP troops by remaining in remote, mountainous areas until ready to stage an attack. For an assault, they concentrated their forces, forming companies and sometimes battalions to overwhelm government troopers. Afterward, they dispersed to avoid AFP retaliation.

Isolated government outposts of the constabulary, police, and militia were favorite targets. The NPA also attacked public buildings such as town halls as a demonstration of its power. The property of uncooperative landowners and businessmen was another common target. The communists normally attacked private property to punish owners for alleged abuses or to coerce the payment of "revolutionary taxes." Attacks on the country's infrastructure were rare; the NPA's demolition of several bridges on Luzon's Bicol Peninsula in 1987 created a popular backlash that apparently caused the NPA to abandon the tactic.

The communists' traditionally rural struggle came to the cities in the mid-1980s with the dramatic increase in NPA assassinations. Beginning in 1984, Davao City became the laboratory for the NPA's developing urban warfare strategy. There, armed city partisan units, known popularly as "sparrow teams," murdered local officials, constables, police, and military personnel in a sustained terror campaign. The NPA selectively targeted unpopular officials, claiming that the killings provided revolutionary justice. The NPA's Davao City offensive ended in 1986, but not before Romulo Kintanar, the mastermind of the Davao City offensive and future NPA chief, had initiated a similar operation in Manila. The tempo of sparrow assassinations in the capital increased slowly after 1984, then rose dramatically in 1987. Some 120 officials, including Aquino's secretary of local government, were assassinated by the NPA that year. As sparrow activity escalated, NPA targeting became more indiscriminate.

The guerrillas also targeted Americans in 1987 for the first time since the early 1970s. After threatening to strike official Americans for their support of the Philippine counterinsurgency effort, the NPA killed two United States airmen, an American retiree, and a Filipino outside Clark Air Base in October. In April 1989, NPA assassins struck United States Army Colonel James N. Rowe, a senior officer at the Joint United States Military Advisory Group, on his way to work in Manila. Several other attacks on United States servicemen and contractors followed in 1989 and 1990.

The NPA obtained most weapons from the Philippine military in raids and ambushes. Some guns and ammunition also were purchased locally. As a result, the guerrillas were armed much like the AFP, with an assortment of American-designed small arms, such as the M-16 rifle. NPA commanders complained, however, that weapons shortages hampered their operations. The Philippine military estimated that only one-half to two-thirds of NPA fighters had high-powered rifles. There were no indications in 1990 of foreign-supplied weapons.

Overall, life in the NPA was austere and demanding. Living conditions were harsh, the food generally poor, medical care primitive, and danger constant. The NPA relied on the party's extensive network of peasant supporters in remote villages. The masa (masses) provided food and lodging to mobile guerrilla bands and warned of approaching government troops. The CPP's base also facilitated communication among party and NPA elements through courier, telephone, and telegraph networks. By the late 1980s, NPA communications had become more sophisticated; long-range radios were used more frequently. Although women were given equal status as NPA fighters, they were normally given secondary support roles in guerrilla units. Discipline in the NPA was strict, designed to win the support of the people by ensuring that the NPA was not discredited by its members' misbehavior. Punishment under the CPP's system of revolutionary justice ranged from reprimand to expulsion and execution.

Financing and Foreign Support

The CPP traditionally relied on "revolutionary taxes" as the principal income for what the communists portrayed as a self-sufficient, home-grown movement. In the areas where they were active, CPP and NPA cadres obtained funds from individuals and businesses through a combination of coercion and persuasion. The party's peasant supporters usually were more forthcoming, providing a few pesos and supplies such as rice to local guerrilla fighters. However, the CPP obtained most of its funds by extorting money from businesses--such as logging, mining, and planting--that operated in guerilla zones. NPA units commonly promised not to foment labor strikes, restrict the transport of goods, destroy company property, or assassinate executives in return for money or material support. The communists enforced their threats through NPA attacks on uncooperative owners and businesses. In addition, the rebels derived some revenues from growing and selling marijuana in remote areas.

During the 1980s, foreign non-government financing, mainly from sympathetic leftist groups in Western Europe, but also from the United States, Australia, New Zealand, Japan, and other Asian countries, became increasingly important to the rebels. By 1990 the AFP chief of staff estimated that support from foreign sympathizers netted the CPP from US$6 million to US$9 million annually, an amount that rivaled the estimated US$7.5 to US$10 million that the CPP netted in domestic revenues. Increased foreign donations resulted in part from intensified "international solidarity work" by the communist-controlled National Democratic Front through its international office in the Netherlands. Luis Jalandoni, a former Catholic priest, headed the CPP's fund-raising and international liaison efforts. He was joined in this work by Jose Maria Sison, the CPP's founder and reputed chairman in absentia, following Sison's release by Aquino in 1986. Donated monies frequently were funneled through party front groups, such as the KMU labor federation.

The CPP also began to appeal openly for support from sympathetic foreign governments for the first time during the late 1980s. Although there was no evidence that any foreign government had responded to the CPP's request in 1990, this campaign represented a dramatic departure from the communists' self-reliant approach, long a source of pride. (Two Chinese attempts to ship weapons to the Philippine communists--in 1972 and 1974--were intercepted by the AFP. Chinese support apparently ended in 1975.) The policy reversal resulted from the CPP's conclusion that more and better weapons were needed to escalate the war against government forces and that domestic revenues could not be increased without aggravating growing popular resentment of rebel taxation.

The Moros

The Philippines has had a long history of Moro insurgent movements dating back to Spanish rule. Resistance to colonization was especially strong among the Muslim population of southwestern Mindanao and the Sulu Archipelago. With pride in their cultural heritage and a strong desire for independence, Moros fought Christian and foreign domination. Spanish control over the Moros was never complete, and the Muslim struggle carried over into the United States colonial era. The Moros earned a reputation as fierce fighters in combat against United States troops (see War of Resistance). Following independence, Filipino Muslims continued to resist Manila's rule, leading to widespread conflict in the 1970s.

More immediate causes of insurgency rose out of the increasing lawlessness in the southern Philippines during the late 1960s, when violence associated with political disputes, personal feuds, and armed gangs proliferated. In this climate of civil turmoil, longstanding tensions between Moro and Christian communities escalated. Already in competition over land, economic resources, and political power, the Moros became increasingly alarmed by the immigration of Christians from the north who were making Moros a minority in what they felt was their own land (see Muslim Filipinos). By mid-1972, partisan political violence, generally divided along religious lines, gripped all of Mindanao and the Sulu Archipelago. After martial law was declared in September 1972 and all civilians were ordered to surrender their guns, spontaneous rebellions arose among Moros, who traditionally had equated the right to carry arms with their religious heritage and were suspicious of the government's intentions toward them.

In its initial phases, the rebellion was a series of isolated uprisings that rapidly spread in scope and size. But one group, the Moro National Liberation Front (MNLF) led by Nur Misuari, managed to bring most partisan Moro forces into the loosely unified MNLF framework. Fighting for an independent Moro nation, the MNLF received support from Muslim backers in Libya and Malaysia. When the conflict reached its peak in 1973-75, the military arm of the MNLF, the Bangsa Moro Army, was able to field some 30,000 armed fighters. The military responded by deploying 70 to 80 percent of its combat forces against the Moros. Destruction and casualties, both military and civilian, were heavy; an estimated 50,000 people were killed. The government also employed a variety of nonmilitary tactics, announced economic aid programs and political concessions, and encouraged factionalism and defections in the Muslim ranks by offering incentives such as amnesty and land. The government's programs, and a sharp decrease in the flow of arms from Malaysia, set back the Moro movement. In 1976 the conflict began to wane.

Talks between the government and the Moros began in late 1976 under the auspices of the Organization of the Islamic Conference, a union of Muslim nations to which the Moros looked for support. The talks led to an agreement between the Philippine government and the MNLF signed in Tripoli that year providing for Moro autonomy in the southern Philippines and for a cease-fire. After a lull in the fighting, the truce broke down in 1977 amid Moro charges that the government's automony plan allowed only token self-rule.

The Moro rebellion never regained its former vigor. Muslim factionalism was a major factor in the movement's decline. Differing goals, traditional tribal rivalries, and competition among Moro leaders for control of the movement produced a threeway split in the MNLF during the late 1970s. The first break occurred in 1977 when Hashim Salamat, supported by ethnic Maguindanaos from Mindanao, formed the Moro Islamic Liberation Front, which advocated a more moderate and conciliatory approach toward the government. Misuari's larger and more militant MNLF was further weakened during that period when rival leaders formed the Bangsa Moro Liberation Organization, drawing many Mindanao Maranaos away from the MNLF, dominated by Misuari's Sulu-based Tausug tribe. The Bangsa Moro Liberation Organization eventually collapsed, giving way to the Moro National Liberation Front Reformist Movement. Moro factionalism, compounded by declining foreign support and general war weariness, hurt the Muslim movement both on the battlefield and at the negotiating table. Moro fighting strength declined to about 15,000 by 1983, and Muslim and government forces only occasionally clashed during Marcos's last years in office.

In keeping with her campaign pledge of national reconciliation, Aquino initiated talks with the MNLF--the largest of the three major factions--in 1986 to resolve the conflict with Muslim separatists. Discussions produced a cease-fire in September, followed by further talks under the auspices of the Organization of the Islamic Conference. In January 1987, the MNLF signed an agreement relinquishing its goal of independence for Muslim regions and accepting the government's offer of autonomy. The Moro Islamic Liberation Front, the next largest faction, refused to accept the accord and initiated a brief offensive that ended in a truce later that month. Talks between the government and the MNLF over the proposed autonomous region continued sporadically throughout 1987 but eventually deadlocked. Following the government's successful diplomatic efforts to block the MNLF's latest bid for Organization of the Islamic Conference membership, the MNLF officially resumed its armed insurrection in February 1988, but little fighting resulted.

The government, meanwhile, pressed ahead with plans for Muslim autonomy without the MNLF's cooperation. Article 10 of the 1987 constitution mandates that the new congress establish an Autonomous Region in Muslim Mindanao. In the November 1989 plebiscite, only two Mindanao provinces--Maguindanao and Lanao del Sur--and two in the Sulu Archipelago--Sulu and Tawitawi-- opted to accept the government's autonomy measure. The fragmented four-province Autonomous Region for Muslim Mindanao, with its own governor and unicameral legislature, was officially inaugurated on November 6, 1990.

Armed activity by the Moros continued at a relatively low level through the late 1980s, with sporadic clashes between government and Muslim forces. The military still based army and marine battalions in Moro areas to maintain order in 1990, but far fewer units than it had in the 1970s. (Four battalions were on Jolo Island, a Moro stronghold, down from twenty-four at the rebellion's height.) Most of the endemic violence in Muslim areas was directed at rival clans, not at the military's peacekeeping forces. The Moro movement remained divided along tribal lines in three major factions. Misuari's MNLF forces in the Sulu Archipelago totaled 15,000, and the Mindanao-based Moro Islamic Liberation Front and the MNLF-Reformist Movement fielded around 2,900 and 900 troops, respectively. Weakened by these divisions, Muslim infighting, and the formation of an autonomous region, the Moro armies did not appear to be an imminent threat. Still, the MNLF--which did not recognize the autonomous region--showed no sign of surrendering, and it promised to remain a potent military and political force in the southern Philippines.

Crime

Despite some improvement in law and order, crime remained a major problem through the end of the 1980s. Police attributed the country's chronic crime problems to a variety of social and cultural factors. Widespread poverty and rapid population growth were frequently cited. Population pressures and a shortage of land and jobs in rural areas had produced a steady internal migration to the cities. This urbanization of a traditionally agrarian society was commonly mentioned as cause for increased crime rates. In particular, police pointed to the rapid growth of urban slum and squatter areas; more than 25 percent of the population of Metro-Manila (see Glossary) were thought to be squatters in the late 1980s (see Migration). Widespread possession of firearms--including automatic rifles--was another factor contributing to crime. Undisciplined private armies, usually maintained by local politicians and wealthy families, and numerous organized crime gangs were the biggest violators of firearms laws. The communist and Muslim insurgencies compounded the problem of proliferating guns and violence. Piracy and smuggling also were thriving criminal industries, especially in the southern portions of the archipelago.

According to the police, the incidence of serious crime escalated through the early 1980s, from approximately 250 crimes per 100,000 population in 1979, to a sustained level of around 310 during 1984 through 1987, then declined in 1988 and 1989. In 1988 the crime rate dipped below 300 crimes per 100,000 people, then fell dramatically in 1989 to 251 crimes per 100,000 citizens. Because of differing reporting practices and degrees of coverage, it was difficult to compare Philippine crime rates to those of other countries.

Government officials attributed the decrease in crime to improved police work, but economic conditions appeared to be as important. The deterioration in law and order during the early and mid-1980s accompanied a steadily worsening economy, whereas the improvement in the late 1980s paralleled renewed economic growth under Aquino. Not surprisingly, crime rates were highest in major urban areas, where unemployment was the highest. Regionally, peninsular southern Luzon, the western Visayan islands, and portions of Mindanao--impoverished rural areas where insurgents were active--had the most criminal activity in the mid-1980s.

Drug use and trafficking were growing problems during the 1980s, particularly in marijuana. Cultivation was geographically widespread, but the mountainous portions of northern Luzon and the central Visayas were the major marijuana-growing centers. During the late 1980s, another drug, methamphetamine, was fast becoming a narcotics problem. Known locally as *shabu*, it had generally been smuggled into the country, but domestic production expanded sharply in 1989 to meet growing demand. Coca cultivation was not significant in 1989, and there was no evidence of opium poppy cultivation or heroin manufacture.

The Philippines remained a center of drug trafficking and transshipment. Cannabis growers exported their product to Hong Kong, Japan, Australia, and the United States, and Philippine waters were routinely used by other smugglers as a transshipment point for Southeast Asian marijuana bound for North America. Manila's Ninoy Aquino International Airport, too, was used for transhipment of heroin and marijuana destined for Guam, Australia, Europe, and the United States. Production and trafficking of illegal drugs was accomplished by a variety of domestic and foreign criminal groups, notably Australian, American, and ethnic Chinese Filipinos. Communist insurgents also were involved in marijuana cultivation.

Corruption remained a serious problem in the early 1990s, and its elimination was one of the government's most vexing challenges. Despite persistent efforts, petty graft was commonplace, and high-level corruption scandals periodically rocked the government. As part of its continuing efforts to weed out official malfeasance, the government maintained a special anticorruption court, known as the Sandiganbayan.

Other government initiatives targeted corruption, crime, and terrorism. Peace and Order Councils at the national, regional, and provincial level were rejuvenated under Aquino. By regularly bringing together responsible government, military, and community leaders, the government hoped to improve the effectiveness of its anticrime and counterinsurgency programs. AFP and police commanders also attempted to address the problems of internal corruption and abuse, which, they admitted, undermined public confidence in, and cooperation with, the security forces. Top military leaders routinely publicized retraining programs, the discharge and demotion of scalawags in the ranks, and other measures designed to improve discipline. The military also mounted a counter narcotics effort, spearheaded by the constabulary's Narcotics Command. Government agents more than doubled arrests during 1989 and eradicated millions of marijuana plants, but they still found it difficult to keep pace with the growing drug trade.

Law Enforcement

Until the mid-1970s, when a major restructuring of the nation's police system was undertaken, the Philippine Constabulary alone was responsible for law enforcement on a national level. Independent city and municipal police forces took charge of maintaining peace and order on a local level, calling on the constabulary for aid when the need arose. The National Police Commission, established in 1966 to improve the professionalism and training of local police, had loose supervisory authority over the police. It was widely accepted, however, that this system had several serious defects. Most noteworthy were jurisdictional limitations, lack of uniformity and coordination, disputes between police forces, and partisan political involvement in police employment, appointments, assignments, and promotions. Local political bosses routinely used police as private armies, protecting their personal interests and intimidating political opponents.

In order to correct such deficiencies, the 1973 constitution provided for the integration of public safety forces. Several presidential decrees were subsequently issued, integrating the police, fire, and jail services in the nation's more than 1,500 cities and municipalities. On August 8, 1975, Presidential Decree 765 officially established the joint command structure of the Philippine Constabulary and Integrated National Police. The constabulary, which had a well-developed nationwide command and staff structure, was given the task of organizing the integration. The chief of the Philippine Constabulary served jointly as the director general of the Integrated National Police. As constabulary commander, he reported through the military chain of command, and as head of the Integrated National Police, he reported directly to the minister (later secretary) of national defense. The National Police Commission was transferred to the Ministry (later Department) of National Defense, retaining its oversight responsibilities but turning over authority for training and other matters to the Philippine Constabulary and Integrated National Police.

The Integrated National Police was assigned responsibility for public safety, protection of lives and property, enforcement of laws, and maintenance of peace and order throughout the nation. To carry out these responsibilities, it was given powers "to prevent crimes, effect the arrest of criminal offenders and provide for their detention and rehabilitation, prevent and control fires, investigate the commission of all crimes and offenses, bring the offenders to justice, and take all necessary steps to ensure public safety." In practice, the Philippine Constabulary retained responsibility for dealing with serious crimes or cases involving jurisdictions far separated from one another, and the Integrated National Police took charge of less serious crimes and local traffic, crime prevention, and public safety.

The Integrated National Police's organization paralleled that of the constabulary. The thirteen Philippine Constabulary regional command headquarters were the nuclei for the Integrated National Police's regional commands. Likewise, the constabulary's seventy-three provincial commanders, in their capacity as provincial police superintendents, had operational control of Integrated National Police forces in their respective provinces. Provinces were further subdivided into 147 police districts, stations, and substations. The constabulary was responsible for patrolling remote rural areas. In Metro Manila's four cities and thirteen municipalities, the Integrated National Police's Metropolitan Police Force shared the headquarters of the constabulary's Capital Command. The commanding general of the Capital Command was also the director of the Integrated National Police's Metropolitan Police Force and directed the operations of the capital's four police and fire districts.

As of 1985, the Integrated National Police numbered some 60,000 people, a marked increase over the 1980 figure of 51,000. Approximately 10 percent of these staff were fire and prison officials, and the remainder were police. The Philippine National Police Academy provided training for Integrated National Police officer cadets. Established under the Integrated National Police's Training Command in 1978, the academy offered a bachelor of science degree in public safety following a two-year course of study. Admission to the school was highly competitive.

Integrated National Police was the subject of some criticism, and the repeated object of reform. Police were accused of involvement in illegal activities, violent acts and abuse. Charges of corruption were frequent. To correct the Integrated National Police's image problem, the government sponsored programs to identify and punish police offenders, and training designed to raise their standard of appearance, conduct, and performance.

Dramatic changes were planned for the police in 1991. The newly formed Philippine National Police was to be a strictly civilian organization, removed from the armed forces and placed under a new civilian department known as the Department of the Interior and Local Government.

Local police forces were supported at the national level by the National Bureau of Investigation. As an agency of the Department of Justice, the National Bureau of Investigation was authorized to "investigate, on its own initiative and in the public interest, crimes and other offenses against the laws of the Philippines; to help whenever officially requested, investigate or detect crimes or other offenses; (and) to act as a national clearing house of criminal records and other information." In addition, the bureau maintained a scientific crime laboratory and provided technical assistance on request to the police and constabulary.

Local officials also played a role in law enforcement. By presidential decree, the justice system in the *barangays* empowered village leaders to handle petty and less serious crimes. The intent of the program was to reinforce the authority of local officials and to reduce the workload on already overtaxed Philippine law enforcement agencies.

Penal Law

The Philippine legal system was a hybrid, reflecting the country's cultural and colonial history. The system combined elements of Roman civil law from Spain, Anglo-American common law introduced by the United States, and the customary systems used by minorities. The influence of Spanish law was slowly fading but was clearly evident in private law, including family relations, property matters, and contracts. The influence of American law was most visible in constitutional and corporate law, and taxation and banking (see National Government). Evidentiary rules also were adopted from the American system. In the Muslim areas of the south, Islamic law was employed.

Philippine law dates to the nation's independence from Spain at the end of the nineteenth century. Statutes were enacted by the colonial Philippine legislature (1900-35), the commonwealth legislature (1935-46), and by the republic, beginning July 4, 1946. Many modern laws were patterned after the United States, and United States case law was cited and given persuasive effect in Philippine courts. As of the mid-1980s, there were twenty-six codes in effect. These included the 1930 revised penal code, in effect since January 1, 1932, and the civil code, which replaced the Spanish civil code on July 1, 1950. In addition, numerous presidential decrees issued during and after the martial law period (1972-81) had the effect of law. During this era, President Marcos issued more than 2,000 decrees. Although some were rescinded by Aquino during her first year in office. Rule by presidential decree ended in February 1987 with the ratification of the constitution.

Substantive criminal law was embodied in the revised penal code, as amended, and based chiefly on the Spanish penal code of 1870, which took effect in 1887. The penal code set forth the basic principles affecting criminal liability, established a system of penalties, and defined classes of crimes. It also provided for aggravating and mitigating circumstances, stating, for instance, that age, physical defect, or acting under "powerful impulse causing passion or obfuscation" can affect criminal liability. Insanity or acting under irresistible force or uncontrollable fear were regarded by law as exempting circumstances. Under the code, penalties were classified as capital (requiring a death sentence), afflictive (six years to life imprisonment), correctional (one month to six years), and light (up to thirty days). These correspond to the classification of crimes as grave felonies, punishable by capital or afflictive penalties; less grave felonies, punishable by correctional penalties; and light felonies, punishable by light penalties. The 1987 constitution, however, outlaws the death penalty unless provided for by subsequent legislation.

Criminal Procedure

The sources of procedural criminal law were the constitution, the revised penal code of 1930, the New Rules of Court of 1964, special laws, and certain presidential orders and letters of instruction. These governed the pleading, practice, and procedure of all courts as well as admission to the practice of law. All had the force and effect of law.

The rights of the accused under Philippine law are guaranteed under Article 3 of the 1987 constitution and include the right to be presumed innocent until proven guilty, the right to enjoy due process under the law, and the right to a speedy, public trial. Those accused must be informed of the charges against them and must be given access to competent, independent counsel, and the opportunity to post bail, except in instances where there is strong evidence that the crime could result in the maximum punishment of life imprisonment. Habeas corpus protection is extended to all except in cases of invasion or rebellion. During a trial, the accused are entitled to be present at every proceeding, to compel witnesses, to testify and cross-examine them and to testify or be exempt as a witness. Finally, all are guaranteed freedom from double jeopardy and, if convicted, the right to appeal.

Criminal action can be initiated either by a complaint--a sworn statement by the offended party, a witness, or a police officer--or by "information." Information consists of a written accusation filed with the court by a prosecutor, known as a fiscal at the provincial levels of government and below. No information can be filed unless investigation by a judge, fiscal, or state prosecutor establishes a prima facie case. Warrant for arrest is issued by a judge. Warrantless arrest by a police officer can be made legally only under extraordinary circumstances. Aquino immediately discontinued Marcos-era practices of presidentially ordered searches and arrests without judicial process and prolonged "preventative detention actions."

Trial procedure consists of arraignment, trial, and the court's judgment and sentencing. The accused must be arraigned in the court where the complaint or information is filed. A defendant must be present to plead to the charge, except in certain minor cases where a lawyer can appear for him or her. All offenses are bailable, save the most serious cases when strong evidence of guilt exists. If a defendant has no lawyer, the court is required to supply one. Prosecution is carried out by the state prosecutor or provincial fiscal, who exercises broad discretion in screening cases and affixing charges. No jury is employed; the judge determines all questions of law and fact and passes sentence. A written sentence must be read to the court. Afterward, either party may appeal.

The Correctional System

In the late 1980s, institutions for the confinement of convicts and the detention of those awaiting trial included a variety of national prisons and penal farms as well as numerous small local jails and lockups. In general, the national prisons housed more serious offenders, and those serving short-term sentences were held in local facilities. The prison system at the national level was supervised by the Bureau of Prisons of the Department of Justice. The bureau was responsible for the safekeeping of prisoners and their rehabilitation through general and moral education and technical training in industry and agriculture. The bureau also oversaw the operation of prison agro-industries and the production of food commodities. In 1991 the newly formed Philippine National Police took over administration of local jails.

The government maintained six correctional institutions and penal farms. The nation's largest prison was the National Penitentiary at Muntinlupa, Rizal Province, near Manila, which also operated the Manila City Jail. The penitentiary served as the central facility for those sentenced to life imprisonment or long-term incarceration. It was divided into two camps to separate those serving maximum and minimum penalties. The Correctional Institution for Women was located in Metropolitan Manila. Combination prison and penal farms also were located in Zamboanga City, and in Palawan, Mindoro Occidental, and in several Mindanao provinces. Prison conditions in the Philippines were generally poor, and prison life was harsh.

Some prison inmates were eligible for parole and probation. Before serving their sentence, felons, who were not charged with subversion or insurgency, or had not been on probation before, could apply for probation. Probationers were required to meet with their parole officers monthly, to avoid any further offense, and to comply with all other court-imposed conditions. After serving an established minimum sentence, certain prisoners could apply to their parole board for release. The board could also recommend pardon to the president for prisoners it believed to have reformed and who presented no menace to society.

In 1991 crime still was a serious, if somewhat reduced, threat to the general peace and security of society and was aggravated by corruption in the police and court systems. The politicization of the military was seen as a long-term problem and the threat of a military coup remained significant. The threat of a CPP-led takeover seemed to be receding as NPA guerrilla strength ebbed. The socioeconomic roots of the revolutionary movement remained and promised to make the insurgency a problem for some time to come, despite its slow decline. The government also recognized the continuing threat posed by well-armed Filipino Muslim rebels, although few feared a near-term resurgent Moro uprising. External security threats were not perceived.

* * *

A series of well-researched books published in the late 1980s added immensely to the available body of work on the Philippine communist insurgency. William Chapman's *Inside the Philippine Revolution* offers unique insights on the revolutionary movement. Richard Kessler's *Rebellion and Repression in the Philippines* provides a thorough review of the insurgency, especially its social and cultural roots. Gregg Jones's *Red Revolution* combines discussions of the CPP's historical development with revealing interviews with communist leaders and first-hand reports on guerrilla commanders and political cadres in the field. Although predictably dogmatic, books by CPP founder Jose Maria Sison--*Philippine Society and Revolution* and *The Philippine Revolution*--present the theoretical underpinnings of the insurgency (the former appears under his nom de guerre, Amado Guerrero). Annual updates on the progress of the communist movement can be found in the *Yearbook on International Communist Affairs*.

Comprehensive studies of the Philippine military are few. Richard Kessler's *Rebellion and Repression in the Philippines* provides the most thorough examination of the Armed Forces of the Philippines and their strengths and weaknesses. The history of Philippine civil-military relations is explored by two doctoral dissertations: Donald L. Berlin's "Prelude to Martial Law" and Carolina Hernandez's "The Extent of Civilian Control of the Military in the Philippines." More current information on the military's role in politics can be found in the *Far Eastern Economic Review, Asian Defence Journal*, and *Pacific Defence Reporter*.

Standard references on military capabilities include annual editions of *The Military Balance*, prepared by the International Institute for Strategic Studies, and the United States Arms Control and Disarmament Agency's *World Military Expenditures and Arms Transfers. Jane's Infantry Weapons, Jane's Armour and Artillery, Jane's All the World's Aircraft*, and *Jane's Fighting Ships* also are useful. The military's human rights performance is reviewed annually by the *Amnesty International Report* and by the United States Department of State's *Country Reports on Human Rights Practices*.

GLOSSARY

barangay Malay term for boat; also came to be used for the communal settlements established by migrants who came from the Indonesian archipelago and elsewhere. The term replaces the word *barrio*, formerly used to identify the lowest political subdivision in the Philippines.

Brady Plan A plan proposed by United States Treasury secretary Nicholas Brady for lending by the International Monetary Fund (*q.v.*), World Bank (*q.v.*), and creditor governments to finance debtor country purchase of their foreign- currency debt at the discounted prices at which the debt instruments were trading in secondary markets.

colorums Folk Christian religious communities derived from the 1839-41 Cofradía de San José movement, which spread through the islands thereafter and were the focus of resistance to American rule in the early twentieth century. Term derived from the phrase *per omnia saecula saeculorum* (world without end), which Roman Catholic priests used to close their Latin prayers.

Cominform (Communist Information Bureau) An international organization of communist parties, founded and controlled by the Soviet Union in 1947 and dissolved in 1956. The Cominform published propaganda touting international communist solidarity but was primarily a tool of Soviet foreign policy.

crony A term used to describe an individual who was able to exploit connections with former President Marcos to gain wealth and economic position.

current account Exports and imports of goods and services, net factor income from abroad, and unilateral transfers (gifts and foreign aid).

EDSA Revolution The February 1986 uprising, also called People's Power (*q.v.*), that ousted President Ferdinard E. Marcos. EDSA stands for Epifanio de los Santos, a ring road around Manila that was the site of confrontation between pro-Marcos and anti- Marcos forces.

exclusive economic zone (EEZ) A wide belt of sea and seabed adjacent to the national boundaries where the state claims preferential fishing rights and control over the exploitation of mineral and other natural resources. Boundary disagreements with neighboring states sometimes prevent the extension of the EEZ to the full limits claimed. The Philippines claims a 200-nautical mile EEZ, now considered the international standard.

fiscal year (FY) Calendar year.

gross domestic product (GDP) A value measure of the flow of domestic goods and services produced by an economy over a period of time, such as a year. Only output values of goods for final consumption and investment are included because the values of primary and intermediate production are assumed to be included in final prices. GDP is sometimes aggregated and shown at market prices, meaning that indirect taxes and subsidies are included; when these have been eliminated, the result is GDP at factor cost. The word *gross* indicates that deductions for depreciation of physical assets have not been made. *See also* gross national product.

gross national product (GNP) Gross domestic product (*q.v.*) plus the net income or loss stemming from transactions with foreign countries. GNP is the broadest measurement of the output of goods and services of an economy. It can be calculated at market prices, which include indirect taxes and subsidies. Because indirect taxes and subsidies are only transfer payments, GNP is often calculated at factor cost by removing indirect taxes and subsidies.

Huks, or Huk Short form of Hukbalahap, itself the abbreviated form of the Tagalog name for the guerrilla force established in 1942, known as the People's Anti-Japanese Army (Hukbong Bayan Laban sa Hapon). In 1946 renamed the People's Liberation Army (Hukbong Mapagpalaya ng Bayan).

ilustrados Literally, enlightened ones, the Philippine elite during the Spanish colonial period.

International Monetary Fund (IMF) Established along with the World Bank (*q.v.*) in 1945, the IMF is a specialized agency affiliated with the United Nations and is responsible for stabilizing international exchange loans to its members (including industrialized and developing countries) when they experience balance of payments difficulties. These loans frequently carry conditions that require substantial internal economic adjustments by the recipients, most of which are developing countries.

liberation theology An activist movement led by Roman Catholic clergy who trace their inspiration to Vatican Council II (1963-65), where some church views were liberalized, and the Second Latin American Bishops' Conference in Medellín, Colombia (1968), which endorsed greater direct efforts to improve the lot of the poor. Advocates of liberation theology have introduced a radical interpretation of the Bible, one that employs Marxist terminology to analyze and condemn the wide disparities between the wealthy elite and the impoverished masses in most underdeveloped countries. This reflection often leads advocates to organize to improve living standards through cooperatives and civic improvement projects.

mestizos The offspring of Filipino and non-Filipino marriages; includes those of Spanish-Filipino parentage (Spanish mestizos) and Chinese-Filipino parentage (Chinese mestizos).

Metro Manila Metropolitan Manila; also called the National Capital Region. Includes the cities of Manila, Pasay, Caloocan, and Quezon City and several other major population centers.

Moro Spanish word for Moor; name given by Spanish to Muslim Filipinos and still used. Moros mostly inhabit southern and eastern Mindanao, the Sulu Archipelago, and Palawan and have not become assimilated into the mainstream of Philippine society.

net domestic product/net national product (NDP/NNP) Gross national product (*q.v.*) or gross domestic product (*q.v.*) less capital consumption allowance and indirect taxes or subsidies.

People's Power The popular uprising that ousted President Ferdinard E. Marcos in February 1986. The movement was best known as People's Power in the United States, but in the Philippines it was also referred to as the EDSA Revolution (*q.v.*).

peso (P) Philippine currency, which is subdivided into 100 centavos. In December 1991, the official exchange rate was US$1 equals P26.70.

structural adjustment loan A program loan, often by the World Bank (*q.v.*), to effect a structural adjustment program to liberalize an economy. Programs involve maintaining a flexible exchange rate, lowering tariffs, removing quantitative restrictions on international trade, and relaxing price and other market controls.

Sunni (from *sunna*, orthodox) A member of the larger of the two great divisions of Islam.

Tagalog Large ethnolinguistic group indigenous to central and southern Luzon, particularly around Manila. The Tagalog language is the basis for Pilipino, the national language of the Philippines.

terms of trade The average price of exports divided by the average price of imports; the quantity of imports that can be purchased per unit of exports.

value added Price of output less purchased inputs; valuation of contribution by enterprise to the product; sum of wages, interest, rent, and profit.

World Bank Informal name used to designate a group of three affiliated international institutions: the International Bank for Reconstruction and Development (IBRD), the International Development Association (IDA), and the International Finance Corporation (IFC). The IBRD, established in 1945, has the primary purpose of providing loans to developing countries for productive projects. The IDA, a legally separate loan fund but administered by the staff of the IBRD, was set up in 1960 to furnish credits to the poorest developing countries on much easier terms than those of conventional IBRD loans. The IFC, founded in 1956, supplements the activities of the IBRD through loans and assistance designed specifically to encourage the growth of productive private enterprises in the less developed countries. The president and certain senior officers of the IBRD hold the same positions in the IFC. The three institutions are owned by the governments of the countries that subscribe their capital. To participate in the World Bank group, member states must first belong to the International Monetary Fund (IMF--*q.v.*).

INDEX

human rights, 17, 21, 30, 32, 71, 73, 157, 179, 180, 181, 187, 188, 194, 195, 196, 210, 212, 218, 228

I

Iglesia ni Kristo, 26, 96, 159
ilustrados, 30, 31, 42, 43, 44, 45, 47, 49, 53, 90, 100, 230
immigration, 41, 56, 59, 80, 87, 221
independent judiciary, 30, 36, 156
independent Muslim state, 4
indigenous groups, 18
Indonesia, 9, 10
inflation rate, 29, 70
inflation, 29, 32, 35, 36, 61, 70, 117, 118, 127, 198
Integrated National Police, 28, 200, 208, 209, 214, 224, 225
intelligence operations, 10
Interfaith Group, 21
intermarriage, 81, 82, 85, 87
International Monetary Fund (IMF), 29, 35, 74, 99, 108, 111, 114, 116, 118, 122, 124, 125, 134, 144, 145, 148, 149, 150, 154, 181, 229, 230, 231
international organizations, 28
international terrorism, 3
Islam, 18, 21
Islamic faith, 17
Islamic law, 19, 51, 84, 226

J

Jaena, Graciano Lopez, 45
Jamiatul Philippine al-Islamia, 98
Janjalani, Abubakar, 5
Japan, 13, 14, 27, 38, 46, 48, 58, 59, 60, 61, 71, 106, 129, 136, 143, 146, 147, 148, 152, 153, 181, 183, 185, 189, 191, 220, 223
Jesuits, 38, 43, 94
jihad, 7
Johnson, President Lyndon, 67
Jolo Island, 4, 7, 84, 222
Jones Act, 54, 55
judicial system, 19

K

Kabisig, 174
Kansas, 5
Khalifa, Mohammed Jamal, 6, 7
kidnappings, 3, 5, 6, 7
Kilusang Mayo Uno, 139, 160, 218

L

Laban Demokratikong Pilipino (LDP) party, 35
Lakas ng Edsa-National Union of Christian Democrats, 34
Lakas-NUCD, 27, 34
leftist groups, 10
Liberal Party, 27, 32, 35, 54, 62, 65, 66, 68, 173
liberation theology, 218, 230
Libya, 5, 7, 9, 68, 84, 186, 221
literacy levels, 92, 101
López de Legazpi, Miguel, 30, 37, 94
Luzon, 18, 25, 28, 29, 31, 35, 37, 38, 39, 40, 41, 42, 50, 51, 56, 57, 58, 61, 63, 64, 65, 67, 72, 73, 78, 79, 81, 82, 83, 85, 86, 96, 101, 111, 122, 123, 126, 131, 133, 167, 183, 190, 197, 201, 202, 204, 206, 214, 215, 217, 219, 223, 231

M

Macapagal, Diosdado, 66, 190
Macapagal,-Arroyo Gloria, 17, 19
Macapagal-Arroyo, President Gloria, 3
MacArthur, General Douglas, 60
Magellan, 37
Magsaysay, Ramon, 65, 175, 190
Malacañang Palace, 65, 68, 76, 135, 193
Malaysia, 4, 7, 8, 9, 10, 16, 36, 46, 66, 67, 68, 84, 184, 191, 212, 221
Malolos Constitution, 49, 157
Manila, 6, 7, 9, 10
Marcos, Ferdinand E., 30, 31, 36, 67, 70, 71, 77, 105, 155, 170, 172, 175, 188, 190
Marcos, Imelda, 29, 34, 68, 69, 70, 72, 161, 165
marijuana, 220, 223, 224
martial law, 30, 31, 32, 36, 67, 68, 69, 71, 72, 73, 74, 76, 84, 85, 108, 109, 123, 125, 126, 139, 146, 155, 158, 161, 162, 166, 168, 169, 175, 176, 178, 180, 188, 190, 192, 212, 221, 226
Mecca, 19
medical treatment, 32, 71, 72, 104
Middle East, 5, 6
Military Bases Agreement, 34, 63, 71, 103, 183, 198, 210, 211
military bases, 10, 11, 14, 35, 66, 71, 99, 160
military cooperation, 3
military equipment, 8, 9
military rebellions, 214
Mindanao peace process, 21
Mindanao, 4, 5, 6, 7, 8, 9, 10, 12, 13, 18, 19, 20, 21, 25, 33, 35, 37, 40, 41, 46, 51, 55, 56, 58, 65, 66, 68, 77, 78, 80, 81, 82, 83, 84, 85, 86, 92, 93, 96,